Cisco Router Troubleshooting Handbook

Cisco Router Troubleshooting Handbook

Peter Rybaczyk

M&T Books
An imprint of Wiley Publishing, Inc.

Cisco Router Troubleshooting Handbook

Published by

M&T Books

An imprint of Wiley Publishing, Inc.

111 River Street

Hoboken, NJ 07030

www.wiley.com

For general information on our other products
and services or to obtain technical support,
please contact our Customer Care Department
within the U.S. at 800-762-2974, outside the
U.S. at 317-572-3993, or fax 317-572-4002.

Wiley also publishes its books in a variety of
electronic formats. Some content that appears in
print may not be available in electronic books.

Library of Congress Cataloging-in-Publication
Data:

Library of Congress Control Number: 00-100274

ISBN: 0-7645-4647-3

1O/RX/QY/QR/FC

 is a trademark of
Wiley Publishing, Inc.

About the Author

Peter Rybaczyk has been an internetworking consultant and a technical trainer since 1990. He is the president of Global InterNetworking Services, Inc., located in Bazeman, Montana. His clients include network equipment vendors, ISPs, Voice over IP providers, law firms, and auto dealerships. Rybaczyk is a former programmer, network administrator, and technical manager for a publishing house, Summit University Press. He first became involved with networks in 1986 and has designed and installed numerous LANs and WANs.

Over the last decade, Rybaczyk has taught over 150 seminars on routing protocols, TCP/IP, Cisco routers and switches, network management, and network design. He also developed custom courses on Cisco WAN management products, OSPF, and rapid development tools, which he delivered to audiences in the United States, Canada, Europe, and Australia.

Rybaczyk holds a B.S. degree in physics and is the author of Novell's *Internet Plumbing Handbook* and a co-author of *PC Network Administration*. Rybaczyk is a Cisco Certified System Instructor and holds CCNA and CCNP certifications. Since early 2000, Rybaczyk has been involved in the design and deployment of a nationwide VoIP network in the U.S. He is actively working toward becoming a CCIE and can be reached at `psram@globalins.com`

Credits

Acquisitions Editor
Jim Sumser

Project Editor
Robert MacSweeney

Technical Editor
Louis W. Gilman

Copy Editor
Chandani Thapa

Project Coordinators
Linda Marousek
Louigene A. Santos

Proofreading and Indexing
York Production Services

Quality Control Specialists
Chris Weisbart
Laura Taflinger

Graphics and Production Specialists
Jude Levinson
Michael Lewis
Ramses Ramirez
Victor Perez-Varela
Dina F. Quan

Book Designer
Kurt Krames

Illustrator
Shelley Norris

To Maria, Yeshe, and Jaques

Preface

With the new millenium upon us, it's hard to remember what life was like without the Internet. Instantaneous global communication by e-mail, online shopping, research, entertainment, you name it: it's all there and taken for granted. The Internet has become a social and economic phenomenon changing the way we communicate, live, and earn a living. It is also a technological feat that's glued together by routers and switches, many of which sport the Cisco Systems logo.

About this Book

Welcome to the *Cisco Router Troubleshooting Handbook*. Cisco's routers range from low-end access devices to high-capacity modular switch-routers deployed in the core of the Internet. Cisco's IOS is a complex operating system that must be activated by network administrators through configuration. When the increasingly complex router hardware is combined with the feature-laden IOS, the probability of something somewhere not working quite right increases. That's where the Cisco Router Troubleshooting Handbook comes in.

This is the book you can turn to when routers and internetworks that are supposed to be running smoothly are having hiccups instead. There are hundreds of ways to misconfigure a router, but only a few to configure it correctly. Some misconfigurations are not permitted by the IOS. Others, however, are silent. Only the bad results that they produce (packets unable to reach destinations, bottlenecks, unusually high router utilization, routing loops) indicate that something is wrong.

It's those silent misconfigurations and pitfalls degrading your network that are cracked and explained in the pages that follow. The uniqueness of this book lies in the approach taken in isolating, correcting, and avoiding problems. The bad stuff is analyzed side by side with the good. You will learn about the undesirable symptoms and their causes. You will also observe the process of eliminating them. You will study the logical approaches to troubleshooting that, with time and practice, lead to intuition. And intuition is often what you need most when the pressure is on to get the best from your network.

Is This Book for You?

A well-functioning routed internetwork is an ultimate example of teamwork. It's like a symphony orchestra where the network administrator is the conductor. If you are a network administrator dedicated to setting up and maintaining a well-tuned network, this book is for you.

How This Book is Organized

This book is organized into three parts as follows.

Part I – Troubleshooting Tools and Philosophy (Chapters 1-3)

Chapter 1 is a warm-up but not an introduction. It delves immediately into common misconfiguration problems related to encapsulation mismatches, access control lists, autonomous system numbers, and OSPF area IDs. In Chapter 2, the troubleshooting philosophy and varying approaches to troubleshooting are examined. Chapter 3 explores IOS troubleshooting tools like the show command, ping, and telnet in the context of a sudden malfunction in a routed internetwork.

Part II – Troubleshooting the Bottom Layers (Chapters 4-6)

Chapters 4 though 6 focus on spotting problems related to the Physical, Data Link, and Network Layers. Physical problems are examined in the context of access and high-end Cisco 12000 series routers. Data Link Layer issues are covered as the network administrator stumbles through optimization of an undocumented and poorly performing internetwork.

In Chapter 6, the focus is on duplicate addressing and masks. Normal and inverted masks are discussed in the context of numerous IOS configuration commands.

Part III – Troubleshooting Routing Protocols (Chapters 7-11)

The last part of the book deals with troubleshooting routing protocols: IGRP/EIGRP, OSPF, RIP, and BGP. The last chapter is dedicated to the analysis of the redistribution pitfalls between them. With tens of thousands of networks comprising the global Internet, no one routing protocol is best for every environment. All routing protocols share the common characteristic of populating routing tables and exchanging updates between routers. But successful deployment of routing protocols demands clear understanding of their unique characteristics. And in multiprotocol environments, the peculiarities of their interactions must also be understood. These are the issues addressed in this part of the book.

Appendixes

The back of the book consists of three appendixes that include a bibliography, a guide to acronyms, and a summary of troubleshooting tips and issues. The summary of the troubleshooting tips and issues in Appendix C is the essence of the many topics covered in greater detail in the body of the book.

Acknowledgments

Many thanks to everyone who helped with this writing project: Jim Sumser who continues to amaze me by still believing that I can write, Lou Gilman for his eagle eye and technical insight, and Bob MacSweeney and Chandani Thapa for their patience and excellent editorial suggestions and corrections.

I also would like to acknowledge my parents, Anna and Henryk Rybaczyk, and my cousin Wladzia for the example and the vision that they've held for me, and my three sisters: Elizabeth, Barbara, and Dorothy. Many thanks to all of my family members and friends who've offered encouragement and moral support during these arduous months of writing: Rachel, Lawrence, Clarissa, Sophia, and Athena Pollack, Barbara and John Reark, Dorothy, Pramod, Bogdan, Leszek and Ania Pathak, Jack and Arlene McShea, Andres and Kathleen Fortino, Andrew and Kathleen Karlsen, Edward and Eileen Francis, Michael and Monica McKeever, Will and Denise Adams, Craig and Jo-Anne Woodland, Barbara and Clyde Laakso, Susan and Vernon Hamilton, and Simon and Chantal Hale. Thanks a bunch everyone. It takes support from family and friends like you to write a book.

Many thanks to my friend and colleague, Randy Schumacher of Care Technologies, for covering for me during these critical months. And thank you to all of my clients for your understanding in working with me while I was under the pressure of meeting the writing deadlines.

Last, but not least, I would like to express my love and profound gratitude to my wife, Maria for her phenomenal patience and loving support during this writing project.

Contents at a Glance

Contents

Part I

Troubleshooting Tools and Philosophy

Chapter 1

Let's Warm Up: Common Router Misconfiguration Problems

This chapter is a troubleshooting "warm-up." It offers an overview of the most common router misconfiguration problems and the troubleshooting techniques needed to identify and correct them. Common misconfiguration problems in routed internetworks result from Data Link Layer encapsulation mismatches, improper use of access control lists, and dynamic routing protocols unable to exchange routing updates. This chapter illustrates why these common problems occur and how to avoid them.

Encapsulation Mismatches on LAN Links

In the context of the Open-Systems Interconnection model (OSI), encapsulation or framing is one of the responsibilities of the Data Link Layer of a networking technology. If all of the LAN technologies followed the same framing rules, there would be no need for a discussion about encapsulation mismatches. However, framing rules at the Data Link Layer vary from one LAN technology to another. Framing rules also vary within the same networking technology as a function of Network Layer protocols and network operating systems deployed on a LAN.

At the Data Link Layer, frames are the "vehicles" into which the packets that are arriving from the Network Layer are packaged or encapsulated for transit across a physical subnet. These vehicles or frames must match if neighboring devices are expected to communicate with one another. However, with many different frame types available on both LANs and WANs, an encapsulation mismatch preventing neighboring routers from talking to one another or to other network devices is not uncommon.

Cisco routers and switches support all of the dominant LAN technologies: Ethernet, Token Ring, and FDDI. All of these technologies come in several different flavors. The differences within a LAN technology such as Ethernet, for example, stem from its support of multiple transmission media (twisted-pair, coax, or fiber), different transmission methods (half-duplex or full duplex), and varying operational speeds (from 10 to 1000Mbps). Collectively, the LAN technologies provide the physical infrastructure over which operating systems like Windows NT, NetWare, Mac OS, or Unix can support user applications.

The combination of the operating system, the supported Network Layer protocols, and the networking technology over which they operate determines the type of frames that will be present on a LAN. In turn, the types of frames resulting from the preceding combination determine what type of encapsulation needs to be configured on a router's interface. This is where your knowledge of Data Link Layer framing really comes in handy. With Ethernet being by far the most popular LAN technology, the different types of Ethernet frames are explored in detail.

Ethernet Frame Types

The four most common frame types found on Ethernet LANs hosting multiple operating systems are as follows.

- Espec-2 or Ethernet_II
- 802.2
- Ethernet_SNAP
- 802.3 "Raw" used with IPX

Cisco routers support all of these Ethernet frame types using configuration keywords, *arpa, sap, snap,* and *novell-ether*, respectively. The reasons why these frame types are supported could evolve into a lengthy history lesson about the ever-evolving LAN standards. They are summarized briefly.

Espec-2 Frame

Prior to 1982, multiple Ethernet frame choices in Cisco's IOS did not exist. That's because Cisco did not exist, Cisco's IOS did not exist, and the only frame type that was available on the Ethernets of those days was Espec-2. The structure of the Espec-2 frame is part of an Ethernet Version 2.0 industry specification. This specification was developed by DEC, Intel, and Xerox. It was published in 1982.

The Espec-2 frame's header consists of two hardware addresses and a type field. The type field identifies the protocol that created the packet that's encapsulated inside of the frame. The type field is effectively a pointer or an interface via which the Data Link Layer knows what's inside a frame and how to pass the frame's contents up the protocol stack. But what's clearly missing from the frame's header is how long the frame is.

To compute the length of the frame, the Data Link Layer has to "peek" into the frame's contents — the header of a packet created by a higher layer protocol. From the OSI point of view, this is a no-no and a clear "violation" of separation between protocol layers. The Data Link Layer should not have to examine higher layer contents to do its job.

802.2 Frame

At the same time that DEC, Intel, and Xerox were working on their Ethernet specifications, the Institute of Electrical and Electronics Engineers (IEEE) started the 802 Project with the intent of producing internationally accepted LAN standards. By 1983, one of the IEEE subcommittees finalized a new LAN standard, 802.3. The Ethernet Version 2.0 specification was used as a foundation for the new standard. However, in the 802.3 standard, the Espec-2 frame's type field was changed to a length field indicating the length of the frame. This change solved the problem of not having a length field in the Espec-2 frame, but it also created a new problem.

The Data Link Layer lost the ability to know what's inside the frame. And without knowing what's inside the frame the Data Link Layer could not pass its content up the protocol stack to a higher layer protocol. Naturally, something had to be added to the 802.3 frame to compensate for the replacement of the type field with a length field. A new set of fields, intended to restore the functionality of the type field, was defined by another IEEE standard, 802.2. The problem was solved temporarily and a new type of frame, 802.2, was created. The 802.2 frame combined the 802.3 header (two hardware addresses and the length field) with the new fields defined by the 802.2 standard.

The 802.2 standard — also referred to as the Logical Link Control (LLC) — introduced the concept of Service Access Points (SAPs). The SAPs were the equivalent of the type field in the Espec-2 frame with some additional functionality. But there was a fundamental problem with the SAPs. The type field in the Espec-2 frame was two bytes long. Put on your binary hat: Two-byte binary can represent decimal numbers between 0 and 65,535. That's a very large number of higher layer protocols that could be represented by the type field in the Espec-2 frame.

The SAPs, on the other hand, could represent only a very limited number of protocols. For reasons best left to the judgement of history, the LLC standard includes two SAPs, a Source SAP (SSAP), and a Destination SAP (DSAP), identifying the sending and the receiving processes from the higher layers. Each SAP is also only one byte long with a couple of bits reserved, which leaves only six bits in each SAP to represent a higher layer protocol. Put on your binary hat again: Six bits can represent 64 decimal values per SAP.

If you are wondering what's going on here, you're probably not alone. Why is there a need for a Source SAP and a Destination SAP? Under what conditions would the two SAPs be different? It seems to make sense that the same Network Layer protocol in one device would be communicating with the same Network Layer protocol in another device. If that's the case, then the Source and the Destination SAPs should be identical. Then why have two SAPs? The answers to these questions may well be found in the details of the 802.2 standard.

Compared to the type field in the Espec-2 frame, SAPs reduced the number of protocols used in the LLC standard by three orders of magnitude, from 65,536 to 64, to be exact. But since SAPs were primarily intended for protocols approved by IEEE, from the IEEE point of view, having a limited number of SAP values was not necessarily a problem. However, there are hundreds of other non-IEEE-approved protocols wanting to use Ethernet with the 802.2 encapsulation. A compromise was needed.

Ethernet_SNAP Frame

If you snap your fingers at this point, you'll know what the compromise was: SNAP! Subnetwork Access Protocol (SNAP). A certain value of SAP, AA hex, would be used to represent another set of fields in the frame header known as SNAP. Inside the SNAP portion of the header, a two-byte type field was reintroduced. And the Ethernet_SNAP frame type was born.

802.3 "Raw" Frame

When IPX was developed and incorporated into early versions of NetWare, it was the only Network Layer protocol supported by the NetWare operating system. When an operating system supports only one protocol, it can use the 802.3 frame type (without the LLC or SNAP fields). Hence, the IPX Ethernet_802.3 frame or the "IPX raw" frame, as it is commonly called, came about. In older versions of NetWare, 3.11 and below, the default encapsulation for the IPX protocols was the IPX Ethernet_802.3. Beginning with NetWare 3.12, the default encapsulation is IEEE 802.2. This means that the IPX protocol has been assigned a global SAP value. An honor indeed.

Common Network Protocols on Ethernet

Given the multi-operating system environment on many of today's LANs, it is not uncommon for a shared-medium LAN to host several different frame types. For example, consider an Ethernet LAN as shown in Figure 1.1. This LAN has a Cisco router, a Windows NT server, a NetWare 4.11 server, a Windows 95 workstation, and a Macintosh attached to the same physical medium.

The three popular protocol stacks present on the LAN in Figure 1.1 are as follows:

- TCP/IP
- IPX/SPX
- AppleTalk

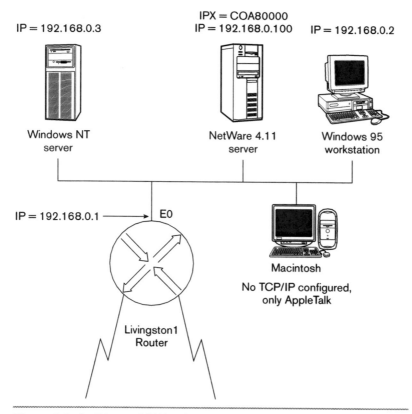

Figure 1.1 *An Ethernet LAN hosting multiple operating systems*

The presence of these three protocol stacks on the LAN in Figure 1.1 creates a potential for all four of the Ethernet frame types discussed in the preceding section to be in use on that LAN. There is also the potential for encapsulation mismatches in this scenario. You can avoid encapsulation mismatches between the different devices by paying attention to the default frame types that are used by each operating system, and by configuring your Cisco router accordingly.

Ethernet Encapsulation of IP Traffic

Cisco's IOS defaults to the Espec-2 frame type for the IP protocol configured on Ethernet interfaces. Cisco's keyword for this type of encapsulation is *arpa*. ARPA stands for Advanced Research Projects Agency, and the story of ARPA and the Internet could evolve into another history lesson, but not here. The use of ARPA encapsulation is demonstrated in the partial output from a show interface e0 command after Ethernet0 has already been configured with an IP address.

```
Ethernet0 is up, line protocol is up

  Hardware is Lance, address is 0000.0c4a.d136 (bia 0000.0c4a.d136)

  Internet address is 192.168.0.1/24

  MTU 1500 bytes, BW 10000 Kbit, DLY 1000 usec,

    reliability 255/255, txload 1/255, rxload 1/255

  Encapsulation ARPA, loopback not set, keepalive set (10 sec)

  ARP type: ARPA, ARP Timeout 04:00:00

  Last input 00:02:21, output 00:00:01, output hang never
```

In fact, when you are assigning an IP address to an Ethernet interface, the IOS will not even allow you to specify an encapsulation type because it defaults to ARPA. An error results if you try. The key to preventing encapsulation mismatches for IP is to make sure that Windows NT and NetWare servers will use the Espec-2 frame type for their TCP/IP traffic on Ethernet interfaces.

Windows NT defaults to Espec-2 frame type for IP on Ethernet interfaces. However, NetWare must be specifically configured with the Espec-2 frame type before its TCP/IP stack will interoperate with all of the other devices. The configuration of the frame type on a NetWare server typically takes place inside the AUTOEXEC.NCF file or via the INETCFG utility.

The following trace is from the show ARP display on router Livingston1 in Figure 1.1. The Windows NT server (192.168.0.3), the NetWare 4.11 server (192.168.0.100), and the Windows 95 workstation (192.168.0.2) are all attached to the same subnet. Livingston1's E0 interface is assigned the IP address of 192.168.0.1. The ARP cache entry for the router's interface does not have an age associated with it because it's always there.

```
Livingston1# show arp

Protocol  Address         Age (min)  Hardware Addr   Type   Interface

Internet  192.168.0.100          23  00a0.240f.fae6  ARPA   Ethernet0

Internet  192.168.0.1             -  0000.0c4a.d136  ARPA   Ethernet0
```

```
Internet  192.168.0.2        11  0060.9755.1d36  ARPA   Ethernet0
Internet  192.168.0.3         2  0000.c02c.c344  ARPA   Ethernet0
Livingston1#
```

Notice the ARPA encapsulation type for all of the devices configured for TCP/IP on the 192.168.0.0/24 subnet. That's what you want to see if you expect the devices to communicate using IP. When the IP frame type on the NetWare server (192.168.0.100) was changed from Espec-2 to SNAP — and the ARP cache was cleared on the router — the NetWare server never made it back into the ARP cache.

That's because an encapsulation mismatch was introduced between the router's Ethernet interface and the NetWare server for passing IP traffic. The router and the NetWare server were no longer communicating via IP. However, not communicating via IP does not preclude the router and the NetWare server from communicating via IPX, provided that the IPX encapsulation is configured properly.

Ethernet Encapsulation of IPX Traffic

When IPX routing is activated on a Cisco router (via the global configuration command IPX routing) and an IPX network address is being assigned to an Ethernet interface, there are multiple encapsulation options available as shown in the following trace:

```
Livingston1(config)#inter e1
Livingston1(config-if)#ipx network C0A080100 encapsulation ?
   arpa         IPX Ethernet_II
   hdlc         HDLC on serial links
   novell-ether IPX Ethernet_802.3
   novell-fddi  IPX FDDI RAW
   sap          IEEE 802.2 on Ethernet, FDDI, Token Ring
   snap         IEEE 802.2 SNAP on Ethernet, Token Ring, and FDDI
```

The first column of the preceding trace contains Cisco's keywords for identifying the encapsulations that correspond to frame types described in the second column. The technical differences between the frames have been explained in preceding sections. What you must decide is which encapsulation option to choose for IPX on your router. Your decision will depend on which version of NetWare you are running on your server and which frame types have been used for the IPX on the server and the workstations.

NetWare servers 3.12 and above use the 802.2 frame type as a default which corresponds to Cisco's SAP encapsulation. The default encapsulation on Cisco routers for IPX is Novell-Ether corresponding to the IPX "raw" or 802.3 frame. If you just stick with defaults, in the case where a Cisco router needs to talk IPX to a NetWare server 3.12 or above, you are in trouble.

On the other hand, if your Cisco router needs to pass IPX traffic generated by an older version of NetWare (below 3.12) and the default framing is used on the NetWare server, along with the default encapsulation on your Cisco router, you will actually be alright. However, what you need to consider is what happens when several NetWare servers are attached to the same segment using different frame types. Your router needs to be configured properly to handle such a scenario.

Effectively, if you have different IPX frame types on a single physical segment, you have multiple logical IPX networks on that segment. On a Cisco router you can assign one or more IPX network numbers to a single interface. If you are assigning a single network number to an interface, the configuration command is:

Ipx network *number* **encapsulation** *encapsulation-type*

where the *number* is the eight-digit hexadecimal number representing an IPX network, and the *encapsulation-type* is ARPA, SAP, SNAP, or Novell-Ether on an Ethernet interface. If there is a need to have more IPX addresses assigned to the same interface, it can be accomplished via the same command followed by a keyword *secondary*.

Ipx network *number* **encapsulation** *encapsulation-type* **secondary**

The use of secondary IPX network addresses is the solution to the issue raised in the preceding paragraph about how a router should handle different IPX frame types on the same physical segment. Suppose that you have an older version of NetWare (prior to 3.12) using the default frame type, which is IPX "raw" or IPX 802.3. Also, suppose you have another server attached to the same segment (IntraNetWare) using default frame type, 802.2. All of the NetWare clients are configured to recognize both frame types. Your Cisco router must also be configured to recognize both frame types.

The only way to accomplish this is through the use of secondary addresses as shown in the configuration example that follows:

```
interface Ethernet0
 ipx network C0A80000 encapsulation SAP
 ipx network C0A80001 encapsulation NOVELL-ETHER secondary
!
```

In this example, the router will be able to exchange IPX traffic over its E0 interface with servers and workstations that are using either 802.2 frames (SAP encapsulation on the router) or IPX 802.3 "raw" frames (Novell-Ether encapsulation on the router). Otherwise, if only one IPX network number were configured on the router with a single encapsulation type, an encapsulation mismatch would occur between the router and one of the Novell servers. For configuration details of NetWare servers, please refer to other volumes on such topics listed in the bibliography (Appendix A).

Ethernet Encapsulation of AppleTalk Traffic

The term AppleTalk refers not so much to a single protocol but rather to the entire computer architecture developed by Apple Computer. AppleTalk encompasses many different protocols, and the Network Layer protocol that corresponds to IP and IPX is actually the Datagram Delivery Protocol (DDP). However, nobody talks about DDP routing the way we talk about IP or IPX routing. When it comes to Apple protocols, it's AppleTalk routing.

AppleTalk routing and encapsulation are relatively simple as long as you do not try to mix AppleTalk Phase I with AppleTalk Phase II in a multivendor environment. But if your Macintoshes are running EtherTalk Version 2.0 or higher, and it's a matter of passing AppleTalk traffic between them across a Cisco router, the configuration is minimal. First, you enable AppleTalk on your router via the global configuration command `AppleTalk routing`. Second, you assign AppleTalk networks to interfaces via an interface configuration command `AppleTalk cable-range` *start-end*, where *start-end* represents the range of AppleTalk network numbers. Third, you assign AppleTalk zones to interfaces via another interface configuration command `AppleTalk zone` *zone-name*, where *zone-name* represents an AppleTalk zone.

Caution

AppleTalk encapsulation on Cisco routers is SNAP by default, not giving you the opportunity to make a mistake. However, if you have Macintoshes on the same segment as a NetWare server that's been configured to support the MAC name space, be sure to configure your NetWare server with the Ether_SNAP frame for AppleTalk protocol. That's if you expect to access it from your Macintosh workstations.

Token Ring and FDDI Encapsulations

There are fewer options with Token Ring and FDDI encapsulations than there are with Ethernet. The default and only Token Ring encapsulation for IP traffic is SNAP. The default Token Ring encapsulation for IPX traffic is SAP with SNAP available as the remaining option. With FDDI, it's either SNAP for IP or SAP, SNAP or Novell-FDDI for IPX. The Novell-FDDI for IPX is the equivalent of the IPX 802.3 or IPX "raw" frame on Ethernet networks. AppleTalk uses SNAP encapsulation on all media.

Encapsulation Rules of Thumb for Ethernet

An effective mnemonic device for Ethernet encapsulation rules: When considering IP encapsulation, think ARPA. ARPA is the name of the computer network that preceded the Internet. ARPA and IP are old buddies. They go back to the late 1970s before there were any IEEE standards like 802.3 or 802.2.

And when you think IPX, think SAP. NetWare uses the Service Advertising Protocol (SAP) to discover network services, and Cisco conveniently uses a keyword *sap* for the 802.2 encapsulation, which is the default IPX encapsulation with NetWare 3.12 and higher.

When you think AppleTalk, think SNAP. Imagine yourself snapping an apple from a tree. Also, another way to associate SNAP with AppleTalk is to consider that AppleTalk is very much a proprietary protocol; that is, not an IEEE-approved protocol. Consequently, if you want to operate it over 802-compliant media without a global SAP value assigned to AppleTalk, you have to use SNAP.

As a general rule of thumb for Ethernet networks, the encapsulation is ARPA for IP, SAP for IPX, and SNAP for AppleTalk.

Encapsulation Mismatch on WAN Links

Consider now Figure 1.2. As an internetwork grows and becomes more complex, the potential for encapsulation mismatches will increase.

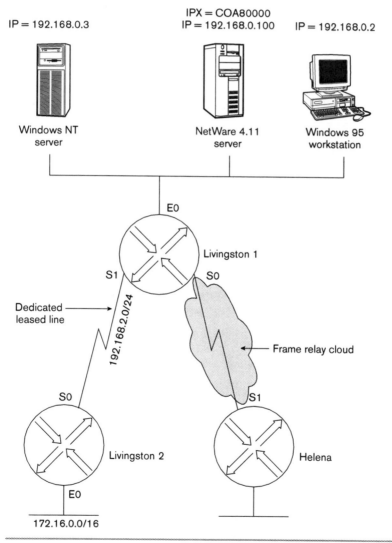

Figure 1.2 *A multi-protocol LAN with WAN connections to other LANs*

Two WAN links have been configured from the central office router (Livingston1) to routers in branch offices. One branch office is located in the same city, within a couple of miles of the central location (Livingston2). The other branch office router is located hundreds of miles away (Helena).

Economic analysis of WAN link options has revealed that a different WAN technology should be used for each WAN link. It's most cost-effective for the link to the branch office located in the same city to be a dedicated leased line. The WAN link to the branch office hundreds of miles away will be a Frame Relay connection. To avoid configuration snags in this scenario, the network administrator must be mindful that the encapsulation will be different for each WAN link.

The dedicated leased line is operating between the serial1 interface on the Livingston1 router and serial0 interface on the Livingston2 router. The network administrator is aware that on dedicated point-to-point links, a High-Level Data Link Control (HDLC) or a Point-to-Point Protocol (PPP) encapsulation can be used. The network administrator is also aware that Cisco defaults to HDLC encapsulation for serial links. This means that when no encapsulation is configured explicitly, HDLC will be used.

The administrator decides to experiment with the different encapsulations and chooses the default HDLC encapsulation on Livingston1's s1 by omitting the encapsulation command entirely, while configuring the Livingston2's s0 interface with PPP. Note that the s0 interface on Livingston1 has not been configured yet for Frame Relay. To his surprise, the configuration does not work. The problem is that a WAN encapsulation mismatch occurred. The solution is to configure both routers with the same encapsulation. The following example shows the initial misconfiguration for the dedicated leased line link.

Livingston1 initial configuration

```
!
hostname Livingston1
!
interface Ethernet0
 ip address 192.168.0.1 255.255.255.0
!
interface Serial1
 ip address 192.168.2.2 255.255.255.0
!
```

Livingston2 initial configuration

```
!
hostname Livingston2
!
interface Ethernet0
 ip address 172.16.0.1 255.255.0.0
!
interface Serial0
 ip address 192.168.2.1 255.255.255.0 encapsulation ppp
 clockrate 2000000
!
```

That a configuration mismatch has occurred can be verified by looking at the routing tables for both routers. Both routers, if correctly configured, should have a directly connected route to serial network 192.168.2.0/24. A quick look at the following traces shows that neither does:

```
Livingston1#sh ip route
Codes: C - connected,

Gateway of last resort is not set

C    192.168.0.0/24 is directly connected, Ethernet0
Livingston1#

Livingston2#sh ip route
Codes: C - connected,

Gateway of last resort is not set

C    172.16.0.0/16 is directly connected, Ethernet0
Livingston2#
```

The only routes that show up are the directly connected Ethernet networks attached to Ethernet0 interface on each router. The reason that 192.168.2.0/24 didn't show up in the route table is that the Link Layer never came up; thus, the Network Layer couldn't come up.

The obvious solution is either to take out the encapsulation statement on Livingston2, which will result in Cisco's default HDLC encapsulation on both routers, or to add PPP encapsulation on Livingston1. Note the change in the routing tables when either one of these conditions occurs.

```
Livingston1#sh ip route
Codes: C - connected,


Gateway of last resort is not set


C    192.168.0.0/24 is directly connected, Ethernet0
     192.168.2.0/24 is variably subnetted, 2 subnets, 2 masks
C       192.168.2.0/24 is directly connected, Serial1
C       192.168.2.1/32 is directly connected, Serial1
Livingston1#


Livingston2#sh ip route
Codes: C - connected,


Gateway of last resort is not set


C    172.16.0.0/16 is directly connected, Ethernet0
     192.168.2.0/24 is variably subnetted, 2 subnets, 2 masks
C       192.168.2.2/32 is directly connected, Serial0
C       192.168.2.0/24 is directly connected, Serial0
Livingston2#
```

In addition to the directly connected Ethernets, the routing tables for Livingston1 and Livingston2 now show the serial link between the two routers, 192.168.2.0/24.

Cisco actually makes it difficult to misconfigure encapsulation on dedicated leased lines by defaulting to Cisco's HDLC without any explicit encapsulation statement. However, if you find yourself in a multi-vendor environment, relying on Cisco's default encapsulation may become a problem for you. Experience dictates that it's best to take a proactive attitude, and to explicitly configure matching encapsulations on serial links. The serial link between Livinsgton1 and Helena is going to be Frame Relay.

Frame Relay configuration can be tricky and is prone to more errors than configuring a dedicated leased line. Potential Frame Relay pitfalls and misconfigurations are covered in later chapters.

Improper Use of Access Control Lists

Access control lists (ACLs) are intended to filter a certain amount of traffic passing through a router. The fundamental problem with ACLs is that when they are implemented improperly, they filter either too much traffic or not enough. When ACLs accidentally filter too much, they prevent legitimate traffic from reaching its intended destination. When they don't filter enough, they allow unintended traffic to get through a router. In either case it's a problem. Improper use of ACLs creates either too much security or a false sense of security.

Types of Access Control Lists

Cisco's IOS supports a wide range of ACLs, which are identified by numbers from pre-assigned ranges. ACLs differ from one another by capability (standard or extended) and by the protocols they filter (IP, IPX, DECnet, and so on). The following trace illustrates the available ACLs on a Cisco router licensed for the Enterprise edition of IOS.

```
victory#conf t
victory(config)#access-list ?
  <1-99>       IP standard access list
  <100-199>    IP extended access list
  <1000-1099>  IPX SAP access list
  <1100-1199>  Extended 48-bit MAC address access list
  <1200-1299>  IPX summary address access list
  <200-299>    Protocol type-code access list
  <300-399>    DECnet access list
  <400-499>    XNS standard access list
  <500-599>    XNS extended access list
  <600-699>    Appletalk access list
```

```
<700-799>    48-bit MAC address access list

<800-899>    IPX standard access list

<900-999>    IPX extended access list
```

Note that a similar display on routers with other flavors of IOS (IP only, IP with IPX, or Desktop) would yield a smaller group of available ACLs. Conceptually, the use of ACLs is simple; you use them to permit or deny incoming or outgoing traffic. But, the numerous options available within ACLs (the order in which the lists are listed in the configuration, the application of lists to either inbound or outbound traffic, and the rather primitive editing capabilities of ACL configurations) make their deployment tricky and prone to errors.

Anatomy of a Standard IP ACL

Perhaps the simplest of all of the ACLs is the standard IP access list. The configuration format of a standard IP access lists is as follows.

Access-list *number* **{permit | deny}** *source wild-card-mask*

The *number* represents a number between 1 and 99, the *source* represents a single or a group of IP addresses, and the *wild-card-mask* allows the representation of multiple IP addresses in the *source*. A configuration of a standard IP ACL on the E1 port of a 2-port Ethernet router is shown below.

```
interface Ethernet0

 ip address 192.168.0.1 255.255.255.0

!

interface Ethernet1

 ip address 192.168.1.1 255.255.255.0

 ip access-group 88 in

!

access-list 88 deny    192.168.1.100

access-list 88 permit 192.168.1.0 0.0.0.255
```

The preceding configuration shows only the router configuration statements needed for discussion of ACLs. The standard IP access list 88 and the ip access-group command in the interface Ethernet1 section are intended to deny inbound traffic from host 192.168.1.100, permit inbound traffic from all other hosts on subnet 192.168.1.0/24, and deny inbound traffic from any other source. The physical layout corresponding to the preceding configuration is illustrated in Figure 1.3.

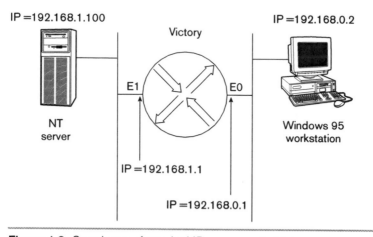

IP=192.168.1.100

Victory

IP=192.168.0.2

E1   E0

NT
server

Windows 95
workstation

IP=192.168.1.1

IP=192.168.0.1

Figure 1.3 *Sample use of standard IP access control list*

Consider now the flow of traffic in Figure 1.3. The IP address in the access-list statement represents the source address in the IP packet header.

If the Windows NT server (192.168.1.100) is originating any traffic, the IP packets will have the address of 192.168.1.100 as the source address in the IP header. If this traffic is destined for networks reachable via router Victory's Ethernet1 interface, this traffic will be denied passage through router Victory. This is accomplished by the `access-list 88 deny 192.168.1.100` statement applied to the Ethernet1 interface via `ip access-group 88` with the keyword *in*.

If a workstation from subnet 192.168.0.0 attempts to access the Windows NT server, the traffic destined for the server will reach it, but the return traffic will be stopped. Effectively, the return traffic is traffic originating on the NT server. The net result: no communication between the NT server and the workstations on subnet 192.168.0.0. If that's what was intended, then the preceding configuration is correct.

In addition, traffic from any subnet other than 192.168.1.0 will be denied entry through router Victory when arriving at the Ethernet1 interface.

That's because there is an implicit *Deny all* statement at the end of the ACL. The implicit *Deny all* is something to be mindful of when configuring ACLs. It's implicit because you don't see it, but it's there, doing its work.

Consider then what kind of traffic will flow through router Victory in this scenario. Router Victory will not block any traffic from passing through it as long as it arrives via Ethernet0. The reason for this is that the ip access-group 88 in statement with the *in* keyword is applied only to Ethernet1 interface. Ethernet0 interface has no restrictions on any incoming or outgoing traffic.

Also, no traffic will be blocked from leaving via Ethernet1. If any traffic that's blocked from arriving via Ethernet1 arrives via Ethernet0 instead, then the *in* keyword applied to Ethernet1 will not prevent it from leaving via Ethernet1. What will stop traffic from leaving through Ethernet1 is another ip access-group statement, but this time with the *out* keyword, that is, ip access-group 88 out. The remaining traffic that will be able to pass through Victory is from the devices on subnet 192.168.1.0 with IP addresses other than 192.168.1.100.

With a basic example of how a standard IP access control list operates, consider the potential pitfalls of its application:

- The order in which the *permit* and *deny* statements are arranged in the list
- Improper application of the wild card mask
- Confusion about the effects of inbound versus outbound filtering

Incorrect List Order

Consider what would happen if the order of the *permit/deny* statements in the IP access list 88 were reversed and the configuration was as follows:

```
interface Ethernet0
 ip address 192.168.0.1 255.255.255.0
!
interface Ethernet1
 ip address 192.168.1.1 255.255.255.0
 ip access-group 88 in
!
access-list 88 permit 192.168.1.0 0.0.0.255
access-list 88 deny   192.168.1.100
```

The second statement `access-list 88 deny 192.168.1.100` would have no effect. When the source IP addresses of arriving packets are checked against the ACL, the list is scanned from top to bottom. If a match occurs, the remainder of the list is not checked. If the intent of this configuration was to deny inbound traffic from server 192.168.1.100, then this configuration would fail. The first statement in the list would match the server's address and traffic originating on the server would pass through.

Now, suppose that all you want to do is to deny inbound traffic from server 192.168.1.100 and the only statement that you place in the list is the *deny* statement. The configuration appears as follows:

```
interface Ethernet0
 ip address 192.168.0.1 255.255.255.0
!
interface Ethernet1
 ip address 192.168.1.1 255.255.255.0
 ip access-group 88 in
!
access-list 88 deny    192.168.1.100
```

You've denied all traffic from getting into the router Victory via Ethernet1 through the preceding configuration. Remember that there is an implicit *Deny all* at the end of the list. The list is scanned until there is a match on the source address. If the server originates traffic, the match will occur on the first statement and since it's a *deny* statement, the traffic from the server will not be allowed to enter the router via the Ethernet1 interface.

If the traffic originates from any other source, there will not be a match on the first statement, but there will be a match on the implicit *Deny all*, and that traffic will be denied. A helpful rule: If you have only *deny* statements in your list without any *permit* statements, you are in effect denying all traffic from entering or leaving via an interface.

 Note

Final reminder: The order of *permit/deny* statements is vital in an access control list.

Improper Application of the Wild Card Mask

The wild card mask is the last component in the configuration statement. It typically begins with 0s and ends with 1s in binary, and it's expressed in dotted decimal notation just like IP addresses, subnet masks, and other masks that use the dotted decimal notation. But the wild card mask does not have to be contiguous 0s ending with contiguous 1s. Ultimately, in this mask, it's the 0 bits that matter. Which means the bits in the source address in the header and the IP address in the list statement must be the same in all of the positions where the bits are 0 in the mask. Consider the following statement:

```
access-list 88 permit 192.168.1.0 0.0.0.255
```

The source address in the IP header and the address in the access list must have the same first three bytes for a match to take place, which means that all of the devices on subnet 192.168.1.0 will match. Assume now that your goal is to allow traffic from all devices on subnet 192.168.1.0 to reach router Victory via Ethernet1 interface, but your configuration is as follows:

```
interface Ethernet0
 ip address 192.168.0.1 255.255.255.0
!
interface Ethernet1
 ip address 192.168.1.1 255.255.255.0
 ip access-group 88 in
!
access-list 88 permit 192.168.1.0 0.0.0.127
```

The result is that all devices that have their last dotted decimal greater than 128 will not match on the *permit* statement, and consequently will be subject to the implicit *Deny all* statement.

Consider what happens if your access list statement looked as follows:

```
access-list 88 permit 192.168.1.0 0.0.0.240
```

The statement is not incorrect, but it's rather confusing. It's not that hard to get the inverted mask (beginning with 0s) and the normal mask (beginning with 1s) mixed up. In this case, it seems that it's the last byte of the mask that's mixed up. Instead of 240 it's supposed to be 15.

However, if it were really meant to be 240 in the last byte, it would mean that only those devices on subnet 192.168.1.0 whose four lowest-order bits are not set would match this statement. The last byte in binary for these devices would have to be a multiple of 16, between 0 and 240. You decide if there is a potential for pitfalls and mistakes with using wild cards in access control lists.

Inbound versus Outbound Filtering

Inbound versus outbound filtering is implemented via the *in* and *out* keywords at the end of the access list statement. Perhaps the easiest way to remember how it works and avoid mistakes is through a couple of simple associations.

The keyword *in* only has impact on the traffic attempting to come into the router through the interface on which the access list is applied. It has no impact on the traffic attempting to leave through the same interface, that is, traffic that made it into the router through some other interface. It has no impact on traffic attempting to enter through any other interface.

The keyword *out* only has impact on traffic attempting to leave the router through the interface on which the access list is applied. It has no impact on traffic attempting to enter through the same interface. It has no impact on traffic attempting to leave through any other interface on the router.

It may be obvious but perhaps it bears repeating: Access control lists are applied to router interfaces, not to routers.

Access Control List Verification

To verify the ACL configuration, use the `show access-list` command to produce a trace, such as the one that follows for the access list 88 used in preceding examples:

```
victory#show access-list
Standard IP access list 88
    deny    192.168.1.100
    permit 192.168.1.0, wildcard bits 0.0.0.255
```

To verify the application of the ACL to an interface, the `show ip interface` command is required. The partial output from the command `show ip interface e1` is displayed for the example used in this section.

```
victory#sh ip interface e1
Ethernet1 is up, line protocol is up
  Internet address is 192.168.1.1/24
  Broadcast address is 255.255.255.255
  Address determined by non-volatile memory
  MTU is 1500 bytes
  Helper address is not set
  Directed broadcast forwarding is enabled
  Multicast reserved groups joined: 224.0.0.5 224.0.0.6
  Outgoing access list is not set
  Inbound  access list is 88
  Proxy ARP is enabled
  .
  .
victory#
```

The preceding traces confirm that access list 88 is applied to Ethernet1 interface inbound. The list consists of two statements, one *deny* and one *permit*, which are used in the configuration example at the beginning of this section.

Autonomous System Number Mismatch in IGRP and EIGRP

Dynamic routing protocols like Interior Gateway Routing Protocol (IGRP), Enhanced IGRP (EIGRP), or Open Shortest Path First (OSPF) — commonly referred to as Interior Gateway Protocols (IGPs) — can be misconfigured to such an extent that neighboring routers running one of these protocols don't exchange any routing updates with one another. And when routing updates are not exchanged between routers, their routing tables will not be accurate.

Routing tables can be populated either with static routes or with routes derived from one or more dynamic routing protocols configured on a router. When routers rely exclusively on static routes, the network administrator who's configured the static routes effectively assumes the role of a routing protocol. It behooves the network administrator to be fully aware of an internetwork's topology and configure the static routes accordingly.

Reliance on static routes is common in simple single path networks. However, in complex internetworks with hundreds of routers and multiple paths between them, strict reliance on static routes deprives you of the key benefit that dynamic routing protocols provide: re-routing around failed links.

Cisco's two proprietary routing protocols are IGRP and EIGRP. The activation of these protocols on a Cisco router is almost trivial compared to some of their operational complexities. The protocol needs to be enabled with a configuration command in the router configuration mode and the routing process needs to be told which networks it's going to be routing for as shown below:

```
Router IGRP as_number

Network  y.y.y.y

Network  z.z.z.z
```

The *as_number* represents an autonomous system (AS) number and *y.y.y.y and z.z.z.z* represent classful network addresses. One *Network* statement is used for each classful network. Multiple *Network* statements are used to tell IGRP about all of the networks it will route for.

In IGRP or EIGRP, it is the autonomous system number (ASN) that can be easily misunderstood and misconfigured. Note that this is Cisco's autonomous system number as opposed to the ASN used in BGP. The autonomous system number used by IGRP and EIGRP is a mechanism of grouping IGRP/EIGRP routers into smaller groups for the purpose of exchanging routing updates only within these groups. Autonomous system numbers used with IGRP and EIGRP have nothing to do with the autonomous systems and autonomous system numbers used with BGP.

In BGP, the autonomous system number is used in reference to a routing domain that may include multiple IGPs on the inside, but appears to have a uniform routing policy from the outside. A uniform routing policy in BGP reflects the purpose of an internetwork. An example of a BGP internetwork with a uniform routing policy is a major ISP acting as a transit provider for other ISPs. The same ISP that's acting as transit provider could have multiple IGRP autonomous systems inside its BGP AS. See Chapter 10 for more information on BGP.

Total Mismatch in AS Numbers

In the scenario shown in Figure 1.4, three routers (Bozeman, Livingston, and Helena) are fully meshed via serial links. These three routers have been configured with IGRP, but each router has been configured with a different autonomous system number. The net result is that there simply is no exchange of routing updates between these routers. From IGRP's perspective, these three routers may as well not be connected.

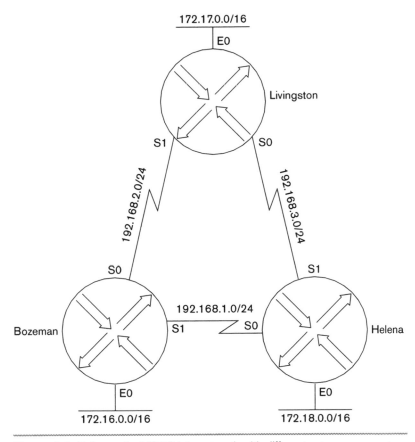

Figure 1.4 *Fully meshed IGRP internetwork with different autonomous system numbers*

The initial interface and protocol configurations of the three routers are shown in the traces that follow:

Bozeman router initial IGRP configuration

```
hostname Bozeman
!
interface Ethernet0
 ip address 172.16.0.1 255.255.0.0
!
interface Serial0
 description serial link to Livingston
 ip address 192.168.2.1 255.255.255.0
 clockrate 2000000
!
interface Serial1
 description serial link to Helena
 ip address 192.168.1.2 255.255.255.0
!
router igrp 1
 network 172.16.0.0
 network 192.168.1.0
 network 192.168.2.0
```

Livingston router initial IGRP configuration

```
hostname Livingston
!
interface Ethernet0
 ip address 172.17.0.1 255.255.0.0
!
interface Serial0
 description serial link to Helena
 ip address 192.168.3.1 255.255.255.0
 clockrate 2000000
!
interface Serial1
```

```
description serial link to serial link to Bozeman

ip address 192.168.2.2 255.255.255.0

!

router igrp 2

network 172.17.0.0

network 192.168.2.0

network 192.168.3.0
```

Helena router initial IGRP configuration

```
!

hostname Helena

!

interface Ethernet0

 ip address 172.18.0.1 255.255.0.0

!

interface Serial0

 description serial link to Bozeman

 ip address 192.168.1.1 255.255.255.0

 clockrate 2000000

!

interface Serial1

 description serial link to Livingston

 ip address 192.168.3.2 255.255.255.0

!

router igrp 3

 network 172.18.0.0

 network 192.168.1.0

 network 192.168.3.0
```

Displaying routes on each router reveals that only the directly connected networks (one Ethernet and two serial) show up in each router's routing table as demonstrated in the traces that follow. No IGRP routes are visible.

```
Bozeman#sh ip route


Codes: C - connected,
```

```
C    172.16.0.0/16 is directly connected, Ethernet0
C    192.168.1.0/24 is directly connected, Serial1
C    192.168.2.0/24 is directly connected, Serial0
Bozeman#
```

```
Livingston#show ip route
Codes: C - connected,
```

```
C    172.17.0.0/16 is directly connected, Ethernet0
C    192.168.2.0/24 is directly connected, Serial1
C    192.168.3.0/24 is directly connected, Serial0
Livingston#
```

```
Helena#sh ip route
Codes: C - connected,
```

```
C    172.18.0.0/16 is directly connected, Ethernet0
C    192.168.1.0/24 is directly connected, Serial0
C    192.168.3.0/24 is directly connected, Serial1
Helena#
```

The reason for the lack of IGRP routes is simple: autonomous system number mismatch. Each router is configured with a different autonomous system number. Livingston is configured with AS 1, Bozeman with AS 2, and Helena with AS 3.

Total Match in AS Numbers

Notice what happens to the routing table on all of the routers when the autonomous system number is changed to the same value on all three routers. The AS number in the IGRP section was changed to 2 on all three routers.

```
Bozeman#sh ip route
Codes: C - connected, S - static, I - IGRP,
```

Gateway of last resort is not set

I   **172.17.0.0/16 [100/8576] via 192.168.2.2, 00:00:32, Serial0**

C   172.16.0.0/16 is directly connected, Ethernet0

I   **172.18.0.0/16 [100/10576] via 192.168.2.2, 00:00:32, Serial0**

C   192.168.1.0/24 is directly connected, Serial1

C   192.168.2.0/24 is directly connected, Serial0

I   **192.168.3.0/24 [100/10476] via 192.168.2.2, 00:00:32, Serial0**

Bozeman#

Livingston#**sh ip route**

Codes: C - connected, S - static, I - IGRP,

Gateway of last resort is not set

C   172.17.0.0/16 is directly connected, Ethernet0

I   **172.16.0.0/16 [100/8576] via 192.168.2.1, 00:01:26, Serial1**

I   **172.18.0.0/16 [100/8576] via 192.168.3.2, 00:01:06, Serial0**

I   **192.168.1.0/24 [100/10476] via 192.168.2.1, 00:01:26, Serial1**

                  [100/10476] via 192.168.3.2, 00:01:06, Serial0

C   192.168.2.0/24 is directly connected, Serial1

C   192.168.3.0/24 is directly connected, Serial0

Livingston#

Helena#**sh ip route**

Codes: C - connected, S - static, I - IGRP,

Gateway of last resort is not set

I   **172.17.0.0/16 [100/8576] via 192.168.3.1, 00:01:22, Serial1**

I   **172.16.0.0/16 [100/8576] via 192.168.1.2, 00:01:18, Serial0**

C   172.18.0.0/16 is directly connected, Ethernet0

C   192.168.1.0/24 is directly connected, Serial0

I   **192.168.2.0/24 [100/10476] via 192.168.1.2, 00:01:18, Serial0**

```
                [100/10476] via 192.168.3.1, 00:01:23, Serial1
C    192.168.3.0/24 is directly connected, Serial1
Helena#
```

All Ethernet LANs shown in Figure 1.4 are now reachable from each router. In addition, the serial network to which each router is not directly connected also becomes visible in the routing table. In the case of the Helena router, the serial link 192.168.2.0/24 is accessible via two paths at the same cost. Doing a traceroute to an IP address on that link as shown in the following trace reveals load sharing as successive packets generated by the traceroute utility.

```
Helena#traceroute 192.168.2.1

Type escape sequence to abort.
Tracing the route to 192.168.2.1

  1 192.168.1.2 4 msec
    192.168.3.1 4 msec
    192.168.1.2 8 msec
Helena#
```

This output from the traceroute utility may not seem very dramatic, but it clearly illustrates the load-sharing principle. Traceroute sends out three successive ICMP probes with increasing Time to Live (TTL) counters until the destination is reached. The destination of 192.168.2.1 is reachable via one hop, but as the three probes are sent out they alternate the paths they take. The first probe goes out via 192.168.1.2 (Bozeman), second via 192.168.3.1 (Livingston) and the third via Bozeman again. In the scenario depicted in Figure 4.1, the load generated by traceroute to a destination on 192.168.2.0/24 is split over the two serial links to which Helena router is attached.

Partial Match or Partial Mismatch in AS Numbers (Your Choice)

Given how easy it is to mismatch the autonomous system numbers in IGRP, you may wonder why Cisco allows them to be different in the first place. Having a choice in the autonomous system number allows for the definition of multiple IGRP processes on the same router.

Suppose that you want the Livingston router to have access to the Ethernet networks attached to the Bozeman and Helena routers, but you do not want the Bozeman router to know about the Ethernet attached to Helena and vice versa. This would effectively create a hub-and-spoke scenario where the Livingston router is a hub and the Bozeman and Helena routers are spokes.

The hub has access to all networks. The spokes have access only to their own networks and the hub's networks, but not to each other's networks. There are certainly many different ways of creating a hub-and-spoke scenario, but one way is via the judicious use of IGRP autonomous system numbers.

Following are the changes to the initial configurations from the "Total Mismatch in AS Numbers" section. The configuration of the Bozeman and Helena routers (the spokes) stays the same. But on the Livingston router there are now two IGRP processes. One has the same AS number as Helena, the other the same AS number as Bozeman.

Bozeman router configuration for partial IGRP AS match

```
!
hostname Bozeman
!
interface Ethernet0
 ip address 172.16.0.1 255.255.0.0
!
interface Serial0
 description serial link to Livingston
 ip address 192.168.2.1 255.255.255.0
 clockrate 2000000
!
interface Serial1
 description serial link to Helena
 ip address 192.168.1.2 255.255.255.0
!
router igrp 1
```

```
network 172.16.0.0
network 192.168.1.0
network 192.168.2.0
!
```

Livingston router configuration for partial IGRP AS match

```
!
hostname Livingston
!
interface Ethernet0
 ip address 172.17.0.1 255.255.0.0
!
interface Serial0
 description serial link to Helena
 ip address 192.168.3.1 255.255.255.0
 clockrate 2000000
!
interface Serial1
 description serial link to Bozeman
 ip address 192.168.2.2 255.255.255.0
!
router igrp 1                    Note changes to IGRP configuration on Livingston
 network 172.17.0.0
 network 192.168.2.0
!
router igrp 3
 network 172.17.0.0
 network 192.168.3.0
```

Helena router configuration for partial IGRP AS match

```
!
hostname Helena
!
interface Ethernet0
```

```
ip address 172.18.0.1 255.255.0.0
!
interface Serial0
 description serial link to Bozeman
 ip address 192.168.1.1 255.255.255.0
 clockrate 2000000
!
interface Serial1
 description serial link to Livingston
 ip address 192.168.3.2 255.255.255.0
!
router igrp 3
 network 172.18.0.0
 network 192.168.1.0
 network 192.168.3.0
```

The net result of this configuration is best viewed by looking at the routing tables.

```
Livingston#sh ip route

Codes: C - connected, S - static, I - IGRP,

Gateway of last resort is not set

C    172.17.0.0/16 is directly connected, Ethernet0
I    172.16.0.0/16 [100/8576] via 192.168.2.1, 00:00:57, Serial1
I    172.18.0.0/16 [100/8576] via 192.168.3.2, 00:01:07, Serial0
I    192.168.1.0/24 [100/10476] via 192.168.2.1, 00:00:57, Serial1
                    [100/10476] via 192.168.3.2, 00:01:07, Serial0
C    192.168.2.0/24 is directly connected, Serial1
C    192.168.3.0/24 is directly connected, Serial0
Livingston#
```

It may be interesting to note that the Livingston IGRP configuration changed but its routing table did not. That's because Livingston is now in two autonomous systems (1 and 3) while Bozeman is only in autonomous system 1 and Helena in autonomous system 3. Reviewing the routing tables for Helena and Bozeman reveals that only the directly connected networks and the Livingston Ethernet are reachable from each router.

```
Bozeman#sh ip route
Codes: C - connected, S - static, I - IGRP,


Gateway of last resort is not set


I    172.17.0.0/16 [100/8576] via 192.168.2.2, 00:00:33, Serial0
C    172.16.0.0/16 is directly connected, Ethernet0
C    192.168.1.0/24 is directly connected, Serial1
C    192.168.2.0/24 is directly connected, Serial0
Bozeman#


Helena#sh ip route
Codes: C - connected, S - static, I - IGRP,


Gateway of last resort is not set


I    172.17.0.0/16 [100/8576] via 192.168.3.1, 00:00:13, Serial1
C    172.18.0.0/16 is directly connected, Ethernet0
C    192.168.1.0/24 is directly connected, Serial0
C    192.168.3.0/24 is directly connected, Serial1
Helena#
```

The point of this discussion on mismatched autonomous system numbers is that a mismatch may be a source of problems or it may actually serve a purpose, as shown in the preceding section. The key is to understand how it works.

Redistribution between AS Numbers

A technique that allows for AS numbers to be different while still maintaining full reachability is redistribution. Note changes to the configuration of the Livingston router and observe their effect on the routing tables in Bozeman and Helena.

Livingston router configuration for IGRP redistribution

```
!
hostname Livingston
!
interface Ethernet0
 ip address 172.17.0.1 255.255.0.0
!
interface Serial0
 description serial link to Helena
 ip address 192.168.3.1 255.255.255.0
 clockrate 2000000
!
interface Serial1
 description serial link to Bozeman
 ip address 192.168.2.2 255.255.255.0
!
router igrp 1
 redistribute igrp 3       Note changes to IGRP configuration on Livingston
 network 172.17.0.0
 network 192.168.2.0
!
router igrp 3
 redistribute igrp 1
 network 172.17.0.0
 network 192.168.3.0
```

The Helena and Bozeman routing tables now once again have knowledge of all of the networks identified in Figure 1.4, as shown in the traces that follow:

```
Bozeman#sh ip route
Codes: C - connected, S - static, I - IGRP,
```

```
Gateway of last resort is not set


I    172.17.0.0/16 [100/8576] via 192.168.2.2, 00:00:03, Serial0

C    172.16.0.0/16 is directly connected, Ethernet0

I    172.18.0.0/16 [100/10576] via 192.168.2.2, 00:00:03, Serial0

C    192.168.1.0/24 is directly connected, Serial1

C    192.168.2.0/24 is directly connected, Serial0

I    192.168.3.0/24 [100/10476] via 192.168.2.2, 00:00:03, Serial0

Bozeman#


Helena#sh ip route

Codes: C - connected, S - static, I - IGRP,


Gateway of last resort is not set


I    172.17.0.0/16 [100/8576] via 192.168.3.1, 00:00:25, Serial1

I    172.16.0.0/16 [100/10576] via 192.168.3.1, 00:00:26, Serial1

C    172.18.0.0/16 is directly connected, Ethernet0

C    192.168.1.0/24 is directly connected, Serial0

I    192.168.2.0/24 [100/10476] via 192.168.3.1, 00:00:26, Serial1

C    192.168.3.0/24 is directly connected, Serial1

Helena#
```

What's different about these routing tables when compared to the routing tables in the "Total Match in AS Numbers" section is the metric or cost of reaching the spoke Ethernet networks. From Helena's point of view, the IGRP metric of reaching 172.16.0.0 (Bozeman Ethernet) is now 10,576. And this network is reachable via Livingston, next hop of 192.168.3.1. In the "Total Match in AS Numbers" section, the same network, 172.16.0.0, was reachable at a cost of 8,576 and via Bozeman.

The effect of redistribution here is that the hub-and-spoke scenario is preserved but there is full reachability between all networks unlike in the "Partial Match or Partial Mismatch in AS Numbers" section. The Livingston router, however, remains a hub. The Helena and Bozeman routers remain as spokes. Traffic from Helena must go through Livingston to reach Bozeman and vice versa. But at least with redistribution and different

AS numbers, they can talk to each other through the hub router, although at a higher cost than if all of the routers shared the same AS number.

Area ID Misconfigurations in OSPF

OSPF is a popular link-state protocol with scalability advantages over distance vector protocols like RIP or IGRP. Large OSPF routing domains can be broken into smaller pieces (OSPF areas) to reduce the amount of routing updates that are transferred between OSPF routers. OSPF areas are represented by an area ID that's typically expressed in a dotted decimal notation, just like IP addresses. However, the area ID can assume the form of a single decimal number as well.

No matter how large or small the OSPF internetwork is, one area that should always be present in an OSPF routing domain is a backbone area, area zero, or 0.0.0.0. As you will see in a subsequent example in this section, OSPF can function under certain conditions without the presence of area 0.0.0.0. However, OSPF configuration without area 0.0.0.0 is not recommended.

OSPF is activated on a Cisco router in a similar manner to IGRP via a router command from the configuration mode:

```
Router OSPF xx
```

Here, *xx* is a process ID. The process ID in OSPF does not have the same meaning as the autonomous system number in IGRP or EIGRP. Different routers can use different process IDs and still be able to exchange routing updates. However, the presence of a process ID allows for multiple OSPF processes to be activated on the same router.

After the OSPF process is activated on a Cisco router, the interfaces over which OSPF will route must be assigned to OSPF area(s). This step is accomplished via the **network** command. The syntax for the assignment of interfaces to OSPF areas from the command line is:

```
network address inverted_mask area area_ID
```

Here, *address* is the IP address of the interface(s), *inverted_mask* is a wild card allowing multiple interfaces to be assigned to the same area, and *area_ID* represents the area to which interfaces are being assigned.

For OSPF to function properly, the area IDs must match for all router interfaces belonging to a particular area. In an OSPF network where only a single backbone area is present, it may be easy to avoid mistakes with mismatched area IDs. However, in an OSPF internetwork with multiple areas, the potential for errors increases. The additional factor that contributes to mistakes in assigning interfaces to OSPF areas is the use of an inverted mask in the `network` statement.

Generally speaking, the use of a mask (normal or inverted) with an IP address is an indication that multiple addresses can hide behind the mask. In the case of OSPF interfaces being assigned to areas, it means that it's possible to assign more than one interface to an area with a single `network` statement. But this shortcut is also prone to errors.

Single Area 0.0.0.0

Consider a scenario as depicted in Figure 1.5 with three routers (Bozeman, Livingston, and Helena) fully meshed via serial links and Ethernet network(s) at each location.

If all of the routers belong to the same area zero, then the interface assignment is quite simple. Since the IP addresses of all interfaces begin either with 192.168 or with 172, the interface assignment on all three routers could be identical, and the OSPF configuration statements on each router would be as follows:

Bozeman router initial OSPF configuration:

```
!
hostname Bozeman
!
interface Ethernet0
 ip address 172.16.0.1 255.255.0.0
!
interface Serial0
 description serial link to Livingston
 ip address 192.168.2.1 255.255.255.0
 clockrate 2000000
!
```

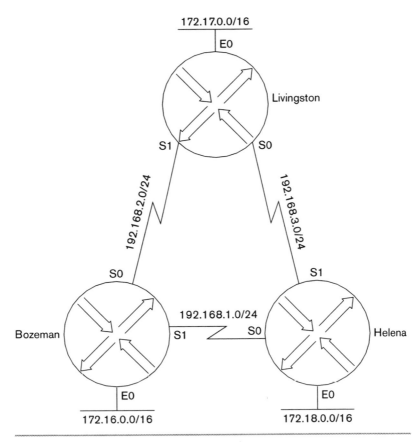

Figure 1.5 *Fully meshed OSPF internetwork*

```
interface Serial1
description serial link to Helena
ip address 192.168.1.2 255.255.255.0
!
router ospf 1
network 172.0.0.0 0.255.255.255 area 0.0.0.0
network 192.168.0.0 0.0.255.255 area 0.0.0.0
!
```

Livingston router initial OSPF configuration

```
!
hostname Livingston
!
interface Ethernet0
 ip address 172.17.0.1 255.255.0.0
!
interface Serial0
 description serial link to Helena
 ip address 192.168.3.1 255.255.255.0
 clockrate 2000000
!
interface Serial1
 description serial link to Bozeman
 ip address 192.168.2.2 255.255.255.0
!
router ospf 1
 network 172.0.0.0 0.255.255.255 area 0.0.0.0
 network 192.168.0.0 0.0.255.255 area 0.0.0.0
!
```

Helena router initial OSPF configuration

```
!
hostname Helena
!
interface Ethernet0
 ip address 172.18.0.1 255.255.0.0
!
interface Serial0
 description serial link to Bozeman
 ip address 192.168.1.1 255.255.255.0
 clockrate 2000000
!
 interface Serial1
```

```
description serial link to Livingston
ip address 192.168.3.2 255.255.255.0
!
router ospf 1
network 172.0.0.0 0.255.255.255 area 0.0.0.0
network 192.168.0.0 0.0.255.255 area 0.0.0.0
!
```

The resulting routing tables from the preceding configuration are shown in the traces that follow:

```
Bozeman#sh ip route

Codes: C - connected, S - static, I - IGRP, R - RIP, M - mobile, B - BGP
       D - EIGRP, EX - EIGRP external, O - OSPF,
Gateway of last resort is not set


O    172.17.0.0/16 [110/74] via 192.168.2.2, 00:06:23, Serial0
C    172.16.0.0/16 is directly connected, Ethernet0
O    172.18.0.0/16 [110/74] via 192.168.1.1, 00:06:23, Serial1
C    192.168.1.0/24 is directly connected, Serial1
C    192.168.2.0/24 is directly connected, Serial0
O    192.168.3.0/24 [110/128] via 192.168.1.1, 00:06:23, Serial1
                    [110/128] via 192.168.2.2, 00:06:23, Serial0
Bozeman#


Livingston#sh ip route
Codes: C - connected, S - static, I - IGRP, R - RIP, M - mobile, B - BGP
       D - EIGRP, EX - EIGRP external, O - OSPF,


Gateway of last resort is not set


C    172.17.0.0/16 is directly connected, Ethernet0
O    172.16.0.0/16 [110/74] via 192.168.2.1, 00:06:37, Serial1
O    172.18.0.0/16 [110/74] via 192.168.3.2, 00:06:37, Serial0
O    192.168.1.0/24 [110/128] via 192.168.3.2, 00:06:37, Serial0
```

```
                   [110/128] via 192.168.2.1, 00:06:37, Serial1
C     192.168.2.0/24 is directly connected, Serial1
C     192.168.3.0/24 is directly connected, Serial0
Livingston#


Helena#sh ip route
Codes: C - connected, S - static, I - IGRP, R - RIP, M - mobile, B - BGP
       D - EIGRP, EX - EIGRP external, O - OSPF,


Gateway of last resort is not set


O     172.17.0.0/16 [110/74] via 192.168.3.1, 00:06:57, Serial1
O     172.16.0.0/16 [110/74] via 192.168.1.2, 00:06:58, Serial0
C     172.18.0.0/16 is directly connected, Ethernet0
C     192.168.1.0/24 is directly connected, Serial0
O     192.168.2.0/24 [110/128] via 192.168.3.1, 00:06:58, Serial1
                      [110/128] via 192.168.1.2, 00:06:58, Serial0
C     192.168.3.0/24 is directly connected, Serial1
Helena#
```

Note that in each case, the serial network not directly connected to the router is reachable via two paths, which would result in load balancing for destinations on that subnet. The preceding scenario is an example of a correctly configured OSPF internetwork with all router interfaces belonging to the single backbone area 0.0.0.0.

Multiple Areas with Area 0.0.0.0

Assume now that the serial mesh between the routers is going to compose area 0.0.0.0 and each site is going to have its own area. The configuration statements on each router would have to change. The areas are going be defined as shown in Figure 1.6.

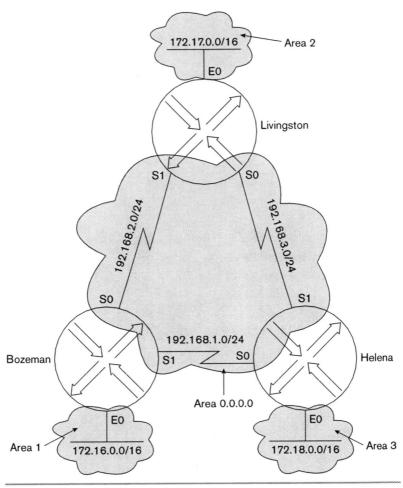

Figure 1.6 *Fully meshed OSPF internetwork broken into areas*

The interface and OSPF configuration for the respective routers is as follows:

Bozeman router configuration with multiple OSPF areas

```
!
hostname Bozeman
!
```

```
interface Ethernet0
 ip address 172.16.0.1 255.255.0.0
 !
interface Serial0
 description serial link to Livingston
 ip address 192.168.2.1 255.255.255.0
 clockrate 2000000
 !
 interface Serial1
 description serial link to Helena
 ip address 192.168.1.2 255.255.255.0
 !
router ospf 1                         Note configuration change on Bozeman
 network 172.0.0.0 0.255.255.255 area 1
 network 192.168.0.0 0.0.255.255 area 0.0.0.0
 !
```

Livingston router configuration with multiple OSPF areas

```
!
hostname Livingston
!
interface Ethernet0
 ip address 172.17.0.1 255.255.0.0
 !
interface Serial0
 description serial link to Helena
 ip address 192.168.3.1 255.255.255.0
 clockrate 2000000
 !
interface Serial1
 description serial link to Bozeman
 ip address 192.168.2.2 255.255.255.0
 !
router ospf 1                         Note configuration change on Livingston
```

```
network 172.0.0.0 0.255.255.255 area 2
network 192.168.0.0 0.0.255.255 area 0.0.0.0
!
```

Helena router configuration with multiple OSPF areas

```
!
hostname Helena
!
interface Ethernet0
 ip address 172.18.0.1 255.255.0.0
!
interface Serial0
 description serial link to Bozeman
 ip address 192.168.1.1 255.255.255.0
 clockrate 2000000
!
 interface Serial1
 description serial link to Livingston
 ip address 192.168.3.2 255.255.255.0
!
router ospf 1                          Note configuration change on Helena
 network 172.0.0.0 0.255.255.255 area 3
 network 192.168.0.0 0.0.255.255 area 0.0.0.0
!
```

The resulting routing tables from this configuration are shown in the traces that follow. They reflect full reachability between all of the networks in different areas. Notice, however, a change in the designation of some of the routes.

```
Bozeman#sh ip route
Codes: C - connected, S - static, I - IGRP, R - RIP, M - mobile, B - BGP
       D - EIGRP, EX - EIGRP external, O - OSPF, IA - OSPF inter area

Gateway of last resort is not set
```

```
O IA 172.17.0.0/16 [110/74] via 192.168.2.2, 00:18:30, Serial0
C    172.16.0.0/16 is directly connected, Ethernet0
O IA 172.18.0.0/16 [110/74] via 192.168.1.1, 00:18:30, Serial1
C    192.168.1.0/24 is directly connected, Serial1
C    192.168.2.0/24 is directly connected, Serial0
O    192.168.3.0/24 [110/128] via 192.168.2.2, 00:18:30, Serial0
                    [110/128] via 192.168.1.1, 00:18:30, Serial1
Bozeman#


Livingston#sh ip route
Codes: C - connected, S - static, I - IGRP, R - RIP, M - mobile, B - BGP
       D - EIGRP, EX - EIGRP external, O - OSPF, IA - OSPF inter area


Gateway of last resort is not set


C    172.17.0.0/16 is directly connected, Ethernet0
O IA 172.16.0.0/16 [110/74] via 192.168.2.1, 00:18:38, Serial1
O IA 172.18.0.0/16 [110/74] via 192.168.3.2, 00:18:38, Serial0
O    192.168.1.0/24 [110/128] via 192.168.2.1, 00:18:38, Serial1
                    [110/128] via 192.168.3.2, 00:18:38, Serial0
C    192.168.2.0/24 is directly connected, Serial1
C    192.168.3.0/24 is directly connected, Serial0
Livingston#


Helena#sh ip route
Codes: C - connected, S - static, I - IGRP, R - RIP, M - mobile, B - BGP
       D - EIGRP, EX - EIGRP external, O - OSPF, IA - OSPF inter area


Gateway of last resort is not set


O IA 172.17.0.0/16 [110/74] via 192.168.3.1, 00:18:55, Serial1
O IA 172.16.0.0/16 [110/74] via 192.168.1.2, 00:18:55, Serial0
C    172.18.0.0/16 is directly connected, Ethernet0
C    192.168.1.0/24 is directly connected, Serial0
O    192.168.2.0/24 [110/128] via 192.168.1.2, 00:18:55, Serial0
```

```
                [110/128] via 192.168.3.1, 00:18:55, Serial1
C    192.168.3.0/24 is directly connected, Serial1
Helena#
```

Take particular note of the routes with the IA designation. The designation of IA in front of some of the routes indicates an Inter Area route. From any router's point of view, an Inter Area route represents a destination that's in an area different than the areas to which this router's interfaces are assigned. In the example in Figure 1.6, the Helena router has interfaces in area 0.0.0.0 and in area 3. Consequently, networks in areas 1 and 2 will appear as Inter Area routes in Helena router's routing table. Since all of the routers in Figure 1.6 have some interfaces in the backbone area, none of the backbone destinations will appear in them as Inter Area routers. All of the backbone destinations will appear either as directly connected routes or just plain OSPF routes designated only with the "O" character.

Missing Area 0.0.0.0

Let's see what happens to OSPF now if, let's say, you took the configuration from the preceding section and replaced area 0.0.0.0 with another area ID, say 10. The configuration would look as follows:

Bozeman router OSPF configuration with area 0.0.0.0 missing

```
!
hostname Bozeman
!
interface Ethernet0
 ip address 172.16.0.1 255.255.0.0
!
interface Serial0
 description serial link to Livingston
 ip address 192.168.2.1 255.255.255.0
 clockrate 2000000
!
 interface Serial1
 description serial link to Helena
 ip address 192.168.1.2 255.255.255.0
!
```

```
router ospf 1                          Note configuration change on Bozeman
 network 172.0.0.0 0.255.255.255 area 1
 network 192.168.0.0 0.0.255.255 area 10
!
```

Livingston router OSPF configuration with area 0.0.0.0 missing

```
!
hostname Livingston
!
interface Ethernet0
 ip address 172.17.0.1 255.255.0.0
!
interface Serial0
 description serial link to Helena
 ip address 192.168.3.1 255.255.255.0
 clockrate 2000000
!
interface Serial1
 description serial link to Bozeman
 ip address 192.168.2.2 255.255.255.0
!
router ospf 1                          Note configuration change on Livingston
 network 172.0.0.0 0.255.255.255 area 2
 network 192.168.0.0 0.0.255.255 area 10
!
```

Helena router OSPF configuration with area 0.0.0.0 missing

```
!
hostname Helena
!
interface Ethernet0
 ip address 172.18.0.1 255.255.0.0
!
interface Serial0
```

```
description serial link to Bozeman

ip address 192.168.1.1 255.255.255.0

clockrate 2000000

!

interface Serial1

description serial link to Livingston

ip address 192.168.3.2 255.255.255.0

!

router ospf 1                          Note configuration change on Helena

network 172.0.0.0 0.255.255.255 area 3

network 192.168.0.0 0.0.255.255 area 10
```

The resulting routing tables are shown in the traces that follow:

Bozeman#sh ip route

```
Codes: C - connected, S - static, I - IGRP, R - RIP, M - mobile, B - BGP
       D - EIGRP, EX - EIGRP external, O - OSPF, IA - OSPF inter area


Gateway of last resort is not set


C    172.16.0.0/16 is directly connected, Ethernet0
C    192.168.1.0/24 is directly connected, Serial1
C    192.168.2.0/24 is directly connected, Serial0
O    192.168.3.0/24 [110/128] via 192.168.2.2, 00:03:12, Serial0
                    [110/128] via 192.168.1.1, 00:03:12, Serial1
Bozeman#
```

```
Livingston#sh ip route
Codes: C - connected, S - static, I - IGRP, R - RIP, M - mobile, B - BGP
       D - EIGRP, EX - EIGRP external, O - OSPF, IA - OSPF inter area


Gateway of last resort is not set


C    172.17.0.0/16 is directly connected, Ethernet0
O    192.168.1.0/24 [110/128] via 192.168.2.1, 00:03:32, Serial1
                    [110/128] via 192.168.3.2, 00:03:32, Serial0
```

```
C    192.168.2.0/24 is directly connected, Serial1

C    192.168.3.0/24 is directly connected, Serial0

Livingston#


Helena#sh ip route

Codes: C - connected, S - static, I - IGRP, R - RIP, M - mobile, B - BGP

       D - EIGRP, EX - EIGRP external, O - OSPF, IA - OSPF inter area


Gateway of last resort is not set


C    172.18.0.0/16 is directly connected, Ethernet0

C    192.168.1.0/24 is directly connected, Serial0

O    192.168.2.0/24 [110/128] via 192.168.1.2, 00:03:58, Serial0

                    [110/128] via 192.168.3.1, 00:03:58, Serial1

C    192.168.3.0/24 is directly connected, Serial1

Helena#
```

What's noteworthy about this configuration is that the only routes that appear in the routing tables of all three routers are for directly connected networks and for networks within the area that's shared by all of the routers, in this case area 10. What has been lost as a result of this misconfiguration is the reachability to destinations within areas to which a particular router is not interfaced. It may seem surprising that OSPF functions at all without the backbone area.

Single OSPF Area Other than 0.0.0.0

Note what happens when all of the interfaces on the three routers are assigned to the same area, but other than 0.0.0.0. In the example that follows, it's area 10. The OSPF configuration on all three routers would be as follows:

Bozeman router OSPF configuration with a single non 0.0.0.0 area

```
!

hostname Bozeman

!

interface Ethernet0

 ip address 172.16.0.1 255.255.0.0
```

```
!
interface Serial0
 description serial link to Livingston
 ip address 192.168.2.1 255.255.255.0
 clockrate 2000000
!
 interface Serial1
 description serial link to Helena
 ip address 192.168.1.2 255.255.255.0
!
router ospf 1
 network 172.0.0.0 0.255.255.255 area 10
 network 192.168.0.0 0.0.255.255 area 10
!
```

Livingston router OSPF configuration with a single non 0.0.0.0 area

```
!
hostname Livingston
!
interface Ethernet0
 ip address 172.17.0.1 255.255.0.0
!
interface Serial0
 description serial link to Helena
 ip address 192.168.3.1 255.255.255.0
 clockrate 2000000
!
interface Serial1
 description serial link to Bozeman
 ip address 192.168.2.2 255.255.255.0
!
router ospf 1
 network 172.0.0.0 0.255.255.255 area 10
 network 192.168.0.0 0.0.255.255 area 10
!
```

Helena router OSPF configuration with a single non 0.0.0.0 area

```
!
hostname Helena
!
interface Ethernet0
 ip address 172.18.0.1 255.255.0.0
!
interface Serial0
 description serial link to Bozeman
 ip address 192.168.1.1 255.255.255.0
 clockrate 2000000
!
 interface Serial1
 description serial link to Livingston
 ip address 192.168.3.2 255.255.255.0
!
router ospf 1
 network 172.0.0.0 0.255.255.255 area 10
 network 192.168.0.0 0.0.255.255 area 10
!
```

The routing tables for all three routers are shown in the traces that follow:

```
Bozeman#sh ip route
Codes: C - connected, S - static, I - IGRP, R - RIP, M - mobile, B - BGP
       D - EIGRP, EX - EIGRP external, O - OSPF,
Gateway of last resort is not set


O    172.17.0.0/16 [110/74] via 192.168.2.2, 00:18:35, Serial0
C    172.16.0.0/16 is directly connected, Ethernet0
O    172.18.0.0/16 [110/74] via 192.168.1.1, 00:18:35, Serial1
C    192.168.1.0/24 is directly connected, Serial1
C    192.168.2.0/24 is directly connected, Serial0
O    192.168.3.0/24 [110/128] via 192.168.1.1, 00:18:35, Serial1
                    [110/128] via 192.168.2.2, 00:18:35, Serial0
Bozeman#
```

```
Livingston#sh ip route

Codes: C - connected, S - static, I - IGRP, R - RIP, M - mobile, B - BGP

       D - EIGRP, EX - EIGRP external, O - OSPF,


Gateway of last resort is not set


C    172.17.0.0/16 is directly connected, Ethernet0

O    172.16.0.0/16 [110/74] via 192.168.2.1, 00:19:00, Serial1

O    172.18.0.0/16 [110/74] via 192.168.3.2, 00:19:00, Serial0

O    192.168.1.0/24 [110/128] via 192.168.3.2, 00:19:00, Serial0
                    [110/128] via 192.168.2.1, 00:19:00, Serial1

C    192.168.2.0/24 is directly connected, Serial1

C    192.168.3.0/24 is directly connected, Serial0

Livingston#


Helena#sh ip route

Codes: C - connected, S - static, I - IGRP, R - RIP, M - mobile, B - BGP

       D - EIGRP, EX - EIGRP external, O - OSPF,


Gateway of last resort is not set


O    172.17.0.0/16 [110/74] via 192.168.3.1, 00:19:17, Serial1

O    172.16.0.0/16 [110/74] via 192.168.1.2, 00:19:17, Serial0

C    172.18.0.0/16 is directly connected, Ethernet0

C    192.168.1.0/24 is directly connected, Serial0

O    192.168.2.0/24 [110/128] via 192.168.1.2, 00:19:17, Serial0
                    [110/128] via 192.168.3.1, 00:19:17, Serial1

C    192.168.3.0/24 is directly connected, Serial1

Helena#
```

What's interesting about the preceding routing tables is that they are identical to the routing tables resulting from the assignment of all of the router interfaces to area 0.0.0.0. The lesson here is that OSPF still functions without area 0.0.0.0 being present as long as all of the router interfaces in the internetwork are assigned to the same area. However, it's vital to understand that in OSPF configuration, OSPF routing updates between areas are always exchanged through area 0.0.0.0. Without area 0.0.0.0, different OSPF areas are, in effect, isolated from one another. Routers that have all interfaces in one area will have no way of reaching networks in another area. This condition does not occur in the presence of area 0.0.0.0 if at least one router from each area has at least one interface in area 0.0.0.0.

Chapter Summary

In this chapter you were introduced to the basic misconfiguration issues related to Data Link Layer encapsulation on LANs and WANs, the application of access control lists to router interfaces, the use of AS numbers in IGRP and EIGRP, and the use of area ID in OSPF.

Cisco uses keywords like *arpa, sap, snap,* or *novell-ether* to indicate encapsulation. These keywords correspond to frame types. Encapsulation must match between neighboring routers. Cisco encapsulation must match the frame types configured on other network devices.

The order of statements in an access control list is important. Be mindful of the implicit *Deny all* statement at the end of a list. Wild card mask in an access list is an inverted mask where zero bits compare. Access lists are applied to interfaces, not entire routers. The keywords *in* and *out* are used to implement inbound and outbound filtering.

The autonomous system number in IGRP or EIGRP must match between neighboring routers for routing updates to be exchanged. Mismatch in the autonomous system number can be accidental or purposeful. Redistribution can be used between different autonomous systems.

In OSPF, router interfaces are assigned to areas. OSPF backbone area, 0.0.0.0, should be always configured in an OSPF internetwork. In a multi-area OSPF internetwork, routing updates between areas are exchanged through the backbone area.

Chapter 2

Troubleshooting Philosophy

Routers and internetworks need troubleshooting when they are not working properly. From a user's perspective, the manifestations of malfunctioning routers and internetworks are very simple: inability to access data or poor network performance. From the network administrator's perspective there is a multitude of reasons why a network is slow or users can't access their resources.

This chapter focuses on the philosophy and approach to troubleshooting. Specific troubleshooting scenarios and tools are explored in later chapters. As a network administrator, you understand very well that when network problems occur, you are expected to fix them quickly. To do so, it's vital that your approach to finding and correcting the problem be proven and effective. Troubleshooting network problems without a game plan can be a time sink and produce no positive results.

As technical backgrounds vary and the underlying causes that can slow down or disable a network are numerous, no two network administrators will approach a problem in exactly the same way. When troubleshooting network problems, success is a goal, not a guarantee. However, your success in troubleshooting can be enhanced by developing an individual approach that's based on experience and a proven, common-sense methodology.

What if Routers Were Perfect?

If routers' hardware were perfect and never failed there would be less need for troubleshooting. If Cisco's IOS never contained any bugs, the need for troubleshooting would be reduced even further. And if network administrators never made router configuration errors, the need for troubleshooting might be eliminated entirely.

However, we live in an imperfect world that doesn't stand still. Hardware fails, new releases of IOS introduce new bugs even as they squash some old ones, and network administrators make configuration errors. When dealing with an internetwork or routers that are not functioning correctly, the vital first step is to quickly identify where the problems lie.

The expression "Let's fix it" holds the key to successful troubleshooting. The "Let's" stands for Localize, Eliminate, Test, and Support. You localize or find the problem, you eliminate or correct it, you test your work to ensure the problem is really gone, and you continue to support your installation in a proactive way.

Localizing the Problem

The four broad categories of problems with routers and internetworks are:

- Hardware problems
- A buggy IOS
- Misconfigurations
- Incorrect interactions between routers in an internetwork

These broad categories can be broken down further into subcategories and areas, all the way to individual hardware components or configuration statements. Figure 2.1 is a graphical, non-linear, and high-level outline that can be used as an aid in locating the cause of problems affecting your router or internetwork.

Figure 2.1 is dynamic. It is intended to grow. As you gain experience with troubleshooting and come across new problems afflicting routers and internetworks, you are encouraged to add your own branches to this troubleshooting schematic.

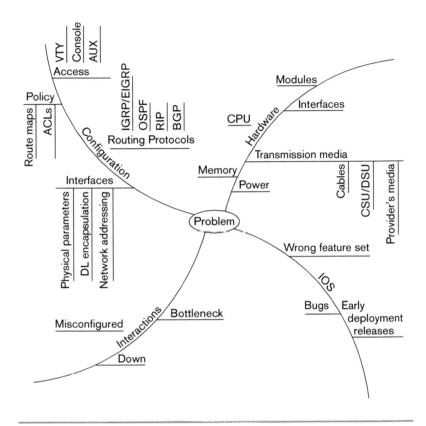

Figure 2.1 *Graphical outline of potential problem areas on routers and internetworks*

Hardware Problems

Routers are computers. Their hardware problems could be related to memory, the power subsystem, the CPU, LAN/WAN interfaces, or the transmission media interfacing them to the rest of the network. Cisco routers are either modular or they come with fixed configurations. The trend is toward modularity with redundant, hot-swappable modules. On a modular router, hardware problems can often be corrected by swapping modules without having to shut the router down.

If you suspect a hardware problem with a router, it's important to locate the component that must be replaced. You should also assess whether the problem affects the entire router or just one of its modules or interfaces.

Hardware problems relating to power, memory, or the CPU can prevent a router from booting. Examples of hardware problems affecting the entire router include intermittent memory problems that cause a router to reboot periodically for no apparent reason. Failure of the blower modules in higher-end routers (12000 series) will result in a critical alarm and a potential rise in temperature to the point where a router will initiate a shutdown if action is not taken to cool it off.

Malfunctioning or misconfigured interfaces can prevent a router from functioning properly after it boots. Bad cables or poor quality cables will also impact a router's operation after it's up and running. However, hardware problems with interfaces or cables are more localized. They impact a router's operation on specific subnets. A router can still function on other subnets.

In the context of the OSI model, hardware problems are considered to be Physical Layer problems. The Physical Layer must function properly if you expect a router to perform its functions at higher layers. Chapter 4 deals with specific Physical Layer troubleshooting issues.

Buggy IOS

Cisco puts out lengthy Field Notices about problems that are discovered in the IOS. Search the Cisco Web site for "Cisco IOS Field Notices" to get an idea of the number of problems that are uncovered and resolved in the IOS.

The sheer number of Field Notes is not surprising, considering that Cisco's IOS is a complex operating system that must handle functions related to the operations of the Physical, Data Link, and Network layer operations in switches and routers. Think of the IOS as a living organism. It grows and evolves with new product lines and the growing demand for Internet and LAN bandwidth.

High-speed technologies like Gigabit Ethernet or Packet-Over-SONET at OC-48 rates are now standardized. The IOS must be continually upgraded to support these and other new technologies in the wide range of Cisco's product lines. When support for these technologies is incorporated into the IOS, bugs will be discovered and resolved as experience with these technologies grows and as the technologies mature.

The second issue that network administrators need to be mindful of regarding the IOS is the feature set that's supported by their version. Given the large number of Cisco product lines (16*xx*, 26*xx*, 75*xx*, 120*xx*, 36*xx* series, to name a few), there are numerous IOS images available for them. A 2500 series router with a couple of Ethernet and serial interfaces does not require the same IOSas a 12000 series with OC-48c/STM-16 or Gigabit Ethernet line cards. Over 60 IOS image files are available in the IOS Release 12.0. It is entirely possible that some problems you may run into are related to an improper IOS feature set installed on your router rather than an IOS bug.

The issue of the correct IOS feature set gains importance as the number of routers in your internetwork grows. Suppose that you have six routers in your internetwork, half of them with the IP feature set and the other half with the Enterprise feature set. Up to this point, you've been routing IP only, but now you must route AppleTalk because Macintoshes have been added to the internetwork.

You look up the AppleTalk configuration commands in a configuration reference manual. You configure AppleTalk routing (globally) and AppleTalk addressing (on the interfaces) on the first router. Everything works fine. You get to the second router and the same commands result in "%Invalid input detected at '∧' marker." You scratch your head and try again, wondering what's going on.

There is nothing wrong with the IOS on the second router for what it was originally intended; that is, IP traffic only. But it's clear that if you want to implement AppleTalk routing on that router, you will need an IOS upgrade. You will need the same upgrade for the other two routers whose IOS feature set supports IP only.

When experiencing problems with a router or an internetwork, take reasonable steps to eliminate the obvious causes related to hardware and configuration. If problems persist, you may have discovered a bug in the IOS. If you have a mixture of routers in your internetwork, you will probably have a mixture of feature sets. Not all functions may be available on all routers. Implementing a new function like AppleTalk routing or IBM connectivity may require that you upgrade the IOS on some of the routers.

Misconfigurations

The number of potential misconfigurations that network administrators can introduce into routed internetworks seems unlimited. Cisco's IOS attempts to minimize the misconfiguration problems through built-in safeguards. Numerous warning messages during router configuration prevent network administrators from doing the absolutely ridiculous. And drastic misconfigurations like an administratively shut down interface or the absence of a routing protocol can usually be detected and corrected quickly.

If you suspect that a problem you are experiencing is due to misconfiguration, it is recommended that you take a layered and/or sectional approach to troubleshooting this broad problem category.

Sectional Approach to Troubleshooting

In the sectional approach, you divide your configuration file into major sections. A typical router configuration file may be broken into sections as follows:

- Administrative (router name, passwords, services, logging)
- Interfaces (addressing, encapsulation, bandwidth, metric cost, authentication)
- Routing Protocols (IGRP, EIGRP, OSPF, RIP, BGP)
- Traffic management (access control lists, communities)
- Routing policies (route maps)
- Out-of-band access (Console, Telnet, dial-up)

This list provides an initial framework for locating the cause of a problem. Understanding the functions that each section is responsible for will help you in the troubleshooting process. Let's walk through a troubleshooting scenario using the sectional approach. Suppose that routing tables are empty, and the `show ip route` command displays only directly connected networks.

The three sections that immediately become suspects are the routing protocols, traffic management or access control lists (ACLs), and interfaces. If no routing protocol is configured on a router, its tables will show only the directly connected and static routes. If ACLs are mistakenly configured to block all routing updates, again the routing tables will not have any dynamically derived entries. And if interfaces are misconfigured with incorrect addresses, masks, or authentication, this can result in the routing tables being empty.

Layered Approach

Now flip a mental switch and look at the same scenario from a layered point of view. In the layered approach, you view a router as a device that spans the bottom three layers of the OSI model: Physical, Data Link, and Network. The simple rule is that if layer 1 (the Physical Layer) is not functional, you can't expect layers 2 and 3 to be functioning properly. And if layer 2 is not functional, you can't expect layer 3 to function.

At the Physical Layer, you are dealing with cables, connectors, signal levels, encoding, clocking, and framing. You look for problems with these configuration parameters that would prevent the interfaces from being up. If interfaces on your router are down, you can't expect it to have much in a routing table.

If you look at the status of the interfaces with the `show ip interface` command and all of the interfaces are up, then in all likelihood you do not have a Physical Layer problem. The exception to this is a Frame Relay environment where your interfaces are up but there is a Physical Layer problem with the providers' network. Chapter 4 is dedicated to troubleshooting the Physical Layer.

Next, consider the functions of the Data Link Layer. Encapsulation mismatch is the most common cause of problems at the Data Link Layer. When the output from `show interfaces` indicates that the interfaces and protocols are up, then you can reasonably expect that the Data Link Layer is operational. If interfaces are up but protocols are down, there is a Data Link Layer problem and empty routing tables are a symptom of that problem.

Link utilization is also associated with the Data Link Layer. The interfaces and protocols may be up but the links may be overutilized. Overutilized links will normally not result in empty routing tables but cause intermittent loss of connectivity and poor performance. Non-routable protocols like LAT or NetBEUI are considered to be Data Link Layer protocols. They either have to be encapsulated inside of routable protocols or you may have to enable bridging, which is also a Data Link Layer function. This is discussed in Chapter 5, which deals with troubleshooting the Data Link Layer.

Lastly, look at the functions of the Network Layer. Incorrect addresses and subnet masks are a common problem. Duplicate addresses throughout the internetwork are another potential Network Layer issue. Routing protocols are also considered to be part of Network Layer operations. Their operation needs to be verified. Chapter 6 covers troubleshooting the Network Layer, and Part III of this book is dedicated to troubleshooting routing protocols.

Router misconfigurations can occur simultaneously at all layers. Encoding may be misconfigured at the Physical Layer, encapsulation at the Data Link Layer, and addressing at the Network Layer. The layered approach to troubleshooting is most useful in these situations, as it enables you to localize problems in an organized and structured fashion. Ideally, when troubleshooting and reconfiguring a router, you want to change only one variable at a time before testing if the symptoms have disappeared. Changing several variables at once may fix the problem but you will never be sure what the cause of it was. It may also introduce other problems even as the existing problems are fixed.

Incorrect Interactions

A properly functioning routing domain is like a well-tuned musical instrument. A single misconfigured or malfunctioning router can introduce problems that reverberate throughout the domain. Your router may experience problems as a result of other routers being down, misconfigured, or overutilized. A scenario leading to the discovery of a misconfigured router in a remote location is developed in Chapter 3, which is dedicated to the IOS troubleshooting tool.

Eliminating the Problem

Remember what the "Let's" stands for in "Let's fix it" — Localize, Eliminate, Test, and Support. The preceding sections dealt with the "L" portion of troubleshooting or problem localization. The next phase in troubleshooting is to eliminate or correct the problem.

Eliminating a problem depends on the nature of the problem. Correcting hardware problems may involve swapping a power supply, replacing a memory chip, or changing a malfunctioning line card. Documentation for your specific router model should be consulted for the exact procedure involving any hardware repairs. In many instances, routers have to be shut down to perform hardware maintenance. On the higher-end modular routers, modules that are redundant and hot swappable can be replaced without bringing a router down.

You will have to involve Cisco's technical support to eliminate bugs in the IOS. If you expect prompt action on your bug request, document the exact conditions under which a bug occurs. Being able to duplicate a bug consistently is very helpful in getting it resolved. Depending on your relationship with Cisco, you may be able to get an interim IOS build, especially if your IOS is an Early Deployment Release. General Deployment releases tend to be more stable.

Generally, misconfiguration problems can be corrected by making changes to the running configuration without bringing a router down. Remember to save those changes to the startup configuration if you are satisfied with them. Also, if possible, it's best to reload a router after making configuration changes to ensure that all of the changes take effect.

If your operating environment does not permit you to reload the router after making configuration changes, be mindful of those commands that do not take immediate effect even though they appear in the running configuration. In Chapter 10, there is a discussion about route maps used in BGP with the `neighbor` command. Newly configured route maps have no effect unless a BGP session is first cleared with the neighbor to whom the route maps will be applied. The route maps still appear in the running configuration file.

Changing the default metric when doing protocol redistribution also has no immediate effect unless the `redistribute` command is removed and placed back in the configuration. When editing access control lists, be mindful that your additions go to the end of the list. The order in which statements appear in an access control list impacts the action of the list.

If it is possible for you to reload your router after making configuration changes, consider using the following procedure. It's one way to avoid quirks in the IOS resulting from making changes only to the running configuration.

1. Make the changes in the text file that stores your configuration on the network.

2. Load the text file into the startup configuration and reload the router.

Correcting problems resulting from interactions with other routers depends on whether the suspect routers are under your control or not. If you control them, then follow the procedures outlined in the preceding sections. If you suspect a problem with a router in another routing domain that's not under your control, inform the network administrator responsible for that domain immediately.

Testing the Solution

After you've eliminated a problem, it's vital that you test your work. To do this, you must know what the symptoms were initially. Observe if the symptoms are gone. If the initial symptoms are gone, the worst thing that can happen is that a new problem may have been introduced as a result of resolving an old one. That's what keeps network administrators in business.

Supporting the Network

Troubleshooting a router or an internetwork requires not only an organized approach but also good record keeping. The troubleshooting process is aided by the presence of existing documentation and a baseline for your system under the normal operating conditions. The issue that network administrators often struggle with is what's considered reasonable documentation and how a system baseline is derived.

Reasonable Documentation

Have you ever heard it said that most of the time, two experts in any field can only agree on what the third expert is doing wrong? There are lots of experts when it comes to documentation and it's hard to find two installations using the same documentation format. There are reasonable standards but no absolute standards in documenting a router or an internetwork. The key to having useful documentation is to be reasonable. Here are some pointers.

Use existing IOS tools to document your router. The output from the `show tech` command may be long, but it's easy to obtain as you only use one command. The `show tech` command is a combination of numerous `show` commands that are most frequently used during the troubleshooting process. If you get Cisco tech support involved in troubleshooting your router, you may be asked to provide it anyway.

Have a hard copy of your documentation along with an electronic version. The `show tech` command displays the configuration file. However, it's advisable that you have the configuration file in a separate text file, both in electronic form and as a hard copy.

Logical and physical diagrams of your networks are invaluable. The logical diagram shows the relationship between routers and networks. All of the network diagrams in this book are logical. The physical diagram identifies the geographic location of routers within buildings. If your internetwork is spread out geographically, be sure to have a list of all of the physical addresses of where the equipment is located. This is vital if you rely on third parties for maintenance.

A complete list of network addresses used throughout the internetwork is essential. It's not sufficient to rely on the addresses in the configuration files for reference. An up-to-date list of addresses will help in avoiding problems with duplicate addresses as your network expands.

A separate list of all of the routers with their purchase dates, IOS versions, model, and serial number is also very helpful. It's important to be able to assess at a glance what IOS feature sets are in use throughout the internetwork. This can save time and headaches when deploying new architectures like Apple or IBM on an existing network.

When configuring router interfaces, use the `description` command to describe the purpose of the interface. This is particularly useful on WAN links to describe the location of the other end.

Some networks and installations are documented up to the last cable and port. It's an individual choice. The most important thing about documentation is that it be kept up to date. If there is too much documentation, it's a given that it won't be regularly updated and will be out of date when most needed. If there is not enough, troubleshooting and maintenance will be more difficult.

Baselining Your System

System baseline normally refers to performance under "normal" conditions. It is intended to be a reference point when changes are implemented or network performance suffers. Performance is a function of time. IOS tools like `show memory, show process cpu,` or `show interfaces` will give you snapshots of memory usage, CPU utilization, and link load at the time that they are executed. `Show process cpu` gives you a snapshot of CPU utilization over short period intervals like five seconds, a minute, or five minutes. But to get a baseline for link load, CPU utilization, or memory usage, this information needs to be collected periodically and graphed as a function of time.

The output from the show tech command has a lot of information that can be used to develop a baseline for your router or internetwork. Suppose that you collect output from show tech that's executed on every router in your internetwork every hour on the hour for one week. Using a script to extract the CPU utilization, memory usage, and link load could give you a pretty good sense of your internetwork performance. Then, if a change in performance is detected, you will have a point of reference with which to isolate the router or an individual link that may be overutilized.

Chapter Summary

The four broad categories of problems with routers and internetworks are hardware, buggy IOS, misconfigurations, and interactions with other routers. Sectional and layered approaches can be used when troubleshooting misconfigurations. "Let's fix it" holds the key to successful troubleshooting. The "Let's" stands for Locate, Eliminate, Test, and Support. Locate the problem, eliminate it, test your work, and support your installation in a proactive way. Reasonable documentation and system baseline are great aids in troubleshooting.

Chapter 3

IOS Troubleshooting Tools

Cisco incorporates very effective troubleshooting tools into its Internetworking Operating System (IOS). After a router boots and the IOS is running, the use of a few commands can help you discover its configuration, view its routing tables, observe what routing protocols are operational, discover who its neigbors are, and more. The IOS troubleshooting tools discussed in this chapter include ping, telnet, Cisco's Discovery Protocol (CDP), the show command, traceroute, and debug.

The Ping Utility

The ping utility allows you to verify if there is IP connectivity between a router and a desired destination. Ping is a well-known utility available in most TCP/IP implementations. It's a combination of Internet Control Message Protocol (ICMP) echo request and echo reply functions. ICMP is part of the TCP/IP protocol suite.

Ping is very useful in indicating whether there is a problem between a source and a destination, but it's not very useful at pinpointing the problem. Think of ping as a verification tool. If you have isolated and fixed a problem, use ping to verify that your remedy worked.

Consider the scenario shown in Figure 3.1.

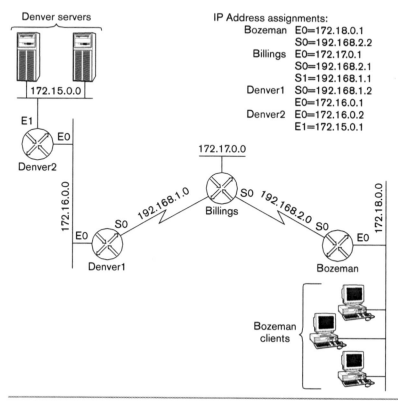

IP Address assignments:

Bozeman	E0=	172.18.0.1
	S0=	192.168.2.2
Billings	E0=	172.17.0.1
	S0=	192.168.2.1
	S1=	192.168.1.1
Denver1	S0=	192.168.1.2
	E0=	172.16.0.1
Denver2	E0=	172.16.0.2
	E1=	172.15.0.1

Figure 3.1 *Internetwork for analysis of IOS troubleshooting tools*

Assume that you are a network administrator located in Bozeman and the internetwork as shown in Figure 3.1 is functioning properly. This is a relatively small internetwork and it is not managed by the Simple Network Management Protocol (SNMP). All the servers on subnet 172.15.0.0 in Denver are reachable from Bozeman. Then, suddenly the Bozeman users accessing the Denver servers start complaining that they can't get to their databases. From the Bozeman router, you ping all interfaces on the Denver2 router.

```
Bozeman#ping 172.16.0.2


Type escape sequence to abort.

Sending 5, 100-byte ICMP Echos to 172.16.0.2, timeout is 2 seconds:

.....
```

```
Success rate is 0 percent (0/5)

Bozeman#

Bozeman#ping 172.15.0.1


Type escape sequence to abort.

Sending 5, 100-byte ICMP Echos to 172.15.0.1, timeout is 2 seconds:

.....

Success rate is 0 percent (0/5)
```

The pings fail. You know you have a problem but you don't really know where it lies. You suspect that the Denver2 router has crashed. You ping the interfaces on the Denver1 router. They respond.

```
Bozeman#ping 192.168.1.2


Type escape sequence to abort.

Sending 5, 100-byte ICMP Echos to 192.168.1.2, timeout is 2 seconds:

!!!!!

Success rate is 100 percent (5/5), round-trip min/avg/max = 4/5/8 ms


Bozeman#ping 172.16.0.1


Type escape sequence to abort.

Sending 5, 100-byte ICMP Echos to 172.16.0.1, timeout is 2 seconds:

!!!!!

Success rate is 100 percent (5/5), round-trip min/avg/max = 4/4/8 ms
```

You are now convinced that the Denver2 router has crashed. But that may be a dangerous conclusion. What you've just confirmed is that you can't ping the interfaces on the Denver2 router, no more, no less. The ping identifies a connectivity problem, but not the cause of the problem.

You do not have physical access to the Denver routers. Since the internetwork is not managed by SNMP, you do not have a management station giving you an overview of the entire network. It's time to think about what to do next. The ping has identified a problem area, but other tools are now required to isolate the cause of the problem. If you can't ping a router, you certainly will not be able to telnet into it. However, if telnet has been configured on all of the routers in the internetwork, the next best thing to do is to telnet into the problem router's neighbor.

Telnet

Before continuing with the troubleshooting example from the preceding section, review the process of enabling telnet on a Cisco router. You want to test telnet access under normal operating conditions before you find yourself in a situation where you must access a router remotely to resolve a critical problem.

Telnet access can be enabled from the configuration mode. On a Cisco 2500 series router, five telnet access lines can be configured: *vty 0* through *vty 4*. Each line can be configured with its own password. It's common, however, to configure the same password for all five lines. Defining telnet or virtual terminal lines access is part of the *line access* configuration, which also includes access to a router via the console and auxiliary ports.

Observe telnet configuration on the Denver1 router:

```
Denver1#
Denver1#conf t
Enter configuration commands, one per line.  End with CNTL/Z.
Denver1(config)#line vty 0 4
Denver1(config-line)#login
Denver1(config-line)#password let_admin
Denver1(config-line)#^Z
Denver1#
```

The preceding steps enabled telnet access on the Denver1 router. Setting the password is critical. Note what happens if telnet access is attempted without the password being set:

```
Bozeman#telnet 172.16.0.1
Trying 172.16.0.1 ... Open
Password required, but none set
[Connection to 172.16.0.1 closed by foreign host]
Bozeman#
```

An error message is generated and your telnet connection is closed. Without the password set for the vty lines you can't access a router via telnet. That's a different concept from the console or the privileged mode passwords. If the console password is not set you can access the router via the console port. If the privileged mode (enable) password is not set, you can get into the privileged mode via the `enable` command.

Assume, however, that the telnet access password has been set for all five vty lines on the Denver1 router, as shown in the preceding telnet configuration example. You are now in a position to telnet into the Denver1 router from Bozeman and continue to troubleshoot the problem that developed in the internetwork shown in Figure 3.1.

```
Bozeman#telnet 172.16.0.1
Trying 172.16.0.1 ... Open
User Access Verification

Password:
Denver1>
Denver1>en
% No password set
Denver1>
```

The telnet access password does not echo and is not shown in the trace. But there is a surprise that awaits you after you gain telnet access to Denver1. You can't get into the privileged mode via the `enable` command. That's another caveat to be aware of. If you gain access to a router via telnet, and the enable mode password on that router is not set, you will not be able to get into the enable mode on that router. Your troubleshooting options are more limited without access to the enable mode because you can't display configuration information.

But the situation is not totally hopeless. You've gained access to a router that neighbors the router that has a problem. It's time for the next tool.

Cisco Discovery Protocol (CDP)

Cisco has a proprietary protocol known as Cisco Discovery Protocol, or CDP. CDP is enabled by default and it facilitates the discovery of neighboring routers.

Remember that you are in the midst of troubleshooting a problem with the internetwork in Figure 3.1. You are physically in Bozeman. You just gained telnet access to Denver1 but can't get into its enable mode. Your goal is to find out what's going on with Denver2. Use of the show CDP command will allow you to discover if Denver1 sees Denver2 as a neighbor. You begin by verifying that CDP is active on Denver1.

```
Denver1>show cdp

Global CDP information:

        Sending CDP packets every 60 seconds

        Sending a holdtime value of 180 seconds
```

After verifying that CDP is running on Denver1, you want to see if Denver1 has any CDP neighbors. You are looking for Denver2.

```
Denver1>show cdp neighbor

Capability Codes: R - Router, T - Trans Bridge, B -- Source Route Bridge

                  S - Switch, H - Host, I - IGMP, r - Repeater
```

Device ID	Local Intrfce	Holdtme	Capability	Platform	Port ID
billings	Ser 0	139	R	2522	Ser 1
Denver2	**Eth 0**	**168**	**R**	**2500**	**Eth 0**

```
Denver1>
```

The CDP display indicates that Denver2 is a CDP neighbor to Denver1. That's a good sign. There is a problem with Denver2 but it hasn't crashed as you initially thought; you can see it as a neighbor to Denver1. You proceed with more detailed CDP displays, which can actually tell you the IP address and the IOS version of the neighbors.

```
Denver1>show cdp neighbor detail

-------------------------

Device ID: billings

Entry address(es):
```

```
IP address: 192.168.1.1

Platform: cisco 2522,  Capabilities: Router

Interface: Serial0,  Port ID (outgoing port): Serial1

Holdtime: 175 sec


Version:

Cisco Internetwork Operating System Software

IOS (tm) 3000 Software (IGS-J-L), Version 11.0(9), RELEASE SOFTWARE (fc1)

Copyright (c) 1986-1996 by cisco Systems, Inc.

Compiled Tue 11-Jun-96 00:37 by loreilly


-------------------------

Device ID: Denver2

Entry address(es):

  IP address: 172.16.0.2

Platform: cisco 2500,  Capabilities: Router

Interface: Ethernet0,  Port ID (outgoing port): Ethernet0

Holdtime : 144 sec


Version:

Cisco Internetwork Operating System Software

IOS (tm) 2500 Software (C2500-I-L), Version 11.3(9), RELEASE SOFTWARE (fc1)

Copyright (c) 1986-1999 by cisco Systems, Inc.

Compiled Tue 06-Apr-99 18:58 by dschwart


Denver1>
```

CDP is a Data Link Layer protocol. The neighbor displays confirm that the Data Link Layer between Denver1 and Denver2 is operational. Additionally, CDP recognizes that Denver2's Ethernet0 is configured with an IP address. It's time to go back to the ubiquitous ping. You ping Denver2's Ethernet0 interface from Denver1 and it works.

```
Denver1>ping 172.16.0.2


Type escape sequence to abort.
```

```
Sending 5, 100-byte ICMP Echos to 172.16.0.2, timeout is 2 seconds:
!!!!!
Success rate is 100 percent (5/5), round-trip min/avg/max = 1/3/4 ms
Denver1>
```

You know that if you can ping Denver2 you should be able to telnet into it as well. You telnet into Denver2 from Denver1 and it works.

```
Denver1>
Denver1>telnet 172.16.0.2
Trying 172.16.0.2 ... Open
User Access Verification
Password:
Denver2>
```

You now have telnet access to Denver2. But there is another surprise in store for you. You know that Denver2 is up and running. It means that the problem of not being able to reach the servers on subnet 172.15.0.0 from Bozeman must be related to Denver2's configuration. You try to get into the enable mode on Denver2. It's the same story as on Denver1.

```
Denver2>enable
% No password set
Denver2>
```

The enable password on Denver2 was not set and you can't get into the configuration mode after accessing it via telnet. This is the real cause of the problem. It turns out that the Denver2 location has a new employee who is preparing for a Cisco certification exam. He became interested in exploring the router configurations at that location. After gaining access to the Denver2 router via the console port, this employee realized that the access to the enable mode was not password-protected. He decided to experiment with some recently-learned IOS commands, and accidentally changed the router configuration. However, he did not know how to restore it to the way it was.

Now's your chance to find out exactly what has been changed. Even without access to the enable mode, which allows you to change the configuration, you can get a lot closer to isolating the cause of the problem through the use of the **show** command.

The Show Command

The amount of information that can be gleaned about a router through the use of the show command is outright phenomenal. The show command options are numerous. Certain show command options are available from the user EXEC mode, for others you must be in the privileged mode. Show command options also vary between different router models. The show command can be used for troubleshooting problems at all layers of a router's operation: Physical, Data Link, and Network. About a dozen show commands are explored throughout this section.

At this time you are still troubleshooting the problem with the internetwork in Figure 3.1. Bozeman clients can't access the servers on subnet 172.15.0.0. You are physically in Bozeman. Through the use of ping, telnet, and CDP described in the preceding sections you managed to gain telnet access to Denver2. You can't, however, get into the privileged mode to change Denver2's configuration. The enable password on Denver2 was not set.

You are aware, though, that there are show commands that are available from the user mode that will give you a pretty good idea of where the problem lies. You choose the commands that display the status of interfaces, routing tables, and routing protocols on Denver2 as shown in the traces that follow.

```
Denver2>sh ip interface brief

Interface      IP-Address      OK?    Method   Status                   Protocol

Ethernet0      172.16.0.2      YES    NVRAM    up                       up

Ethernet1      172.15.0.1      YES    manual   up                       up

Serial0        unassigned      YES    unset    administratively down    down

Serial1        unassigned      YES    unset    administratively down    down

Denver2>


Denver2>sh ip route

Codes: C - connected, S - static, I - IGRP, R - RIP, M - mobile, B — BGP
       D - EIGRP, EX - EIGRP external, O - OSPF,

Gateway of last resort is not set
```

```
C    172.15.0.0/16 is directly connected, Ethernet1
C    172.16.0.0/16 is directly connected, Ethernet0
Denver2>


Denver2>sh ip prot
Denver2>
Denver2>
```

The output from the preceding three commands tells the story. The interfaces on Denver2 are up and operational. The routing table has only directly connected networks. That's a sign that something is wrong with routing protocols on Denver2. The last command, show ip protocols, reveals that, in fact, no routing protocols are operational on Denver2.

Congratulations! Through the use of basic IOS troubleshooting tools like ping, telnet, CDP, and the show command, you were able to pinpoint the problem with the internetwork in Figure 3.1. As it turned out, the new employee at the Denver location — who was able to get into the configuration mode on Denver2 due to lack of proper password protection — accidentally removed the entire OSPF section from the router's configuration. This made the 172.15.0.0 subnet inaccessible from Bozeman and left the Denver2 router with only the directly connected networks in its routing table. No one tool gave you that information. It took the judicious use of ping, telnet, CDP, and the show command to zero in on the problem.

To correct the problem you will probably need some physical assistance from that aspiring Cisco expert at the Denver location. The quickest way to do it is to have him set an enable password on Denver2. This will allow you to get into the privileged mode on Denver2 via telnet and reconfigure OSPF. After reconfiguring OSPF, you can change the enable password to limit any further accidental reconfigurations.

The rest of this section discusses some of the remaining show commands, particularly those that are used in the troubleshooting examples in later chapters. They are boldfaced in the display that follows. For the explanation of every keyword associated with the show command, the reader is referred to Cisco documentation available on the Cisco Web site or on the Cisco documentation CD.

Observe the available keywords that can be used with the show command on a Cisco's 2500 series router. The show command is executed from the privileged EXEC mode followed by a "?". Use of a question mark following any Cisco command displays the keywords that are available for use with that command.

Show command options available on a Cisco 2500 series

```
Denver3#show ?
  WORD              Flash device information - format <dev:>[partition]
  access-expression List access expression
  access-lists      List access lists
  accounting        Accounting data for active sessions
  aliases           Display alias commands
  alps              Alps information
  apollo            Apollo network information
  appletalk         AppleTalk information
  arap              Show Appletalk Remote Access statistics
  arp               ARP table
  async             Information on terminal lines used as router interfaces
  bridge            Bridge Forwarding/Filtering Database [verbose]
  bsc               BSC interface information
  bstun             BSTUN interface information
  buffers           Buffer pool statistics
  cdp               CDP information
  clns              CLNS network information
  clock             Display the system clock
  cls               DLC user information
  compress          Show compression statistics
  configuration     Contents of Non-Volatile memory
  controllers       Interface controller status
  debugging         State of each debugging option
  decnet            DECnet information
  dhcp              Dynamic Host Configuration Protocol status
  dialer            Dialer parameters and statistics
  dlsw              Data Link Switching information
  dnsix             Shows Dnsix/DMDP information
```

drip	DRiP DB
dspu	Display DSPU information
dxi	atm-dxi information
entry	Queued terminal entries
flash	System Flash information
flh-log	Flash Load Helper log buffer
frame-relay	Frame-Relay information
fras	FRAS Information
fras-host	FRAS Host Information
history	Display the session command history
hosts	IP domain-name, lookup style, nameservers, and host table
interfaces	**Interface status and configuration**
ip	**IP information**
ipx	Novell IPX information
isis	IS-IS routing information
kerberos	Show Kerberos Values
key	Key information
keymap	Terminal keyboard mappings
lat	DEC LAT information
line	TTY line information
llc2	IBM LLC2 circuit information
lnm	IBM LAN manager
local-ack	Local Acknowledgement virtual circuits
location	Display the system location
logging	Show the contents of logging buffers
memory	**Memory statistics**
modemcap	Show Modem Capabilities database
nbf	NBF (NetBEUI) information
ncia	Native Client Interface Architecture
netbios-cache	NetBIOS name cache contents
node	Show known LAT nodes
ntp	Network time protocol
ppp	PPP parameters and statistics
printers	Show LPD printer information

privilege	Show current privilege level
processes	**Active process statistics**
protocols	**Active network routing protocols**
qllc	Display qllc-llc2 and qllc-sdlc conversion information
queue	Show queue contents
queueing	Show queueing configuration
registry	Function registry information
reload	Scheduled reload information
rhosts	Remote-host+user equivalences
rif	RIF cache entries
rmon	rmon statistics
route-map	**route-map information**
rtr	Response Time Reporter (RTR)
running-config	**Current operating configuration**
sdllc	Display sdlc - llc2 conversion information
services	LAT learned services
sessions	Information about Telnet connections
sgbp	SGBP group information
smds	SMDS information
smf	Software MAC filter
smrp	Simple Multicast Routing Protocol (SMRP) information
sna	Display SNA host information
snapshot	Snapshot parameters and statistics
snmp	snmp statistics
source-bridge	Source-bridge parameters and statistics
spanning-tree	Spanning tree topology
stacks	Process stack utilization
standby	Hot standby protocol information
startup-config	**Contents of startup configuration**
stun	STUN status and configuration
subscriber-policy	Subscriber policy
subsys	Show subsystem information
tacacs	Shows tacacs+ server statistics

tarp	TARP information
tcp	Status of TCP connections
tech-support	**Show system information for Tech-Support**
terminal	Display terminal configuration parameters
tn3270	TN3270 settings
traffic-shape	traffic rate shaping configuration
translate	Protocol translation information
ttycap	Terminal capability tables
users	Display information about terminal lines
version	**System hardware and software status**
vines	VINES information
vpdn	VPDN information
whoami	Info on current tty line
x25	X.25 information
x29	X.29 information
xns	XNS information
xremote	XRemote statistics

```
Denver3#
```

The preceding trace displays a total of 111 keywords that can be used initially with the show command. Most of those keywords are followed by more keywords. All of them are useful, however, some are useful only if certain architectural platforms like IBM, DEC, or Apple are deployed in your internetwork. The ones that are deemed most useful in troubleshooting are boldfaced. You should memorize these, and become familiar with their output.

Notice that all of the keywords that can be used with the show command are listed alphabetically. Whereas an alphabetical listing offers some order to a large number of available keywords, it doesn't mesh with the layered approach to troubleshooting a router. When your router has a problem, what you want to have at your fingertips are the commands that display information about its configuration, software in use, and operation at the Physical, Data Link, and Network layers. See Chapters 4 through 6 for more information.

Configuration Show Commands

The show command keywords for displaying a router's configuration include version, startup-configuration, running-configuration, and tech-support. The use of show with these keywords informs you about a router's IOS version, hardware characteristics (interfaces, processor type, amount of memory installed), software add-ons (X.25, SuperLAT, TN3270 Emulation), and configuration. It also tells you how long a router has been up, how it was brought up, and the actual name of the IOS image file. Take a look at output from the show version command.

```
Denver3#show version

Cisco Internetwork Operating System Software

IOS (tm) 2500 Software (C2500-JS-L), Version 11.3(7)T, RELEASE SOFTWARE (fc1)

Copyright (c) 1986-1998 by cisco Systems, Inc.

Compiled Tue 01-Dec-98 12:44 by ccai

Image text-base: 0x0304CDF0, data-base: 0x00001000


ROM: System Bootstrap, Version 5.2(5), RELEASE SOFTWARE

BOOTFLASH: 3000 Bootstrap Software (IGS-RXBOOT), Version 10.2(5), RELEASE

SOFTWARE (fc1)


Denver3 uptime is 7 hours, 21 minutes

System restarted by power-on

System image file is "flash:c2500-js-l_113-7_T.bin", booted via flash


cisco 2500 (68030) processor (revision D) with 16384K/2048K bytes of memory.

Processor board ID 01879072, with hardware revision 00000000

Bridging software.

X.25 software, Version 3.0.0.

SuperLAT software copyright 1990 by Meridian Technology Corp).

TN3270 Emulation software.

2 Ethernet/IEEE 802.3 interface(s)

2 Serial network interface(s)

32K bytes of non-volatile configuration memory.

16384K bytes of processor board System flash (Read ONLY)
```

```
Configuration register is 0x2102
Denver3#
```

Knowing your router's hardware platform and IOS version is vital when trying to resolve strange or unusual problems with Cisco's technical support. Cisco uses a numbering convention to designate different releases of the IOS. The numbers prior to the number in parentheses indicate a Major Release. The number in parentheses is the maintenance level, which represents periodic revisions to the Major Release. If the numbers are followed by a letter, it represents an Early Deployment or ED release. If no letter follows the IOS version number, the release is considered to be a General Deployment or GD release.

Early Deployment releases are a mechanism for a quick delivery of new IOS features, but to select customers and in limited environments. ED releases normally do not attain GD status. If features introduced in an ED release prove stable, they may be incorporated into a Major General Deployment release. It's natural to expect that ED releases may have more problems then GD releases, given their very nature. The Bozeman router in the preceding show version display is running 11.3(7)T Early Deployment release.

The show running-config command displays the currently running router configuration. Show startup-config displays the contents of the configuration file that's usually stored in non-volatile memory or NVRAM. On some platforms, the CONFIG_FILE environment variable points to the location of the startup configuration file.

The running and startup configuration files are viewed from the privileged mode. It is recommended that network administrators maintain a hardcopy and an electronic (text format) backup of the startup configuration file. In the event of a fatal crash, having a startup configuration file on storage media external to a router allows you to quickly configure a replacement router. A text file residing on external storage media can be sent to a router via tftp or by a cut-and-paste method from a terminal emulator.

It is also recommended that if you make changes to the running configuration, you save those changes to the startup configuration file. When a router is rebooted via a reload or power off/on cycle, the changes to the running configuration are lost.

If you working on a complex problem with Cisco's tech support, you will probably be asked to e-mail them output from show tech-support.

This command incorporates into a single listing the output from many of the show commands discussed in this chapter. For higher-end routers with large configuration files, the output from show tech may be in excess of 100 pages. Use capture tools that come with terminal emulators to redirect output from show tech to a text file. You can then attach it to an e-mail and send it to Cisco's tech support.

Physical Layer Show Commands

The show commands for troubleshooting the Physical Layer include show interfaces, show memory, show process, show controllers, and show buffers. On the higher-end routers (Cisco's 12000 series, for example), quite a few additional Physical Layer troubleshooting commands are available. Show environment and show diag are discussed in Chapter 4.

The show interfaces command displays information that's applicable to the physical, data link, and Network Layers. Take a look at the output from show interface s0 executed on the Bozeman router in the scenario depicted in Figure 3.1. At the Physical Layer you are looking at the bandwidth, delay (used in IGRP/EIGRP metric calculations), reliability, load, input and output errors, carrier transitions, and the DCE/DTE control signals (at the bottom of the display).

```
Bozeman#show interface s0
Serial0 is up, line protocol is up
  Hardware is HD64570
  Internet address is 192.168.2.2/24
  MTU 1500 bytes, BW 1544 Kbit, DLY 20000 usec,
     reliability 255/255, txload 1/255, rxload 1/255
  Encapsulation HDLC, loopback not set, keepalive set (10 sec)
  Last input 00:00:06, output 00:00:00, output hang never
  Last clearing of "show interface" counters never
  Queueing strategy: fifo
  Output queue 0/40, 0 drops; input queue 0/75, 0 drops
  5 minute input rate 0 bits/sec, 0 packets/sec
  5 minute output rate 0 bits/sec, 0 packets/sec
     7990 packets input, 521741 bytes, 0 no buffer
```

```
Received 3907 broadcasts, 0 runts, 0 giants, 0 throttles

0 input errors, 0 CRC, 0 frame, 0 overrun, 0 ignored, 0 abort

8233 packets output, 518712 bytes, 0 underruns

0 output errors, 0 collisions, 2 interface resets

0 output buffer failures, 0 output buffers swapped out

0 carrier transitions

DCD=up  DSR=up  DTR=up  RTS=up  CTS=up
Bozeman#
```

From a physical point of view, this interface is functioning properly. It is up, it has the default Cisco bandwidth for a serial interface (1,544 Kbit), and it correctly shows the default delay of 20,000 microseconds. The default delay for each type of interface is translated into IGRP/EIGRP delay, which is then factored into the IGRP/EIGRP metric calculation (see Chapter 7 for details on IGRP/EIGRP metric). The reliability of this interface is 255/255, which translates into 100 percent reliability. The DCE/DTE signals at the bottom of the display are all up. These signals are discussed in more detail in Chapter 4 in the "Analysis of Show Interface Output" section. Zero input errors, zero output errors, and zero carrier transitions are all signs of good health for a serial interface. WAN circuit faults and problems with CSU/DSUs can result in carrier transitions.

The next Physical Layer command considered here is **show memory**. The output from the **show memory** command goes on for pages. From a network administrator's point of view, the most interesting part of that output is the first two summary lines.

```
Bozeman#show memory
           Head      Total(b)   Used(b)   Free(b)    Lowest(b)   Largest(b)
Processor  9B8B0     16136016   897460    15238556   15188432    15207428
     I/O   4000000   2097152    393032    1704120    1704120     1703812
.

.

Bozeman#
```

If you know that a router experiences peak usage during certain times, try to observe its memory usage during those times. This will clue you in to whether a router needs extra memory or not. Also, if your environment permits, take a look at memory usage before and after certain processes have been activated.

For example, if you are bringing a new router online that's going to be running EIGRP and OSPF, jot down the memory usage on that router before the EIGRP and OSPF routing processes have been activated. Following the activation of the EIGRP and OSPF processes, check the total memory usage again. Check the memory periodically as the routing tables and databases become populated with entries derived via these protocols. It's not an exact science, but it can give you a clue as how much memory is taken up by the process, their routing tables, and databases.

If you are in an environment where your routing tables continue to grow, it's a good idea to have a sense as to the relationship between the routing table size and the memory usage. This can help you determine when extra memory will be required for your router as a function of growth. Of course, you can always install the maximum amount of memory that a router will take. But even with the maximum amount of memory installed, it's a good idea to check memory and CPU usage periodically. Constant high memory usage may be an indication that you need a higher capacity router.

The output from the **show process** cpu command can give you a sense of your router's CPU utilization. This output again stretches on for pages, with the most useful indicator perhaps being on the first line. Observe the output on the Bozeman router.

```
Bozeman#

Bozeman#sh process cpu

CPU utilization for five seconds: 12%/12%; one minute: 21%; five minutes: 21%

PID   Runtime(ms)   Invoked   uSecs   5Sec    1Min    5Min    TTY   Process

  1    14880         7207      2064    0.08%   0.03%   0.02%   0     Load Meter

  2    960           8449      113     0.00%   0.00%   0.00%   0     OSPF Hello

  3    64828         678       95616   0.00%   0.19%   0.17%   0     Check heaps

  .

  .

Bozeman#
```

The Bozeman router does not seem to be heavily utilized. If the utilization was constantly showing 80% or 90% over five-minute intervals, that would be cause for concern. Checking the CPU utilization and the load from the `show interface` command is a good way to determine if your router is potentially a bottleneck.

In a recent situation, users were convinced that a router interfacing their LAN to an ISP for direct Internet access was the bottleneck. With all the users doing downloads and Web browsing (which were indeed happening very slowly), a check of the CPU utilization and the interface load revealed that they were both below 20%. The CPU utilization was 13%, the load was 40/255 or approximately 16%. It was time to look elsewhere for the culprit. It turned out that a misconfigured proxy server was responsible for the poor performance.

The output from the `show controllers` command is again voluminous, but some useful information can be gleaned from it.

```
Bozeman#

Bozeman#show controllers
                            Note: Partial display for Ethernet interface
LANCE unit 0, idb 0xCF4B8, ds 0xD0CD0, regaddr = 0x2130000, reset_mask 0x2
IB at 0x4006F18: mode=0x0000, mcfilter 0000/0002/0100/0080
station address 0000.0c4a.d136  default station address 0000.0c4a.d136
buffer size 1524
.

.

0 missed datagrams, 0 overruns
0 transmitter underruns, 0 excessive collisions
0 single collisions, 0 multiple collisions
0 dma memory errors, 0 CRC errors
0 alignment errors, 0 runts, 0 giants
0 tdr, 0 spurious initialization done interrupts
0 no enp status, 0 buffer errors, 0 overflow errors
0 tx_buff, 0 throttled, 0 enabled
Lance csr0 = 0x73

                            Note: Partial display for serial0 interface
```

```
HD unit 0, idb = 0xDB574, driver structure at 0xE08D0

buffer size 1524  HD unit 0, V.35 DTE cable

cpb = 0x2, eda = 0x2850, cda = 0x2864

.

.

0 missed datagrams, 0 overruns

0 bad datagram encapsulations, 0 memory errors

0 transmitter underruns

0 residual bit errors


                              Note: Partial display for seriall interface
HD unit 1, idb = 0xE4A54, driver structure at 0xE9DB0

buffer size 1524  HD unit 1, No cable

cpb = 0x3, eda = 0x1140, cda = 0x1000

.

.

0 missed datagrams, 0 overruns

0 bad datagram encapsulations, 0 memory errors

0 transmitter underruns

0 residual bit errors


Bozeman#
```

It's not necessarily a network administrator's job to interpret every hexadecimal number that appears in a show command display. Some output from show commands is rightfully reserved for qualified service technicians. The show controllers command output is full of hex numbers that are not shown in the preceding trace.

What's shown for the Ethernet interface is the hex value of the MAC address, the buffer size associated with the interface, and the counters related to Ethernet performance. If you see a lot of non-zero values in those counters, it's a sign that there is a problem with the interface.

For the serial interfaces, you can determine what kind of cable is used, and whether an interface is configured as DCE or DTE. The serial0 interface in the preceding trace uses V.35 cable and is configured as DTE. The seriall interface has no cable attached to it.

The last Physical Layer command examined here is the show buffers command. It displays statistics about public and interface buffers. Interface buffers are permanent and static in size. Public buffers are more dynamic. They can be created and destroyed as necessary by the route processor. Observe the output from the show buffers command executed on the Bozeman router.

```
Bozeman#
Bozeman#show buffers
Buffer elements:
     500 in free list (500 max allowed)
     39498 hits, 0 misses, 0 created

Public buffer pools:
Small buffers, 104 bytes (total 50, permanent 50):
     49 in free list (20 min, 150 max allowed)
     17608 hits, 0 misses, 0 trims, 0 created
     0 failures (0 no memory)
Middle buffers, 600 bytes (total 25, permanent 25):
     25 in free list (10 min, 150 max allowed)
     183 hits, 0 misses, 0 trims, 0 created
     0 failures (0 no memory)
Big buffers, 1524 bytes (total 50, permanent 50):
     50 in free list (5 min, 150 max allowed)
     1469 hits, 0 misses, 0 trims, 0 created
     0 failures (0 no memory)
VeryBig buffers, 4520 bytes (total 10, permanent 10):
     10 in free list (0 min, 100 max allowed)
     0 hits, 0 misses, 0 trims, 0 created
     0 failures (0 no memory)
Large buffers, 5024 bytes (total 0, permanent 0):
     0 in free list (0 min, 10 max allowed)
     0 hits, 0 misses, 0 trims, 0 created
     0 failures (0 no memory)
Huge buffers, 18024 bytes (total 0, permanent 0):
     0 in free list (0 min, 4 max allowed)
```

```
    0 hits, 0 misses, 0 trims, 0 created

    0 failures (0 no memory)


Interface buffer pools:

Ethernet0 buffers, 1524 bytes (total 32, permanent 32):

    8 in free list (0 min, 32 max allowed)

    24 hits, 0 fallbacks

    8 max cache size, 8 in cache

Ethernet1 buffers, 1524 bytes (total 32, permanent 32):

    8 in free list (0 min, 32 max allowed)

    24 hits, 0 fallbacks

    8 max cache size, 8 in cache

Serial0 buffers, 1524 bytes (total 32, permanent 32):

    7 in free list (0 min, 32 max allowed)

    28 hits, 0 fallbacks

    8 max cache size, 8 in cache

Serial1 buffers, 1524 bytes (total 32, permanent 32):

    7 in free list (0 min, 32 max allowed)

    25 hits, 0 fallbacks

    8 max cache size, 8 in cache

Bozeman#

Bozeman#
```

In general, your router is coping well with network traffic when you see
non-zero values only for the "hits" counters as in the show buffers display. When you see high numbers for the "misses" counters in the system
buffers, it's an indication that buffers have been requested by the route processor but none were available in the free list for a particular buffer size. The
"created" counter means that new buffers had to be created as a result of
misses or the number of buffers in the free list dipping below the minimum.

A large number of "misses" and "created" is an indication that you may
be running into performance problems on your router and it may be necessary to increase the number of buffers for a particular size. Buffers can be
adjusted via the buffers configuration command. It's recommended,
however, that you get a second opinion (like talking to Cisco's technical
support) before adjusting buffers on your router. A simple rule of thumb

for reviewing buffer statistics is that "hits" are good and "misses/created" are a red flag.

Data Link Layer Show Commands

At the Data Link Layer you are concerned with encapsulation mismatches. The show interfaces command again comes in very handy. Take a look again at output from show interface s0 on the Bozeman router from the internetwork in Figure 3.1.

```
Bozeman#show interface s0
Serial0 is up, line protocol is up
    Hardware is HD64570
    Internet address is 192.168.2.2/24
    MTU 1500 bytes, BW 1544 Kbit, DLY 20000 usec,
        reliability 255/255, txload 1/255, rxload 1/255
    Encapsulation HDLC, loopback not set, keepalive set (10 sec)
.
.
```

You have already looked at the physical characteristics of this output in the previous section. Here you are looking at the encapsulation, which is HDLC. HDLC is the default Cisco encapsulation for serial links. If you have two Cisco routers communicating over a serial link, leaving the encapsulation at default will work. In a multi-vendor environment, it is recommended that you configure encapsulation explicitly to avoid mismatches. Line Protocol will not be up if there is an encapsulation mismatch between serial neighbors.

Commands related to frame relay operations can be considered as data link Layer commands. They are covered in Chapter 5.

Network Layer Show Command Options

You have already seen some of the Network Layer show commands used in the troubleshooting example earlier in this chapter. They were show ip interfaces brief, show ip route, and show ip protocols. All these commands represent the use of different keywords with the show ip command. The full list of the show ip command keywords is displayed in the following trace.

```
Bozeman#show ip ?
  access-lists          List IP access lists
  accounting            The active IP accounting database
  aliases               IP alias table
  arp                   IP ARP table
  as-path-access-list   List AS path access lists
  bgp                   BGP information
  cache                 IP fast-switching route cache
  community-list        List community-list
  drp                   Director response protocol
  dvmrp                 DVMRP information
  egp                   EGP connections and statistics
  eigrp                 IP-EIGRP show commands
  igmp                  IGMP information
  interface             IP interface status and configuration
  irdp                  ICMP Router Discovery Protocol
  local                 IP local options
  masks                 Masks associated with a network
  mcache                IP multicast fast-switching cache
  mpacket               Display possible duplicate multicast packets
  mroute                IP multicast routing table
  mtag                  IP Multicast Tagswitching TIB
  nat                   IP NAT information
  nhrp                  NHRP information
  ospf                  OSPF information
  pim                   PIM information
  policy                Policy routing
  prefix-list           List IP prefix lists
  protocols             IP routing protocol process parameters and statistics
  redirects              IP redirects
  route                  IP routing table
  rpf                    Display RPF information for multicast source
  rsvp                   RSVP information
  rtp                    RTP/UDP/IP header-compression statistics
  sdr                    Session Directory (SDPv2) cache
```

```
sockets                   Open IP sockets

tcp                       TCP/IP header-compression statistics

traffic                   IP protocol statistics

trigger-authentication    Trigger-authentication host table
```

The list is long (38 keywords), and is organized alphabetically. Many of these keywords are followed by more keywords. Consider that a single keyword, *ip*, from the initial list of 111 keywords resulting from *show ?* can be used with 38 more keywords. It's not difficult to conclude that there are probably thousands of different ways in which the **show** command can be used.

In the preceding display, the routing protocols that will be discussed in later chapters are available as keywords. They include *eigrp*, *ospf*, and *bgp*. Each one of those keywords has more keywords that follow. Take a look at the *bgp*, *ospf*, and *eigrp* keywords.

```
Bozeman#

Bozeman#sh ip bgp ?
  A.B.C.D           Network in the BGP routing table to display

  cidr-only         Display only routes with non-natural netmasks

  community         Display routes matching the communities

  community-list    Display routes matching the community-list

  dampened-paths    Display paths suppressed due to dampening

  filter-list       Display routes conforming to the filter-list

  flap-statistics   Display flap statistics of routes

  inconsistent-as   Display only routes with inconsistent origin ASs

  neighbors         Detailed information on TCP and BGP neighbor connections

  paths             Path information

  peer-group        Display information on peer-groups

  regexp            Display routes matching the AS path regular expression

  summary           Summary of BGP neighbor status

  <cr>


Bozeman#sh ip ospf ?
  <1-4294967295>      Process ID number

  border-routers      Border and Boundary Router Information

  database            Database summary
```

```
interface                    Interface information

neighbor                     Neighbor list

request-list                 Link state request list

retransmission-list          Link state retransmission list

summary-address              Summary-address redistribution Information

virtual-links                Virtual link information

<cr>


Bozeman#sh ip eigrp ?

interfaces                   IP-EIGRP interfaces

neighbors                    IP-EIGRP neighbors

topology                     IP-EIGRP Topology Table

traffic                      IP-EIGRP Traffic Statistics
```

The amount of information that's available from these show commands is staggering. Use these displays as an initial guide to further experiment in environments where these protocols are deployed. The show command that's used most frequently in later chapters on troubleshooting EIGRP, OSPF, and BGP (Chapters 7, 8, and 10) is the display of neighbors for the respective protocols.

Routing Policy Show Commands

Routing policies impact traffic flow. Traffic that meets the routing policy criteria (source address, destination address, type of traffic) may be denied entry or exit through a specific router interface. Traffic may also be influenced as to which way to enter or exit a routing domain, like a BGP autonomous system. See Chapter 10 for a discussion of BGP and autonomous systems. Route maps and access control lists are generic IOS tools that are used to implement routing policies.

The show route-maps and show access-lists commands display the route maps and access lists that are configured on a router. The displays do not tell you whether the route maps or access list have been activated. For that you have to look at displays of IP interface parameters (show ip interfaces), or better yet, at the active router configuration (show running-config).

Access lists must be associated with an interface via the `ip access-group #` command before they take effect. Route maps must be invoked from another configuration command for them to take effect. Route maps are frequently invoked via a `redistribute` command, which performs redistribution between routing protocols. They can also be used with the `neighbor` command in BGP. Route maps perform an action via the `set` keyword upon routing updates that have been identified via the `match` keyword. Access control lists are often used with route maps to match the incoming or outgoing routing updates. Here is a display of a simple standard IP access list:

```
Billings#sh access-lists
Standard IP access list 22
     permit 172.20.0.0, wildcard bits 0.0.255.255
Billings#
```

This display simply tells you that a standard access control list #22 has been configured permitting traffic to or from destinations on network 172.20.0.0. It doesn't tell you in which direction (in or out of the interface) the traffic is permitted. Also, remember that access control lists end with an implicit `deny all` statement. If list 22 is associated with an interface to filter inbound traffic, it will have the effect of denying all traffic arriving on that interface except traffic from hosts on 172.20.0.0. Observe the interface configuration and the corresponding `show ip interface` display to gain a fuller perspective of how this access list is deployed on the Billings router.

```
billings#sh running
Building configuration...


Current configuration:
!
hostname billings
 .
 .
interface Serial1
 ip address 192.168.129.1 255.255.255.0
 ip access-group 22 in
```

```
clockrate 2000000
.

.


billings#sh ip int s1
Serial1 is up, line protocol is up
  Internet address is 192.168.129.1 255.255.255.0
  Broadcast address is 255.255.255.255
  Address determined by non-volatile memory
  MTU is 1500 bytes
  Helper address is not set
  Directed broadcast forwarding is enabled
  Outgoing access list is not set
  Inbound  access list is 22
  .

  .
```

The standard IP access list 22 is configured to filter inbound traffic on serial1 interface on the Billings router. If you do not use the *in* keyword at the end of ip access-group #, the default will be *out*. It means that outbound traffic will be filtered instead of inbound. In the case of the Billings router, only inbound traffic is filtered on s0. The show ip interface s0 display indicates that no outgoing access list is set for that interface.

The route maps that are configured on the Billings router can be viewed via the show route-maps command. The names of these route maps are *set_lp_again* and *set_lp*. They set the BGP attribute local preference to 300 for matching routing updates.

```
billings#show route-map
route-map set_lp_again, permit, sequence 1
  Match clauses:
  Set clauses:
      local-preference 300
  Policy routing matches: 88 packets, 22528 bytes
```

```
route-map set_lp, permit, sequence 1
  Match clauses:
  Set clauses:
     local-preference 300
  Policy routing matches: 26 packets, 3328 bytes
billings#
```

These particular route maps are discussed and analyzed in Chapter 10.

Traceroute

Traceroute, like ping, is another well-known TCP/IP utility that's incorporated into the IOS. Traceroute is a valuable tool in determining traffic patterns in an internetwork. Ping will tell you that a destination can be reached. Traceroute will tell you how a destination can be reached.

Observe an output from *traceroute* executed on the Billings router.

```
billings#traceroute 172.20.0.3

Type escape sequence to abort.
Tracing the route to 172.20.0.3

 1 192.168.1.2   4 msec 4 msec 4 msec
 2 192.168.144.2   4 msec 4 msec 4 msec
 3 172.20.0.3   4 msec 8 msec 4 msec
billings#
```

The interpretation of this output is that to reach destination 172.20.0.3, traffic will flow through router interfaces configured with IP addresses of 192.168.1.2 and 192.168.144.2. There are two routers between Billings and the destination host 172.20.0.3. The IP addresses of the routers identify their inbound interfaces. The number in front of the IP addresses refers to the sequence of ICMP probes that the traceroute utility sends out to trace a path to the destination.

By default, traceroute sends out sets (sequences) of three ICMP probes with increasing Time To Live (TTL) counters. The times in milliseconds refer to the round trip delay between the source and a corresponding IP address for the individual ICMP packets in a set. It's natural that the times should be gradually increasing to reach the routers in the path that are further away from the destination. However, if you observe unusually large delay times in the traceroute, it's an indication of congestion along the path.

If you invoke the `traceroute` command without a destination address or host name, you are able to change the default traceroute settings. Traceroute is available for other network protocols like AppleTalk and VINES. The number of ICMP packets in each sequence can also be set higher to give you a better sense of the delay times. You can also specify a specific path (source route) that you want the traceroute packets to follow to a destination. The traceroute utility is very useful when troubleshooting network performance problems.

Debug

Debug options are very similar to the `show` command options. They are numerous. A note of warning about debug must be sounded from the start: Indiscriminate use of the `debug` command can be dangerous to your router. Debug is a very CPU-intensive process. It's best to experiment with debug in lab environments before using it in live production settings. It's a powerful tool, however, that every network administrator should be aware of.

If you are connected to a router via the console port and you activate debug, you may not be able to deactivate it due to the volume of messages that will be generated to the console. It's always a good idea to have a backup plan. If you are going to use debug, telnet into your router from another terminal. Make sure that the timeout on your telnet session is sufficiently long. Then activate debug from the console port. If you get locked out from the console port due to a large volume of debug messages, you can always turn debug off from your telnet session. That's provided your telnet session allows you access to the privileged mode.

Sometimes, there is so much debugging output that the monitor seems to show a rapidly scrolling bunch of garbage. Remember that the `undebug all` command, or simply `u all` may be entered to stop all debug output. Don't be concerned about all the text flying by. Just type **u all** and it will stop.

A few debug commands are used in Chapters 9 and 10 when troubleshooting RIP and BGP. To display all of the available debug options execute `debug ?` from the privileged mode. 99 debug keywords are available as compared to 111 `show` command keywords on the router from which the traces in this chapter are derived. Debug is often used to resolve subtle problems that cannot be detected from the observation of output from the show commands.

Chapter Summary

IOS has numerous and versatile troubleshooting tools. The combination of ping, telnet, traceroute, CDP, and show commands can be used in troubleshooting problems with internetworks. Numerous show and debug command options are available for troubleshooting individual routers at the physical, data link, and Network Layers. For a complete listing of all available troubleshooting commands, refer to Cisco documentation available on their Web site and on the Cisco Documentation CD.

Part II

Troubleshooting the Bottom Layers

Chapter 4

Troubleshooting the Physical Layer

It is recommended that in the layered approach to troubleshooting routers and internetworks, the troubleshooting process begin with the Physical Layer. The Physical Layer provides the foundation upon which the higher layers depend to perform their functions. If the Physical Layer is not configured and working properly, higher-layer functions will fail.

Physical Layer problems on a router can be detected and diagnosed through a combination of visual inspections, review of IOS-generated system messages, and the use of commands like show or debug. On the higher-end modular routers like Cisco's 7500 or 12000 series, numerous LEDs indicate the operational status of a router's hardware components. A component failure will typically result in the simultaneous color change of an LED and a console error/warning message. The review of system messages requires direct access to the console port or to the location where console messages have been redirected. Debug and certain show commands require access to a router's privileged mode.

Physical Layer problems may be related to power, mulfunctioning interfaces in fixed configuration routers, problems with faulty or unplugged modules in modular routers, faulty transmission media, and malfunctioning or misconfigured components interfacing routers to the transmission media.

Power Problems

Power problems range from no power at all to poor and/or intermittent power being supplied to a router. When no power is supplied to a router, the AC source, the power cable(s), and the power supplies are all suspect. Detecting bad power is not easy. Frequent brownouts can be observed visually. But special power monitoring equipment is required to get a complete picture of all dips, spikes, and brownouts over a period of time. The solution to bad power is to install a power conditioner and/or an Uninterruptible Power Supply (UPS). This section deals with troubleshooting the "no power" conditions.

Troubleshooting Power Problems on Non-Modular Routers (2500 Series)

In the lower-end, fixed-hardware-configuration routers (2500 series, for example), verifying that AC power is being supplied to a router may be as simple as turning on the power switch, listening for the cooling fan to come on, and observing if the power-on LED turns green. If nothing happens when the power switch is turned on, there are several possibilities as to what's wrong.

First, it's possible that the power cable may either be loose at the router end or the wall outlet. Get rid of power cables that do not fit well in the AC outlets or the power socket on a router. They are a source of intermittent router reboots, which occur at the least expected and usually the most undesirable times. Also, they may cause a router not to power up at all when the power switch is turned on.

A second possibility is that a power cable may be bad. Bad power cables are rare, but they do occur. If your power cable fits well into the router and the AC receptacle but nothing happens when the power is turned on, try another cable.

A third possibility is that the AC outlet may be bad. A simple tool for checking AC power should be part of every network administrator's tool kit. If your router is accidentally plugged into an AC outlet that doesn't have any power, it may be that either the outlet itself has a problem or a circuit breaker controlling that outlet has flipped. It's always a good idea to know where the circuit breakers are for circuits supplying power to critical equipment. In most installations, routers tend to fall into the critical equipment category.

There are more possibilities as to what may be wrong if your router does not come on when the power switch is turned on. If the router is plugged into an UPS, verify that the UPS is turned on and functioning properly. Finally, after eliminating all of the possibilities that can be checked and verified easily, suspect a problem with the router power supply.

In the non-modular fixed-hardware-configuration routers, replacing a bad supply may be outside the scope of a network administrator's responsibility and expertise. However, swapping routers is easily done, provided that there is an extra router available. If the new router powers up when plugged into the same AC outlet and using the same power cord, then it's likely that you have a problem with the power supply in the original unit. If you have the expertise, time, and spare parts to replace a malfunctioning power supply, do it. Otherwise, have qualified service personnel take care of the problem.

When hardware failures occur — whether it's the power supply, the individual interfaces, or the CPU — it's vital to have handy all of the relevant information needed to resolve a problem quickly. Relevant information includes your router model and serial #, IOS version, warranty information, and phone numbers for authorized service centers.

Troubleshooting Power Problems on Modular Routers (12000 Series)

Troubleshooting and replacing power supplies in the higher-end routers and switches with multiple, modular, hot-swappable power supplies is actually easier than in the lower-end units with a single built-in power supply. Take, for example, Cisco's top-of-the-line unit, the GSR 12000 series router. The Giga Switch Router (GSR) 12000 series accommodates up to four modular, hot-swappable power supplies. Each power supply has its own power switch and status LED.

Assume that a 12012 model GSR is fully populated with four power supplies. You turn them on one by one and nothing happens. No sounds of blower fans, no LEDs flashing anywhere on a router. That's a fairly clear indication that you have a problem with the power source to the router rather than with the individual power supplies. However, if only one out of the four power supplies does not come on, here's what you can do.

Turn the power switch to the off position on the malfunctioning supply and unplug it. Do the same with one of the functioning power supplies. A Cisco 12000 series router will operate with two power supplies. Swap the two unplugged units between the two empty slots, remembering which power supply is which. It's helpful to label the slots and the power supplies before the swap.

You have two suspects: the power supply and the slot it's in. If the suspect power supply works in the functioning slot, the problem is with the suspect slot. Confirm your finding by making sure that the functioning supply does not work in the suspect slot. If, on the other hand, the functioning supply works in the suspect slot, it's the suspect power supply that has the problem. To confirm this diagnosis, ensure that the suspect power supply does not work in the functioning slot.

From the operational perspective, troubleshooting routers with multiple, modular hot-swappable power supplies is very advantageous. A router can still function while the troubleshooting takes place. For exact instructions on how to change power supplies and what precautions to take when doing so, you should consult the hardware reference manual for your specific router model.

Additionally, on a router like the GSR 12000 series, there are system messages generated to the console if there is a problem with one of the power supplies. Observe the console messages that were generated on a 12000 series router when one of the four power supplies was not operating properly.

Console output for a malfunctioning power supply on a 12000 series router

```
Nov 1 09:38:16.285 MST: %GSR_ENV-0-SHUTDOWN: Slot 26 5V supply at 0 mv < 1000 mv
Nov 1 09:38:16.285 MST: %GSR_ENV-0-SHUTDOWN_PS: Slot 26 Voltage input failed -
48V output= 0 V; Power supply may be unplugged or turned off
Nov 1 09:38:16.285 MST: %GSR_ENV-0-SHUTDOWN: Slot 26 48V supply at 0 V < 39 V
```

The three messages that were generated clearly identify that there is a problem with the power supply in slot 26. That's a lot better feedback than listening to hear if the cooling fan comes on when the power is turned on in lower-end routers. The exact condition resulting in the preceding set of messages was that a power supply in slot 26 was plugged in and turned on, but it was not connected properly to the AC source.

Troubleshooting a Router's Physical Interfaces

During a boot cycle, routers generate numerous console messages. Some of those messages identify the router's hardware configuration. The information that's displayed regarding cards, controllers, ports, and interfaces is your first clue as to what LAN and WAN interfaces are present and recognized by a router.

In modular routers, it's particularly important to pay attention to the version of the Bootstrap ROM. It's the Bootstrap ROM that performs the initial Power-On-Self-Test (POST) diagnostics. As new modules with new interfaces become available for a modular router, the bootstrap ROM may require an update. Otherwise, the new modules may not be recognized.

The interfaces that are identified during the boot cycle may not necessarily be operational once the router is fully booted. They may be disconnected from the transmission media or misconfigured. But the very first step in troubleshooting an interface is to make sure that it's recognized during the POST. Troubleshooting a router's interface is a multi-layer process, as described in Chapter 2. In this chapter, the emphasis is on the Physical Layer. Data Link and Network Layer troubleshooting are discussed in Chapters 5 and 6.

Interfaces on Modular Routers (12000 Series)

Observe a portion of a trace that was generated on 12000 series router during a boot cycle.

Portion of boot trace identifying hardware components on a 12000 series

```
Cisco 12012/GRP (R5000) processor (revision 0x01) with 262144K bytes of memory.

R5000 CPU at 200Mhz, Implementation 35, Rev 2.1, 512KB L2 Cache

Last reset from power-on


1 Route Processor Card

2 Clock Scheduler Cards

3 Switch Fabric Cards
```

```
1 four-port OC3 POS controller (4 POS).

2 Single Port Gigabit Ethernet/IEEE 802.3z controllers (2 GigabitEthernet).

1 Ethernet/IEEE 802.3 interface(s)

2 GigabitEthernet/IEEE 802.3 interface(s)

4 Packet over SONET network interface(s)

507K bytes of non-volatile configuration memory.


20480K bytes of Flash PCMCIA card at slot 0 (Sector size 128K).

8192K bytes of Flash internal SIMM (Sector size 256K).
```

The boot trace from the 12000 series router identifies the cards, controllers, and interfaces that are present in the router. Cards and controllers are all pluggable modules. A total of nine modules are present in this configuration (six cards and three controllers).

The Route Processor Card, also known as the Gigabit Route Processor or GRP, is the module responsible for calculating the routing table. To optimize the 12000's performance, the GRP distributes the routing table to all of the line cards (LC) identified in the trace as controllers.

Controllers are typically modules with ports that allow routers to interface to LANs and WANs. A total of seven interfaces are identified in the trace. Notice that there are references to both ports and interfaces in the trace. Ports and interfaces are often used interchangeably in routing jargon.

In general, an interface is used in reference to a Physical Layer characteristic of a port, that is, the type of connector that's built into a router or present on a controller. A port normally identifies a Data Link Layer technology (Gigabit Ethernet, Ethernet, OC3 Packet-Over-SONET or POS) or a function (console, auxiliary, and so on). However, when Data Link Layer technologies become identified with the media and connectors that they use, ports and interfaces often become synonymous.

A single controller can have multiple ports. The trace identifies that each of the Ethernet Gigabit controllers has a single Gigabit Ethernet port. The OC-3 controller has four ports or four Packet-Over-SONET (POS) interfaces. The last interface that's identified in the trace is the Ethernet 802.3. There is no separate controller for this interface. It resides on the Route Processor Card. After gleaning what you can from the boot trace, review other indicators about the status of interfaces.

Take, for example, the four-port OC3 POS controller. The full official name for it is OC-3c/STM-1c Packet-Over-SONET line card. Each port on this line card has status LEDs associated with it. They are labeled Active, Carrier, and RX PKT, indicating whether a port is active (normally this means connected to the transmission media), whether it is detecting a carrier signal, or whether it is receiving packets. There isn't any single indicator for the entire line card.

However, the one card not identified in the trace, which is a vital hardware troubleshooting aid, is the alarm card. The alarm card can detect problems with the line cards sporting the LAN/WAN interfaces. The alarm card plugs into its own unique slot on the GSR 12000. The alarm card has LEDs labeled critical, major, and minor alarms.

The alarm card is interfaced to the maintenance bus on the GSR. The GRP and the line cards also interface to the maintenance bus. If there is a Physical Layer problem with one of the line cards (an out-of-range voltage condition or an excessively high temperature), the LEDs on the alarm will change color from green to red or amber, depending on the severity of the condition. An audible alarm can also be configured to go off on the alarm card.

The alarm card is also equipped with LEDs that identify the status of the clock and scheduler cards (CSCs) and the switch fabric cards (SFCs). The CSCs and SFCs provide an internal switch fabric for the GSR 12000. The switch fabric is used for fast and optimized communications between the GRP and the line cards.

Additionally, the clock and scheduler card is responsible for clock synchronization between the GPR and the line cards. It also schedules the distribution of the routing table from the GRP to the line cards. At least one clock and scheduler card must be present for a GSR 12000 to function properly. If two are present, there is redundancy.

The physical indicators for troubleshooting interfaces on the 12000 are complemented by IOS tools as well. The IOS tools include commands like show diag, diag, show interfaces, and show environment.

Observe a partial output from the show diag command executed on a 12000 series that analyzes a Gigabit Ethernet controller.

```
Big_Router#show diag
.
.
```

```
SLOT 4   (RP/LC 4 ): 1 Port Gigabit Ethernet
  MAIN: type 43,  800-3955-02 rev B0 dev 16777215
        HW config: 0x00    SW key: FF-FF-FF
  PCA:  73-3302-03 rev C0 ver 3
        HW version 1.1  S/N CAB03161GXW
  MBUS: MBUS Agent (1)   73-2146-07 rev B0 dev 0
        HW version 1.2  S/N CAB03222374
        Test hist: 0xFF    RMA#: FF-FF-FF    RMA hist: 0xFF
  DIAG: Test count: 0xFFFFFFFF    Test results: 0xFFFFFFFF
  MBUS Agent Software version 01.36 (RAM) (ROM version is 02.00)
  Using CAN Bus A
  ROM Monitor version 10.00
  Fabric Downloader version used 13.04 (ROM version is 13.04)
  Primary clock is CSC 1
  Board is analyzed
  Board State is Line Card Enabled (IOS  RUN )
  Insertion time: 00:00:08 (5w1d ago)
  DRAM size: 134217728 bytes
  FrFab SDRAM size: 134217728 bytes, SDRAM pagesize: 8192 bytes
  ToFab SDRAM size: 134217728 bytes, SDRAM pagesize: 8192 bytes
  0 crashes since restart
```

The show diag output identifies the slot in which the controller resides, serial numbers, maintenance bus (MBUS) agent software version, clock source, and more. Perhaps most importantly, the bottom of the trace identifies that the card has had no crashes since restart.

Overall, the troubleshooting tools for the top-of-the-line routers are much more sophisticated and plentiful than for the lower-end fixed hardware configuration units.

Interfaces on Non-modular Routers (2500 Series)

Now take a look at the boot trace from a 2500 series router.

Portion of a boot trace identifying hardware components on a 2500 series

```
cisco 2522 (68030) processor (revision E) with 16384K/2048K bytes of memory.

Processor board ID 03858157, with hardware revision 00000002

Bridging software.

SuperLAT software copyright 1990 by Meridian Technology Corp).

X.25 software, Version 2.0, NET2, BFE and GOSIP compliant.

TN3270 Emulation software (copyright 1994 by TGV Inc).

Basic Rate ISDN software, Version 1.0.

1 Ethernet/IEEE 802.3 interface.

2 Serial network interfaces.

8 Low-speed serial(sync/async) network interfaces.

1 ISDN Basic Rate interface.

32K bytes of non-volatile configuration memory.

8192K bytes of processor board System flash (Read ONLY)
```

There are no references to cards and controllers in the power-on trace from a 2500 series router. Only interfaces are referenced. All of the interfaces on the 2522 from which the trace was taken are built-in. The 2522 is not a modular router. There are also no `diag` or `show diag` commands available on this router. Your best bet for the next step is to verify the status of the interfaces via a `show interface` command once the router has booted.

Analysis of Show Interface Output

When a router has a dozen or more interfaces, like the Cisco 2522, the output from the `show interface` command is voluminous. The 2522 has ten serial interfaces, one Ethernet, and one ISDN Basic Rate Interface (BRI). A partial output from the `show interface` command executed on a 2522 follows. All of the information displayed is useful, but the information that's boldfaced is most relevant to the troubleshooting at the Physical Layer. The interfaces shown in the following trace differ in type and status. One Ethernet and three serial interfaces are displayed. The Ethernet interface is up and functioning properly. The three serial interfaces are up, down, and administratively down.

The first line of output from the `show interface` command for each interface tells you whether the interface is up or down and whether the protocol associated with the interface is up or down. The possible combinations for the interface and the protocol are:

- Interface is up and line protocol is up
- Interface is up and line protocol is down
- Interface is down and line protocol is down
- Interface is administratively down and line protocol is down

Show interface output from a Cisco 2522

```
Test_router#show interface
.

.

Ethernet0 is up, line protocol is up
  Hardware is Lance, address is 0000.0c92.1bbc (bia 0000.0c92.1bbc)
  Internet address is 172.16.0.1 255.255.0.0
  MTU 1500 bytes, BW 10000 Kbit, DLY 1000 usec, rely 255/255, load 1/255
  Encapsulation ARPA, loopback not set, keepalive set (10 sec)
  ARP type: ARPA, ARP Timeout 4:00:00
  Last input 0:00:18, output 0:00:03, output hang never
  Last clearing of "show interface" counters never
  Output queue 0/40, 0 drops; input queue 0/75, 0 drops
  5 minute input rate 0 bits/sec, 0 packets/sec
  5 minute output rate 0 bits/sec, 0 packets/sec
     128 packets input, 29621 bytes, 0 no buffer
     Received 128 broadcasts, 0 runts, 0 giants
     0 input errors, 0 CRC, 0 frame, 0 overrun, 0 ignored, 0 abort
     0 input packets with dribble condition detected
     342 packets output, 31454 bytes, 0 underruns
     0 output errors, 0 collisions, 2 interface resets, 0 restarts
     0 output buffer failures, 0 output buffers swapped out
.

.

Serial0 is up, line protocol is up
```

```
Hardware is HD64570

Internet address is 192.168.1.1 255.255.255.0

MTU 1500 bytes, BW 1544 Kbit, DLY 20000 usec, rely 255/255, load 1/255

Encapsulation HDLC, loopback not set, keepalive set (10 sec)

Last input 0:00:00, output 0:00:04, output hang never

Last clearing of "show interface" counters never

Output queue 0/40, 0 drops; input queue 0/75, 0 drops

5 minute input rate 0 bits/sec, 0 packets/sec

5 minute output rate 0 bits/sec, 0 packets/sec

   80 packets input, 4783 bytes, 0 no buffer

   Received 62 broadcasts, 0 runts, 0 giants

   0 input errors, 0 CRC, 0 frame, 0 overrun, 0 ignored, 0 abort

   97 packets output, 6163 bytes, 0 underruns

   0 output errors, 0 collisions, 70 interface resets, 0 restarts

   0 output buffer failures, 0 output buffers swapped out

   9 carrier transitions

   DCD=up  DSR=up  DTR=up  RTS=up  CTS=up
```

.

.

```
Serial1 is down, line protocol is down

Hardware is HD64570

Internet address is 192.168.129.1 255.255.255.0

MTU 1500 bytes, BW 1544 Kbit, DLY 20000 usec, rely 255/255, load 1/255

Encapsulation HDLC, loopback not set, keepalive set (10 sec)

Last input 0:35:09, output 0:35:04, output hang never

Last clearing of "show interface" counters never

Input queue: 0/75/0 (size/max/drops); Total output drops: 0

Output queue: 0/64/0 (size/threshold/drops)

   Conversations  0/1 (active/max active)

   Reserved Conversations 0/0 (allocated/max allocated)

5 minute input rate 0 bits/sec, 0 packets/sec

5 minute output rate 0 bits/sec, 0 packets/sec

   176 packets input, 10196 bytes, 0 no buffer

   Received 127 broadcasts, 0 runts, 0 giants

   0 input errors, 0 CRC, 0 frame, 0 overrun, 0 ignored, 0 abort
```

```
171 packets output, 10558 bytes, 0 underruns

0 output errors, 0 collisions, 138 interface resets, 0 restarts

0 output buffer failures, 0 output buffers swapped out

16 carrier transitions

DCD=up  DSR=up  DTR=down  RTS=down  CTS=up
.

.


Serial3 is administratively down, line protocol is down

Hardware is CD2430 in sync mode

MTU 1500 bytes, BW 115 Kbit, DLY 20000 usec, rely 255/255, load 1/255

Encapsulation HDLC, loopback not set, keepalive set (10 sec)

Last input never, output never, output hang never

Last clearing of "show interface" counters never

Input queue: 0/75/0 (size/max/drops); Total output drops: 0

Output queue: 0/64/0 (size/threshold/drops)

    Conversations  0/0 (active/max active)

    Reserved Conversations 0/0 (allocated/max allocated)

5 minute input rate 0 bits/sec, 0 packets/sec

5 minute output rate 0 bits/sec, 0 packets/sec

    0 packets input, 0 bytes, 0 no buffer

    Received 0 broadcasts, 0 runts, 0 giants

    0 input errors, 0 CRC, 0 frame, 0 overrun, 0 ignored, 0 abort

    0 packets output, 0 bytes, 0 underruns

    0 output errors, 0 collisions, 15 interface resets, 0 restarts

    0 output buffer failures, 0 output buffers swapped out

    0 carrier transitions

DCD=down  DSR=down  DTR=down  RTS=down  CTS=down
.

.

.
```

Interface Is Up and Line Protocol Is Up

This is the condition that you ultimately want to see for each interface that's supposed to be operational. It's the condition that's displayed for Ethernet0 and Serial0 in the preceding trace. If an interface is up and the line protocol is up, the next step is to review the details in the display. Numerous counters at the bottom of the display for each interface convey useful information about its physical health.

For example, on the Ethernet0 display, the counter statistics look good. There are no errors. However, assume for a moment that there were numerous input errors related to the CRC. You should suspect either the transmission media (cabling), ports on switches or concentrators, a transceiver for AUI interfaces using twisted pair cabling, or the interface itself as the culprit.

Troubleshooting involves testing and elimination. The rule of thumb is to begin with what's easiest. Swapping a transceiver is easy. Plugging a cable into a different port on a concentrator or a switch is also fairly straightforward. Trying a different cable may or may not be easy depending on the topology and location of the equipment. If there is no improvement after all of these steps are tried, the interface itself may have an intermittent problem, which will require either swapping a router or involving a qualified service technician.

Interface Is Up and Line Protocol Is Down

This is a condition that occurs when an Ethernet interface is disconnected from the transmission media. Observe the trace that was captured from the Ethernet0 interface on the same router after a cable was pulled out from the interface.

```
Test_router#sh int e0

Ethernet0 is up, line protocol is down

   Hardware is Lance, address is 0000.0c92.1bbc (bia 0000.0c92.1bbc)

   Internet address is 172.16.0.1 255.255.0.0

   MTU 1500 bytes, BW 10000 Kbit, DLY 1000 usec, rely 128/255, load 1/255

   Encapsulation ARPA, loopback not set, keepalive set (10 sec)

   ARP type: ARPA, ARP Timeout 4:00:00

   Last input 0:29:12, output 0:00:03, output hang never

   Last clearing of "show interface" counters 0:10:25

   Output queue 0/40, 0 drops; input queue 0/75, 0 drops

   5 minute input rate 0 bits/sec, 0 packets/sec

   5 minute output rate 0 bits/sec, 0 packets/sec

      0 packets input, 0 bytes, 0 no buffer
```

```
Received 0 broadcasts, 0 runts, 0 giants

0 input errors, 0 CRC, 0 frame, 0 overrun, 0 ignored, 0 abort

0 input packets with dribble condition detected

63 packets output, 3797 bytes, 0 underruns

63 output errors, 0 collisions, 0 interface resets, 0 restarts

0 output buffer failures, 0 output buffers swapped out
Test_router#
```

The reliability changed from 255/255 to 128/255. When you see the reliability as other than 255/255, suspect a problem with either the interface or the transmission media. Interface reliability is expressed as a percentage of 255, with 255/255 being 100%.

When you observe the output from a `show interface` display with output errors, it's safe to assume there is a problem with the transmission media. In the preceding case, the router was completely disconnected from the network. But a bad cable or a crossover cable connecting the router to a switch or a concentrator could produce the same result. A bad port on a concentrator or a switch could also result in a similar display.

Interface Is Down and Line Protocol Is Down

When this condition occurs on an Ethernet interface, you can bet that the interface itself has a problem. When it occurs on a serial interface, something else may be causing the problem. Serial interfaces operate in pairs, and normally there are CSU/DSUs between them along with transmission media that may be spanning the globe. You have to start looking at some of details in the display to determine why the interface is not up.

The serial0 interface in the trace is operating properly but the serial1 interface is down with the line protocol also down. What you want to examine next are the conditions of the various signals at the bottom of the display. They are as follows:

- DCD – Data Carrier Detect
- DSR – Data Set Ready
- DTR – Data Terminal Ready
- RTS – Request to Send
- CTS – Clear to Send

From a network administrator's perspective, it's important to understand which end of the connection is responsible for what signals. If two routers are directly connected via a crossover serial cable, one of the routers will have to act as Data Terminal Equipment (DTE), the other as Data Circuit-terminating Equipment (DCE). The DCE router will have to configure clocking for its serial interface via the `clockrate` command. When routers are connected via WAN transmission lines, both routers are configured as DTEs. The CSU/DSUs act as DCEs.

The breakdown of the signal (DCD, DSR, DTR, RTS, CTS) between DTE and DCE is as follows. DTE is responsible for DTR and RTS. DCE is responsible for DCD, DSR, and CTS.

Observe the signal display from serial0 interface on Test_router in the portion reproduced below.

```
Serial0 is up, line protocol is up
  Hardware is HD64570
  Internet address is 192.168.1.1 255.255.255.0
  .

  .

  9 carrier transitions

  DCD=up  DSR=up  DTR=up  RTS=up  CTS=up
```

All signals are up. That's a sign of a properly operating serial link at the physical level. Now take a look at the display from theSerial1 interface on Test_router reproduced in part below.

```
Serial1 is down, line protocol is down
  Hardware is HD64570
  Internet address is 192.168.129.1 255.255.255.0
  .

  .

  16 carrier transitions

  DCD=up  DSR=up  DTR=down  RTS=down  CTS=up
```

On serial1, the DCE signals are up but the DTE signals are down. This is rather unusual, but remember that routers can be connected directly via a serial cable. What the serial1 display indicates is that the router with serial1 is acting as the DCE and is connected to the DTE router that's down.

When two routers are connected via WAN lines with CSU/DSUs between them, and there is a problem with the transmission media, you can expect a combination of signals as displayed below.

```
Router1#sh inter s0
Serial0 is down, line protocol is down
  Hardware is HD64570
  Internet address is 192.168.1.2/24
  MTU 1500 bytes, BW 1544 Kbit, DLY 20000 usec, rely 255/255, load 1/255
  Encapsulation HDLC, loopback not set, keepalive set (10 sec)
  Last input 00:02:09, output 00:02:09, output hang never
  Last clearing of "show interface" counters never
  Input queue: 0/75/0 (size/max/drops); Total output drops: 0
  Queueing strategy: weighted fair
  Output queue: 0/1000/64/0 (size/max total/threshold/drops)
     Conversations  0/1/256 (active/max active/max total)
     Reserved Conversations 0/0 (allocated/max allocated)
  5 minute input rate 0 bits/sec, 0 packets/sec
  5 minute output rate 0 bits/sec, 0 packets/sec
     43 packets input, 2707 bytes, 0 no buffer
     Received 28 broadcasts, 0 runts, 0 giants, 0 throttles
     0 input errors, 0 CRC, 0 frame, 0 overrun, 0 ignored, 0 abort
     34 packets output, 2127 bytes, 0 underruns
     0 output errors, 0 collisions, 5 interface resets
     0 output buffer failures, 0 output buffers swapped out
     1 carrier transitions
     DCD=down  DSR=down  DTR=up  RTS=up  CTS=down
Router1#
```

Notice that up/down signals are opposite in this display for serial0 on Router1 compared to what they were for serial1 on Test_router. The signals that are up are DTR and RTS. These are signals generated by a DTE. Router1 is a DTE. Even though the interface serial0 on Router1 is down and the line protocol is down, the problem lies elsewhere. It's either with a CSU/DSU or the transmission media between the two routers. In the case of two routers being directly connected via a serial cable, the problem may be that the router configured as the DCE is turned off.

Interface Is Administratively Down and Line Protocol Is Down

When the `show interfaces` command displays that an interface is administratively down, you don't have to look very far for the problem. Check the router configuration file and make sure that the `shutdown` command is removed from the appropriate interface section. The trace generated for Test_router shows interface serial3 as being administratively down. A portion of that trace is reproduced below.

```
Serial3 is administratively down, line protocol is down
  Hardware is CD2430 in sync mode
  MTU 1500 bytes, BW 115 Kbit, DLY 20000 usec, rely 255/255, load 1/255
  .

  .

    0 carrier transitions
    DCD=down  DSR=down  DTR=down  RTS=down  CTS=down
```

All of the DTE/DCE signals are down. There is also no sign of IP address assignment to this interface. Everything points to the interface not having been activated via configuration.

Troubleshooting the Transmission Media

Collectively, the transmission media represent the physical path between any two routers. The critical issue to consider when troubleshooting the transmission media is their accessibility and ownership. A general rule of thumb is that LAN owners own the LAN media. The WAN media are typically owned by telcos. In a typical LAN/WAN environment, multiple parties own the transmission media. The LAN media tend to be more accessible to network administrators, which is useful during troubleshooting. If you suspect a problem with your WAN circuits, you will have to get your provider involved.

If two routers are not talking to each other across a circuit provided by a telco, it's recommended that for purposes of troubleshooting you mentally break the path between them into multiple segments, as shown in the scenario in Figure 4.1.

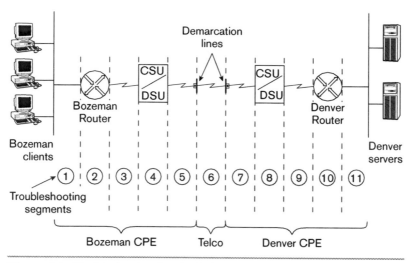

Figure 4-1 *Troubleshooting the physical media scenario*

In Figure 4.1, there are at least a half-dozen potential problem areas to consider at the Physical Layer if there is no communication between the Bozeman clients and the Denver servers. They are as follows:

- Cables interfacing each router to the LAN (segments 1 and 11)
- Cables interfacing routers to CSU/DSUs (segments 3 and 9)
- Cables interfacing CSU/DSUs to telco outlets (segments 5 and 7)
- WAN circuit (segment 6)
- The CSU/DSUs (segments 4 and 8)
- The router interfaces (segments 2 and 10)

What you need to be very clear about at this point is that you are verifying the operation of the Physical Layer. If the Bozeman clients can't communicate with the Denver servers, there could be many reasons for it stretching all the way up to the top layer of the OSI model. There could be problems with encapsulation at the Data Link Layer, improper addressing at the Network Layer, and improper access rights at the higher layers. What you are verifying at the Physical Layer is cabling, CSU/DSUs, and router physical interfaces. Troubleshooting router interfaces was discussed in a previous section in this chapter. CSU/DSUs are discussed in the next section. The emphasis in this section is on cabling.

Bad Cables

The life of a troubleshooter is made easier (not easy!) by hard component failures. When a hard failure occurs (as opposed to an intermittent failure) it is obvious either by visual inspection or the use of testing tools which component has failed. Cables that are outright bad are easier to isolate than poor quality cables. Tools for testing cables range from simple continuity and wire map testers to sophisticated cable scanners.

In Figure 4.1, there are three types of cables involved: the cables between LAN devices (clients, servers) and the routers, the cables between the routers and the CSU/DSUs, and the cables between the CSU/DSU and the telco's outlet at the demarcation line. Additionally, there is the WAN cabling provided by the telco. All equipment and cabling up to the demarcation line is considered to be Customer Premises Equipment (CPE). If you verify that all equipment and cabling on customer premises is functional, the only other suspect that's left is the WAN circuit. You will have to get the WAN provider involved at this point to continue with troubleshooting.

The LAN cabling is typically CAT5 twisted pair. If these cables are purchased from reputable vendors, they are generally very reliable. A simple cable tester will check for continuity and alert you if cable pairs don't match between the cable ends. If you don't have continuity, or cable pairs are mismatched, LAN cabling must be replaced or repaired. See Appendix A for references on cabling standards.

The next type of cable in Figure 4.1 is the cabling between the router and the CSU/DSU. These cables are normally available from either the router or the CSU/DSU vendor. The greatest challenge that a network administrator faces here is not so much the quality of the cable as choosing the right cable to interface the router to a CSU/DSU. Make sure you know the type of connectors that you have on your router and the CSU/DSU. Cables conforming to V.35, X.21, or G.703 standards are commonly in use between routers and CSU/DSUs.

The third type of cable in use in Figure 4.1 is the cable between CSU/DSU and the telco jack. For 56K, leased T1, least fractional T1, Frame Relay, ISDN or switched 56K, the jack will be labeled either RJ-48C or RJ-48S. A straight-through 4-pair cable conforming to EIA/TIA 568A/B standard can be used here. Different cable pairs will be used for signals in these connections for different circuits. But as long as all four pairs in the cable are wired according to the EIA/TIA 568A/B standard, your cable will function. Bad cables should be eliminated through the use of a cable tester or scanner.

Poor Quality Cables

A simple cable tester will not tell you anything about the quality of the cables or their lengths. If you are observing frequent interface resets rather than a hard down state on a router interface, it's possible that there is an intermittent problem with the cables.

For LAN cables, a cable scanner like Microtest's PentaScanner can be used to perform more sophisticated cable testing. A cable scanner will test for cable length, attenuation, and Near-End Cross Talk (NEXT). Experience dictates that most of the intermittent cabling problems on the LAN side result from poor terminations at the patch panel and wall jacks. Occasionally, in larger buildings, the standards-permitted cable lengths could be exceeded, causing intermittent problems as well.

Attenuation, NEXT loss, or cable lengths that exceed the recommended standards will cause individual cables or the entire cable plant to fail the CAT5 certification test. No easy fixes are available in those situations. Cables will have to be replaced, patch panels and jacks reconnectorized properly. It is recommended that network administrators be familiar with cabling standards, use the highest quality cable available on the market, and work with professional cable installers to avoid intermittent problems related to cabling.

When Good Cables Are a Problem

It is possible to use perfectly good cables but in a wrong places. RJ-45 connectorized cables come in several different pinouts. RJ-45 connectors are used with 10BaseT Ethernet, 100BaseTX Ethernet, UPT Token Ring, and ISDN BRI, as well as for console and AUX port access.

Straight-through Cables

For LAN connections, straight-through cabling is used between a router and a concentrator or a switch. Take for example, an RJ-45 connectorized cable complying with the EIA/TIA 568B standard. This cable will work fine between a 10BaseT or a 100BaseT interface on a router and a concentrator. However, don't try to use it when connecting two 10BaseT router ports back-to-back; a crossover cable is required in that situation. The outer appearance of a crossover cable is identical to that of a straight-through cable. Only when you start looking at the connectors and comparing the pinouts can you tell the difference between a straight-through and a crossover cable.

Crossover Cables

Crossover cables are normally used for connecting two routers back-to-back. If you are creating an Ethernet subnet out of two 10BaseT router ports, you have to use a crossover cable. If you are plugging a workstation or a server directly into a router port, also use a crossover cable. Straight-through cables will not work in these situations.

Cisco Rollover Cable

The Cisco rollover cable is also referred to as a console cable. It's RJ-45-connectorized, but the pinning is entirely different from that of EIA/TIA 568A/B cables. This cable is intended only for accessing the console port. It typically comes with a DB9 and DB25 adapter that's used to connect the console port to a serial port on a dumb terminal or a PC running a terminal-emulation program.

DTE versus DCE Cables on Direct Serial Links

For direct serial links between routers, a combination of a DTE and DCE cable is required. V.35 DCE and DTE cables are commonly used to create a single cable for connecting two routers back-to-back via serial ports. The key issue in using this kind of a cable is that the DCE end of the cable must be connected to a router that defines that clock rate for the serial connection via the `clockrate` IOS command.

BRI Cables

BRI interfaces on Cisco routers use RJ-45 connectors. The danger with the BRI cables is that there are other RJ-45 connectors on a router and the signal levels on the BRI cable, if it is plugged into a non-BRI port on a router, can damage that port. Network administrators ought to be very careful not to plug a BRI cable into a console, AUX, or a 10BaseT port.

CSUs/DSUs

CSU/DSU functionality can be provided either by a separate device that connects to a router, or it can be built into an interface module itself. Fixed hardware configuration Cisco routers require a dedicated CSU/DSU. Modular routers like the 3600 series have WAN modules with CSU/DSU built in.

Whether a CSU/DSU is built into a router module or it's an outside unit, it will have to be configured if you expect a digital serial circuit between two routers to operate. Numerous vendors supply CSU/DSUs along with the exact configuration steps. Vendor manuals should be consulted for detailed configuration information. However, there are three parameters that you will have to configure on any CSU/DSU. They are encoding, framing, and clocking. Other parameters can usually be left at default values.

Encoding

Encoding is used in reference to the representation of digital data via digital signals. The digital data are your e-mail transmissions, results of Web browsing, protocol exchanges between routers, and so on. Digital data can be reduced to zeros and ones. The digital signals are voltage levels operational over a transmission medium. Encoding means the use of digital signals to represent zeros and ones.

On LANs, you do not have to be concerned about encoding. It exists, but it's not an administrator-configurable parameter. On digital WAN circuits, encoding must be configured. The common encoding methods on digital lines are Bipolar 8 Zero Substitution (B8ZS) and Alternate Mark Inversion (AMI). AMI is typically used if a digital circuit will be used for voice transmission, whereas B8ZS is used when a circuit is used for data. On modular routers with a built-in CSU/DSU, encoding is an IOS configurable parameter. For external CSU/DSUs, use the vendor-provided interface to configure encoding.

Framing

Framing defines the Physical Layer frame type for digital transmissions. This is not to be confused with framing at the Data Link Layer. At the

Physical Layer, it's strictly bits. Two Physical Layer frames that are commonly used in digital serial transmissions are Extended Super Frame (ESF) or a Super Frame normally abbreviated as D4. ESF is normally used for digital data circuits. The frame type is another parameter that must be configured on a CSU/DSU.

Clocking

The clocking parameter is used to define who provides the clocking signal. Either the internal or network clock can be used. Network clock in this context means that the clock signal is provided by the telco. If you are provisioning a digital circuit, you must work out with your provider who will supply the clock signal for the line.

On short distance digital lines — sometimes referred to as dry lines — you are responsible for providing the clock signal. This means that one of the CSU/DSUs must be configured to that effect, that is, internal clocking. Only one, not both CSU/DSUs need to be configured to provide clocking on a dry line. If the telco is providing clocking, then both of the CSU/DSUs need to be configured to reflect this, normally with the clocking parameter set to network.

IOS Physical Layer Troubleshooting Tools

The IOS Physical Layer troubleshooting tools vary as a function of the Cisco router series. On the higher-end modular routers, **show** command options are available that do not exist on the lower-end models. One such command that's available on the Cisco 12000 that's not available on the lower-end units is **show environment**. A partial output from the **show environment** command follows.

```
Big_Router#show environment all

Slot #  Hot Sensor     Inlet Sensor
         (deg C)         (deg C)


0         35.0           30.0
```

4	31.0	25.5
5	34.5	27.5
6	33.0	28.0
16	31.0	28.0
17	31.0	28.0
18	30.0	27.0
19	29.5	26.0
20	29.0	25.5
24	NA	25.0
26	NA	25.0
28	NA	24.5
29	NA	24.5

Slot #	3V (mv)	5V (mv)	MBUS 5V (mv)
0	3288	5008	5080
4	3296	5032	5152
5	3284	5000	5136
6	3272	5016	5144
16	3292	NA	5040
17	3300	NA	5048
18	3288	NA	5144
19	3292	NA	5136
20	3300	NA	5152
28	NA	NA	5104
29	NA	NA	5104

Slot #	5V (mv)	MBUS 5V (mv)	48V (Volt)	AMP_48 (Amp)
24	5552	5128	52	5
26	5568	5136	52	5

Slot #	Fan 0	Fan 1	Fan 2

```
        (RPM)   (RPM)   (RPM)

28      2559    2646    2577

29      2565    2619    2562


Slot #  Card Specifc Leds

16      Mbus OK

17      Mbus OK

18      Mbus OK

19      Mbus OK

20      Mbus OK

24      Input Ok

26 @code 80:Input Ok
```

On the 12012 GSR, certain slot numbers are allocated to certain components. The line cards and the GRP go into slots 0 through 11. On the 7500 series, specific slots are reserved for the RSP. That's not the case on the GSR. The GRP and the line cards can go into any of the slots numbered 0 through 11. The remaining slots are allocated to the CSCs (slots 16 and 17), SFCs (slots 18, 19, and 20), power supplies (slots 24 through 27), and blowers (slots 28 and 29).

In the preceding trace, it looks like only 4 out of the 12 slots allocated to the GRP and the line cards are occupied. Slots 16 through 20 are fully populated with CSCs and SFCs affording this particular unit the maximum aggregate capacity for the internal switch fabric. Two power supplies and two blower modules are present. The 12000 can have either four AC power supplies or two DC supplies.

Knowing what modules go into which slots is vital to the correct interpretation of the **show environment all** output. What additionally helps with the interpretation is the display of the environment table that's available via the **show environment table** command. The output from **show environment table** follows.

```
Big_Router# show environment table
Hot Sensor Temperature Limits (deg C):
                        Warning Critical Shutdown
```

GRP/GLC	(Slots 0-15)	40	46	57
CSC	(Slots 16-17)	46	51	65
SFC	(Slots 18-20)	41	46	60

Inlet Sensor Temperature Limits (deg C):

		Warning	Critical	Shutdown
GRP/GLC	(Slots 0-15)	35	40	52
CSC	(Slots 16-17)	40	45	59
SFC	(Slots 18-20)	37	42	54

3V Ranges (mv):

		Warning		Critical		Shutdown	
		Below	Above	Below	Above	Below	Above
GRP/GLC	(Slots 0-15)	3200	3400	3100	3500	3050	3550
CSC	(Slots 16-17)	3200	3400	3100	3500	3050	3550
SFC	(Slots 18-20)	3200	3400	3100	3500	3050	3550

5V Ranges (mv):

	Warning		Critical		Shutdown	
	Below	Above	Below	Above	Below	Above
GRP/GLC (Slots 0-15)	4850	5150	4750	5250	4680	5320

MBUS_5V Ranges (mv):

		Warning		Critical		Shutdown	
		Below	Above	Below	Above	Below	Above
GRP/GLC	(Slots 0-15)	5000	5250	4900	5350	4750	5450
CSC	(Slots 16-17)	4820	5150	4720	5250	4750	5450
SFC	(Slots 17-20)	5000	5250	4900	5350	4750	5450

Blower Operational Range (RPM):

Top Blower:

	Warning	Critical
	Below	Below
Fan 0	1000	750
Fan 1	1000	750

```
Fan 2          1000      750


Bottom Blower:
               Warning   Critical
               Below     Below
Fan 0          1000      750
Fan 1          1000      750
Fan 2          1000      750
```

The output from the show environment table command displays the temperature, voltage, and fan RPM ranges that will result in warnings, critical alarms, and shutdowns. Assume, for example, that the inlet sensor temperature on the line card occupying slot 3 exceeded 40 degrees centigrade. That would be cause for a critical alarm. The line cards are interfaced to the maintenance bus over which this information could be conveyed to the alarm card. If an alarm card were present on the Big_Router, one of the alarm LEDs would turn from green to red. At the same time a warning message would be printed to the console. The environmental values on the Big_Router are all within the acceptable ranges. No cause for alarms here.

One IOS command that's extremely useful in troubleshooting Physical Layer problems and that's available on all router platforms is show interfaces. The output from this command was already discussed and analyzed earlier in this chapter. Other commands include show controller, diag, and show diag.

There are over 60 image files supporting different feature sets in IOS Release 12.0. You are encouraged to investigate your particular feature set and use the reference documentation that comes with your router to derive the maximum benefit from your hardware/IOS combination.

Chapter Summary

Troubleshooting the Physical Layer is accomplished via a combination of visual inspections, review of console messages, and the use of IOS commands. More tools are available for troubleshooting router interfaces on the high-end modular routers (12000 series) than on the lower-end fixed hardware configuration units. Several pinouts are in use for RJ-45 connectorized cables. Good cables can be used in wrong places if cables are not clearly labeled. Familiarity with cabling standards is important for network administrators. CSU/DSUs can be built into router modules or come as external units from third-party vendors.

Chapter 5

Troubleshooting the Data Link Layer

The functions of the Data Link Layer include addressing, framing, error checking/correction, and media access. These functions are incorporated into the IOS and require minimal if any configuration. The addressing at the Data Link Layer refers to hardware addressing. Routers come with unique pre-assigned hardware addresses for their LAN interfaces. Address duplication at the Data Link Layer is a non-issue except in rare circumstances where local hardware addressing is used. IEEE standards allow for the use of locally defined hardware addresses.

Network administrators can monitor Data Link Layer errors that are reported by the IOS. Often, those errors are the result of malfunctioning interface controllers, weak transceivers, and/or poor transmission media. However, network administrators have no influence over the media access techniques used by Data Link Layer technologies. A token-passing media access method is used with Token Ring and FDDI. Carrier Sense Multiple Access Collision Detection (CSMA/CD) is used with the various flavors of Ethernet.

Network administrators have choices in the configuration of framing or encapsulation on WANs. Encapsulation on LANs is primarily automatic. The most notable exception is the IPX protocol that allows several different frame types to be defined. Misconfigured encapsulation will disable a WAN and usually cause a partial loss of connectivity on a LAN.

The Data Link Layer is probably the easiest of the bottom layers discussed in this book to troubleshoot. If you handle the encapsulation correctly, then it's mostly a matter of monitoring the Data Link Layer indicators for excessive utilization, cyclical redundancy check (CRC) errors, framing errors, or LMI mismatches in Frame Relay WANs.

Troubleshooting the Data Link Layer on LANs

A very useful IOS command for troubleshooting the Data Link Layer on LANs and WANs is show interfaces. You've seen the output from show interfaces in Chapter 4 in the context of discussing the Physical Layer. Different elements of the display are examined in this section. Take a look at the output from the show interfaces command for an Ethernet interface.

```
Router#show int e0
Ethernet0 is up, line protocol is up
   Hardware is Lance, address is 0000.0c4a.3dae (bia 0000.0c4a.3dae)
   Internet address is 172.16.152.1/24
   MTU 1500 bytes, BW 10000 Kbit, DLY 1000 usec, rely 255/255, load 1/255
   Encapsulation ARPA, loopback not set, keepalive set (10 sec)
   ARP type: ARPA, ARP Timeout 04:00:00
   Last input 00:02:16, output 00:00:00, output hang never
   Last clearing of "show interface" counters never
   Queueing strategy: fifo
   Output queue 0/40, 0 drops; input queue 0/75, 0 drops
   5 minute input rate 31000 bits/sec, 2 packets/sec
   5 minute output rate 31000 bits/sec, 2 packets/sec
      1044 packets input, 1419106 bytes, 0 no buffer
      Received 102 broadcasts, 0 runts, 0 giants, 0 throttles
      15 input errors, 4 CRC, 0 frame, 0 overrun, 0 ignored, 0 abort
      0 input packets with dribble condition detected
      1875 packets output, 1494166 bytes, 0 underruns
      0 output errors, 3 collisions, 4 interface resets
      1 babbles, 0 late collision, 0 deferred
      0 lost carrier, 0 no carrier
```

```
            0 output buffer failures, 0 output buffers swapped out
Router#
```

When you see collisions, interface resets, babbles, or CRC errors it's a sign of potential problems with the interface or the transmission media.

Excessive Collisions on Ethernet

The LAN Controller for Ethernet (LANCE) reports errors that are related to the malfunctioning of Ethernet interfaces. About a dozen errors are reported by LANCE. LANCE errors are reported to the console, and some of them are reflected in the counters at the bottom of show interfaces display. Most of the LANCE errors that are reported to t he console are cause for concern and typically require the repair or replacement of the controller. Collisions don't mean a problem with the router, but rather a problem elsewhere on the LAN.

Collisions are unavoidable on shared Ethernet LANs, but the collisions counter in the show interfaces display has to be put in perspective. It's an indication that a router had to make retransmissions due to collisions. If a router makes only an occasional transmission onto a LAN but continues to report collisions, take it as clue that you have a physical problem with the LAN.

Problems with the LAN can stem from violating wiring specifications. Cables may be too long or there may be too many repeaters or concentrators with a high latency between any two communicating devices, including the router. An Ethernet LAN has a diameter that can be defined in bit times or in units of time. The diameter for a 10Mbps Ethernet LAN is 25.6 microseconds between any two devices. You can add up the latencies of all the LAN components (cables, hubs, and device NICs) between any two devices and see if the diameter is being exceeded.

If the collisions counter on your router continues to grow, investigate the physical infrastructure of your LAN. Cable scanners are very useful in determining cable lengths and quality. Also, vendors specify the latencies for LAN devices, which can help you determine the LAN diameter. Poor LAN infrastructure may lead to another set of problems reported by a router, namely, CRC errors.

Cyclical Redundancy Check (CRC) Errors

A CRC error is an indication that the frame that was received differs from the frame that was sent. Something in the contents of the frame has changed during its transition through the media between the sender to the receiver. Imagine if the frame carries financial information: A number in the wrong place can make a big difference in someone's finances.

CRC errors are mostly related to problems with the transmission media. The cause of the problem is usually poor quality cabling or violations of the cabling specification rules. If the CRC errors counter continues to grow on your router, it's another clue that it's time to investigate your physical infrastructure.

When troubleshooting the Data Link Layer, it's hard to separate it from the Physical Layer. They are closely related in the sense that problems at those layers usually represent hardware problems as opposed to configuration problems. But there are configuration problems at the Data Link Layer as well. Data Link Layer configuration problems tend to be more pronounced on WANs than LANs.

Troubleshooting the Data Link Layer on WANs

Data Link Layer problems on WANs include encapsulation mismatches, excessive utilization, keepalive mismatches, and LMI-type mismatches on Frame Relay WANs. Consider an internetwork as shown in Figure 5.1.

In the internetwork in Figure 5.1, three locations (Bozeman, Livingston, and Helena) are fully meshed via a Frame Relay cloud. There is an additional point-to-point backup link between Bozeman and Helena. The internetwork offers full connectivity between all locations, but there are complaints from the users about performance.

The network administrator has been on the job for only a couple of weeks and is physically located in Bozeman. The previous administrator left no documentation regarding the WAN. The new administrator decides to document the WAN as well as optimize its performance. He begins by checking the status of interfaces and reviewing the configuration files.

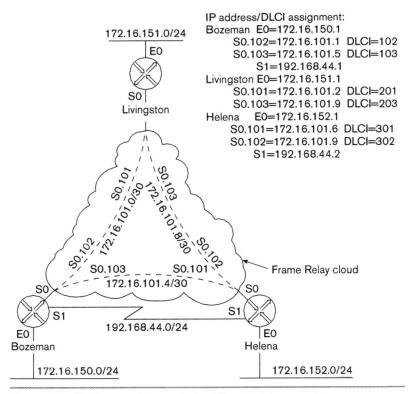

Figure 5.1 *WAN network for analysis of Data Link Layer problems*

```
Bozeman#sh ip int b
```

Interface	IP-Address	OK?	Method	Status	Protocol
Ethernet0	172.16.150.1	YES	manual	up	up
Serial0	unassigned	YES	unset	up	up
Serial0.102	172.16.101.1	YES	manual	up	up
Serial0.103	172.16.101.5	YES	manual	up	up
Serial1	192.168.44.1	YES	manual	up	up

```
Bozeman#


Livingston#sh ip int b
```

```
Interface               IP-Address     OK? Method Status        Protocol
Ethernet0               172.16.151.1   YES manual up            up
Serial0                 unassigned     YES unset  up            up
Serial0.101             172.16.101.2   YES manual up            up
Serial0.103             172.16.101.9   YES manual up            up
Livingston#


Helena#sh ip int b
Interface               IP-Address     OK? Method Status        Protocol
Ethernet0               172.16.152.1   YES manual up            up
Serial0                 unassigned     YES unset  up            up
Serial0.101             172.16.101.6   YES manual up            up
Serial0.102             172.16.101.10  YES manual up            up
Serial1                 192.168.44.2   YES manual up            up
Helena#
```

The trace from the show ip interface brief command confirms
that all of the interfaces are up. The administrator feels somewhat relieved.
The use of ping and traceroute confirms that each location can communicate directly with every other location, which eliminates the possibility of a
link being down and all traffic flowing through a single router that could
potentially turn into a bottleneck. However, the preceding display does not
tell the administrator anything about where the potential bottleneck is. It's
time to review the configurations.

Bozeman initial configuration

```
hostname Bozeman
!
enable password cisco
!
interface Ethernet0
 ip address 172.16.150.1 255.255.255.0
!
interface Ethernet1
 no ip address
```

```
 shutdown
!
interface Serial0
 no ip address
 encapsulation frame-relay
 no ip mroute-cache
 frame-relay lmi-type cisco
!
interface Serial0.102 point-to-point
 description 64K link to Livingston
 ip address 172.16.101.1 255.255.255.252
 bandwidth 64
 frame-relay interface-dlci 102
!
interface Serial0.103 point-to-point
 description 64K link to Helena
 ip address 172.16.101.5 255.255.255.252
 bandwidth 64
 frame-relay interface-dlci 103
!
interface Serial1
 description 64K leased line to Helena
 ip address 192.168.44.1 255.255.255.0
 clockrate 64000
 bandwidth 64
!
router ospf 1
 network 172.16.101.1 0.0.0.0 area 0.0.0.0
 network 172.16.101.5 0.0.0.0 area 0.0.0.0
 network 172.16.150.0 0.0.0.255 area 0.0.0.0
!
ip classless
!
```

Livingston initial configuration

```
!
hostname Livingston
!
enable password cisco
!
interface Ethernet0
 ip address 172.16.151.1 255.255.255.0
!
interface Ethernet1
 no ip address
 shutdown
!
interface Serial0
 no ip address
 encapsulation frame-relay
 no ip mroute-cache
 no fair-queue
 frame-relay lmi-type cisco
!
interface Serial0.101 point-to-point
 description 64K link to Bozeman
 ip address 172.16.101.2 255.255.255.252
 bandwidth 64
 frame-relay interface-dlci 201
!
interface Serial0.103 point-to-point
 description 64K link to Helena
 ip address 172.16.101.9 255.255.255.252
 bandwidth 64
 frame-relay interface-dlci 203
!
interface Serial1
 no ip address
```

```
  shutdown
!
router ospf 1
  network 172.16.101.2 0.0.0.0 area 0.0.0.0
  network 172.16.101.9 0.0.0.0 area 0.0.0.0
  network 172.16.151.0 0.0.0.255 area 0.0.0.0
!
no ip classless
!
```

Helena initial configuration

```
!
hostname Helena
!
enable password cisco
!
ip subnet-zero
!
interface Ethernet0
  ip address 172.16.152.1 255.255.255.0
!
interface Serial0
  no ip address
  encapsulation frame-relay
  no ip mroute-cache
  no fair-queue
  frame-relay lmi-type cisco
!
interface Serial0.101 point-to-point
  description 64K link to Bozeman
  ip address 172.16.101.6 255.255.255.252
  bandwidth 64
  frame-relay interface-dlci 301
!
```

```
interface Serial0.102 point-to-point
 description 64K link to Livingston
 ip address 172.16.101.10 255.255.255.252
 bandwidth 64
 frame-relay interface-dlci 302
!
interface Serial1
 description 64K leased line to Bozeman
 ip address 192.168.44.2 255.255.255.0
 bandwidth 64
!
router ospf 1
 network 172.16.101.6 0.0.0.0 area 0.0.0.0
 network 172.16.101.10 0.0.0.0 area 0.0.0.0
 network 172.16.152.0 0.0.0.255 area 0.0.0.0
!
ip classless
!
```

Reviewing the configurations, the administrator notices that no encapsulation has been configured on the point-to-point link between Bozeman and Helena. He is aware that if no encapsulation is configured on a serial link, Cisco uses the default HDLC encapsulation. However, he decides to experiment with the standard Point-to-Point Protocol (PPP) encapsulation in the hope of determining which one offers better performance.

Encapsulation Mismatches

The following is the configuration change on the Bozeman router that the administrator implements.

```
Bozeman#
Bozeman#conf t
Enter configuration commands, one per line.  End with CNTL/Z.
Bozeman(config)#inter s0
Bozeman(config-if)#encapsulation ppp
```

```
Bozeman(config-if)#^Z
Bozeman#
```

Within seconds of the change, the phone begins to ring. Nobody in Bozeman can get through to any other locations. Calls are coming in from other locations as well. No one can communicate with Bozeman. The administrator realizes that something is drastically wrong. The PPP encapsulation was supposed to be configured on s1 not s0 interface. This seemingly innocuous error exposed a preexisting problem in the internetwork and taught the administrator a valuable lesson.

The preexisting problem was that the backup link between Bozeman and Helena was not operational. The lesson that the administrator had to learn was a hard one. Upon recognizing that the experiment with the PPP encapsulation took place on a wrong interface, he quickly goes back into configuration mode and corrects the encapsulation to Frame Relay, just as it was in the initial configuration.

```
Bozeman#
Bozeman#conf t
Enter configuration commands, one per line.  End with CNTL/Z.
Bozeman(config)#inter s0
Bozeman(config-if)#encapsulation frame-relay
Bozeman(config-if)#^Z
Bozeman#
```

But to his surprise, there is no change. The reconfiguration of the encapsulation back to Frame Relay on the s0 interface has no impact on the state of the internetwork. Something else is wrong. A check of the interfaces in the brief mode reveals something unexpected. The two subinterfaces over which PVCs were defined to the other locations show up with a *deleted* status.

```
Bozeman#sh ip int b
Interface        IP-Address      OK? Method Status                Protocol
Ethernet0        172.16.150.1    YES NVRAM  up                    up
Ethernet1        unassigned      YES unset  administratively down  down
Serial0          unassigned      YES unset  up                    down
Serial0.102      unassigned      YES NVRAM  deleted               down
```

```
Serial0.103              unassigned      YES NVRAM  deleted              down
Serial1                  192.168.44.1    YES manual up                   up
Bozeman#
```

A check of the running configuration further confirms that indeed the subinterfaces are gone.

```
Bozeman#sh run
Building configuration...
Current configuration:
!
version 11.3
!
hostname Bozeman
!
enable password cisco
!
interface Ethernet0
 ip address 172.16.150.1 255.255.255.0
!
interface Ethernet1
 no ip address
 shutdown
!
interface Serial0
 no ip address
 encapsulation ppp
 no ip mroute-cache
!
interface Serial1
 ip address 192.168.44.1 255.255.255.0
 bandwidth 64
 clockrate 64000
!
router ospf 1
 network 172.16.101.1 0.0.0.0 area 0.0.0.0
```

```
network 172.16.101.5 0.0.0.0 area 0.0.0.0

network 172.16.150.0 0.0.0.255 area 0.0.0.0

!

no ip classless

!
```

And the Bozeman routing table shows only the directly connected networks.

```
Bozeman#sh ip route

Codes: C - connected,


Gateway of last resort is not set


C    192.168.44.0/24 is directly connected, Serial1

     172.16.0.0/24 is subnetted, 1 subnets

C        172.16.150.0 is directly connected, Ethernet0

Bozeman#
```

It turns out that when Frame Relay encapsulation is changed and then reconfigured on a serial interface from which subinterfaces are derived, the IOS deletes the subinterfaces in the process. The administrator decides it is time to put the subinterfaces back in. Before doing so, he checks the status of the Frame Relay PVCs via the show frame-relay pvc command.

```
Bozeman#

Bozeman#sh frame-relay pvc


PVC Statistics for interface Serial0 (Frame Relay DTE)


DLCI = 102, DLCI USAGE = UNUSED, PVC STATUS = ACTIVE, INTERFACE = Serial0


  input pkts 109        output pkts 0        in bytes 10727

  out bytes 0           dropped pkts 0       in FECN pkts 0

  in BECN pkts 0        out FECN pkts 0      out BECN pkts 0

  in DE pkts 0          out DE pkts 0

  out bcast pkts 0       out bcast bytes 0        Num Pkts Switched 0

  pvc create time 00:15:44, last time pvc status changed 00:15:44
```

```
DLCI = 103, DLCI USAGE = UNUSED, PVC STATUS = ACTIVE, INTERFACE = Serial0

  input pkts 110          output pkts 0           in bytes 10888

  out bytes 0             dropped pkts 0          in FECN pkts 0

  in BECN pkts 0          out FECN pkts 0         out BECN pkts 0

  in DE pkts 0            out DE pkts 0

  out bcast pkts 0         out bcast bytes 0          Num Pkts Switched 0

  pvc create time 00:15:45, last time pvc status changed 00:15:45
Bozeman#

Bozeman#
```

The DLCI usage shows the status of *UNUSED* for the two DLCIs defined in the initial configuration, further confirming that the mistake of configuring PPP encapsulation on a wrong interface has wider implications than was initially thought. Now the problem is bigger than just an encapsulation mismatch. Fortunately, the administrator has the printouts of the initial configuration files to assist with the reconfiguration of the subinterfaces.

```
Bozeman#conf t

Enter configuration commands, one per line.  End with CNTL/Z.

Bozeman(config)#inter s0.102 point-to-point

Bozeman(config-subif)#description 64 K link to Livingston

Bozeman(config-subif)#ip address 172.16.101.1 255.255.255.252

Bozeman(config-subif)#bandwidth 64

Bozeman(config-subif)#frame-relay interface-dlci 102

Bozeman(config-fr-dlci)#inter s0.103

Bozeman(config-subif)#ip address 172.16.101.5 255.255.255.252

Bozeman(config-subif)#description 64 K link to Helena

Bozeman(config-subif)#bandwidth 64

Bozeman(config-subif)#frame-relay interface-dlci 103

Bozeman(config-fr-dlci)#^Z

Bozeman#
```

Upon reconfiguration, a check of the routing table on Bozeman, along with a few pings and traceroutes, reveals that reachability throughout the internetwork is restored.

```
Bozeman#sh ip route

Codes: C - connected, S - static, I - IGRP, R - RIP, M - mobile, B - BGP

       D - EIGRP, EX - EIGRP external, O - OSPF,


Gateway of last resort is not set


C    192.168.44.0/24 is directly connected, Serial1

     172.16.0.0/16 is variably subnetted, 6 subnets, 2 masks

O       172.16.152.0/24 [110/1572] via 172.16.101.6, 01:03:48, Serial0.103

C       172.16.150.0/24 is directly connected, Ethernet0

O       172.16.151.0/24 [110/1572] via 172.16.101.2, 01:03:48, Serial0.102

O       172.16.101.8/30 [110/3124] via 172.16.101.2, 01:03:48, Serial0.102

                        [110/3124] via 172.16.101.6, 01:03:48, Serial0.103

C       172.16.101.0/30 is directly connected, Serial0.102

C       172.16.101.4/30 is directly connected, Serial0.103

Bozeman#
```

The administrator decides to forgo further experimentation with encapsulation. He also realizes that there is another problem he has to solve. The backup link between Bozeman and Helena is not doing its job. It turns out to be a higher layer problem. Review of the initial configuration files shows that the network 192.168.44.0 is not assigned to OSPF, which is the routing protocol configured in the internetwork in Figure 5.1.

The serial link between Bozeman and Helena was functional at the Data Link Layer, but not useful in the context of the larger internetwork without being advertised by a dynamic routing protocol. The administrator decides to correct the problem and move on with further experiments at optimizing performance.

LMI Type Mismatches on Frame Relay WANs

Assume at this point that the internetwork in Figure 5.1 has been restored to its initial configuration. The following trace shows the configuration steps that were required to fix the problem with the backup link. The problem was discovered during the encapsulation experiment. The administrator wants to have the backup link between Bozeman and Helena operational, in case the Frame Relay links shut down again.

```
Bozeman#conf t

Enter configuration commands, one per line.  End with CNTL/Z.

Bozeman(config)#router ospf 1

Bozeman(config-router)#network 192.168.44.0 0.0.0.255 area 0.0.0.0

Bozeman(config-router)#^Z

Bozeman#


Helena#conf t

Enter configuration commands, one per line.  End with CNTL/Z.

Helena(config)#router ospf 1

Helena(config-router)#network 192.168.44.0 0.0.0.255 area 0.0.0.0

Helena(config-router)#^Z

Helena#
```

And the Frame Relay links are indeed in danger as the administrator moves on with attempts to optimize the internetwork. He decides to configure a different LMI type on the Bozeman router. Local Management Interface (LMI) is an add-on to the original Frame Relay specification that operates between a router and a Frame Relay switch. Three types of LMIs are available: Cisco, ansi, and q933a. The LMI type must match between a router and a switch. Not being fully aware of the LMI type requirements, the administrator decides to change it on the Bozeman router in an effort to determine which LMI type offers best performance.

```
Bozeman#

Bozeman#conf t

Enter configuration commands, one per line.  End with CNTL/Z.

Bozeman(config)#inter s0

Bozeman(config-if)#frame-relay lmi-type ansi

Bozeman(config-if)#^Z

Bozeman#
```

The phone begins to ring again. But this time it is different. Users can get through to other locations, but it is very slow. The administrator investigates by reviewing the status of the PVCs, the LMI, and the routing table on the Bozeman router.

```
Bozeman#show frame-relay pvc


PVC Statistics for interface Serial0 (Frame Relay DTE)


DLCI = 102, DLCI USAGE = LOCAL, PVC STATUS = DELETED, INTERFACE = Serial0.102


    input pkts 869          output pkts 715         in bytes 89352

    out bytes 73610         dropped pkts 2          in FECN pkts 0

    in BECN pkts 0          out FECN pkts 0         out BECN pkts 0

    in DE pkts 0            out DE pkts 0

    out bcast pkts 715       out bcast bytes 73610

    pvc create time 02:05:25, last time pvc status changed 00:02:55

DLCI = 103, DLCI USAGE = LOCAL, PVC STATUS = DELETED, INTERFACE = Serial0.103


    input pkts 856          output pkts 697         in bytes 87369

    out bytes 71532         dropped pkts 0          in FECN pkts 0

    in BECN pkts 0          out FECN pkts 0         out BECN pkts 0

    in DE pkts 0            out DE pkts 0

    out bcast pkts 697       out bcast bytes 71532

    pvc create time 02:05:27, last time pvc status changed 00:02:57

Bozeman#
```

When the PVC status shows DELETED, do not expect your Frame Relay connection to work. A check of the LMI status shows a mismatch between the number of status inquiries sent and received. It also shows timeouts. These are additional signs to watch out for when troubleshooting Frame Relay connections. If no problems occur between a router and a Frame Relay switch, you should expect the numbers for *Num Status Enq. Sent* and *Num Status msgs Rcvd* to be the same.

```
Bozeman#show frame-relay lmi


LMI Statistics for interface Serial0 (Frame Relay DTE) LMI TYPE = ANSI

    Invalid Unnumbered info 0        Invalid Prot Disc 0

    Invalid dummy Call Ref 0         Invalid Msg Type 0
```

```
Invalid Status Message 0          Invalid Lock Shift 0

Invalid Information ID 0          Invalid Report IE Len 0

Invalid Report Request 0         Invalid Keep IE Len 0

Num Status Enq. Sent 756         Num Status msgs Rcvd 713

Num Update Status Rcvd 0         Num Status Timeouts 42
```

The administrator is now convinced that attempts to optimize the network by changing the encapsulation or the LMI type are to no avail. But the fact that the network still functions — however slow — puzzles him. A check of the routing table shows that all of the networks previously reachable are still reachable.

```
Bozeman#

Bozeman#show ip route

Codes: C - connected, S - static, I - IGRP, R - RIP, M - mobile, B - BGP
       D - EIGRP, EX - EIGRP external, O - OSPF,


Gateway of last resort is not set


C    192.168.44.0/24 is directly connected, Serial1

     172.16.0.0/16 is variably subnetted, 4 subnets, 2 masks
O       172.16.152.0/24 [110/1572] via 192.168.44.2, 00:03:05, Serial1
C       172.16.150.0/24 is directly connected, Ethernet0
O       172.16.151.0/24 [110/3134] via 192.168.44.2, 00:03:05, Serial1
O       172.16.101.8/30 [110/3124] via 192.168.44.2, 00:03:05, Serial1

Bozeman#
```

All destinations are reachable but via the backup serial link, that is, the Serial1 interface on the Bozeman router. The Frame Relay links from Bozeman to Livingston and Helena defined over s0 are again shut down. Now it really makes sense that there was reachability, but performance was worse than before the optimization efforts started. The backup link was excessively utilized.

Excessive Utilization

Excessive utilization on serial WAN links leads to performance problems. You can check if a WAN link is excessively utilized by displaying the information about an interface via the `show interfaces` command. Take a look at the s1 interface following the experiment with the LMI type in the previous section. The backup link between Bozeman and Helena appears to be very highly utilized.

```
Bozeman#sh int s1
Serial1 is up, line protocol is up
  Hardware is HD64570
  Internet address is 192.168.44.1/24
  MTU 1500 bytes, BW 64 Kbit, DLY 20000 usec,
     reliability 255/255, txload 245/255, rxload 245/255
  Encapsulation HDLC, loopback not set, keepalive set (10 sec)
  Last input 00:00:03, output 00:00:00, output hang never
  Last clearing of "show interface" counters never
  Input queue: 0/75/0 (size/max/drops); Total output drops: 0
  Queueing strategy: weighted fair
  Output queue: 0/1000/64/0 (size/max total/threshold/drops)
     Conversations  0/2/256 (active/max active/max total)
     Reserved Conversations 0/0 (allocated/max allocated)
  5 minute input rate 61000 bits/sec, 7 packets/sec
  5 minute output rate 61000 bits/sec, 7 packets/sec
     2819 packets input, 762760 bytes, 0 no buffer
     Received 1155 broadcasts, 0 runts, 0 giants, 0 throttles
     0 input errors, 0 CRC, 0 frame, 0 overrun, 0 ignored, 0 abort
     2832 packets output, 764485 bytes, 0 underruns
     0 output errors, 0 collisions, 6 interface resets
     0 output buffer failures, 0 output buffers swapped out
     8 carrier transitions
     DCD=up  DSR=up  DTR=up  RTS=up  CTS=up
Bozeman#
```

When you see a load of 245/255, which translates into about 96 percent utilization, you have a problem with that link. When the link capacity is 64K and you observe input and output rates in the range of 61,000 bits/sec, that's another clue that utilization is in the high 90s. Anytime the WAN link utilization is consistently over 50 percent, it should raise a red flag. It's time to start thinking about expanding the capacity of the link. A few other problems with that link are evident from the preceding display. They are interface resets and carrier transitions.

These two phenomena are closely related and occur as a result of missed keepalive messages, which can occur due to excessive utilization or a mismatch in the keepalive interval. At a certain point, it becomes a vicious circle. Excessive utilization leads to missed keepalives, leading to interface resets, which in turn leads to carrier transitions, causing still greater utilization.

Keepalive Mismatches

In the show interface s1 display in the previous section, the encapsulation was HDLC and the keepalive interval was set to ten seconds. When keepalive messages are missed due to excessive utilization or the mismatch in the keepalive interval, the interface becomes unstable. From the user's perspective, the effects are sporadic hang-ups, lost connections to servers, or poor performance.

Observe what happens when a mismatch in the keepalive interval is introduced for the s1 interface on the Bozeman router. It's necessary to use debug for the serial interfaces to get a perspective of the level of activity and instability that's occurring on the interface. Increasing the keepalive interval from 10 to 60 was the latest attempt by the network administrator to improve performance. After all, fewer keepalive messages on the serial link means more user data can go through.

```
Bozeman#debug serial interface
Serial network interface debugging is on
Bozeman#
04:13:54: HD(0): New serial state = 0x0115

04:13:54: HD(1): got an interrupt state = 0x8055
04:13:54: HD(1): New serial state = 0x0055

04:13:54: HD(1): DTR is down.
04:13:54: HD(0): New serial state = 0x0115

04:13:54: HD(1): got an interrupt state = 0x805F
```

```
04:13:54: HD(1): New serial state = 0x005F


04:13:54: HD(1): DTR is up.
04:14:04: Serial1 - Keepalive time mismatch - should be 60 secs, is 20
04:14:14: Serial1 - Keepalive time mismatch - should be 60 secs, is 9
04:14:23: Serial1: HDLC myseq 18, mineseen 18*, yourseen 1513, line up
04:14:25: Serial1 - Keepalive time mismatch - should be 60 secs, is 10
04:14:35: Serial1 - Keepalive time mismatch - should be 60 secs, is 10
04:14:45: HD(0): New serial state = 0x0115


04:14:45: HD(1): got an interrupt state = 0x8055
04:14:45: HD(1): New serial state = 0x0055


04:14:45: HD(1): DTR is down.
04:14:45: HD(0): New serial state = 0x0115


04:14:45: HD(1): got an interrupt state = 0x805F
04:14:45: HD(1): New serial state = 0x005F


04:14:45: HD(1): DTR is up.
04:14:55: HD(0): New serial state = 0x0115


04:14:55: HD(1): got an interrupt state = 0x8055
04:14:55: HD(1): New serial state = 0x0055


04:14:55: HD(1): DTR is down.
04:14:55: HD(0): New serial state = 0x0115


Bozeman#undebug all
All possible debugging has been turned off
Bozeman#
```

When you see DTR going up and down, as in the preceding trace, it's not hard to conclude that the interface has a problem. Think about what's occurring here. The Bozeman router has a keepalive interval of 60 for its s1 interface. The Helena's s1 interface stays at 10. When Helena misses three consecutive keepalives from Bozeman, it will reset its interface. This will in turn cause a carrier transition on Bozeman.

If you were to monitor the interface resets and carrier transitions on Helena and Bozeman, the interface reset counter would be going up on Helena and the carrier transitions would be increasing on Bozeman. Bozeman will not be resetting its interface because its keepalive interval is much larger than Helena's is. But from the user's point of view, it's purely academic as to which router has a reset and which a carrier transition; the effects on the users are the same. Observe a few successive pings from Bozeman to Helena's s1 interface.

```
Bozeman#ping 192.168.44.2


Type escape sequence to abort.

Sending 5, 100-byte ICMP Echos to 192.168.44.2, timeout is 2 seconds:

.....

Success rate is 0 percent (0/5)
Bozeman#ping 192.168.44.2


Type escape sequence to abort.

Sending 5, 100-byte ICMP Echos to 192.168.44.2, timeout is 2 seconds:

....!

Success rate is 20 percent (1/5), round-trip min/avg/max = 28/28/28 ms
Bozeman#ping 192.168.44.2


Type escape sequence to abort.

Sending 5, 100-byte ICMP Echos to 192.168.44.2, timeout is 2 seconds:

..!!!

Success rate is 60 percent (3/5), round-trip min/avg/max = 28/28/28 ms
```

The pings show 0 percent, 20 percent, and 60 percent success rates. If the pings were to continue, the success rate would go back to 0 percent and then up again and down again. Imagine what this feels like to network users who are relying on that link for their communications.

Keepalive intervals for serial links are set to default values. They can be increased to offer a minimal improvement in performance on heavily utilized links. Be sure, however, to set the same keepalive interval on both serial neighbors. Mismatch in a keepalive interval causes serial links to behave like yo-yos, up and down.

Non-Routable Protocols

Non-routable protocols need extra help to get through a router. They do not have Network Layer addressing and can't be routed in the traditional sense of the word. But it doesn't mean that it's impossible to pass them through a router. They can be bridged or encapsulated into a routable protocol. The internetwork in Figure 5.2 uses Windows NT servers and a combination of Windows 95/98 and Windows 2000 workstations. It's a very simple internetwork. There are only two sites. One site has the server and workstations; the other has workstations only.

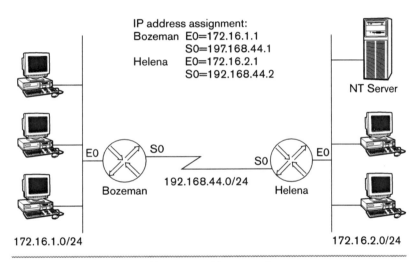

Figure 5.2 *Internetwork with non-routable protocols*

If you want to configure this internetwork as a Windows workgroup only, you can disable IP routing on both routers and configure them as bridges. The global command to disable IP routing is no IP routing. Using the interface command bridge-group, you can configure the routers as bridges. This allows NETBEUI, which is considered a Data Link Layer protocol used in the Windows environments, to operate between the workstations at both sites as though they were attached to the same single physical segment.

But suppose now that you want to route TCP/IP on the internetwork in Figure 5.2. You also want to configure the Windows NT server at the Helena site as a Dynamic Host Configuration Protocol (DHCP) server. DHCP operation relies on the use of the IP broadcast address, 255.255.255.255, that's not forwarded by routers by default. This broadcast address is a local IP broadcast as opposed to a directed broadcast. Directed broadcasts are broadcasts for specific subnets and are forwarded by default.

Cisco provides a way out of this situation through the `ip helper-address` command. The `ip helper-address` *address* command allows for local broadcasts to be forwarded to specific addresses. It's an interface configuration command and multiple helper addresses can be defined. Apply this now to the internetwork in Figure 5.2.

The clients at the Bozeman site will be issuing local broadcasts to get authenticated by the NT server and to be assigned an IP address. To take advantage of the DHCP server in Helena, you need to define a helper address (the IP address of the NT server) on the e0 interface of the Bozeman router. If you don't configure the helper address, the Bozeman router and the Bozeman clients will be able to ping the NT server, but when it comes to the Bozeman clients logging onto the server, they will not be able to do so.

The `ip helper-address` command is closely related to the `ip forward-protocol` command. The `ip forward-protocol` {udp [*port*] | nd | sdns} command allows IP broadcasts encapsulated into UDP packets — with port numbers specified by the *port* variable — to be forwarded across routers. It's a global configuration command as opposed to the `ip helper-address` command, which is applied to an interface.

The use of the `ip forward-protocol udp` command without any *port* options enables forwarding of UDP broadcasts for a group of default ports, which includes the ports responsible for DHCP traffic. The use of the `ip helper-address` command automatically enables IP forwarding of the default UDP ports. It also makes the forwarding process more discriminatory. The broadcasts are sent only to pre-defined addresses.

To take advantage of the DHCP server in Figure 5.2, you can configure a helper address of the NT server on the Bozeman e0 interface and make sure that IP forwarding is enabled on the Helena router.

Fragmentation

Routers may have to engage in fragmentation whenever there is a difference between the size of the MTUs on their interfaces. The MTU represents the maximum amount of data from the Network and higher layers that can be packaged into a Data Link Layer frame. For Espec-2 Ethernet, the MTU is 1500 bytes. Data Link Layer technologies like Token Ring or FDDI can support larger MTUs. 16 Mbps Token Ring can support MTUs of up to 17,800 bytes. A typical Token Ring MTU on a Cisco router is 4464 bytes.

When a router engages in constant fragmentation due to an MTU mismatch, its overall performance will suffer. Some router interfaces support user-settable MTU via the mtu interface configuration command, others do not. Experiment with your own model to determine where the MTU setting is supported. For interfaces that support setting the MTU, it's possible for you to adjust it. But remember that routers are only intermediate devices passing packets between end systems like servers and workstations.

It's best to adjust MTUs or frame sizes on the devices (servers or workstations) that originate them. An MTU mismatch will not disable your internetwork. TCP/IP routers are designed to perform fragmentation. But fragmentation is an issue to be aware of. It's related to the Data Link Layer and if it's excessive, it can have an impact on your router's performance.

Chapter Summary

Common problems at the Data Link Layer stem from encapsulation mismatches, excessive utilization, or interface controller failures. The best way to improve performance on overutilized WAN links is to increase their capacity. An LMI type mismatch between a router and a Frame Relay switch will disable Frame Relay links. The `show interface` and `show frame-relay` commands are useful IOS tools for troubleshooting Data Link Layer problems. Non-routable protocols can be bridged. Local IP broadcasts can be forwarded across routers if configured to do so. Excessive fragmentation impacts a router's performance.

Chapter 6

Troubleshooting IP

IP is one of several protocols operating at the network layer. Problems with IP stem mostly from misconfigurations. By the time you get to troubleshooting IP and the Network Layer, you should be certain that the Physical and Data Link Layers on your router or internetwork are working properly. Common problems with the IP and the Network Layer in general include address duplication and misconfigured masks.

Duplicate IP Addresses

IP address duplication can take place between subnets or within a subnet. Common causes of duplicate addresses are oversight, poor address management procedures, and network merges. Fast-growing, dynamic, large internetworks are in a greater danger of address duplication than their smaller, more stable counterparts. To avoid address duplication — and its consequences — it behooves network administrators to manage their address space effectively.

Duplicate Addresses within a Subnet

Duplicate addresses within a subnet occur when two or more routers that are interfaced to a subnet are assigned the same IP address. Subnets with duplicate addresses can either be LAN segments or serial WAN links. On LANs, IOS usually warns you about a duplicate address but still allows you to assign it. On serial links you don't even get a warning.

On transit subnets that are interconnecting multiple network segments, the final effect of address duplication is usually a loss of IP connectivity between the interconnected segments. The intermediate effects of address duplication—leading to the loss of IP connectivity—depend on the routing protocols that are deployed on a transit subnet. For example, OSPF neighbors will lose their adjacency if they are reconfigured with the same IP addresses on the interfaces over which they are adjacent. And without adjacency they won't be able to exchange routing updates.

Observe what happens when a duplicate address is assigned an Ethernet interface. Address 172.17.16.2 has already been configured on another router interfaced to the same Ethernet subnet.

```
Denver1#conf t
Enter configuration commands, one per line.  End with CNTL/Z.
Denver1(config)#inter e0
Denver1(config-if)#ip address 172.17.16.2 255.255.240.0
Denver1(config-if)#
08:48:18: %IP-4-DUPADDR: Duplicate address 172.17.16.2 on Ethernet0, sourced by
0000.0c4a.d136
Denver1(config-if)#
```

IOS accepts the `ip address` configuration command, but responds with a message that another device already has the same IP address. The warning message also tells you the hardware address of that device, which in this case is 0000.0c4a.d136. Knowing the hardware address of a device with the duplicate IP address is helpful in troubleshooting duplicate addresses. ARP tables associate hardware addresses with the IP addresses and the router's interfaces. Displaying the ARP tables on all of the neighboring routers can help pinpoint the interface with the duplicate address. An ARP table on a router can be viewed via the `show arp` command.

Notice that there is no warning from the IOS when a duplicate IP address is configured on the s0 interface of the same router. Denver1's neighbor over s0 has an address of 192.168.1.1/24 configured at the other end of the serial link.

```
Denver1#conf t
Enter configuration commands, one per line.  End with CNTL/Z.
Denver1(config)#inter s0
```

```
Denver1(config-if)#ip address 192.168.1.1 255.255.255.0
Denver1(config-if)#^Z
Denver1#
```

However, unbeknownst to the administrator who was changing the s0 address, there was an established BGP session between Denver1 and its s0 neighbor. Changing the s0 address to be the same as the neighbor's address tore down the TCP connection over which the BGP session was established. This is another example of the drastic effect of address duplication. If Denver1 was relying on BGP updates from its s0 neighbor, those updates just stopped coming. The net effect on network users is inability to reach certain destinations.

If you suspect a duplicate address on a subnet, you can use the Cisco Discovery Protocol (CDP) to find out the IP addresses of all your neighbors. CDP is a Data Link Layer protocol, so it operates even if there is address duplication between neighbors. Observe the output from the CDP display on the Denver1 router. By now Denver1 has been configured with two duplicate addresses (e0 and s0) and is getting quite isolated. A quick way to check for address duplication is to display a router's interfaces in a brief mode and follow it with show cdp neighbor detail display as demonstrated in the following traces.

```
Denver1#
Denver1#sh ip inter br
Interface          IP-Address      OK? Method Status           Protocol
Ethernet0          172.17.16.2     YES manual up               up
Serial0            192.168.1.1     YES manual up               up
Denver1#


Denver1#sh cdp neigh det
-------------------------
Device ID: billings
Entry address(es):
  IP address: 192.168.1.1
Platform: cisco 2522,  Capabilities: Router
Interface: Serial0,  Port ID (outgoing port): Serial0
Holdtime : 148 sec
```

```
Version :

Cisco Internetwork Operating System Software

IOS (tm) 3000 Software (IGS-J-L), Version 11.0(9), RELEASE SOFTWARE (fc1)

Copyright (c) 1986-1996 by cisco Systems, Inc.

Compiled Tue 11-Jun-96 00:37 by loreilly




-------------------------

Device ID: Denver3

Entry address(es):

  IP address: 172.17.16.2

Platform: cisco 2500,  Capabilities: Router

Interface: Ethernet0,  Port ID (outgoing port): Ethernet0

Holdtime : 166 sec


Version :

Cisco Internetwork Operating System Software

IOS (tm) 2500 Software (C2500-JS-L), Version 11.3(7)T,  RELEASE SOFTWARE (fc1)

Copyright (c) 1986-1998 by cisco Systems, Inc.

Compiled Tue 01-Dec-98 12:44 by ccai


Denver1#
```

The preceding traces reveal that Denver1 has 172.17.16.2 assigned to e0, but its neighbor Denver3 has the same address assigned to its e0. Denver1 has 192.168.1.1 assigned to s0 and so does its neighbor Billings. When you see the same addresses in the show ip interface brief display and in the show cdp neighbor detail, you know that you have address duplication that must be corrected before your internetwork will work properly.

Duplicate Subnets

Duplicate subnets are a less frequent phenomenon than duplicate addresses within a subnet. It takes considerable mismanagement of an address space within a company to end up with duplicate subnets. But duplicate subnets can occur, for example, when two companies using the same private addressing merge their networks.

The effects of duplicate subnets differ from duplicate addresses on a subnet. With duplicate addresses, traffic does not reach its intended destination due to loss of IP connectivity, and with duplicate subnets, traffic ends up going to the wrong place. It's like having imposters on the network intercepting your communications. Consider an internetwork as illustrated in Figure 6.1.

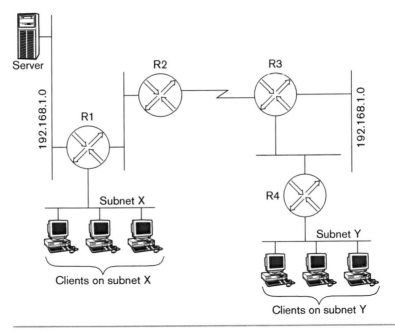

Figure 6.1 *Example of duplicate subnets*

Figure 6.1 points to the problem with duplicate subnets. Any one of the routing protocols could be operating on the internetwork in Figure 6.1 producing the same results. Suppose that the clients from subnets X and Y are trying to reach a server on network 192.168.1.0. The problem is that there are two networks 192.168.1.0 in this internetwork. One is attached to router R1 and has been there for a while. The other subnet is attached to router R3 and has been introduced into the internetwork just recently. The server that clients from X and Y are trying to reach is on the 192.168.1.0 network that's attached to R1.

Clients from subnet X will probably get to their right destinations, but clients from subnet Y will be banging on the wrong door. The network 192.168.1.0 that's attached to R3 is closer to clients from Y than the same network attached to R1. It will take a high layer indicator like the inability to log on to alert clients on Subnet Y that something is wrong.

The best way to avoid situations with duplicate subnets is to manage your address space well. If you suspect a problem with duplicate subnets, use the traceroute utility to help you identify traffic paths. A logical layout of your network — as recommended in Chapter 2 — can also be an invaluable tool in this process.

If you discover that you have duplicate subnets in your internetwork, the solution is to change addresses on one of the subnets so that all of the addresses are unique.

Misconfigured Masks

Masks are used with numerous IOS configuration commands. They take on two forms: normal or inverted. Normal masks begin with 1s and end with 0s. Inverted masks are just the opposite; they begin with 0s and end with 1s.

Normal Masks

Examples of normal mask usage include the assignment of IP addresses to interfaces, definition of static routes, OSPF summarization, and BGP aggregation. Optionally, normal masks are used with the assignment of networks to IGRP, EIGRP, or RIP processes and the advertising of networks into BGP. Depending on where a mask is used, it's referred to by different names.

When assigning addresses to interfaces, the mask is referred to as the subnet mask. The mask identifies the subnet to which the interface belongs. When performing OSPF summarization, the mask is referred to as the summarization mask. The summarization mask differs from the subnet mask of the summarized networks. It is shorter than the subnet mask. With BGP aggregation, the mask is referred to as the aggregation mask.

Again, it's different from the subnet masks that are in use inside a BGP autonomous system.

When normal masks are used in IOS configuration statements, they end up being associated with routing table entries. The subnet masks that are assigned to a router's interfaces show up as the masks for its directly connected networks. The OSPF summarization mask configured on Area Border Routers (ABRs) shows up in other routers' tables with the routing table entry for the summarized route. The aggregation mask in BGP is very similar to the summarization mask in OSPF. It shows up in other routers' routing tables with the aggregate route entry.

The principle behind the normal mask is that it identifies a portion of the IP address that's going to be used in routing decisions. If the normal mask is longer than a default mask for a particular IP address class, then it's a subnet mask. Subnetting allows for creation of multiple logical networks out of a single class A, B, or C network. If the normal mask is shorter than a default mask for a particular address class, it's often referred to as a supernet mask.

Supernetting allows multiple networks from an address class to be represented with a single routing table entry. OSPF summarization and BGP aggregation are a form of supernetting when multiple addresses from an address class become summarized or aggregated. In those cases, the summarization or aggregation masks will be shorter than the default masks. However, OSPF summarization can be used on subnets of a classful address without the summarization mask becoming a supernet mask. OSPF summarization is discussed in Chapter 8.

Subnet Masks (Assignment of Addresses to Interfaces)

IP addresses are assigned to interfaces via the `ip address` *ip-address mask* command. The *mask* defines the subnet to which an interface belongs. Before assigning IP addresses to router interfaces, it's important that network administrators develop an addressing plan for their internetwork. Having a list of addresses that have already been used is vital and is considered to be a part of reasonable documentation, as discussed in Chapter 2. This can prevent address duplication and minimize the potential for errors with masks.

On networks where a single router is connecting a few subnets together, occasionally you may be able to get away with a misconfigured subnet mask on your router. But when more routers are present in an internetwork and dynamic routing protocols are in use, subnet mask misconfigurations are very unforgiving. Take a look at the very simple internetwork shown in Figure 6.2.

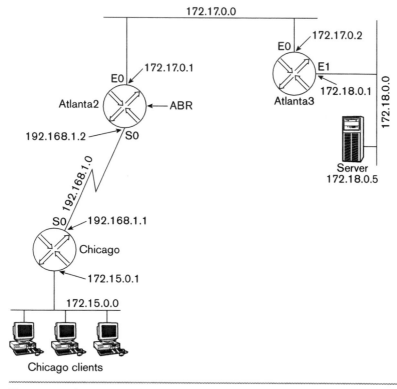

Figure 6.2 *Internetwork for misconfigured subnet mask analysis*

OSPF is configured on all routers in Figure 6.2. Subnet 172.17.0.0 is a transit subnet, which means that for Chicago clients to reach the Atlanta servers, traffic must go through 172.17.0.0. It also means that Atlanta2 and Atlanta3 must see each other as OSPF neighbors on subnet 172.17.0.0.

The following traces display the relevant portions of initial working configurations for Atlanta2 and Atlanta3, the routing table for Chicago, the OSPF neighbor display on Atlanta2, and a ping trace from Chicago to the server on 172.18.0.0.

```
Atlanta2#show run
Building configuration...
.
hostname Atlanta2
!
enable password cisco
!
ip subnet-zero
!
interface Ethernet0
 ip address 172.17.0.1 255.255.0.0
!
interface Serial0
 ip address 192.168.1.2 255.255.255.0
!
router ospf 10
 network 172.17.0.0 0.0.255.255 area 0.0.0.0
 network 192.168.1.0 0.0.0.255 area 0.0.0.0
.

.


Atlanta3#show run
Building configuration...
!
hostname Atlanta3
!
interface Ethernet0
 ip address 172.17.0.2 255.255.0.0
!
interface Ethernet1
```

```
  ip address 172.18.0.1 255.255.0.0
 !
 .

 .

router ospf 10
  network 172.17.0.0 0.0.255.255 area 0.0.0.0
  network 172.18.0.0 0.0.255.255 area 0.0.0.0
 !



Atlanta2#show ip ospf neigh


Neighbor ID     Pri   State        Dead Time   Address        Interface
172.18.0.1       1    FULL/DR      00:00:39    172.17.0.2     Ethernet0
192.168.1.1      1    FULL/  -     00:00:33    192.168.1.1    Serial0
Atlanta2#



Chicago#sh ip route
Codes: C - connected, S - static, I - IGRP, R - RIP, M - mobile, B - BGP
       D - EIGRP, EX - EIGRP external, O - OSPF,


Gateway of last resort is not set


C    192.168.1.0 is directly connected, Serial0
C    172.15.0.0 is directly connected, Ethernet0
O    172.17.0.0 [110/74] via 192.168.1.2, 00:34:35, Serial0
O    172.18.0.0 [110/84] via 192.168.1.2, 00:34:35, Serial0


Chicago#ping 172.18.0.5
Type escape sequence to abort.
Sending 5, 100-byte ICMP Echos to 172.18.0.5, timeout is 2 seconds:
!!!!!
Success rate is 100 percent (5/5), round-trip min/avg/max = 4/5/8 ms
Chicago#
```

The preceding traces reflect a properly configured internetwork. The Atlanta server is reachable from Chicago as shown in the ping. Observe now the reconfiguration of the subnet mask on Atlanta2's Ethernet0 interface from 255.255.0.0 to 255.255.255.0. Compare the neighbor display, the routing table, and the ping that follow with those from the preceding set of traces.

```
Atlanta2#conf t
Enter configuration commands, one per line.  End with CNTL/Z.
Atlanta2(config)#
Atlanta2(config)#inter e0
Atlanta2(config-if)#ip address 172.17.0.1 255.255.255.0
Atlanta2(config-if)#^Z
Atlanta2#


Atlanta2#sh ip ospf neighbor


Neighbor ID     Pri   State        Dead Time   Address       Interface
192.168.1.1      1    FULL/  -     00:00:36    192.168.1.1   Serial0
Atlanta2#


Chicago#sh ip route
Codes: C - connected, S - static, I - IGRP, R - RIP, M - mobile, B - BGP
       D - EIGRP, EX - EIGRP external, O - OSPF,


Gateway of last resort is not set


C    192.168.1.0 is directly connected, Serial0
C    172.15.0.0 is directly connected, Ethernet0
     172.17.0.0 255.255.255.0 is subnetted, 1 subnets
O       172.17.0.0 [110/74] via 192.168.1.2, 00:00:28, Serial0
Chicago#


Chicago#ping 172.18.0.5
Type escape sequence to abort.
Sending 5, 100-byte ICMP Echos to 172.18.0.5, timeout is 2 seconds:
```

```
.....
Success rate is 0 percent (0/5)
Chicago#
```

The repercussions from the misconfigured subnet mask on Atlanta2 router are quite dramatic. OSPF is no longer functional on transit subnet 172.17.0.0 (Atlanta2 and Atlanta3 do not see each other as neighbors). Subnet 172.18.0.0 is no longer in Chicago's routing table. And Chicago clients can no longer get to the Atlanta server located on subnet 172.18.0.0. There was no warning from the IOS that this would be the impact on the internetwork when the subnet mask was accidentally changed on Atlanta2.

There are some instances where the IOS tries to give you a hint that the mask you are putting in is going to cause a problem. Observe what happens, for example, on the Atlanta2 router when an inverted mask or a mask of all 0s or all 1s is used.

```
Atlanta2#conf t
Enter configuration commands, one per line.  End with CNTL/Z.
Atlanta2(config)#inter e0
Atlanta2(config-if)#ip address 172.17.0.1 0.0.255.255
Bad mask 0xFFFF for address 172.17.0.1
Atlanta2(config-if)#
Atlanta2(config-if)#ip address 172.17.0.1 0.0.0.0
Bad mask /0 for address 172.17.0.1
Atlanta2(config-if)#
Atlanta2(config-if)#ip address 172.17.0.1 255.255.255.255
Bad mask /32 for address 172.17.0.1
Atlanta2(config-if)#ip address 172.17.0.1 255.255.255.240
Atlanta2(config-if)#^Z
Atlanta2#
```

The IOS will prevent you from doing the extreme and the ridiculous but it will not prevent you from doing damage to your internetwork due to lack of planning or proper documentation. The error messages that IOS generated for the bad masks are boldfaced. Notice, however, that the last attempt to assign a mask in the preceding trace was successful from IOS' point of view. But the mask of 255.255.255.240 that was assigned would have the same consequences as the mask of 255.255.255.0 which, as you observed, resulted in wreaking havoc even in a simple internetwork.

Masks Used with Static and Default Routes

Static and default routes are defined via the `ip route` *prefix mask* [address | interface] command where the mask specifies the length of the prefix that will be used in making routing decisions. Unlike the subnet mask used with the assignment of addresses to interfaces in the previous section, the mask in the `ip route` command can assume values of all zeros and all ones. You want to be sure that you know what those values represent and when to use them.

When using a mask of all 1s with the `ip route` command, you are creating a host-specific route. This means that only one IP address will match this entry in the routing table. This address should belong to a host like a workstation or a server; it should not be a router interface. Routers and networks are only the facilitators for the exchange of information between workstations and servers that are attached to the networks.

What you also want to avoid in defining a static route is using an IP address of a network with an all-1s mask. IOS will allow you to do it, but the entry will be useless. Networks themselves do not initiate packets and network addresses are not normally found in the destination address field of the IP header.

Consider the four examples of static routes configuration shown in the following trace. Two have resulted in an error. IOS accepted the other two. Only one of the two configuration statements accepted by IOS is meaningful.

```
Atlanta2#

Atlanta2#conf t

Enter configuration commands, one per line.  End with CNTL/Z.

Atlanta2(config)#ip route 192.168.7.0 255.255.255.255 s0

Atlanta2(config)#

Atlanta2(config)#ip route 192.168.8.0 255.255.0.0 s0

%Inconsistent address and mask

Atlanta2(config)#

Atlanta2(config)#ip route 192.168.8.0 255.255.255.0 s0

Atlanta2(config)#

Atlanta2(config)#ip route 192.168.9.0 0.0.0.0 s0
```

```
%Inconsistent address and mask
Atlanta2(config)#
Atlanta2(config)#^Z
Atlanta2#
```

The `ip route` entry for 192.168.7.0 with an all-1s mask was accepted. But it's rather meaningless. You can certainly execute a ping or a traceroute to a network address, but user packets typically have host addresses for their destinations. Some IOS versions will not even allow you to use an invalid host address with a host-specific mask.

The `ip route` entry for 192.168.8.0 with a mask of 255.255.0.0 resulted in an error. The IOS is preventing you from using a default class B mask for a class C address. If this mask were accepted, the net effect would be that all traffic destined to any class C network beginning with 192.168 would be forwarded out of the s0 interface, not just the traffic for 192.168.8.0. Using a mask shorter than the class default for a static route prefix effectively means attempting aggregation, and IOS prevents you from doing it.

The next `ip route` entry for 192.168.8.0 with 255.255.255.0 was accepted. This is a meaningful entry. The mask could be longer, realistically up to 255.255.255.252. An increasingly longer mask will mean that fewer and fewer destinations will match the route.

The last `ip route` entry attempts to use an all-0s mask. An error results. The all-0s mask can be used when defining a static route, but only when the prefix is also all 0s. When this occurs, the prefix matches all addresses and the static route becomes a default route.

Observe the definition of a default route in the next series of traces. Also take a look at what happens when a prefix of 0.0.0.0 is used with a mask of 255.255.255.255. The fact that IOS accepts both entries is a common source of confusion.

```
Atlanta2#conf t
Enter configuration commands, one per line.  End with CNTL/Z.
Atlanta2(config)#ip route 0.0.0.0 0.0.0.0 s0
Atlanta2(config)#
Atlanta2(config)#ip route 0.0.0.0 255.255.255.255 s0
Atlanta2(config)#
Atlanta2(config)#^Z
Atlanta2#
```

What you want to notice, however, is how those two entries are show-ing up in the routing table.

```
Atlanta2#sh ip route
Codes: C - connected, S - static, I - IGRP, R - RIP, M - mobile, B - BGP
       D - EIGRP, EX - EIGRP external, O - OSPF, IA - OSPF inter area
       N1 - OSPF NSSA external type 1, N2 - OSPF NSSA external type 2
       E1 - OSPF external type 1, E2 - OSPF external type 2, E - EGP
       i - IS-IS, L1 - IS-IS level-1, L2 - IS-IS level-2, * - candidate default
       U - per-user static route, o - ODR


Gateway of last resort is 0.0.0.0 to network 0.0.0.0


S    192.168.8.0/24 is directly connected, Serial0
     172.17.0.0/28 is subnetted, 1 subnets
C       172.17.0.0 is directly connected, Ethernet0
O    172.16.0.0/16 [110/74] via 192.168.1.1, 02:25:59, Serial0
     192.168.7.0/32 is subnetted, 1 subnets
S       192.168.7.0 [1/0] via 192.168.1.1
C    192.168.1.0/24 is directly connected, Serial0
S    0.0.0.0/32 is directly connected, Serial0
S*   0.0.0.0/0 is directly connected, Serial0
```

Both entries for the prefix 0.0.0.0 are present in the routing table. The entry with an all-0s mask is flagged as the default. The entry with an all-1s mask causes no harm but is rather meaningless. You will a not find many networks with packets that have the destination IP address of all 0s. The correct way to install a default route is via ip address 0.0.0.0 0.0.0.0 [address | interface] and not ip address 0.0.0.0 255.255.255 [address | interface].

OSPF Summarization Mask

OSPF summarization is implemented on Area Border Routers via the area area_ID range address mask command. The mask represents the length of the common part or the prefix of all of the networks that are be-ing summarized. It's a normal mask beginning with 1s and ending with 0s.

An attempt to use an inverted mask in the summarization statement results in an error message. Observe the configuration of summarization on
the Atlanta2 router in Figure 6.3.

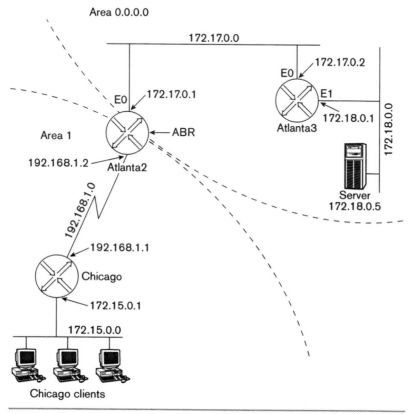

Figure 6.3 *OSPF internetwork for summarization mask analysis*

Atlanta2 will summarize the networks 172.17.0.0 and 17.18.0.0, which
are located in area 0.0.0.0, and inject them into area 10. The common prefix
for these networks is 172.16.0.0. The longest normal mask for this prefix is
255.252.0.0 or /14, and the shortest normal mask for this prefix is
255.240.0.0 or /12. The inverted masks would be 0.3.255.255 and
0.15.255.255, correspondingly. Now suppose that you forgot that OSPF
summarization uses a normal mask and you tried to use an inverted mask. Or
perhaps you mistakenly try to use a mask that's shorter than /12 or longer
than /14. Observe what happens.

```
Atlanta2#conf t

Enter configuration commands, one per line.  End with CNTL/Z.

Atlanta2(config)#router ospf 10

Atlanta2(config-router)#area 0.0.0.0 range 172.16.0.0 0.3.255.255

% OSPF: Inconsistent address/mask 172.16.0.0 0x3FFFF for area range

Atlanta2(config-router)#

Atlanta2(config-router)#area 0.0.0.0 range 172.16.0.0 255.252.0.0

Atlanta2(config-router)#

Atlanta2(config-router)#area 0.0.0.0 range 172.16.0.0 255.0.0.0

% OSPF: Inconsistent address/mask 172.16.0.0/8 for area range

Atlanta2(config-router)#

Atlanta2(config-router)#area 0.0.0.0 172.16.0.0 255.224.0.0

% OSPF: Inconsistent address/mask 172.16.0.0/11 for area range

Atlanta2(config-router)#

Atlanta2(config-router)#area 0.0.0.0 range 172.16.0.0 255.240.0.0

Atlanta2(config-router)#
```

IOS warns you if you try to use an inverted mask (first error message in the trace). It also warns you if you try to use a mask that does not match the prefix (second and third error messages in the trace). In the example, masks 255.0.0.0 and 255.224.0.0 do not match the prefix, that is, if those masks are logically ANDed with the prefix, the result is different than the prefix. But IOS does not warn you when your masks match the prefix. In the example, two masks matching the prefix were used: 255.252.0.0 and 255.240.0.0. Both masks were accepted and both configuration statements appear in the OSPF section of the configuration file.

If different masks are accepted by the IOS for the same prefix, the issue becomes which mask is the correct one to use. You want to use the longest mask which when ANDed with the networks being summarized will result in the common prefix. In the example, it's 255.252.0.0. If you configure summarization with that mask, then the other summarization statement (in the example, area 0.0.0.0 range 172.16.0.0 255.240.0.0) will have no effect even though it appears in the configuration file. In the event that you remove the statement with the longest valid mask, the summarization statement with the next longest valid mask will take effect.

The preceding configuration on the Atlanta2 router results in the following routing table on the Chicago router.

```
Chicago#
Chicago#sh ip route
Codes: C - connected, S - static, I - IGRP, R - RIP, M - mobile, B - BGP

       D - EIGRP, EX - EIGRP external, O - OSPF, IA - OSPF inter area
       E1 - OSPF external type 1, E2 - OSPF external type 2, E - EGP
       i - IS-IS, L1 - IS-IS level-1, L2 - IS-IS level-2, * - candidate default

Gateway of last resort is not set

C    192.168.1.0 is directly connected, Serial0
C    172.15.0.0 is directly connected, Ethernet0
O IA 172.16.0.0 255.252.0.0 [110/74] via 192.168.1.2, 00:02:11, Serial0
```

The entry 172.16.0.0 in Chicago's routing table has a mask of 255.252.0.0, which is the longer of the valid two summarization masks that were configured on the Atlanta2 router. Atlanta2, being an ABR, advertises the summary route to Chicago. Now observe what happens to the Chicago routing table when the configuration statement area 0.0.0.0 range 172.16.0.0 255.252.0.0 is removed on the Atlanta2 router. Remember that Atlanta2 has two summarization statements in its configuration file as shown.

```
Atlanta2#sh run
Building configuration...

Current configuration:
hostname Atlanta2
!
enable password cisco
!
ip subnet-zero
!
```

```
interface Ethernet0

 ip address 172.17.0.1 255.255.0.0

!

interface Serial0

 ip address 192.168.1.2 255.255.255.0

!

router ospf 10

 network 172.17.0.0 0.0.255.255 area 0.0.0.0

 network 192.168.1.0 0.0.0.255 area 10

 area 0.0.0.0 range 172.16.0.0 255.252.0.0

 area 0.0.0.0 range 172.16.0.0 255.240.0.0

!



Atlanta2#

Atlanta2#conf t

Enter configuration commands, one per line.  End with CNTL/Z.

Atlanta2(config)#router ospf 10

Atlanta2(config-router)#no area 0.0.0.0 range 172.16.0.0 255.252.0.0

Atlanta2(config-router)#^Z

Atlanta2#


Chicago#sh ip route

Codes: C - connected, S - static, I - IGRP, R - RIP, M - mobile, B - BGP

       D - EIGRP, EX - EIGRP external, O - OSPF, IA - OSPF inter area

       E1 - OSPF external type 1, E2 - OSPF external type 2, E - EGP

       i - IS-IS, L1 - IS-IS level-1, L2 - IS-IS level-2, * - candidate default


Gateway of last resort is not set


C    192.168.1.0 is directly connected, Serial0

C    172.15.0.0 is directly connected, Ethernet0

O IA 172.16.0.0 255.240.0.0 [110/74] via 192.168.1.2, 00:00:17, Serial0

Chicago#
```

Chicago's routing table now has an entry for 172.16.0.0 with a 255.240.0.0 mask. This entry is actually a summary route for all networks ranging from 172.16.0.0 to 172.31.0.0. This is the new summary route that's now being advertised to Chicago by Atlanta2 following the removal of a summarization statement with a longer mask on Atlanta2. But only two networks in this range are accessible from Atlanta2. This means that if traffic for any networks in that range other than 172.17.0.0 and 172.18.0.0 is sent from Chicago to Atlanta2, and Atlanta2 does not have a default route, that traffic will get lost.

IOS shields you from configuring OSPF summarization using an inverted mask or a mask that doesn't match the prefix. The only danger that's left is that the mask may end up being too long or too short. If you do err, it's far better to make the mask too long than too short. In the preceding example, if the mask were taken to the extreme of all 1s, the effect would be no summarization. Atlanta2 would be advertising networks 172.17.0.0 and 172.18.0.0 to Chicago with their default class B masks. That's far better than advertising networks you don't know about, which is what happens when the summarization mask is too short.

The general guideline for OSPF summarization is to use the longest valid summarization mask possible. A shorter valid mask means that the ABR will advertise networks that are not in the area it represents. This leads to problems with the delivery of traffic to the correct destinations. See Chapter 8 for more details on OSPF summarization pitfalls.

BGP Aggregation Mask

BGP aggregation is very similar to OSPF summarization except that it's occurring with a different routing protocol. BGP aggregation is implemented via the `aggregate-address` *address mask* [options] command. This command takes a normal mask, but unlike with OSPF summarization, no error message is generated when an inverted mask is used.

When an inverted mask is used accidentally with the BGP aggregation command, IOS changes the summary address to a default route of 0.0.0.0 and keeps the inverted mask. For example, the correct aggregation command usage might be `aggregate-address   172.16.0.0 255.240.0.0`. The incorrect usage would be `aggregate-address 172.16.0.0 0.15.155.255`, which is translated by IOS into `aggregate-address 0.0.0.0 0.15.255.255`.

Consider a BGP internetwork as shown in Figure 6.4.

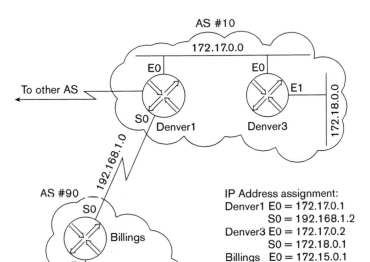

Figure 6.4 *BGP internetwork for aggregation mask analysis*

Denver1 is going to perform aggregation for networks 172.17.0.0 and 172.18.0.0. These are the same networks that were used with the OSPF summarization mask examples in the preceding section. The valid aggregation mask can be anything between /12 and /14 or 255.240.0.0 and 255.252.0.0. The initial configuration on Denver1 is as follows:

```
Denver1#sh run
Building configuration...

Current configuration:
hostname Denver1
!
enable password cisco
!
ip subnet-zero
!
```

```
interface Ethernet0
 ip address 172.17.0.1 255.255.0.0
!
interface Serial0
 ip address 192.168.1.2 255.255.255.0
!
interface Serial1
 ip address 192.168.144.1 255.255.255.0
 clockrate 2000000
!
router ospf 10
 network 172.17.0.0 0.0.255.255 area 0.0.0.0
!
router bgp 10
 redistribute ospf 10
 neighbor 172.18.0.1 remote-as 10
 neighbor 192.168.1.1 remote-as 90
 neighbor 192.168.144.2 remote-as 20
!
```

The next step is to configure BGP aggregation on Denver1.

```
Denver1#
Denver1#conf t
Enter configuration commands, one per line.  End with CNTL/Z.
Denver1(config)#router bgp 10
Denver1(config-router)#aggregate-address 172.16.0.0 0.15.255.255
Denver1(config-router)#^Z
Denver1#
```

The only problem here is that the administrator mistakenly used an inverted mask instead of a normal mask. There was no warning from the IOS, but look what happened to that configuration statement when the running configuration is displayed.

```
Denver1#sh run
Building configuration...
```

```
Current configuration:
hostname Denver1
.

.

.

router bgp 10
  aggregate-address 0.0.0.0 0.15.255.255
  redistribute ospf 10
  neighbor 172.18.0.1 remote-as 10
  neighbor 192.168.1.1 remote-as 90
  neighbor 192.168.144.2 remote-as 20
!
```

The address 172.16.0.0 was translated into 0.0.0.0 without any warning. It's a meaningless aggregation statement. The next example shows you how to remove it from the configuration.

```
Denver1#conf t
Enter configuration commands, one per line.  End with CNTL/Z.
Denver1(config)#router bgp 10
Denver1(config-router)#no aggregate-address 0.0.0.0 0.15.255.255
Denver1(config-router)# ^Z
Denver1#
```

When it comes to error messages relating to BGP aggregations, the IOS programmers should be commended for having a sense of humor. When you try to enter a default route as a BGP aggregate, you get an error message that's self-explanatory. Observe what happens when you try to aggregate a default route.

```
Denver1#conf t
Enter configuration commands, one per line.  End with CNTL/Z.
Denver1(config-router)#aggregate-address 0.0.0.0 0.0.0.0
Aggregating to create default makes no sense,
use a network statement instead.
Denver1(config-router)# ^Z
Denver1#
```

Now that you've been told point-blank that what you are doing makes no sense, try doing aggregation the right way.

```
Denver1#
Denver1#conf t
Enter configuration commands, one per line.  End with CNTL/Z.
Denver1(config)#router bgp 10
Denver1(config-router)#aggregate-address 172.16.0.0 255.252.0.0
Denver1(config-router)#^Z
Denver1#sh
```

IOS has now accepted the aggregation command with the correct mask, as shown in the final configuration on Denver1.

```
Denver1#sh run
Building configuration...


Current configuration:
hostname Denver1
!
enable password cisco
!
ip subnet-zero
!
interface Ethernet0
 ip address 172.17.0.1 255.255.0.0
!
interface Serial0
 ip address 192.168.1.2 255.255.255.0
.
.
.
router bgp 10
 aggregate-address 172.16.0.0 255.252.0.0
 redistribute ospf 10
 neighbor 172.18.0.1 remote-as 10
```

```
neighbor 192.168.1.1 remote-as 90
neighbor 192.168.144.2 remote-as 20
!
```

The danger in misconfiguring the aggregation mask boils down to using a normal mask that's too short, resulting in a router aggregating more routes than it can reach. You end up aggregating someone else's routes. This aspect of BGP troubleshooting is explored in Chapter 10.

Suppose that a range of class C networks from 192.168.0.0 to 192.168.255.0 is deployed in a BGP internetwork composed of multiple autonomous systems. If all of the BGP routers performed aggregation with a /16 mask, the aggregation statement would be aggregate-address 192.168.0.0 255.255.0.0. In reality, this would not be a problem.

BGP aggregation without a *summary-only* keyword creates an aggregate, but the individual routes composing the aggregate continue to be advertised. However, if those statements were used with the *summary-only* keyword, then real havoc would result in the internetwork. Only the aggregates would be advertised and each router would be advertising the same aggregate. Misdelivered traffic in that internetwork is almost a certainty.

Advertising of Networks into BGP

The BGP process on a router must be told about the networks that it's going to route for. This can be accomplished either via redistribution or advertising. Redistribution takes place via the `redistribute` command and advertising takes place via a `network` command. Redistribution is considered a dynamic injection of routes into BGP whereas advertising is static. BGP aggregation, discussed in the preceding section, takes place after the BGP process has been told about networks to route for either via redistribution or advertising.

If you review the configuration file on Denver1 from the preceding section, you will notice that under the BGP process definition there is a `redistribute` command performing redistribution of OSPF into BGP. All the networks that OSPF knows about on Denver1 are injected into BGP via the redistribution process. If Denver1 learns about more networks via OSPF, there is no need for the administrator to change its configuration. All of those newly learned networks will be made known to BGP. That's the advantage of redistribution.

The disadvantage of redistribution is that some undesirable networks can be learned via an IGP like OSPF and an administrator may have to set up policies to prevent them from being redistributed into BGP. Consequently, there is an alternative for injecting networks into BGP. The `redistribute` command can be replaced with one or more `network` commands. The syntax for the `network` command is `network` *network_address* [`options`]. One of the optional keywords is *mask* followed by a mask value.

Anytime that a mask can be used in any configuration statement, it is subject to misuse and misconfiguration. Consider the internetwork in Figure 6.5.

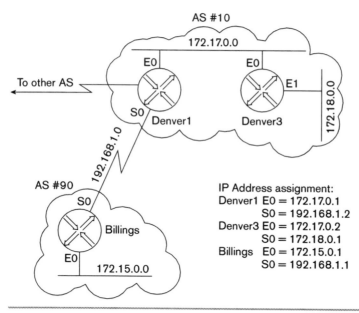

Figure 6.5 *Internetwork for analysis of mask usage with the BGP network command*

The purpose of the mask with the BGP `network` command is to identify the exact prefix (*network_address*) that you want to have advertised into BGP. This prefix can be a classful address, a subnet of a classful address, or even an OSPF summary route. BGP will advertise the prefix to its neighbors provided that it first finds it in the IP routing table. The implication of this condition is simple. If the *mask_value* you use in the `network` *network_address* `mask` *mask_value* command identifies a prefix that's not in the IP routing table, the network command will have no effect. This is where there is the greatest potential for misconfiguration.

In Figure 6.5, Denver1 wants to tell its neighbors about networks 172.17.0.0 and 172.18.0.0. These are classful networks. If you are advertising only classful networks, the default mask is assumed and you don't have to use it in the network statement. The initial Denver1 configuration before the advertising takes place is as follows.

```
Denver1#

Denver1#show run

Building configuration...


Current configuration:

hostname Denver1

!

enable password cisco

!

ip subnet-zero

!

interface Ethernet0

 ip address 172.17.0.1 255.255.0.0

!

interface Serial0

 ip address 192.168.1.2 255.255.255.0

!

router ospf 10

 network 172.17.0.0 0.0.255.255 area 0.0.0.0

!

router bgp 10

 neighbor 172.18.0.1 remote-as 10

 neighbor 192.168.1.1 remote-as 90

 neighbor 192.168.144.2 remote-as 20

!
```

The routing table on Billings knows nothing about the networks 172.17.0.0 and 172.18.0.0 as shown below. It only knows about its directly connected networks at this point.

```
billings#sh ip route
Codes: C - connected, S - static, I - IGRP, R - RIP, M - mobile, B - BGP
       D - EIGRP, EX - EIGRP external, O - OSPF,


Gateway of last resort is not set


C    192.168.1.0 is directly connected, Serial0
C    172.15.0.0 is directly connected, Ethernet0
billings#
```

Observe now the configuration steps on Denver1 that do not involve the use of the mask with the **network** command.

```
Denver1#conf t
Enter configuration commands, one per line.  End with CNTL/Z.
Denver1(config)#router bgp 10
Denver1(config-router)#network 172.17.0.0
Denver1(config-router)#network 172.18.0.0
Denver1(config-router)#^Z
Denver1#
```

As these two networks are both present in the IP routing table on Denver1, you can expect them to appear in the Billings routing table as well. See the displays of the Denver1 and Billings routing tables that follow.

```
Denver1#sh ip route
Codes: C - connected, S - static, I - IGRP, R - RIP, M - mobile, B - BGP
       D - EIGRP, EX - EIGRP external, O - OSPF,


Gateway of last resort is not set


B    172.15.0.0/16 [20/0] via 192.168.1.1, 00:11:26
C    172.17.0.0/16 is directly connected, Ethernet0
O    172.18.0.0/16 [110/20] via 172.17.0.2, 00:08:50, Ethernet0
C    192.168.1.0/24 is directly connected, Serial0
Denver1#
```

```
billings#sh ip route
Codes: C - connected, S - static, I - IGRP, R - RIP, M - mobile, B - BGP
       D - EIGRP, EX - EIGRP external, O - OSPF,

Gateway of last resort is not set

C    192.168.1.0 is directly connected, Serial0
C    172.15.0.0 is directly connected, Ethernet0
B    172.17.0.0 [20/0] via 192.168.1.2, 00:01:01
B    172.18.0.0 [20/20] via 192.168.1.2, 00:00:01
billings#
```

Injecting classful networks into BGP is the easy part, offering little opportunity for misconfiguration. Assume that the network addressing is different now, as shown in Figure 6.6.

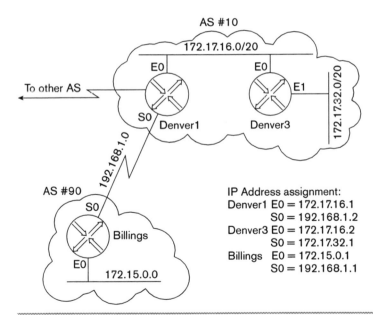

Figure 6.6 *Internetwork with subnets for analysis of mask usage with the BGP network command*

First, the network statements that were just put in are removed.

```
Denver1#
Denver1#conf t
Enter configuration commands, one per line.  End with CNTL/Z.
Denver1(config)#router bgp 10
Denver1(config-router)#no network 172.17.0.0
Denver1(config-router)#no network 172.18.0.0
Denver1(config-router)#^Z
Denver1#
```

The routing table on Denver1 shows two subnets of 172.17.0.0.

```
Denver1#
Denver1#sh ip route
Codes: C - connected, S - static, I - IGRP, R - RIP, M - mobile, B - BGP
       D - EIGRP, EX - EIGRP external, O - OSPF,

Gateway of last resort is not set

B    172.15.0.0/16 [20/0] via 192.168.1.1, 01:26:39
     172.17.0.0/20 is subnetted, 2 subnets
O       172.17.32.0 [110/20] via 172.17.16.2, 00:03:53, Ethernet0
C       172.17.16.0 is directly connected, Ethernet0
C    192.168.1.0/24 is directly connected, Serial0
Denver1#
```

This is where the advertising of networks into BGP gets tricky. Suppose that you advertise only the classful 172.17.0.0 without the mask. The result will be that IOS will accept it and the Billings router will have a BGP entry to 172.17.0.0. You are now including subnets in the advertisement that your router does not know about. Conceptually, a form of aggregation is taking place here that includes subnets that may be used elsewhere in the internetwork. What you want to do is advertise those two subnets with their exact masks.

Suppose, however, that mistakenly you advertise the two subnets with a longer mask of 255.255.255.0 as shown in the configuration that follows.

```
Denver1#conf t
Enter configuration commands, one per line.  End with CNTL/Z.
Denver1(config)#router bgp 10
Denver1(config-router)#network 172.17.16.0 mask 255.255.255.0
Denver1(config-router)#network 172.17.32.0 mask 255.255.255.0
Denver1(config-router)#^Z
Denver1#
```

The effect of this configuration is nil. When you apply those masks to the addresses, you end up with subnets 172.17.16.0/24 and 172.17.32.0/24. But these subnets are not present in Denver1's routing table and they will not be advertised to Billings. The Billings routing table reflects this.

```
billings#sh ip route
Codes: C - connected, S - static, I - IGRP, R - RIP, M - mobile, B - BGP
       D - EIGRP, EX - EIGRP external, O - OSPF,

Gateway of last resort is not set

C    192.168.1.0 is directly connected, Serial0
C    172.15.0.0 is directly connected, Ethernet0
billings#
```

The Billings routing table only knows about its directly connected networks, just like in the very beginning of this exercise. The correct configuration is to advertise those subnets with a /20 mask or 255.255.240.0 as shown next.

```
Denver1#conf t
Enter configuration commands, one per line.  End with CNTL/Z.
Denver1(config)#router bgp 10
Denver1(config-router)#network 172.17.16.0 mask 255.255.240.0
Denver1(config-router)#network 172.17.32.0 mask 255.255.240.0
Denver1(config-router)#^Z
Denver1#
```

The effects of this configuration are that Billings now has a BGP route to the two subnets as shown in its routing table.

```
billings#sh ip route
Codes: C - connected, S - static, I - IGRP, R - RIP, M - mobile, B - BGP
       D - EIGRP, EX - EIGRP external, O - OSPF, IA - OSPF inter area
       E1 - OSPF external type 1, E2 - OSPF external type 2, E - EGP
       i - IS-IS, L1 - IS-IS level-1, L2 - IS-IS level-2, * - candidate default


Gateway of last resort is not set


C    192.168.1.0 is directly connected, Serial0
C    172.15.0.0 is directly connected, Ethernet0
     172.17.0.0 255.255.240.0 is subnetted, 2 subnets
B       172.17.32.0 [20/20] via 192.168.1.2, 00:03:23
B       172.17.16.0 [20/0] via 192.168.1.2, 00:03:23
billings#
```

The rule for applying a mask to the network command in BGP is simple. If you don't know what it is, look at the mask in the routing table for the networks that you want to advertise. Use that mask. You don't have to use a mask if you are advertising an entire major class A, B, or C network.

Inverted Masks

If you take a normal mask and flip all of its bits around (make 1s, 0s and 0s, 1s) you end up with an inverted mask. The binary sum of a normal mask and its inverted counterpart is always 255.255.255.255. The perceptual difference between a normal mask and an inverted mask is that a normal mask begins with 1s and ends with 0s and the inverted mask begins with 0s and ends with 1s. But the normal and inverted masks serve different purposes in configuration commands.

Think of the inverted masks as wild cards. The use of a wild card typically means a shortcut. When you are using a shortcut, it also means that it's possible to do something the long way. The results of commands that use inverted masks can be accomplished via a shortcut or through a lengthy and tedious configuration. That's not the case with the commands that use normal masks.

Two configuration commands that involve the use and potential misuse of inverted masks are examined here. They are the definition of access control lists and the assignment interfaces to OSPF areas.

Access Control List Mask

Access control lists are used to block traffic from flowing into or out of a router interface. When you use a standard IP access control list to block traffic from coming through a router's interface, you must somehow identify that traffic. If there are two hundred stations on a subnet from which traffic is supposed to be blocked, it is possible to define a list that has two hundred statements in it, one for each of the two hundred stations. Or you can define a list that has a single statement identifying all of the stations on that subnet with a wild card, which in IOS happens to be an inverted mask. Observe the configuration that follows:

```
Chicago#conf t
Enter configuration commands, one per line.  End with CNTL/Z.
Chicago(config)#access-list 33 deny 172.18.0.0 0.0.255.255
Chicago(config)#access-list 33 permit any
Chicago(config)#inter s0
Chicago(config-if)#ip access-group 33 in
Chicago(config-if)#^Z
Chicago#
```

In the preceding configuration statements, list 33 is defined and applied to interface s0. This configuration blocks traffic originating on 172.18.0.0 (or any of its subnets) from coming into the router via the s0 interface. Theoretically, there are 65,534 possible hosts that can be defined on network 172.18.0.0. And theoretically, you could put 65,534 statements into the access control lists identifying each of those hosts individually. The configuration would look something like this.

```
Chicago#conf t
Enter configuration commands, one per line.  End with CNTL/Z.
Chicago(config)#access-list 33 deny 172.18.0.1 0.0.0.0
Chicago(config)#access-list 33 deny 172.18.0.2 0.0.0.0
Chicago(config)#access-list 33 deny 172.18.0.3 0.0.0.0
Chicago(config)#access-list 33 deny 172.18.0.4 0.0.0.0
```

.

.

.

```
Chicago(config)#access-list 33 deny 172.18.255.254 0.0.0.0
Chicago(config)#access-list 33 permit any
```

Those three dots separating the configuration statements represent in excess of 60,000 statements defining the access control list. But that's theory. In practice, you will not find a single logical network that has 65,534 hosts on it, and routers are not configured with 60,000+ statements in an access control list. The principle, however, is well illustrated. You can waste a lot of time and router memory putting tons of statements into an access control list, or you can use a shortcut.

The number of 0s in the inverted masks defines the portions of the addresses in the access list configuration statements that are used to match the incoming traffic. This means that an all-0s inverted mask will match a single IP address. An all-1s inverted mask will match all IP addresses.

The danger with inverted masks is that if they are not calculated and applied correctly, they will either do too much or not enough. Take, for example, another configuration that IOS does not block you from doing nor does it warn you about its consequences. This time it's list 34 that's defined with the intent of blocking traffic from network 172.18.0.0. The administrator got carried away and used 255.255.255.255 for the mask. Observe the configuration.

```
Chicago#conf t
Enter configuration commands, one per line.  End with CNTL/Z.
Chicago(config)#access-list 34 deny 172.18.0.0 255.255.255.255
Chicago(config)#access-list 34 permit any
Chicago(config)#
Chicago(config)#inter s0
Chicago(config-if)#ip access-group 34 in
Chicago(config-if)#^Z
Chicago#
```

The IOS has accepted your configuration statements without a warning. Your intent was to define a list that blocks traffic from any host on 172.18.0.0. What you've done, in reality, is block all traffic from coming via interface s0. When you have an all-1s inverted mask that's used in an ACL with a *deny* keyword, there is nothing to match or compare. Any traffic is denied. IOS actually translates `access-list 34 deny 172.18.0.0 255.255.255.255` into `access-list 34 deny any`. Take a look at the output from the `show access-list` command and a portion of the running config file resulting from the preceding configurations.

```
Chicago#
Chicago#sh access-l
Standard IP access list 33
    deny    172.18.0.0, wildcard bits 0.0.255.255
    permit any
Standard IP access list 34
    deny    any
    permit any
Chicago#


Chicago#show run
Building configuration...

Current configuration:
!
hostname Chicago
!
interface Ethernet0
 ip address 172.15.0.1 255.255.0.0
!
interface Serial0
 ip address 192.168.1.1 255.255.255.0
 ip access-group 34 in
 no fair-queue
 clockrate 2000000
!
.
.
```

```
access-list 33 deny    172.18.0.0 0.0.255.255
access-list 33 permit any
access-list 34 deny    any
access-list 34 permit any
.

.

Chicago#
```

As list 34 is now applied to the s0 interface, all traffic will be blocked from coming into that interface. Access control lists are examined in the order in which the statements appear from top to bottom. When the first statement denies all traffic, it does not matter what follows that statement, even if it is a statement that permits all traffic.

The pitfall you want to avoid with inverted masks is to be clear that an all-0s inverted mask is the most specific mask corresponding to a single address. All bits in the incoming address are compared to the address that's in the list. As you add 1s to the mask, there are fewer and fewer bits in the incoming addresses that are compared with the address in the list.

This means that the inverted mask covers more and more incoming addresses. When the inverted mask eventually becomes a complete wild card (255.255.255.255), it matches all incoming addresses. If it's used with a deny keyword as in the preceding configurations, then it will deny all traffic.

Assignment of OSPF Interfaces to Areas

Unlike the network command in BGP, the network command in OSPF uses an inverted mask. The discussion about the use of inverted masks in the access control list mask section illustrated that the configurations involving inverted masks can be done the long way or via a shortcut.

Suppose that you are running OSPF on a router that has a dozen serial interfaces. All interfaces are going to be assigned to the same OSPF backbone area zero, or 0.0.0.0. The IP addresses for all of those interfaces are derived from a single major class C network, 192.168.1.0, subnetted with a /30 mask. Each interface is assigned to a different subnet to avoid address duplication. The addresses are 192.168.1.1, 192.168.1.5, 192.168.1.9, and so on.

The choice in the OSPF configuration section is to have one network statement per interface (12 network statements for 12 interfaces) or a single network statement for all 12 interfaces. The syntax for assigning interfaces to OSPF areas is network *address inverted_mask* area *area_id*. When you assign only a single interface to an area you can use the most specific inverted mask, which is 0.0.0.0. It's important, however, that you do not confuse the *area_id* with the *inverted_mask* in those cases.

The long configuration process is shown next.

```
Router#conf t
Enter configuration commands, one per line.  End with CNTL/Z.
Router(config)#router ospf 10
Router(config-router)#network 192.168.1.1 0.0.0.0 area 0.0.0.0
Router(config-router)#network 192.168.1.5 0.0.0.0 area 0.0.0.0
Router(config-router)#network 192.168.1.9 0.0.0.0 area 0.0.0.0
Router(config-router)#network 192.168.1.13 0.0.0.0 area 0.0.0.0
.
.
Router(config-router)#network 192.168.1.45 0.0.0.0 area 0.0.0.0
```

If you want to take a shortcut you can use the inverted mask as a wild card and assign all of the 12 interfaces to area 0.0.0.0 with a single statement. To do so, however, you must calculate the inverted mask that covers those interfaces. One way to calculate the mask is to find the common part between the highest and the lowest IP addresses of your interfaces, which would be 192.168.1.0/26. If you convert the highest and the lowest addresses into binary, the first 26 bits in each address are the same. This mean that six of the lowest order bits can vary. The inverted mask or wild card would have 0s for the first 26 bits and 1s for the remaining six. The dotted decimal value of the mask in this case would be 0.0.0.63. The corresponding configuration would be as follows.

```
Router#conf t
Enter configuration commands, one per line.  End with CNTL/Z.
Router(config)#router ospf 10
Router(config-router)#network 192.168.1.0 0.0.0.63 area 0.0.0.0
Router(config-router)#^Z
Router#
```

There is, of course, a potential for misconfiguration here. What if you were off by one bit and instead of calculating the inverted mask as 0.0.0.63

you came up with 0.0.0.31. The interfaces beginning with 192.168.1.33 and higher would have been missed. Your router would not be running OSPF on the subnets with those interfaces.

There is less danger in making the mask less specific. Even without any calculations you could have glanced at all of the IP addresses and recognized that they all begin with 192.168.1. You could have used a class C inverted mask of 0.0.0.255 to assign them all to OSPF area 0.0.0.0. The problem with making a mask less specific is that if you try to assign an interface to another area that's covered by the less specific mask, you will get an error message.

Consider a router with interfaces as shown in Figure 6.7.

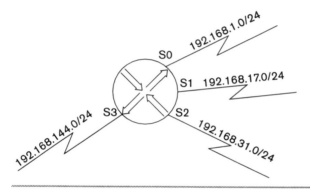

Figure 6.7 *Router with serial interfaces for analysis of inverted mask usage in OSPF*

Glancing at the network addresses, you detect that they all have 192.168 in common. The inverted mask for assignment of all of the interfaces to area 0.0.0.0 could be 0.0.255.255. But later, one of the interfaces must be assigned to a different area. Observe the configuration process and effects.

```
Router#conf t
Enter configuration commands, one per line.  End with CNTL/Z.
Router(config)#router ospf 10
Router(config-router)#network 192.168.0.0 0.0.255.255 area 0.0.0.0
Router(config-router)#^Z
Router#
```

The initial OSPF configuration worked fine through the use of a short-cut. But in this case the addresses are so spread out that a shortcut (less specific mask) may not be the best action. As the internetwork grows, it turns out that one of the interfaces has to be reassigned to another area. You proceed with the reconfiguration process as follows:

```
Router#conf t
Enter configuration commands, one per line.  End with CNTL/Z.
Router(config)#router ospf 10
Router(config-router)#network 192.168.144.0 0.0.0.255 area 10
Router(config-router)#
% OSPF: "network 192.168.144.0 0.0.0.255 area 10" is ignored. It is a subset of
a previous entry.
Router(config-router)#^Z
Router#
```

IOS does not allow you to assign the interface that's on subnet 192.168.144.0 to another area. What you will have to do to correct the situation is remove the statement assigning all interfaces to area 0.0.0.0 with the 0.0.255.255 mask. Then you can assign each interface to its respective area with the mask of 0.0.0.255.

The use of shortcuts translates into less specific masks. These shortcuts are effective if the addresses are from neighboring subnets. Otherwise, assign interfaces to OSPF areas the long way from the start.

Chapter Summary

Duplicate addresses and misconfigured masks are a common source of problems with IP and the network layer. Masks can be normal or inverted. Normal masks are used in numerous configuration commands as either required or optional parameters. Regardless of where normal masks are used, they end up defining the length of routing prefixes. Inverted masks are used as wild cards. The use of less specific inverted masks can reduce the number of configuration statements in access control lists. IOS issues some warnings about bad masks, but misconfigurations involving masks are common.

Part III

Troubleshooting Routing Protocols

Chapter 7

Troubleshooting IGRP and EIGRP

IGRP and EIGRP are Cisco's proprietary routing protocols. IGRP is a distance vector protocol developed by Cisco in the 1980s to transcend some of the limitations of RIP. Those limitations include a very small internetwork diameter of 15 hops, a very simple metric based on the hop count, and a frequent update interval. IGRP has a default hop count limit of 100, which can be increased through configuration to 255. It has a sophisticated metric, which by default is a function of the bandwidth and delay characteristics of the transmission media, and can be configured to take into account network load and media reliability. IGRP optimizes the use of network bandwidth by increasing its update interval to three times that of RIP. Finally, IGRP can be configured to place unequal-cost routes to the same destinations into the routing table, which allows for unequal-cost load sharing. However, IGRP retains the limitation of being a classful protocol and as a distance vector protocol it is subject to the split horizon rule.

EIGRP is best described as a hybrid protocol. It has characteristics of both distance-vector and link-state protocols. Trying to pin a label on it is a futile exercise. A characteristic behavior of distance-vector protocols is that they periodically transmit the entire contents of their routing tables to all of their directly connected neighbors. EIGRP optimizes and departs from this classic distance vector behavior in several ways. EIGRP's updates are non-periodic — they occur only when there is a metric or a topology change. EIGRP's updates are partial — only the affected routes are transmitted rather than a full table. And finally, EIGRP's updates are bounded — they are only transmitted to routers that need to know about them rather than to all routers. EIGRP's metric is similar in composition to that of IGRP's, but it has a higher granularity. It is IGRP's metric multiplied by 256. EIGRP, just like IGRP, supports unequal-cost load sharing.

A link-state feature of EIGRP that further differentiates it from IGRP is its reliance on Hello messages to discover its neighbors. EIGRP also maintains a topological database and supports Variable Length Subnet Masking (VLSM). In a significant behavioral contrast to IGRP, EIGRP is a classless protocol.

Classful Routing Protocol Updates

One defining feature of classful routing protocols is that their routing updates do not carry a subnet mask. Another feature is that under certain conditions they perform automatic summarization on major network boundaries. The implication stemming from these simple facts is that if certain addressing and configuration guidelines are not observed with a protocol such as IGRP or RIP, an internetwork deploying a classful protocol will end up with destinations that are unreachable. And in routing, not being able to reach a destination is generally considered very undesirable, unless access to such a destination is deliberately restricted.

As no direct information about a subnet mask is passed between routers in classful routing updates, a classful routing process receiving an update must derive that information from secondary sources. The rule for this determination is simple. A classful router assumes either a default mask for a major network or a mask that's been configured on one of its interfaces. The question is, when does a router assume a default mask versus a mask that's configured on its interfaces?

Assume a configuration as shown in Figure 7.1.

In Figure 7.1, router DC1 has two Ethernet interfaces over which it is a neighbor with routers DC2 and DC3. It also has two point-to-point serial links to routers Boston and Atlanta. The Ethernets are subnets of a major network 172.16.0.0 and the serial links are subnets of 192.168.1.0. When router DC1 advertises its directly connected networks to DC2 and DC3, it will automatically summarize the serial subnets on the Class C boundary and advertise them as a single classful route of 192.168.1.0. Routers DC2 and DC3 receiving this update will assume a default Class C mask for that route. However, DC1 also needs to pass information about 172.16.1.0/24 to DC3 and about 172.16.2.0/24 to DC2. These updates will be handled differently than the update about the subnets of 192.168.1.0.

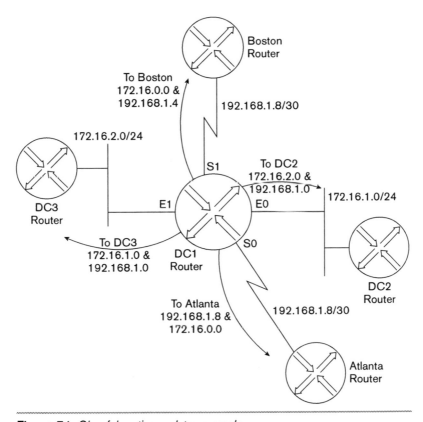

Figure 7.1 *Classful routing updates example*

Because DC2 and DC3 are directly connected neighbors with DC1 over the subnets of 172.16.0.0, the actual subnets — not a summary — will be advertised to them by DC1. DC2 and DC3 will interpret those subnets according the masks configured on their own interfaces. As classful routing protocols do not support VLSM, the mask for 172.16.0.0 on all of the routers throughout the internetwork must be the same. DC2 will interpret the update about 172.16.2.0 as having a /24 mask. Likewise, DC3 will interpret the update about 172.16.1.0 as also having a /24 mask.

Now, when DC1 advertises the directly connected subnets 172.16.1.0 and 172.16.2.0 to Boston and Atlanta, it will recognize that it does not share any subnets of 172.16.0.0 with them. Consequently, it will advertise the two subnets as a single summary route of 172.16.0.0, and both Boston and Atlanta will interpret that advertisement with a default mask for a Class B address.

Let's explore and summarize this example further. DC1 will advertise 172.16.0.0 and 192.168.1.4 to Boston. 172.16.0.0 represents the summary of 172.16.1.0 and 172.16.2.0 because DC1 and Boston do not share any subnets of 172.16.0.0. 192.168.1.4 represents a subnet, because DC1 and Boston share another subnet of 192.168.1.0. DC1 will advertise 172.16.0.0 and 192.168.1.8 to Atlanta for the same reasons. DC1 will advertise 192.168.1.0 and 172.16.1.0 to DC3. And it will advertise 192.168.1.0 and 172.16.2.0 to DC2.

The manner in which the routing updates are passed between classful protocol routers, and the difference in the way that routing tables are examined between these two categories of protocols, are the cause of common misconfigurations which are explored throughout the remainder of this chapter.

Classful versus Classless Routing Behavior

Classful versus classless behavior in routing has to do with the way routing tables are examined when a router attempts to forward a packet to a destination. When classful routing is enabled (a default with Cisco routers) a router will attempt to match the destination on a major network number. A major network number is a Class A, B, or C. If there is no match on the major network, the packet is dropped. If there is a match on the major network, then the next action depends on whether the destination network is directly connected or not, and if it is directly connected, whether it is subnetted or not. This means there are three possibilities for the next action.

First, if there is a match on the major network number that's not directly connected, the packet is forwarded according to the best metric for that destination. A network that's not directly connected cannot appear subnetted in a classful routing table due to the automatic summarization explained in the previous section.

Second, if the destination network is directly connected, and it's not subnetted, a router will deliver the packet to the destination.

Third, if the destination network is directly connected and subnetted, then an attempt is made to match the destination packet to a subnet, according to the subnet mask configured on this router's interfaces. If a match is made on a subnet, then the packet is forwarded onto the appropriate subnet. If there is no match on any subnet, the packet is dropped.

Notice there has been no mention here about using a default route in case a destination cannot be matched either on the major network portion or on the subnet. That's because classful routing does not rely on default routes.

The use of default routes is part of classless routing behavior. When classless routing is enabled via the global configuration command `ip classless`, then the routing behavior changes. When a packet needs to be forwarded to a destination, a router will attempt to match the most specific subnet for that destination in its table. If the match fails, the default route will be used to forward the packet.

In a small isolated internetwork, the use of default routes may not be necessary. But in an internetwork where access to external networks is necessary and you do not want to import all external destinations into your routing tables, the use of default routes is vital.

Classful Misconfigurations in IGRP

The issue of classful routing has several implications. First, if by chance different subnet masks are used with a classful protocol such as IGRP, there is going to be a loss of reachability to some destinations. Second, if subnets of a major network are separated by another major network, there is again a loss of reachability and a potential for misdelivery of packets. Consider the internetwork shown in Figure 7.2.

In Figure 7.2, a major network 172.16.0.0 is fixed-length and subnetted with a /24 mask. A review of the configuration files reveals that IGRP is configured properly. All interfaces on all three routers have been configured with a /24 mask. The major network, 172.16.0.0, has been properly assigned to the IGRP process. The autonomous system numbers match between the IGRP processes on all the routers. Only subnets from the one major network are in use throughout the internetwork. All destinations are reachable from anywhere in the internetwork. This scenario represents the baseline for a discussion of potential problems and misconfigurations with IGRP. See the following initial configurations and the routing tables for this "perfect" scenario.

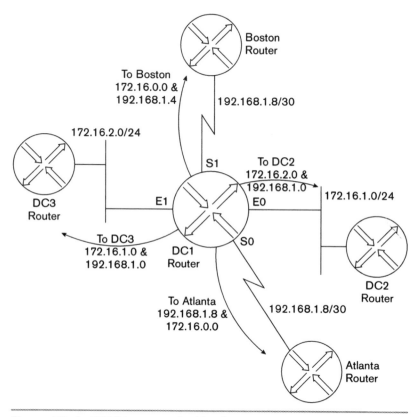

Figure 7.2 *An IGRP internetwork with a fixed-length, subnetted single major network*

Bozeman router fixed-length subnetting, single major network configuration

```
hostname Bozeman
!
interface Ethernet0
 ip address 172.16.150.1 255.255.255.0
```

```
!
interface Serial0
 no ip address
 encapsulation frame-relay
 frame-relay lmi-type cisco
!
interface Serial0.102 point-to-point
 description 64K link to Livingston
 ip address 172.16.101.1 255.255.255.0
 bandwidth 64
 frame-relay interface-dlci 102
!
interface Serial0.103 point-to-point
 description 64K link to Helena
 ip address 172.16.102.1 255.255.255.0
 bandwidth 64
 frame-relay interface-dlci 103
!
router igrp 1
 network 172.16.0.0
!
```

Livingston router fixed-length subnetting, single major network configuration

```
hostname Livingston
!
interface Ethernet0
 ip address 172.16.151.1 255.255.255.0
!
interface Serial0
 no ip address
 encapsulation frame-relay
 frame-relay lmi-type cisco
!
```

```
interface Serial0.101 point-to-point
 description 64K link to Bozeman
 ip address 172.16.101.2 255.255.255.0
 bandwidth 64
 frame-relay interface-dlci 201
!
interface Serial0.103 point-to-point
 description 64K link to Helena
 ip address 172.16.103.1 255.255.255.0
 bandwidth 64
 frame-relay interface-dlci 203
!
router igrp 1
 network 172.16.0.0
!
```

Helena router fixed-length subnetting, single major network configuration

```
hostname Helena
!
interface Ethernet0
 ip address 172.16.152.1 255.255.255.0
!
interface Serial0
 no ip address
 encapsulation frame-relay
 frame-relay lmi-type cisco
!
interface Serial0.101 point-to-point
 description 64K link to Bozeman
 ip address 172.16.102.2 255.255.255.0
 bandwidth 64
 frame-relay interface-dlci 301
!
interface Serial0.102 point-to-point
 description 64K link to Livingston
```

```
ip address 172.16.103.2 255.255.255.0

bandwidth 64

frame-relay interface-dlci 302

!

router igrp 1

network 172.16.0.0

!
```

All of the relevant portions of the configurations pertaining to the proper functioning of IGRP are shown in bold in the preceding configuration files. They include the routing process, network assignment to the routing process, and the IP address assignment to the interfaces. Contents of the routing tables below show entries for directly connected network and routes derived via IGRP. Each subnet in Figure 7.2 is reachable from every router in the internetwork.

```
Bozeman router's table for the fixed-length subnetting, single major network
configuration:Bozeman#sh ip route
Codes: C - connected, S - static, I - IGRP,


Gateway of last resort is not set


     172.16.0.0/24 is subnetted, 6 subnets
I       172.16.152.0 [100/158350] via 172.16.102.2, 00:00:25, Serial0.103
C       172.16.150.0 is directly connected, Ethernet0
I       172.16.151.0 [100/158350] via 172.16.101.2, 00:00:54, Serial0.102
C       172.16.101.0 is directly connected, Serial0.102
C       172.16.102.0 is directly connected, Serial0.103
I       172.16.103.0 [100/160250] via 172.16.102.2, 00:00:25, Serial0.103
                     [100/160250] via 172.16.101.2, 00:00:54, Serial0.102
```

Livingston router's table for the fixed-length subnetting, single major network configuration

```
Livingston#sh ip route
Codes: C - connected, S - static, I - IGRP,
```

```
Gateway of last resort is not set

     172.16.0.0/24 is subnetted, 6 subnets
I       172.16.152.0 [100/158350] via 172.16.103.2, 00:00:39, Serial0.103
I       172.16.150.0 [100/158350] via 172.16.101.1, 00:01:11, Serial0.101
C       172.16.151.0 is directly connected, Ethernet0
C       172.16.101.0 is directly connected, Serial0.101
I       172.16.102.0 [100/160250] via 172.16.103.2, 00:00:39, Serial0.103
                     [100/160250] via 172.16.101.1, 00:01:11, Serial0.101
C       172.16.103.0 is directly connected, Serial0.103
Livingston#
```

Helena router's table for the fixed-length subnetting, single major network configuration

```
Helena#sh ip route
Codes: C - connected, S - static, I - IGRP,

Gateway of last resort is not set

     172.16.0.0/24 is subnetted, 6 subnets
C       172.16.152.0 is directly connected, Ethernet0
I       172.16.150.0 [100/158350] via 172.16.102.1, 00:00:17, Serial0.101
I       172.16.151.0 [100/158350] via 172.16.103.1, 00:00:06, Serial0.102
I       172.16.101.0 [100/160250] via 172.16.103.1, 00:00:06, Serial0.102
                     [100/160250] via 172.16.102.1, 00:00:17, Serial0.101
C       172.16.102.0 is directly connected, Serial0.101
C       172.16.103.0 is directly connected, Serial0.102
```

Now, assume that a network administrator realized that in the internetwork shown in Figure 7.2, a lot of addresses were being wasted on the serial links by using a /24 mask, and instead decides to use VLSM.

Using VLSM with a Classful Protocol

Instead of continuing with the /24 mask on the serial links in the scenario in Figure 7.2, the administrator changes it to /30, not being fully aware that IGRP is a classful protocol and that classful routing is the default on Cisco routers unless modified. The implications of such a change become obvious very quickly. The entries for all of the /24 networks that are not directly connected will disappear from the routing tables on all three routers. This means that from the Helena router, it will no longer be possible to reach the Bozeman Ethernet, 172.16.150.0, or the Livingston Ethernet, 172.16.151.0. Likewise, the Livingston and Helena Ethernets will not be reachable from the Bozeman router, nor will the Bozeman and Helena Ethernets be reachable from the Livingston router.

If the changes to the subnet masks are done dynamically, there will be a period of time when the disappearing table entries will remain in the table with the "possibly down" message until the IGRP flush timer of 630 seconds expires. Following the expiration of the flush timer, those entries will permanently disappear from the routing tables. The following traces reflect the configuration changes and corresponding routing tables on all three routers after IGRP has converged.

Bozeman router VLSM subnetting, single major network configuration

```
hostname Bozeman
!
interface Ethernet0
 ip address 172.16.150.1 255.255.255.0
!
interface Serial0
 no ip address
 encapsulation frame-relay
 frame-relay lmi-type cisco
!
interface Serial0.102 point-to-point
 description 64K link to Livingston
```

```
  ip address 172.16.101.1 255.255.255.252      Note mask change

  bandwidth 64

  frame-relay interface-dlci 102

 !

interface Serial0.103 point-to-point

  description 64K link to Helena

  ip address 172.16.102.1 255.255.255.252      Note mask change

  bandwidth 64

  frame-relay interface-dlci 103

 !

router igrp 1

  network 172.16.0.0

 !
```

Livingston router VLSM subnetting, single major network configuration

```
hostname Livingston

 !

interface Ethernet0

  ip address 172.16.151.1 255.255.255.0

 !

interface Serial0

  no ip address

  encapsulation frame-relay

  frame-relay lmi-type cisco

 !

interface Serial0.101 point-to-point

  description 64K link to Bozeman

  ip address 172.16.101.2 255.255.255.252   Note mask change

  bandwidth 64

  frame-relay interface-dlci 201

 !

interface Serial0.103 point-to-point

  description 64K link to Helena
```

```
ip address 172.16.103.1 255.255.255.252  Note mask change

bandwidth 64

frame-relay interface-dlci 203

!

router igrp 1

 network 172.16.0.0
```

Helena router VLSM subnetting, single major network configuration

```
hostname Helena

!

interface Ethernet0

 ip address 172.16.152.1 255.255.255.0

!

interface Serial0

 no ip address

 encapsulation frame-relay

 frame-relay lmi-type cisco

!

interface Serial0.101 point-to-point

 description 64K link to Bozeman

 ip address 172.16.102.2 255.255.255.252  Note mask change

 bandwidth 64

 frame-relay interface-dlci 301

!

interface Serial0.102 point-to-point

 description 64K link to Livingston

 ip address 172.16.103.2 255.255.255.252  Note mask change

 bandwidth 64

 frame-relay interface-dlci 302

!

router igrp 1

 network 172.16.0.0
```

Compare the routing tables from the original configuration (fixed-length subnetting, single major network) for the internetwork in Figure 7.2 with the routing tables that follow. There is a warning sign here for anyone troubleshooting a classful routing protocol. In the routing tables from the "perfect configuration," the network 172.16.0.0 was announced as follows: `172.16.0.0/24 is subnetted, 6 subnets`. In the routing tables that follow, after the internetwork has been variably subnetted, the 172.16.0.0 network is announced as: `172.16.0.0/16 is variably subnetted, 4 subnets, 2 masks`. Whenever you see a major network that is announced as being *variably subnetted*, and routing is taking place with a classful routing protocol, it should be a sign that some destinations are not going to be reachable. What makes troubleshooting tricky in this case is that you may not necessarily know which ones are the unreachable destinations.

Bozeman router's table following reconfiguration of the internetwork with VLSM:

```
Bozeman#sh ip route

Codes: C - connected, S - static, I - IGRP,

Gateway of last resort is not set

     172.16.0.0/16 is variably subnetted, 4 subnets, 2 masks
C       172.16.150.0/24 is directly connected, Ethernet0
C       172.16.101.0/30 is directly connected, Serial0.102
C       172.16.102.0/30 is directly connected, Serial0.103
I       172.16.103.0/30 [100/160250] via 172.16.102.2, 00:00:00, Serial0.103
                        [100/160250] via 172.16.101.2, 00:00:32, Serial0.102
```

Livingston router's table following reconfiguration of the internetwork with VLSM

```
Livingston#sh ip route

Codes: C - connected, S - static, I - IGRP,

Gateway of last resort is not set

     172.16.0.0/16 is variably subnetted, 4 subnets, 2 masks
C       172.16.151.0/24 is directly connected, Ethernet0
```

```
C       172.16.101.0/30 is directly connected, Serial0.101

I       172.16.102.0/30 [100/160250] via 172.16.101.1, 00:00:25, Serial0.101

C       172.16.103.0/30 is directly connected, Serial0.103
```

Helena router's table following reconfiguration of the internetwork with VLSM

```
Helena#sh ip route

Codes: C - connected, S - static, I - IGRP

Gateway of last resort is not set

     172.16.0.0/16 is variably subnetted, 4 subnets, 2 masks
C       172.16.152.0/24 is directly connected, Ethernet0

I       172.16.101.0/30 [100/160250] via 172.16.102.1, 00:00:40, Serial0.101

C       172.16.102.0/30 is directly connected, Serial0.101

C       172.16.103.0/30 is directly connected, Serial0.102
```

If the "perfect configuration" (fixed-length subnetting, single major network) was not there to act as a foundation for this misconfiguration of VLSM being used with a classful protocol, it might not even be obvious that there is a problem to begin with. After all, you have to know that a network is supposed to be in a routing table before you can detect that it's missing.

Major Network Segmentation

Consider a scenario as depicted in Figure 7.3. It is similar to the one depicted in Figure 7.2 except that there are more LANs at each location and a different major network separates all three locations. The WAN cloud subnets are derived from a Class C address subnetted with a /30 and the LAN subnets are derived from a Class B address subnetted with a /24.

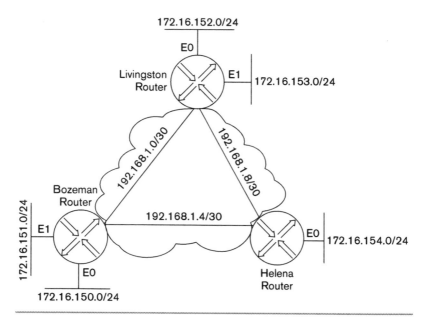

Figure 7.3 *IGRP internetwork with multiple major networks*

The configuration for the scenario in Figure 7.3 follows next.

Bozeman router configuration with multiple major networks

```
hostname Bozeman
!
ip subnet-zero
!
interface Ethernet0
 ip address 172.16.150.1 255.255.255.0
 no shut
!
interface Ethernet1
 ip address 172.16.151.1 255.255.255.0
 no shut
!
interface Serial0
 no ip address
```

```
  encapsulation frame-relay

  frame-relay lmi-type cisco

  no shut

!

interface Serial0.102 point-to-point

  description 64K link to Livingston

  ip address 192.168.1.1 255.255.255.252

  bandwidth 64

  frame-relay interface-dlci 102

!

interface Serial0.103 point-to-point

  description 64K link to Helena

  ip address 192.168.1.5 255.255.255.252

  bandwidth 64

  frame-relay interface-dlci 103

!

router igrp 1

  network 172.16.0.0

  network 192.168.1.0

!
```

Livingston router configuration with multiple major networks

```
!

hostname Livingston

!

ip subnet-zero

!

interface Ethernet0

  ip address 172.16.152.1 255.255.255.0

  no shut

!

interface Ethernet1

  ip address 172.16.153.1 255.255.255.0

  no shut
```

```
!
interface Serial0
 no ip address
 encapsulation frame-relay
 frame-relay lmi-type cisco
 no shut
!
interface Serial0.101 point-to-point
 description 64K link to Bozeman
 ip address 192.168.1.2 255.255.255.252
 bandwidth 64
 frame-relay interface-dlci 201
!
interface Serial0.103 point-to-point
 description 64K link to Helena
 ip address 192.168.1.9 255.255.255.252
 bandwidth 64
 frame-relay interface-dlci 203
!
router igrp 1
 network 172.16.0.0
 network 192.168.1.0
!
```

Helena router configuration with multiple major networks

```
hostname Helena
!
ip subnet-zero
!
interface Ethernet0
 ip address 172.16.154.1 255.255.255.0
 no shut
!
interface Serial0
```

```
no ip address

encapsulation frame-relay

frame-relay lmi-type cisco

no shut

!

interface Serial0.101 point-to-point

description 64K link to Bozeman

ip address 192.168.1.6 255.255.255.252

bandwidth 64

frame-relay interface-dlci 301

!

interface Serial0.102 point-to-point

description 64K link to Livingston

ip address 192.168.1.10 255.255.255.252

bandwidth 64

frame-relay interface-dlci 302

!

router igrp 1

 network 172.16.0.0

 network 192.168.1.0

!
```

Given the above configuration, you might reasonably expect that there would be reachability throughout the internetwork. Autonomous system numbers match between all of the routers, networks are properly assigned to the routing process, and no VLSM subnetting is taking place. However, an examination of the routing tables reveals that something is wrong.

Bozeman router's table for IGRP reconfiguration with multiple major networks

```
Bozeman#sh ip route

Codes: C - connected, S - static, I - IGRP,

Gateway of last resort is not set

     172.16.0.0/24 is subnetted, 2 subnets
```

```
C       172.16.150.0 is directly connected, Ethernet0
C       172.16.151.0 is directly connected, Ethernet1
     192.168.1.0/30 is subnetted, 3 subnets
I       192.168.1.8 [100/160250] via 192.168.1.6, 00:00:13, Serial0.103
                    [100/160250] via 192.168.1.2, 00:01:14, Serial0.102
C       192.168.1.0 is directly connected, Serial0.102
C       192.168.1.4 is directly connected, Serial0.103
```

Livingston router's table for IGRP reconfiguration with multiple major networks

```
Livingston#sh ip route
Codes: C - connected, S - static, I - IGRP

Gateway of last resort is not set

172.16.0.0/24 is subnetted, 2 subnets
C       172.16.152.0 is directly connected, Ethernet0
C       172.16.153.0 is directly connected, Ethernet1
     192.168.1.0/30 is subnetted, 3 subnets
C       192.168.1.8 is directly connected, Serial0.103
C       192.168.1.0 is directly connected, Serial0.101
I       192.168.1.4 [100/160250] via 192.168.1.10, 00:00:32, Serial0.103
                    [100/160250] via 192.168.1.1, 00:00:39, Serial0.101
```

Helena router's table for IGRP reconfiguration with multiple major networks

```
Helena#sh ip route
Codes: C - connected, S - static, I - IGRP,

Gateway of last resort is not set

172.16.0.0/24 is subnetted, 1 subnets
C       172.16.154.0 is directly connected, Ethernet0
     192.168.1.0/30 is subnetted, 3 subnets
```

```
C      192.168.1.8 is directly connected, Serial0.102
I      192.168.1.0 [100/160250] via 192.168.1.5, 00:00:54, Serial0.101
               [100/160250] via 192.168.1.9, 00:00:18, Serial0.102
C      192.168.1.4 is directly connected, Serial0.101
```

The routing tables on each router do not show the subnets derived from the 172.16.0.0 major network, except for the ones directly connected to each router. This is the result of IGRP's performing summarization on major network boundaries. Although IGRP routers advertise three different types of routes—local, system, and external—and thereby indirectly convey minimal subnet masking information, it's not sufficient to prevent the problem of an incomplete routing table for the scenario depicted in Figure 7.3.

IGRP local routes are defined as subnets of a major network that are advertised to a neighbor sharing at least one other subnet of the same major network with the advertising router. In the example in Figure 7.3, the Bozeman router is directly connected to subnets 192.168.1.0/30 and 192.168.1.4/30. The Bozeman router will advertise 192.168.1.0/30 as a local route to Helena as both Bozeman and Helena are neighbors over 192.168.1.4/30. The Bozeman router will advertise 192.168.1.4 /30 to Livingston as both Bozeman and Livingston are neighbors over 192.168.1.0/30. Consequently, when local routes are advertised, it is understood that their subnet mask will be the same as that of another directly connected subnet of the advertised major network. The local route represents IGRP's implementation of a mechanism to advertise a subnet by a classful protocol, a concept that was explained earlier in the "Classful Routing Protocol Updates" section.

The system route in IGRP is defined as a major network that's advertised to a neighbor where the advertising router and the neighbor do not share a subnet of the advertised major network. In Figure 7.3, the Bozeman router will advertise the subnets 172.16.150.0 and 172.16.151.0 as a single system route, 172.16.0.0/16, to both of its neighbors. Bozeman is a neighbor to Livingston and Helena but only on subnets of 192.168.1.0. Even though Livingston and Helena are directly connected to subnets of 172.16.0.0, they do not share subnets of 172.16.0.0 with the Bozeman router.

Both Livingston and Helena routers will receive an update from the Bozeman router about 172.16.0.0, but this update will be with the default mask for a Class B address. Consequently, Livingston and Helena will ignore the Bozeman update about 172.16.0.0 as they are both directly connected to other subnets of 172.16.0.0 with a /24 mask. The longer mask wins. With no default routes installed and the classful routing behavior not taking advantage of the default routes, the net result is a loss of reachability in the scenario depicted in Figure 7.3. The preceding routing tables reflect this loss of reachability between the locations. The system route in IGRP is the implementation of the concept of the summary route that, again, was discussed earlier in the "Classful Routing Protocol Updates" section.

The bottom line is this; with classful routing protocols, avoid separating subnets of a major network with other major networks. Otherwise, you will be faced with the consequences of not being able to reach some destinations.

Here are two ground rules for configuring internetworks with classful routing protocols. First, use a single major network with fixed-length subnetting or multiple major networks without subnetting. Either one will work. Second, don't use a classful protocol — use a classless routing protocol such as OSPF or EIGRP. With EIGRP, however, you will have to watch out for one of its features known as auto summary. Even though EIGRP is a classless routing protocol and it supports VLSM, if you don't disable the auto summary feature you may end up with the same kind of mess on your hands as depicted in the preceding scenario.

Auto Summary Implications in EIGRP

EIGRP is a classless protocol. It might seem that by simply changing from IGRP to EIGRP in the Figure 7.3 scenario, the problem of not being able to reach certain networks would disappear. Think again. The configuration from the scenario has been changed so that instead of IGRP, EIGRP is now running on all three routers. Take a look at the new configuration and the resulting routing tables.

Bozeman router initial EIGRP configuration with multiple major networks

```
hostname Bozeman
!
ip subnet-zero
!
interface Ethernet0
 ip address 172.16.150.1 255.255.255.0
 no shut
!
interface Ethernet1
 ip address 172.16.151.1 255.255.255.0
 no shut
!
interface Serial0
 no ip address
 encapsulation frame-relay
 frame-relay lmi-type cisco
 no shut
!
interface Serial0.102 point-to-point
 description 64K link to Livingston
 ip address 192.168.1.1 255.255.255.252
 bandwidth 64
 frame-relay interface-dlci 102
!
interface Serial0.103 point-to-point
 description 64K link to Helena
 ip address 192.168.1.5 255.255.255.252
 bandwidth 64
 frame-relay interface-dlci 103
!
router eigrp 7              Note change from IGRP to EIGRP
```

```
network 172.16.0.0

network 192.168.1.0
```

Livingston router initial EIGRP configuration with multiple major networks

```
hostname Livingston
!
enable password cisco
!
ip subnet-zero
!
interface Ethernet0
 ip address 172.16.152.1 255.255.255.0
 no shut
!
interface Ethernet1
 ip address 172.16.153.1 255.255.255.0
 no shut
!
interface Serial0
 no ip address
 encapsulation frame-relay
 frame-relay lmi-type cisco
 no shut
!
interface Serial0.101 point-to-point
 description 64K link to Bozeman
 ip address 192.168.1.2 255.255.255.252
 bandwidth 64
 frame-relay interface-dlci 201
!
interface Serial0.103 point-to-point
 description 64K link to Helena
 ip address 192.168.1.9 255.255.255.252
 bandwidth 64
```

```
frame-relay interface-dlci 203
!
interface Serial1
 shut
!
 router eigrp 7                      Note change from IGRP to EIGRP
 network 172.16.0.0
 network 192.168.1.0
```

Helena router initial EIGRP configuration with multiple major networks

```
hostname Helena
!
ip subnet-zero
!
interface Ethernet0
 ip address 172.16.154.1 255.255.255.0
 no shut
!
interface Serial0
 no ip address
 encapsulation frame-relay
 frame-relay lmi-type cisco
 no shut
!
 interface Serial0.101 point-to-point
 description 64K link to Bozeman
 ip address 192.168.1.6 255.255.255.252
 bandwidth 64
 frame-relay interface-dlci 301
!
interface Serial0.102 point-to-point
 description 64K link to Livingston
 ip address 192.168.1.10 255.255.255.252
 bandwidth 64
```

```
frame-relay interface-dlci 302
!
interface Serial1
 shut
!
router eigrp 7                    Note change from IGRP to EIGRP
 network 172.16.0.0
 network 192.168.1.0
```

The routing tables that result from the preceding EIGRP configuration do not have any EIGRP entries for subnets of 172.16.0.0. The only subnets of 172.16.0.0 that appear in any of the routing tables are the ones that are directly connected. This is identical to what was demonstrated with IGRP in the "Major network segmentation" section earlier in this chapter.

Bozeman router's table for EIGRP configuration with multiple major networks

```
Bozeman#sh ip route
Codes: C - connected, S - static, I - IGRP, R - RIP, M - mobile, B - BGP
       D - EIGRP,

Gateway of last resort is not set

     172.16.0.0/16 is variably subnetted, 3 subnets, 2 masks
C       172.16.150.0/24 is directly connected, Ethernet0
C       172.16.151.0/24 is directly connected, Ethernet1
D       172.16.0.0/16 is a summary, 00:11:45, Null0
     192.168.1.0/24 is variably subnetted, 4 subnets, 2 masks
D       192.168.1.8/30 [90/41024000] via 192.168.1.2, 00:11:45, Serial0.102
                       [90/41024000] via 192.168.1.6, 00:11:45, Serial0.103
D       192.168.1.0/24 is a summary, 00:13:42, Null0
C       192.168.1.0/30 is directly connected, Serial0.102
C       192.168.1.4/30 is directly connected, Serial0.103
```

Note that Livingston subnets (172.16.152.0 and 172.16.153.0) and the Helena subnet 172.16.154.0 are all missing from Bozeman's routing table.

Livingston router's table for EIGRP configuration with multiple major networks

```
Livingston#sh ip route
Codes: C - connected, S - static, I - IGRP, R - RIP, M - mobile, B - BGP
       D - EIGRP,


Gateway of last resort is not set


     172.16.0.0/16 is variably subnetted, 3 subnets, 2 masks
C       172.16.152.0/24 is directly connected, Ethernet0
C       172.16.153.0/24 is directly connected, Ethernet1
D       172.16.0.0/16 is a summary, 00:12:06, Null0
     192.168.1.0/24 is variably subnetted, 4 subnets, 2 masks
C       192.168.1.8/30 is directly connected, Serial0.103
D       192.168.1.0/24 is a summary, 00:13:06, Null0
C       192.168.1.0/30 is directly connected, Serial0.101
D       192.168.1.4/30 [90/41024000] via 192.168.1.1, 00:12:06, Serial0.101
                       [90/41024000] via 192.168.1.10, 00:12:06, Serial0.103
```

Note that Bozeman subnets (172.16.150.0 and 172.16.151.0) and the Helena subnet (172.16.154.0) are missing from Livingston's routing table.

Helena router's table for EIGRP configuration with multiple major networks

```
Helena#sh ip route
Codes: C - connected, S - static, I - IGRP, R - RIP, M - mobile, B - BGP
       D - EIGRP,


Gateway of last resort is not set


     172.16.0.0/16 is variably subnetted, 2 subnets, 2 masks
C       172.16.154.0/24 is directly connected, Ethernet0
D       172.16.0.0/16 is a summary, 00:12:20, Null0
     192.168.1.0/24 is variably subnetted, 4 subnets, 2 masks
C       192.168.1.8/30 is directly connected, Serial0.102
D       192.168.1.0/30 [90/41024000] via 192.168.1.9, 00:12:20, Serial0.102
```

```
                        [90/41024000] via 192.168.1.5, 00:12:20, Serial0.101
D       192.168.1.0/24 is a summary, 00:12:25, Null0
C       192.168.1.4/30 is directly connected, Serial0.101
```

Note that Bozeman subnets (172.16.150.0 and 172.16.151.0) and the Livingston subnets (172.16.152.0 and 172.16.153.0) are missing from Helena's routing table.

The problem here is that EIGRP is going to summarize the subnets of a major network at the major network boundary. Effectively, when EIGRP does automatic summarization and routers are separated by another major network, from the point of view of the routing tables there isn't any difference between IGRP and EIGRP. Adding a no auto-summary configuration statement on each router in the EIGRP routing process will change the behavior of EIGRP so that the problem of missing subnets disappears. The configuration files with the no auto-summary statement are not shown here. However, the reconfiguration has resulted in much fuller routing tables, which are displayed next.

Bozeman router's table for EIGRP reconfiguration with no auto-summary

```
Bozeman#sh ip route
Codes: C - connected, S - static, I - IGRP, R - RIP, M - mobile, B - BGP
       D - EIGRP,


Gateway of last resort is not set


     172.16.0.0/24 is subnetted, 5 subnets
D       172.16.152.0 [90/40537600] via 192.168.1.2, 00:00:41, Serial0.102
D       172.16.153.0 [90/40537600] via 192.168.1.2, 00:00:41, Serial0.102
D       172.16.154.0 [90/40537600] via 192.168.1.6, 00:00:41, Serial0.103
C       172.16.150.0 is directly connected, Ethernet0
C       172.16.151.0 is directly connected, Ethernet1
     192.168.1.0/30 is subnetted, 3 subnets
D       192.168.1.8 [90/41024000] via 192.168.1.2, 00:00:41, Serial0.102
                    [90/41024000] via 192.168.1.6, 00:00:41, Serial0.103
C       192.168.1.0 is directly connected, Serial0.102
C       192.168.1.4 is directly connected, Serial0.103
```

Note the presence of the three subnets that were missing without the no
auto-summary in the Bozeman router.

Livingston router's table for EIGRP reconfiguration with no auto-summary

```
Livingston#sh ip route
Codes: C - connected, S - static, I - IGRP, R - RIP, M - mobile, B - BGP
       D - EIGRP,


Gateway of last resort is not set
     172.16.0.0/24 is subnetted, 5 subnets
C       172.16.152.0 is directly connected, Ethernet0
C       172.16.153.0 is directly connected, Ethernet1
D       172.16.154.0 [90/40537600] via 192.168.1.10, 00:00:58, Serial0.103
D       172.16.150.0 [90/40537600] via 192.168.1.1, 00:00:59, Serial0.101
D       172.16.151.0 [90/40537600] via 192.168.1.1, 00:00:59, Serial0.101
     192.168.1.0/30 is subnetted, 3 subnets
C       192.168.1.8 is directly connected, Serial0.103
C       192.168.1.0 is directly connected, Serial0.101
D       192.168.1.4 [90/41024000] via 192.168.1.1, 00:01:01, Serial0.101
                    [90/41024000] via 192.168.1.10, 00:01:01, Serial0.103
```

Note the presence of the three subnets that were missing without the no
auto-summary in the Livingston router.

Helena router's table for EIGRP reconfiguration with no auto-summary

```
Helena#sh ip route
Codes: C - connected, S - static, I - IGRP, R - RIP, M - mobile, B - BGP
       D - EIGRP,


Gateway of last resort is not set


     172.16.0.0/24 is subnetted, 5 subnets
D       172.16.152.0 [90/40537600] via 192.168.1.9, 00:01:18, Serial0.102
D       172.16.153.0 [90/40537600] via 192.168.1.9, 00:01:18, Serial0.102
C       172.16.154.0 is directly connected, Ethernet0
```

```
D       172.16.150.0 [90/40537600] via 192.168.1.5, 00:01:18, Serial0.101
D       172.16.151.0 [90/40537600] via 192.168.1.5, 00:01:18, Serial0.101
     192.168.1.0/30 is subnetted, 3 subnets
C       192.168.1.8 is directly connected, Serial0.102
D       192.168.1.0 [90/41024000] via 192.168.1.9, 00:01:18, Serial0.102
                    [90/41024000] via 192.168.1.5, 00:01:18, Serial0.101
C       192.168.1.4 is directly connected, Serial0.101
```

Note the presence of the four subnets that were missing without the no auto-summary in the Helena router.

There is another caveat here that's worth mentioning. In the EIGRP configurations corresponding to the scenario in Figure 7.3, the ip subnet-zero global command has been used on all the routers. You may have noticed that all of the serial subnets are derived from 192.168.1.0. The zero subnet in the example is 192.168.1.0/30 with the valid interface addresses of 192.168.1.1 and 192.168.1.2 assigned to s0.102 on Bozeman and s0.101 on Livingston, respectively.

If you attempt to assign 192.168.1.1 with a mask of 255.255.255.252 to the s0.102 subinterface on the Bozeman router without the ip subnet-zero command, IOS will notify you that there is a problem by displaying a message "Bad mask /30 for 192.168.1.1". It may not be obvious from this message, however, that you have not used the ip subnet-zero global command.

Missing EIGRP Neighbors

EIGRP is a complex protocol with many capabilities that are explored and discussed in other books. (See Appendix A.) It was mentioned earlier in the chapter that EIGRP is somewhat of a hybrid protocol. It has distance-vector characteristics but it also acts like a link-state protocol because it discovers neighbors dynamically and maintains a topological database. One of the more useful tools in troubleshooting link-state protocols is checking to see if a router has acquired all of its neighbors. With EIGRP, the command for displaying neighbors is show ip eigrp neighbors.

If you expect an EIGRP router to have neighbors but none show up, there could be many reasons for it, for example, an interface on a neighbor could be passive or there could be a mismatch in the EIGRP timers such as the Hello interval and the Hold time. There is a possibility of authentication mismatch as well as access control lists on a neighboring router blocking EIGRP updates from being sent out.

Consider an EIGRP internetwork as shown in Figure 7.4.

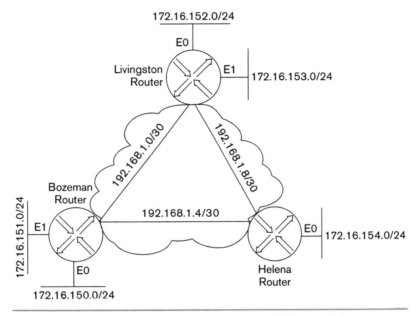

Figure 7.4 *EIGRP internetwork used for missing neighbor analysis*

The configuration files for the three routers in Figure 7.4 are shown next. Here, all of the potential misconfiguration issues addressed up to this point have been taken into account. Autonomous system numbers match among all of the routers. IP addresses are assigned correctly to interfaces. IP subnet-zero is enabled. And the default automatic summarization has been negated with the no auto-summary command. All of the configuration statements relevant to the proper functioning of EIGRP are bold-faced.

Bozeman router initial EIGRP configuration

```
hostname Bozeman
!
```

```
ip subnet-zero
!
interface Ethernet0
 ip address 172.16.150.1 255.255.255.0
 no shut
!
interface Ethernet1
 ip address 172.16.151.1 255.255.255.0
 no shut
!
interface Serial0
 no ip address
 encapsulation frame-relay
 frame-relay lmi-type cisco
 no shut
!
interface Serial0.102 point-to-point
 description 64K link to Livingston
 ip address 192.168.1.1 255.255.255.252
 bandwidth 64
 frame-relay interface-dlci 102
!
interface Serial0.103 point-to-point
 description 64K link to Helena
 ip address 192.168.1.5 255.255.255.252
 bandwidth 64
 frame-relay interface-dlci 103
!
router eigrp 7
 network 172.16.0.0
 network 192.168.1.0
 no auto-summary
```

Livingston router initial EIGRP configuration

```
hostname Livingston
!
enable password cisco
!
ip subnet-zero
!
interface Ethernet0
 ip address 172.16.152.1 255.255.255.0
 no shut
!
interface Ethernet1
 ip address 172.16.153.1 255.255.255.0
 no shut
!
interface Serial0
 no ip address
 encapsulation frame-relay
 frame-relay lmi-type cisco
 no shut
!
interface Serial0.101 point-to-point
 description 64K link to Bozeman
 ip address 192.168.1.2 255.255.255.252
 bandwidth 64
 frame-relay interface-dlci 201
!
interface Serial0.103 point-to-point
 description 64K link to Helena
 ip address 192.168.1.9 255.255.255.252
 bandwidth 64
 frame-relay interface-dlci 203
!
```

```
interface Serial1
 shut
!
router eigrp 7
 network 172.16.0.0
 network 192.168.1.0
 no auto-summary
```

Helena router initial EIGRP configuration

```
hostname Helena
!
ip subnet-zero
!
interface Ethernet0
 ip address 172.16.154.1 255.255.255.0
 no shut
!
interface Serial0
 no ip address
 encapsulation frame-relay
 frame-relay lmi-type cisco
 no shut
!
 interface Serial0.101 point-to-point
 description 64K link to Bozeman
 ip address 192.168.1.6 255.255.255.252
 bandwidth 64
 frame-relay interface-dlci 301
!
interface Serial0.102 point-to-point
 description 64K link to Livingston
 ip address 192.168.1.10 255.255.255.252
 bandwidth 64
 frame-relay interface-dlci 302
```

```
!
interface Serial1
 shut
!
router eigrp 7
 network 172.16.0.0
 network 192.168.1.0
 no auto-summary
```

The Bozeman router from Figure 7.4 has two neighbors as shown in the neighbor display.

```
Bozeman#sh ip eigrp neighbors
IP-EIGRP neighbors for process 7
H   Address              Interface    Hold Uptime    SRTT   RTO  Q  Seq
                                      (sec)          (ms)        Cnt Num
0   192.168.1.2          Se0.102       11 00:52:34   61    2280  0  63
1   192.168.1.6          Se0.103       12 01:08:33   42    2280  0  65
```

The show ip eigrp neighbors command displays nine columns. The H column shows the order in which neighbors were acquired. The Address column shows the IP addresses of neighbors. The Interface column displays the interfaces on the local router (router executing the show command) over which it is a neighbor with other EIGRP routers. The Hold column represents the EIGRP hold time, the amount of time an EIGRP router can be a neighbor without receiving a Hello packet from its neighbor. If existing EIGRP neighbors of a local router stop transmitting Hello packets, they will disappear from the local router's neighbor display after the Hold time has expired. The default Hold time is 15 seconds. The Uptime shows how long a local router has been a neighbor with other routers.

SRTT stands for Smooth Round Trip Time, the amount of time in milliseconds for an EIGRP packet to be transmitted to a neighbor and for the neighbor to acknowledge receipt of that packet. The retransmission time-out (RTO) is measured in milliseconds and represents the amount of time that a local router will wait before sending out a packet to a neighbor from its retransmission queue. The Queue count (Q Cnt) represents the number of various EIGRP packets waiting to be sent. The sequence number (Seq Num) has to do with sequenced exchanges of EIGRP packets between routers and is the last sequence number of an EIGRP packet received from a neighbor.

The routing table on the Bozeman router shows routes for all destinations in Figure 7.4.

Bozeman router's table for initial EIGRP used with missing neighbor analysis

```
Bozeman#sh ip route
Codes: C - connected, S - static, I - IGRP, R - RIP, M - mobile, B - BGP
       D - EIGRP,


Gateway of last resort is not set

     172.16.0.0/24 is subnetted, 5 subnets
D       172.16.152.0 [90/40537600] via 192.168.1.2, 00:52:56, Serial0.102
D       172.16.153.0 [90/40537600] via 192.168.1.2, 00:03:20, Serial0.102
D       172.16.154.0 [90/40537600] via 192.168.1.6, 00:52:56, Serial0.103
C       172.16.150.0 is directly connected, Ethernet0
C       172.16.151.0 is directly connected, Ethernet1
     192.168.1.0/30 is subnetted, 3 subnets
D       192.168.1.8 [90/41024000] via 192.168.1.6, 00:52:56, Serial0.103
                    [90/41024000] via 192.168.1.2, 00:52:56, Serial0.102
C       192.168.1.0 is directly connected, Serial0.102
C       192.168.1.4 is directly connected, Serial0.103
Bozeman#
```

Everything seems to be in order, as it should with the configuration files, the EIGRP neighbor display, and the routing tables. Now, let's consider some of the things that could go wrong.

Passive Interfaces

Suppose that the Livingston and Helena router configurations have been modified with a `passive interface` command on some of their subinterfaces. The Bozeman configuration stays the same, but observe what effect the other configuration changes will have on the Bozeman router.

Livingston EIGRP configuration modified to include a passive interface

```
hostname Livingston
!
enable password cisco
!
ip subnet-zero
!
interface Ethernet0
 ip address 172.16.152.1 255.255.255.0
 no shut
!
interface Ethernet1
 ip address 172.16.153.1 255.255.255.0
 no shut
!
interface Serial0
 no ip address
 encapsulation frame-relay
 frame-relay lmi-type cisco
 no shut
!
interface Serial0.101 point-to-point
 description 64K link to Bozeman
 ip address 192.168.1.2 255.255.255.252
 bandwidth 64
 frame-relay interface-dlci 201
!
interface Serial0.103 point-to-point
 description 64K link to Helena
 ip address 192.168.1.9 255.255.255.252
```

```
bandwidth 64

frame-relay interface-dlci 203

!

interface Serial1

 shut

!

router eigrp 7

passive-interface Serial0.101          Notice modification

network 172.16.0.0

network 192.168.1.0

no auto-summary
```

Helena EIGRP configuration modified to include a passive interface

```
hostname Helena

!

ip subnet-zero

!

interface Ethernet0

 ip address 172.16.154.1 255.255.255.0

 no shut

!

interface Serial0

 no ip address

 encapsulation frame-relay

 frame-relay lmi-type cisco

 no shut

!

interface Serial0.101 point-to-point

description 64K link to Bozeman

ip address 192.168.1.6 255.255.255.252

bandwidth 64

frame-relay interface-dlci 301

!

interface Serial0.102 point-to-point
```

```
description 64K link to Livingston

ip address 192.168.1.10 255.255.255.252

bandwidth 64

frame-relay interface-dlci 302

!

interface Serial1

 shut

!

router eigrp 7

 passive-interface Serial0.101              Notice modification

 network 172.16.0.0

 network 192.168.1.0

 no auto-summary
```

The passive interface modifications took place on the Livingston and Helena routers (the Bozeman router configuration has not been touched), but the effect of the modification is most visible on the Bozeman router. The show ip eigrp neighbors command executed on the Bozeman router shows that the Bozeman router has no EIGRP neighbors.

```
Bozeman#sh ip eigrp neighbors
IP-EIGRP neighbors for process 7
```

The two EIGRP neighbors that Bozeman had before the passive interface was implemented disappeared very quickly. The routing tables on the Bozeman router now show only the directly connected networks.

Bozeman router's table for EIGRP reconfiguration with passive interfaces on Livingston & Helena

```
Bozeman#sh ip route
Codes: C - connected, S - static, I - IGRP, R - RIP, M - mobile, B - BGP
       D - EIGRP,


Gateway of last resort is not set


     172.16.0.0/24 is subnetted, 2 subnets
```

```
C       172.16.150.0 is directly connected, Ethernet0
C       172.16.151.0 is directly connected, Ethernet1
     192.168.1.0/30 is subnetted, 2 subnets
C       192.168.1.0 is directly connected, Serial0.102
C       192.168.1.4 is directly connected, Serial0.103
```

Through the use of a `passive-interface` command, EIGRP routing over a given interface can be disabled. You must consider the impact of this rather powerful command and use it judiciously. In larger internetworks, downstream routers may have no idea what's happening when a `passive-interface` command has been executed on an upstream router's interface.

One result of the use of the `passive-interface` command may be a total isolation as has been demonstrated in the case of a Bozeman router in the scenario depicted in Figure 7.4. Another impact may be a redirection of traffic across a slower link. In the event that there are multiple EIGRP routes to a destination, and the interface associated with a faster path has been effectively shut down through the use of the `passive-interface` command, the slower link may become overloaded with traffic.

It's almost like shutting down an interface with a `shutdown` command or having an interface fail, except that it is more difficult to troubleshoot. When an interface has been shut down administratively or it has failed, it can't be reached at all. Assume for a moment that a `shutdown` command has been executed on the s0.101 subinterfaces on the Livingston and Helena routers. The directly connected subnets of 192.168.1.0/30 and 192.168.1.4/30 would disappear from the Bozeman router's routing tables, and it would be quite clear what's happening. You would not be able to ping from the Bozeman router to the s0.101 subinterfaces on the Helena and Livingston routers. But with the `passive-interface` command the results are more subtle. You can still ping the s0.101 subinterfaces on the Helen and Livingston routers. But no routing is taking place between Bozeman and the other two routers. And you aren't easily able to figure out what's causing the condition on the Bozeman router without examining the configurations of the other routers. There are other misconfigurations that can produce similar results on the Bozeman router.

Mismatch in the EIGRP Timers

The EIGRP timers are best left alone unless you are really concerned about the frequency with which the EIGRP Hello messages are generated. The default Hello interval is five seconds for broadcast networks or LANs, point-to-point serial links, and point-to-point subinterfaces. For physical interfaces connecting into "WAN clouds" (Frame Relay and ATM), and for multipoint subinterfaces, the Hello interval is increased to 60 seconds. The Hold time is three times the Hello interval, or 15 and 180 seconds, respectively.

If an EIGRP router fails to receive a Hello message from a neighbor within a Hold time, it will consider this neighbor as being down, and routing tables will have to be recalculated. The effects of the Hello interval mismatch in EIGRP are somewhat different from the Hello interval mismatch in OSPF (see Chapter 8). In OSPF, the mismatch in the Hello interval will not allow two OSPF routers to become neighbors and establish a FULL adjacency. In EIGRP, the result of a Hello interval mismatch can be route flapping.

The relationship between EIGRP neighbors demonstrating the condition of a Hello interval mismatch is best observed in real time. Neighbors will come and go and the routing tables will keep on changing. Some destinations may disappear from the table only to reappear a few seconds later. Other destinations may become reachable through a different next hop at a different cost, fluctuating back and forth.

The net result is that while reachability throughout the internetwork may be maintained, EIGRP neighbors with the Hello interval mismatch will be doing a lot of extra work recalculating routes. This process may take a toll on the overall network performance.

Observe what happens on the Bozeman router as a result of changing the EIGRP Hello interval on both subinterfaces from the default 5 to 20 seconds. The Bozeman router configuration is shown below. The configurations of the Livingston and Helena routers are the same as in the initial EIGRP configurations associated with Figure 7.4.

Bozeman EIGRP configuration with modified Hello interval timers

```
hostname Bozeman
!
```

```
ip subnet-zero
!
interface Ethernet0
 ip address 172.16.150.1 255.255.255.0
 no shut
!
interface Ethernet1
 ip address 172.16.151.1 255.255.255.0
 no shut
!
interface Serial0
 no ip address
 encapsulation frame-relay
 frame-relay lmi-type cisco
 no shut
!
interface Serial0.102 point-to-point
 description 64K link to Livingston
 ip address 192.168.1.1 255.255.255.252
 ip Hello-interval eigrp 7 20                    Notice modification
 bandwidth 64
 frame-relay interface-dlci 102
!
interface Serial0.103 point-to-point
 description 64K link to Helena
 ip address 192.168.1.5 255.255.255.252
 ip Hello-interval eigrp 7 20                    Notice modification
 bandwidth 64
 frame-relay interface-dlci 103
!
router eigrp 7
 network 172.16.0.0
 network 192.168.1.0
 no auto-summary
```

The syntax for changing the Hello interval value is ip Hello-interval eigrp *xx yy*, where *xx* represents the EIGRP process number (autonomous system number) and *yy* represents the new Hello interval value in seconds. The effects of this change on the Bozeman router can best be observed by viewing its EIGRP neighbors and routing tables over a period of time.

The following displays of EIGRP neighbors on the Bozeman router begin at an arbitrary ground zero time after the changes to the Hello intervals have been configured. The time offset from ground zero referenced throughout this trace is derived from the "uptime" in the neighbor displays.

Ground Zero Neighbor Display on the Bozeman Router

Bozeman router has two neighbors. Uptime with Livingston (192.168.1.2) is 7 seconds, and uptime with Helena (192.168.1.6) is 45 minutes and 44 seconds.

```
Bozeman#sh ip eigrp neighbors

IP-EIGRP neighbors for process 7

H   Address           Interface    Hold Uptime   SRTT   RTO  Q   Seq
                                   (sec)         (ms)       Cnt Num
0   192.168.1.2       Se0.102      11 00:00:07   76    2280  0   358
1   192.168.1.6       Se0.103      10 00:45:44   54    2280  0   188
```

21 seconds from ground zero. Bozeman router still has two neighbors.

```
Bozeman#sh ip eigrp neighbors

IP-EIGRP neighbors for process 7

H   Address           Interface    Hold Uptime   SRTT   RTO  Q   Seq
                                   (sec)         (ms)       Cnt Num
0   192.168.1.2       Se0.102      13 00:00:28   76    2280  0   358
1   192.168.1.6       Se0.103      13 00:46:06   54    2280  0   188
```

22 seconds from ground zero. Bozeman router loses its Helena neighbor (192.168.1.6).

```
Bozeman#sh ip eigrp neighbors
```

```
IP-EIGRP neighbors for process 7
```

H	Address	Interface	Hold (sec)	Uptime	SRTT (ms)	RTO	Q Cnt	Seq Num
0	192.168.1.2	Se0.102	14	00:00:29	62	2280	0	361

24 seconds from ground zero. Bozeman router recovers its Helena neighbor (192.168.1.6).

```
Bozeman#sh ip eigrp neighbors
IP-EIGRP neighbors for process 7
```

H	Address	Interface	Hold (sec)	Uptime	SRTT (ms)	RTO	Q Cnt	Seq Num
1	192.168.1.6	Se0.103	14	00:00:00	0	2000	1	0
0	192.168.1.2	Se0.102	14	00:00:31	62	2280	0	361

43 seconds from ground zero. Bozeman router still has two neighbors.

```
Bozeman#sh ip eigrp neighbors
IP-EIGRP neighbors for process 7
```

H	Address	Interface	Hold (sec)	Uptime	SRTT (ms)	RTO	Q Cnt	Seq Num
1	192.168.1.6	Se0.103	14	00:00:19	60	2280	0	192
0	192.168.1.2	Se0.102	14	00:00:50	59	2280	0	361

44 seconds from ground zero. Bozeman router loses its Livingston neighbor (192.168.1.2). This condition will last for four seconds.

```
Bozeman#sh ip eigrp neighbors
IP-EIGRP neighbors for process 7
```

H	Address	Interface	Hold (sec)	Uptime	SRTT (ms)	RTO	Q Cnt	Seq Num
1	192.168.1.6	Se0.103	14	00:00:20	57	2280	0	195

48 seconds from ground zero. Bozeman router recovers its Livingston neighbor (192.168.1.2).

```
Bozeman#sh ip eigrp neighbors
IP-EIGRP neighbors for process 7
```

H	Address	Interface	Hold Uptime	SRTT	RTO	Q	Seq

			(sec)	(ms)		Cnt	Num
0	192.168.1.2	Se0.102	14 00:00:00	0	2000	1	0
1	192.168.1.6	Se0.103	13 00:00:24	57	2280	0	195

1 minute 16 seconds from ground zero. Bozeman router still maintains two neighbors.

```
Bozeman#sh ip eigrp neighbors

IP-EIGRP neighbors for process 7
```

H	Address	Interface	Hold Uptime	SRTT	RTO	Q	Seq
			(sec)	(ms)		Cnt	Num
0	192.168.1.2	Se0.102	13 00:00:28	690	4140	0	365
1	192.168.1.6	Se0.103	13 00:00:52	60	2280	0	195

1 minute 17 seconds from ground zero. Bozeman router again loses its Helena neighbor (192.168.1.6).

```
Bozeman#sh ip eigrp neighbors

IP-EIGRP neighbors for process 7
```

H	Address	Interface	Hold Uptime	SRTT	RTO	Q	Seq
			(sec)	(ms)		Cnt	Num
0	192.168.1.2	Se0.102	14 00:00:29	456	2736	0	368

1 minute 20 seconds from ground zero. Bozeman router recovers its Helena neighbor.

```
Bozeman#sh ip eigrp neighbors

IP-EIGRP neighbors for process 7
```

H	Address	Interface	Hold Uptime	SRTT	RTO	Q	Seq
			(sec)	(ms)		Cnt	Num
1	192.168.1.6	Se0.103	14 00:00:00	0	2000	1	0
0	192.168.1.2	Se0.102	14 00:00:32	456	2736	0	368

1 minute 40 seconds from ground zero. Bozeman router still has two neighbors.

```
Bozeman#sh ip eigrp neighbors

IP-EIGRP neighbors for process 7
```

H	Address	Interface	Hold Uptime (sec)	SRTT (ms)	RTO	Q Cnt	Seq Num
1	192.168.1.6	Se0.103	13 00:00:20	64	2280	0	199
0	192.168.1.2	Se0.102	13 00:00:52	373	2280	0	368

1 minute 41 seconds from ground zero. Bozeman router loses its Livingston neighbor again (192.168.1.2).

```
Bozeman#sh ip eigrp neighbors
IP-EIGRP neighbors for process 7
```

H	Address	Interface	Hold Uptime (sec)	SRTT (ms)	RTO	Q Cnt	Seq Num
1	192.168.1.6	Se0.103	14 00:00:21	62	2280	1	202

1 minute 44 seconds from ground zero. Bozeman router recovers its Livingston neighbor (192.168.1.2).

```
Bozeman#sh ip eigrp neighbors
IP-EIGRP neighbors for process 7
```

H	Address	Interface	Hold Uptime (sec)	SRTT (ms)	RTO	Q Cnt	Seq Num
0	192.168.1.2	Se0.102	14 00:00:00	0	2000	1	0
1	192.168.1.6	Se0.103	14 00:00:24	80	2280	0	202

By now you get the picture of the havoc that's created by a Hello interval mismatch in EIGRP. It's difficult to imagine that any administrator would be doing this on purpose. However, should you find yourself in a situation where EIGRP neighbors are coming and going and the routing tables are changing accordingly, Hello interval mismatch is definitely something to suspect. A Hello interval mismatch may well be the result of a good intention to minimize the Hello traffic, where one or two routers in an internetwork have not had their intervals changed correctly.

The routing tables for this misconfiguration are not displayed, but you can surmise that they would be changing accordingly. Within 1 minute and 44 seconds, the Bozeman router lost and recovered each of its two neighbors twice. This means that there would have been at least four route re-computations on the Bozeman router with the next hop for the various destinations changing accordingly as its EIGRP neighbors came and went.

Mismatch in EIGRP Authentication

EIGRP supports only MD5 authentication. The configuration of EIGRP authentication is relatively involved compared to other elements of EIGRP configuration. The mismatches in EIGRP authentication are analyzed in the context of the scenario in Figure 7.5.

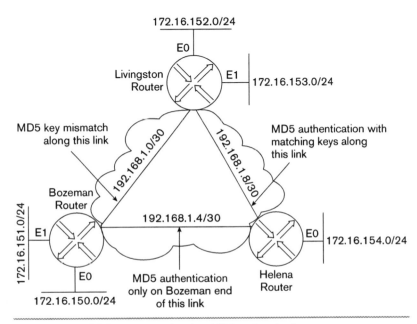

Figure 7.5 *EIGRP internetwork using MD5 authentication*

The configuration files for the three routers in Figure 7.5 are presented next. They literally represent a "three-ring circus." The serial link between the Bozeman and Livingston routers is configured to authenticate EIGRP packets with MD5, but there is a key mismatch between the two routers. The serial link between Livingston and Helena is configured correctly with a matching key. And finally, the serial link between Helena and Bozeman is again misconfigured. The results of the configurations that follow will be reflected in the display of EIGRP neighbors and the routing tables.

The relevant portions of the configuration files pertaining to EIGRP and EIGRP authentication are boldfaced. There are three major steps in configuring EIGRP authentication. First, the MD5 authentication mode must be enabled in the interface configuration mode. Second, a key chain needs to be identified, also in the interface configuration mode. Finally, the key chain must be configured with keys. EIGRP can support multiple keys, but only a single key is used in the example that follows. A key is characterized by a key string, a time interval for sending out the MD5 authenticated messages (send-lifetime), and a time interval for accepting the MD5 authenticated messages (accept-lifetime). The send-lifetime and the accept-lifetime intervals have been identified as beginning at 01:00:00 on 9/9/99 and never ending (infinite). The key strings in the examples are *abc* and *def.*

Bozeman router EIGRP configuration with MD5 authentication

```
hostname Bozeman
!
enable password cisco
!
ip subnet-zero
!
key chain mykey               New section defining the key chain and keys
 key 1
  key-string abc
  accept-lifetime 01:00:00 Sep 9 1999 infinite
  send-lifetime 01:00:00 Sep 9 1999 infinite
!
interface Ethernet0
 ip address 172.16.150.1 255.255.255.0
!
interface Ethernet1
 ip address 172.16.151.1 255.255.255.0
!
interface Serial0
 no ip address
 encapsulation frame-relay
 frame-relay lmi-type cisco
```

```
!
interface Serial0.102 point-to-point
 description 64K link to Livingston
 ip address 192.168.1.1 255.255.255.252
 ip authentication mode eigrp 7 md5         Enabling EIGRP authentication on
s0.102
 ip authentication key-chain eigrp 7 mykey
 bandwidth 64
 frame-relay interface-dlci 102
!
interface Serial0.103 point-to-point
 description 64K link to Helena
 ip address 192.168.1.5 255.255.255.252
 ip authentication mode eigrp 7 md5         Enabling EIGRP authentication on
s0.103
 ip authentication key-chain eigrp 7 mykey
 bandwidth 64
 frame-relay interface-dlci 103
!
interface Serial1
 no ip address
 shutdown
!
router eigrp 7
 network 172.16.0.0
 network 192.168.1.0
 no auto-summary
```

Livingston router EIGRP configuration with MD5 authentication

```
hostname Livingston
!
enable password cisco
!
ip subnet-zero
!
```

```
key chain mykey              New section defining the key chain and keys
 key 1
  key-string def
  accept-lifetime 01:00:00 Sep 9 1999 infinite
  send-lifetime 01:00:00 Sep 9 1999 infinite
!
 interface Ethernet0
 ip address 172.16.152.1 255.255.255.0
!
interface Ethernet1
 ip address 172.16.153.1 255.255.255.0
!
interface Serial0
 no ip address
 encapsulation frame-relay
 frame-relay lmi-type cisco
!
interface Serial0.101 point-to-point
 description 64K link to Bozeman
 ip address 192.168.1.2 255.255.255.252
 ip authentication mode eigrp 7 md5      Enabling EIGRP authentication on
s0.101
 ip authentication key-chain eigrp 7 mykey
 bandwidth 64
 frame-relay interface-dlci 201
!
interface Serial0.103 point-to-point
 description 64K link to Helena
 ip address 192.168.1.9 255.255.255.252
 ip authentication mode eigrp 7 md5      Enabling EIGRP authentication on
s0.103
 ip authentication key-chain eigrp 7 mykey
 bandwidth 64
 frame-relay interface-dlci 203
!
```

```
interface Serial1
 no ip address
 shutdown
!
router eigrp 7
 network 172.16.0.0
 network 192.168.1.0
 no auto-summary
```

Helena router EIGRP configuration with MD5 authentication

```
hostname Helena
!
enable password cisco
!
ip subnet-zero
!
key chain mykey                    New section defining the key chain and keys
 key 1
  key-string def
  accept-lifetime 01:00:00 Sep 9 1999 infinite
  send-lifetime 01:00:00 Sep 9 1999 infinite
!
interface Ethernet0
 ip address 172.16.154.1 255.255.255.0
!
interface Serial0
 no ip address
 encapsulation frame-relay
 frame-relay lmi-type cisco
!
interface Serial0.101 point-to-point
 description 64K link to Bozeman
 ip address 192.168.1.6 255.255.255.252  No EIGRP authentication on s0.101
 bandwidth 64
```

```
  frame-relay interface-dlci 301
!
interface Serial0.102 point-to-point
  description 64K link to Livingston
  ip address 192.168.1.10 255.255.255.252
  ip authentication mode eigrp 7 md5      Enabling EIGRP authentication on s0.102
  ip authentication key-chain eigrp 7 mykey
  bandwidth 64
  frame-relay interface-dlci 302
!
interface Serial1
  no ip address
  shutdown
!
router eigrp 7
  network 172.16.0.0
  network 192.168.1.0
  no auto-summary
```

The routing tables and EIGRP neighbor displays for the three routers confirm the preceding configurations. The serial link shared by the Bozeman and Livingston routers is MD5 authenticated at both ends. However, there is a mismatch in the key string. Bozeman uses *abc* and Livingston uses *def.* Bozeman and Livingston will not become EIGRP neighbors over that link. The serial link shared by the Bozeman and Helena routers is MD5-configured at the Bozeman end, but it has a default configuration at the Helena end. Again, don't expect Bozeman and Helena to become neighbors over that link.

The show ip eigrp neighbors display confirms that the Bozeman router has no EIGRP neighbors.

```
Bozeman#sh ip eigrp neighbors
IP-EIGRP neighbors for process 7
```

The absence of neighbors on the Bozeman router is due to two different types of authentication mismatch. Without any EIGRP neighbors, the Bozeman router's routing table only shows directly connected routes.

Bozeman router's table following misconfiguration of EIGRP authentication

```
Bozeman#sh ip route
Codes: C - connected, S - static, I - IGRP, R - RIP, M - mobile, B - BGP
       D - EIGRP,


Gateway of last resort is not set

     172.16.0.0/24 is subnetted, 2 subnets
C       172.16.150.0 is directly connected, Ethernet0
C       172.16.151.0 is directly connected, Ethernet1
     192.168.1.0/30 is subnetted, 2 subnets
C       192.168.1.0 is directly connected, Serial0.102
C       192.168.1.4 is directly connected, Serial0.103
```

The Livingston router has a key string misconfiguration with the Bozeman router, but it has a correct configuration with the Helena router. Both Livingston and Helena use the same key string, *def.* Consequently, the Livingston router becomes a neighbor with the Helena router but not with the Bozeman router. The show ip eigrp neighbors command confirms that Helena is Livingston's EIGRP neighbor.

```
Livingston#sh ip eigrp neighbors
IP-EIGRP neighbors for process 7
H   Address            Interface     Hold Uptime    SRTT    RTO  Q  Seq
                                     (sec)          (ms)         Cnt Num
0   192.168.1.10       Se0.103         10 00:10:08   424   2544  0  3
```

The routing table on the Livingston router shows some EIGRP derived routes, which are reachable via Helena. But it's not a full table. The Livingston router does not know about the Ethernet networks attached to the Bozeman router. This means that something must be wrong between Helena and Bozeman, and in all likelihood Helena will also not be aware of the Ethernets attached to the Bozeman router.

Livingston router's table following misconfiguration of EIGRP authentication

```
Livingston#sh ip route

Codes: C - connected, S - static, I - IGRP, R - RIP, M - mobile, B - BGP
       D - EIGRP,


Gateway of last resort is not set


     172.16.0.0/24 is subnetted, 3 subnets
C       172.16.152.0 is directly connected, Ethernet0
C       172.16.153.0 is directly connected, Ethernet1
D       172.16.154.0 [90/40537600] via 192.168.1.10, 00:10:12, Serial0.103
     192.168.1.0/30 is subnetted, 3 subnets
C       192.168.1.8 is directly connected, Serial0.103
C       192.168.1.0 is directly connected, Serial0.101
D       192.168.1.4 [90/41024000] via 192.168.1.10, 00:10:12, Serial0.103
```

On the Helena router, the situation seems peculiar. The show ip eigrp neighbors command displays that Helena has two neighbors, both Bozeman (192.168.1.5) and Livingston (192.168.1.9). However, there is something unusual about the Bozeman neighbor display. The SRTT stays at 0, and the Queue count stays at 1. The sequence number is 0. These are all indications that the Bozeman router is not really an EIGRP neighbor with Helena. Subsequent neighbor displays only confirm the problem — Helena does not use any authentication on its link to Bozeman, while Bozeman uses MD5 on its links to Helena.

```
Helena#sh ip eigrp neighbors
IP-EIGRP neighbors for process 7
H   Address              Interface    Hold Uptime    SRTT   RTO  Q  Seq
                                      (sec)          (ms)        Cnt Num
0   192.168.1.5          Se0.101       14 00:01:13     0   5000  1  0
```

```
1   192.168.1.9          Se0.102      10 00:12:17  80  2280  0  42


Helena#sh ip eigrp neighbors

IP-EIGRP neighbors for process 7

H   Address              Interface   Hold Uptime   SRTT   RTO  Q  Seq

                                     (sec)         (ms)        Cnt Num

0   192.168.1.5          Se0.101      13 00:01:18    0   5000  1  0

1   192.168.1.9          Se0.102      14 00:12:22   80   2280  0  42
```

The routing table on Helena only reflects that it is not getting any updates from Bozeman. The only EIGRP-derived routes come from Livingston, with which Helena shares correct authentication.

Helena router's table following misconfiguration of EIGRP authentication

```
Helena#sh ip route

Codes: C - connected, S - static, I - IGRP, R - RIP, M - mobile, B - BGP

       D - EIGRP,


Gateway of last resort is not set


     172.16.0.0/24 is subnetted, 3 subnets

D       172.16.152.0 [90/40537600] via 192.168.1.9, 00:11:12, Serial0.102

D       172.16.153.0 [90/40537600] via 192.168.1.9, 00:11:12, Serial0.102

C       172.16.154.0 is directly connected, Ethernet0

     192.168.1.0/30 is subnetted, 3 subnets

C       192.168.1.8 is directly connected, Serial0.102

D       192.168.1.0 [90/41024000] via 192.168.1.9, 00:11:12, Serial0.102

C       192.168.1.4 is directly connected, Serial0.101
```

The final conclusion that can be drawn about EIGRP authentication is rather intuitive. Authentication type and keys must match between neighboring routers for routing updates to be exchanged. In that sense, authentication is no different from the autonomous system numbers or the EIGRP timers. They all have to match for EIGRP routers to become neighbors and exchange routing updates.

Impact of Bandwidth Parameter on the IGRP/EIGRP Metric

The IGRP/EIGRP metric is complex compared to the simple hop count metric of RIP or even the OSPF metric. Almost all discussion here will center on the IGRP metric, as the EIGRP metric is functionally the same as IGRP except that it's further scaled by a factor of 256 for greater granularity.

The default IGRP metric is a function of two parameters: bandwidth and delay. The bandwidth component of the metric is calculated by dividing 10,000,000 by the bandwidth in Kbps of the slowest link between the router and a destination. The delay component of the metric is derived from the sum of all of delays associated with all links between a router and a destination. Cisco provides standard delays (in microseconds) for different types of network media. The delay component of IGRP metric is the sum of all of the standard individual delays divided by 10.

For example, the bandwidth associated with standard Ethernet is 10,000Kbps, which translates into 1000 for the bandwidth component of IGRP metric. For Fast Ethernet the bandwidth is 100,000Kbps, which translates into 100 as the bandwidth component of IGRP metric. The delay component is 1000 microseconds for Ethernet and 100 microseconds for Fast Ethernet. If a packet had to cross an Ethernet network and a Fast Ethernet network on the way to its destination, the delay component of the IGRP metric would be 110, that is, (1000+100)/10=110. The total IGRP metric for that destination would be the sum of the bandwidth component (1,000) and the delay component (110), which would be 1,110.

Troubleshooting the IGRP metric primarily boils down to understanding how the metric is calculated. The one peculiarity to be aware of is that for serial links, Cisco defaults to the T1 bandwidth of 1544Kbps regardless of the nature of the serial link. The link could be a 56K link, 64K link, 256K link, or a full T1 link, and the default bandwidth for that link would still be 1544Kbps. Consequently, in environments where serial links are involved, it's vital to set the bandwidth through configuration if the link is anything other than a T1. Otherwise slower links may become overutilized, leading to traffic congestion.

Consider a scenario as depicted in Figure 7.6 where 64K fractional frame circuits have been provisioned between locations and the bandwidth parameter has been configured on all of the serial links.

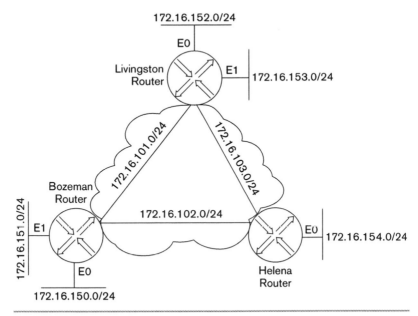

172.16.152.0/24

Figure 7.6 *IGRP internetwork for metric analysis*

The configuration files for the three routers in Figure 7.6 are shown next.

Bozeman router configuration for IGRP metric troubleshooting

```
!
hostname Bozeman
!
enable password cisco
!
interface Ethernet0
 ip address 172.16.150.1 255.255.255.0
 no shut
!
interface Ethernet1
 ip address 172.16.151.1 255.255.255.0
 no shut
!
```

```
interface Serial0
 no ip address
 encapsulation frame-relay
 frame-relay lmi-type cisco
 no shut
!
interface Serial0.102 point-to-point
 description 64K link to Livingston
 ip address 172.16.101.1 255.255.255.0
 bandwidth 64
 frame-relay interface-dlci 102
!
interface Serial0.103 point-to-point
 description 64K link to Helena
 ip address 172.16.102.1 255.255.255.0
 bandwidth 64
 frame-relay interface-dlci 103
!
interface Serial1
 shut
!
router igrp 1
 network 172.16.0.0
!
```

Livingston router configuration for IGRP metric troubleshooting

```
!
hostname Livingston
!
enable password cisco
!
interface Ethernet0
 ip address 172.16.152.1 255.255.255.0
 no shut
!
```

```
interface Ethernet1
 ip address 172.16.153.1 255.255.255.0
 no shut
!
interface Serial0
 no ip address
 encapsulation frame-relay
 frame-relay lmi-type cisco
 no shut
!
interface Serial0.101 point-to-point
 description 64K link to Bozeman
 ip address 172.16.101.2 255.255.255.0
 bandwidth 64
 frame-relay interface-dlci 201
!
interface Serial0.103 point-to-point
 description 64K link to Helena
 ip address 172.16.103.1 255.255.255.0
 bandwidth 64
 frame-relay interface-dlci 203
!
interface Serial1
 shut
!
 router igrp 1
 network 172.16.0.0
!
```

Helena router configuration for IGRP metric troubleshooting

```
hostname Helena
!
enable password cisco
!
```

```
ip subnet-zero
!
interface Ethernet0
 ip address 172.16.154.1 255.255.255.0
 no shut
!
interface Serial0
 no ip address
 encapsulation frame-relay
 frame-relay lmi-type cisco
 no shut
!
 interface Serial0.101 point-to-point
 description 64K link to Bozeman
 ip address 172.16.102.2 255.255.255.0
 bandwidth 64
 frame-relay interface-dlci 301
 !
interface Serial0.102 point-to-point
 description 64K link to Livingston
 ip address 172.16.103.2 255.255.255.0
 bandwidth 64
 frame-relay interface-dlci 302
 !
interface Serial1
 shut
 !
router igrp 1
 network 172.16.0.0
```

The above configurations reflect a properly configured IGRP internet-work operating over a Frame Relay cloud. A single major network has been used with fixed-length subnetting. The routing table on the Helena router that follows indicates that the Bozeman Ethernets (172.16.150.0 and 172.16.151.0) are reachable via Serial0.101 and the Livingston Ethernets are reachable via Serial0.102.

Helena router's table for initial IGRP metric analysis configuration

```
Helena#sh ip route
Codes: C - connected, S - static, I - IGRP, R - RIP, M - mobile, B - BGP
       D - EIGRP,


Gateway of last resort is not set

     172.16.0.0/24 is subnetted, 8 subnets
I       172.16.152.0 [100/158350] via 172.16.103.1, 00:00:10, Serial0.102
I       172.16.153.0 [100/158350] via 172.16.103.1, 00:00:10, Serial0.102
C       172.16.154.0 is directly connected, Ethernet0
I       172.16.150.0 [100/158350] via 172.16.102.1, 00:00:06, Serial0.101
I       172.16.151.0 [100/158350] via 172.16.102.1, 00:00:06, Serial0.101
I       172.16.101.0 [100/160250] via 172.16.102.1, 00:00:06, Serial0.101
                     [100/160250] via 172.16.103.1, 00:00:10, Serial0.102
C       172.16.102.0 is directly connected, Serial0.101
C       172.16.103.0 is directly connected, Serial0.102
```

From the Helena router, the metric to all of the Ethernets in Bozeman and in Livingston is the same. Its value is 158,350. Consider where this metric comes from. To get from Helena to 172.16.150.0, a packet has to cross a serial link between Helena and Bozeman and then get onto the Bozeman Ethernet of 172.16.150.0. The lowest bandwidth along the way is 64K on the serial link. The bandwidth component of the IGRP metric for that route will be 10,000,000/64 or 156,250. The delay in microseconds is 20,000 for the serial link and 1,000 for the Ethernet. The delay component of the metric will be (20,000+1,000)/10=2,100. The total metric, therefore, is 156,250+2,100 or 158,350, as shown in the routing table.

Now, consider what happens if an administrator inadvertently forgets to configure the bandwidth parameter. Bandwidth has not been set on the serial link from Helena to Bozeman and from Bozeman to Livingston. All of the serial circuits have been provisioned as fractional T1 circuits (64K) and the clockrate comes from the Frame Relay switch. There is no immediate indication in the configurations about the capacity of the serial links except for the bandwidth parameter.

The changes to the configuration files are minimal. The No bandwidth 64 command has been executed on the Helena router in the s0.101 interface section and on the Bozeman router in the s0.102 section to simulate this scenario. But the impact on the Helena routing tables is very visible, as reflected in the routing table that follows.

Helena router's table following bandwidth parameter manipulation

```
Helena#sh ip route
Codes: C - connected, S - static, I - IGRP, R - RIP, M - mobile, B - BGP
       D - EIGRP,


Gateway of last resort is not set


     172.16.0.0/24 is subnetted, 8 subnets
I       172.16.152.0 [100/10576] via 172.16.102.1, 00:00:28, Serial0.101
I       172.16.153.0 [100/10576] via 172.16.102.1, 00:00:28, Serial0.101
C       172.16.154.0 is directly connected, Ethernet0
I       172.16.150.0 [100/8576] via 172.16.102.1, 00:00:28, Serial0.101
I       172.16.151.0 [100/8576] via 172.16.102.1, 00:00:28, Serial0.101
I       172.16.101.0 [100/10476] via 172.16.102.1, 00:00:28, Serial0.101
C       172.16.102.0 is directly connected, Serial0.101
C       172.16.103.0 is directly connected, Serial0.102
```

All of the IGRP derived routes are now reachable via serial0.101. There has been no change to the actual capacity of the circuits by the circuit providers. The implication is that a circuit between Helena and Livingston will be underutilized, while the circuit between Helena and Bozeman will be overloaded, as all of the traffic from Helena to Livingston will now be going through Bozeman.

The metric for 172.16.150.0 has changed from 158,350 to 8,576. There has been no change to the delay component of this metric, which was calculated to be 2,100 before the reconfiguration. This leaves 6,476 for the bandwidth component. This is where you have to remember that if the bandwidth configuration parameter is not used, the default bandwidth for a serial link is going to be 1,544K. As 1,544K is the lowest bandwidth along the path to 172.16.150.0 (1,544K bandwidth for the serial is lower than 10,000K bandwidth for Ethernet), the bandwidth component of

IGRP metric for that route will be 10,000,000/1,544 or 6,476. The total metric is 2,100+6,476, as shown in the preceding table.

If EIGRP were running instead of IGRP, the metrics would look 256 times bigger. The impact of the bandwidth parameter on the IGRP/EIGRP metric can be reduced to the following:

- Default metric is a function of bandwidth and delay.

- The bandwidth component comes from taking the bandwidth of the slowest link along the path to destination. If there are dozens of links, remember that none has any impact on the bandwidth component of the metric except the slowest one.

- The delay component for the metric is a sum of the delays associated with each link that a router must pass. The fixed-delay values associated with each link are added up and divided by 10 to give you the delay component of the IGRP metric.

- The final default metric is the sum of the bandwidth and delay components.

- Serial links have a default bandwidth of 1,544 unless modified through configuration.

- Network load and reliability can be taken into account in metric calculation via additional configuration.

Split Horizon Issue in IGRP on a Frame Relay WAN

Split horizon is a loop prevention mechanism in distance vector protocols. It prevents a route from being re-advertised to a neighbor over the same interface on which the route was learned. Split horizon can become a problem on Frame Relay networks when a protocol such as IGRP is used in a partial mesh with multipoint subinterfaces.

When Frame Relay encapsulation is enabled on a physical serial interface, split horizon is automatically disabled. This section addresses the problem of what happens in a Frame Relay network when split horizon is enabled. Split horizon is *enabled* on multipoint subinterfaces when Frame Relay encapsulation is used.

In all of the examples used throughout this chapter, the Frame Relay configurations were using point-to-point subinterfaces. The advantage of point-to-point subinterfaces in a Frame Relay cloud is that the entire cloud becomes a partial or a full mesh of point-to-point links. There is a single Data Link Connection Identifier (DLCI) and a single virtual circuit per point-to-point subinterface. Split horizon is not an issue. The disadvantage of point-to-point subinterfaces is that each subinterface consumes its own subnet and takes up more router memory than, for example, a single multipoint subinterface with multiple DLCIs.

To avoid problems with distance vector protocols on WAN clouds, use point-to-point subinterfaces or multiple physical interfaces with a single DLCI per interface. Otherwise, witness what can happen. Consider the classic hub-and-spoke scenario in Figure 7.7.

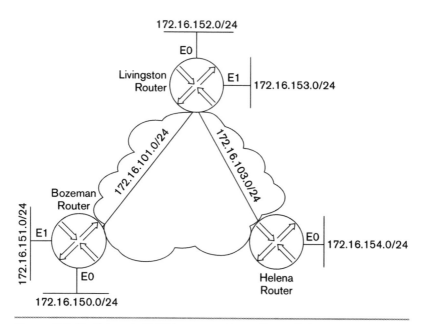

Figure 7.7 *Partial mesh IGRP internetwork over Frame Relay with multipoint subinterfaces used for split horizon analysis*

The Livingston router is a hub. It has a permanent virtual circuit (PVC) to the Bozeman and Helena routers. Helena and Bozeman routers each have a PVC to Livingston but not to each other. The configuration files for the scenario in Figure 7.7 are as follows.

Bozeman router IGRP configuration with multipoint subinterface

```
hostname Bozeman
!
enable password cisco
!
interface Ethernet0
 ip address 172.16.150.1 255.255.255.0
!
interface Ethernet1
 ip address 172.16.151.1 255.255.255.0
!
interface Serial0
 no ip address
 encapsulation frame-relay
 no ip mroute-cache
 frame-relay lmi-type cisco
!
interface Serial0.101 multipoint
 description 64 K link to Livingston
 ip address 172.16.100.1 255.255.255.0
 bandwidth 64
 frame-relay interface-dlci 102
!
interface Serial1
 no ip address
 shutdown
!
router igrp 1
 network 172.16.0.0
```

Livingston router IGRP configuration with multipoint subinterface

```
hostname Livingston
!
enable password cisco
```

```
!
interface Ethernet0
 ip address 172.16.152.1 255.255.255.0
!
interface Ethernet1
 ip address 172.16.153.1 255.255.255.0
!
interface Serial0
 no ip address
 encapsulation frame-relay
 no ip mroute-cache
 frame-relay lmi-type cisco
!
interface Serial0.102 multipoint
 description 64 K links to Bozeman & Helena
 ip address 172.16.100.2 255.255.255.0
 bandwidth 64
 frame-relay interface-dlci 201
 frame-relay interface-dlci 203
!
interface Serial1
 no ip address
 shutdown
!
router igrp 1
 network 172.16.0.0
```

Helena router IGRP configuration with multipoint subinterface

```
hostname Helena
!
enable password cisco
!
ip subnet-zero
!
```

```
interface Ethernet0

 ip address 172.16.154.1 255.255.255.0

!

interface Serial0

 no ip address

 encapsulation frame-relay

 no ip mroute-cache

 frame-relay lmi-type cisco

!

interface Serial0.103 multipoint

 description 64 K link to Livingston

 ip address 172.16.100.3 255.255.255.0

 bandwidth 64

 frame-relay interface-dlci 302

!

interface Serial1

 no ip address

 shutdown

!

router igrp 1

 network 172.16.0.0
```

In the preceding configurations, there are two virtual circuits on the Livingston router identified with DLCIs: 201 for Bozeman and 203 for Helena. The routing protocol, in this case IGRP, knows nothing about Frame Relay virtual circuits. It understands interfaces but not virtual circuits. Therefore with split horizon enabled, an update about 172.16.150.0 and 172.16.151.0 that arrives on the Livingston router from Bozeman will not be propagated to Helena. That's because IGRP on Livingston would be sending this update on the same interface that it was received. Remember that IGRP has no awareness of Frame Relay PVCs. Consequently, the Helena router will not have any awareness of the two Ethernet subnets attached to the Bozeman router. In the same way, the Bozeman router will not know about the Ethernet attached to the Helena router. A look at the routing tables on Bozeman and Helena confirms that neither one knows about the other's directly attached subnets.

Bozeman router's table with missing entries due to split horizon

```
Bozeman#sh ip route
Codes: C - connected, S - static, I - IGRP,


Gateway of last resort is not set


     172.16.0.0/24 is subnetted, 5 subnets
I       172.16.152.0 [100/158350] via 172.16.100.2, 00:00:07, Serial0.101
I       172.16.153.0 [100/158350] via 172.16.100.2, 00:00:07, Serial0.101
C       172.16.150.0 is directly connected, Ethernet0
C       172.16.151.0 is directly connected, Ethernet1
C       172.16.100.0 is directly connected, Serial0.101
```

Note the absence of the Helena Ethernet in Bozeman's routing table.

Helena router's table with missing entries due to split horizon

```
Helena#sh ip route
Codes: C - connected, S - static, I - IGRP,


Gateway of last resort is not set


     172.16.0.0/24 is subnetted, 4 subnets
I       172.16.152.0 [100/158350] via 172.16.100.2, 00:00:29, Serial0.103
I       172.16.153.0 [100/158350] via 172.16.100.2, 00:00:29, Serial0.103
C       172.16.154.0 is directly connected, Ethernet0
C       172.16.100.0 is directly connected, Serial0.103
```

Note the absence of the Bozeman Ethernets in Helena router's table.

It may seem like a lot of work went into proving something that does not work, but the split horizon issue is important because it applies to protocols other than just IP. You must be aware of its effects in WAN clouds. Also, you may use it to your advantage. In the hub-and-spoke scenario shown in Figure 7.7, it may be desirable to have this kind of " misconfiguration" where the spokes know only about their directly connected and hubs' networks, but not about other spokes' networks.

It might be interesting to see what happens when split horizon is disabled on all the multipoint subinterfaces. This is accomplished via the no ip split-horizon configuration command on each router in the multi-point subinterface section. The configuration files are not shown for this change. But take a look at the routing tables again for Bozeman and Helena. The routes that were missing reappear. However, there is another problem lurking here.

Bozeman's routing table following the disabling of split horizon on multipoint subinterfaces

```
Bozeman#sh ip route
Codes: C - connected, S - static, I - IGRP,


Gateway of last resort is not set


     172.16.0.0/24 is subnetted, 6 subnets
I       172.16.152.0 [100/158350] via 172.16.100.2, 00:01:12, Serial0.101
I       172.16.153.0 [100/158350] via 172.16.100.2, 00:01:12, Serial0.101
I       172.16.154.0 [100/160350] via 172.16.100.2, 00:01:12, Serial0.101
C       172.16.150.0 is directly connected, Ethernet0
C       172.16.151.0 is directly connected, Ethernet1
C       172.16.100.0 is directly connected, Serial0.101
```

Helena's Ethernet is back following the disabling of the split horizon on all of the multipoint subinterfaces.

Helena's routing table following the disabling of split horizon on multipoint subinterfaces

```
Helena#sh ip route
Codes: C - connected, S - static, I - IGRP


Gateway of last resort is not set


     172.16.0.0/24 is subnetted, 6 subnets
I       172.16.152.0 [100/158350] via 172.16.100.2, 00:00:18, Serial0.103
I       172.16.153.0 [100/158350] via 172.16.100.2, 00:00:18, Serial0.103
C       172.16.154.0 is directly connected, Ethernet0
I       172.16.150.0 [100/160350] via 172.16.100.2, 00:00:18, Serial0.103
```

```
I       172.16.151.0 [100/160350] via 172.16.100.2, 00:00:18, Serial0.103
C       172.16.100.0 is directly connected, Serial0.103
```

Bozeman Ethernets are also back in Helena's routing table. But appearances are deceiving. There is still a problem with this configuration, the effects of which are even more confusing. Even though there is an entry for the Bozeman Ethernets in Helena's routing table, those networks are not reachable from Helena. Pings from Helena to hosts on 172.16.150.0 and 172.16.151.0 fail. That may seem really deceptive but that's the way it is. And this time it has nothing to do with split horizon, but with the fact that there is no PVC from Bozeman to Helena and all of the traffic must flow through Livingston. Livingston would not have a problem with this if it were configured with multiple subnets for its links to Bozeman and Helena. But when all three routers share a single subnet on the WAN cloud, the effects are the same as though split horizon was enabled, even though entries may appear in the routing tables.

As you can see, the issue of split horizon when combined with partial mesh WAN and multipoint subinterfaces can be messy. Naturally, it's best to avoid certain combinations of protocols, encapsulations, and configuration techniques, but if you can't, then the next best thing is to understand how they interact. The cleanest way to deal with these kinds of problems as demonstrated in this section would be to use a link-state protocol that does not care about split horizon and uses point-to-point subinterfaces. But link-state protocols such as OSPF present their own challenges, as you will see in Chapter 8.

Autonomous System Number Mismatch Issues

Both IGRP and EIGRP use autonomous system (AS) numbers, which allow for the breaking of larger internetworks into smaller groups or process domains. You can think of the AS numbers in these protocols as process domain ID. All routers that use the same AS number will be able to exchange routing updates. If there is a mismatch in the AS number, routers will not exchange updates. In Border Gateway Protocol (BGP), an autonomous system refers to a routing domain with a uniform routing policy where multiple process domains can exist. A BGP autonomous system could include several IGRP or EIGRP process domains, along with internetworks using other routing protocols, such as RIP and OSPF.

The issue of AS number mismatch in IGRP and EIGRP was first discussed in Chapter 1, and this section is intended to reinforce several key points from that discussion.

- AS numbers must match between neighboring IGRP or EIGRP routers if they are to exchange routing updates.

- If an internetwork has been configured with multiple autonomous systems, there needs to be at least one router that's running multiple IGRP/EIGRP processes and performing redistribution if reachability between all networks is expected.

Autonomous system mismatches are one of the easiest problems to troubleshoot in IGRP/EIGRP internetworks.

Chapter Summary

IGRP routers will not exchange routing updates if there is an AS mismatch between them. Separation of major network subnets with another major network leads to problems with classful routing protocols. Do not use VLSM with classful routing protocols. Nothing stops you from doing so, but you will run into problems as a result of it. EIGRP routers will not become neighbors if there is an authentication mismatch or an autonomous system mismatch between them. With a mismatch in EIGRP timers the neighbors may be coming and going, resulting in frequent route re-computations and network instability. IGRP/EIGRP metric is complex. If the bandwidth parameter is not properly configured on serial links, it may lead to underutilization on some links and congestion on others. Be mindful of split horizon behavior on partially meshed WAN clouds. Auto summarization in EIGRP can lead to the same problems as use of classful protocols.

Chapter 8

Troubleshooting OSPF

A link-state protocol like Open Shortest Path First (OSPF) operates quite differently from distance vector protocols such as RIP or IGRP. Distance vector protocols advertise routes (destinations) as vectors — a combination of distance and direction. Distance represents the cost or the metric of reaching a destination, and direction represents the next-hop router through which an advertised route is reachable. Periodically, each router broadcasts its entire routing table to all other routers on each network segment that it is attached to. The update interval varies between the different routing protocols. For RIP, it's 30 seconds, for IGRP, it's 90 seconds, and for IPX RIP, it's 60 seconds. But it's the periodic advertisement of the contents of the entire routing table — regardless of any changes in the topology — that characterizes a distance vector protocol. Each router then updates its routing table based on the information received from all other routers on a segment.

In a link-state protocol such as OSPF, routers that are attached to the same network segment first discover each other dynamically via Hello messages. Then, they establish relationships with other routers on the same segment. The level of a relationship between routers determines what type of information they will exchange with each other. From a troubleshooting perspective, it's important to understand that two OSPF routers will exchange routing updates only if they have formed a FULL adjacency. Any number of misconfigurations can prevent routers attached to the same network segment from establishing a FULL adjacency.

Area ID Mismatch

The issue of area ID mismatch in OSPF was introduced in Chapter 1. The key concepts to be reinforced regarding OSPF area IDs are as follows:

- Area IDs must match among routers sharing the same network segment (broadcast subnet, point-to-point link, or a PVC over a WAN cloud) if routing updates are to be exchanged.

- Area 0.0.0.0 should be configured in every OSPF internetwork if multiple areas are eventually planned.

- When interfaces on a single router are assigned to multiple areas, this router becomes an area border router, or ABR. At least one of the interfaces on an ABR should be in area 0.0.0.0. If an ABR has no interfaces in area 0.0.0.0, it ought to have a virtual link to another ABR that's connected to area 0.0.0.0.

- OSPF routing updates between non-backbone areas are exchanged via the backbone area. The backbone area 0.0.0.0 must be configured in every multi-area OSPF internetwork, otherwise, non-backbone areas become isolated from one another.

Consider now an internetwork as shown in Figure 8.1 and the corresponding configuration files for the Bozeman, Helena, and Livingston routers.

OSPF is properly enabled on all three routers and all interfaces are assigned correctly to area 0.0.0.0 as shown in the configurations that follow. However, there is a problem with OSPF in this configuration, as will be reflected in the routing tables of the three routers.

Bozeman router configuration for OSPF over Frame Relay using subinterfaces

```
hostname Bozeman
!
enable password cisco
!
interface Ethernet0
 ip address 172.16.150.1 255.255.255.0
!
interface Serial0
```

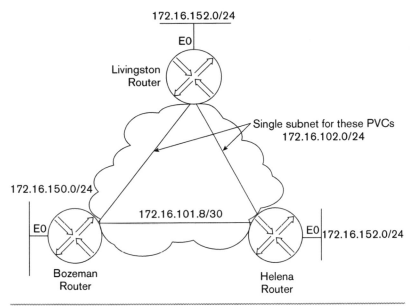

Figure 8.1 *OSPF over Frame Relay configuration using subinterfaces*

```
no ip address
encapsulation frame-relay
frame-relay lmi-type cisco
!
interface Serial0.101 multipoint
 description 64K frame link to Livingston and Helena
 ip address 172.16.102.1 255.255.255.0
 bandwidth 64
 frame-relay interface-dlci 102
 frame-relay interface-dlci 103
!
router ospf 1
 network 172.16.102.1 0.0.0.0 area 0.0.0.0
 network 172.16.150.0 0.0.0.255 area 0.0.0.0
!
```

Livingston router configuration for OSPF over Frame Relay using subinterfaces

```
hostname Livingston
!
enable password cisco
!
interface Ethernet0
 ip address 172.16.151.1 255.255.255.0
!
interface Serial0
 no ip address
 encapsulation frame-relay
 frame-relay lmi-type cisco
!
interface Serial0.101 point-to-point
 description 64K frame link to Bozeman
 ip address 172.16.102.2 255.255.255.0
 bandwidth 64
 frame-relay interface-dlci 201
!
interface Serial0.103 point-to-point
 description 64K frame link to Helena
 ip address 172.16.101.9 255.255.255.252
 bandwidth 64
 frame-relay interface-dlci 203
!
router ospf 1
 network 172.16.102.2 0.0.0.0 area 0.0.0.0
 network 172.16.101.9 0.0.0.0 area 0.0.0.0
 network 172.16.151.0 0.0.0.255 area 0.0.0.0
!
```

Helena router configuration for OSPF over Frame Relay using subinterfaces

```
hostname Helena
!
enable password cisco
!
ip subnet-zero
!
interface Ethernet0
 ip address 172.16.152.1 255.255.255.0
!
interface Serial0
 no ip address
 encapsulation frame-relay
 frame-relay lmi-type cisco
!
interface Serial0.101 point-to-point
 description 64K frame link to Bozeman
 ip address 172.16.102.3 255.255.255.0
 bandwidth 64
 frame-relay interface-dlci 301
!
interface Serial0.102 point-to-point
 description 64K frame link to Livingston
 ip address 172.16.101.10 255.255.255.252
 bandwidth 64
 frame-relay interface-dlci 302
!
router ospf 1
 network 172.16.102.3 0.0.0.0 area 0.0.0.0
 network 172.16.101.10 0.0.0.0 area 0.0.0.0
 network 172.16.152.0 0.0.0.255 area 0.0.0.0
```

On the surface, the preceding configurations appear correct. The output from the `show ip interface brief` command on each router reveals that all of the interfaces and subinterfaces defined in the configuration files are up.

```
Bozeman#sh ip int b

Interface            IP-Address      OK? Method Status           Protocol

Ethernet0            172.16.150.1    YES NVRAM  up               up

Serial0.101          172.16.102.1    YES manual up               up


Livingston#sh ip int b

Interface            IP-Address      OK? Method Status           Protocol

Ethernet0            172.16.151.1    YES manual up               up

Serial0.101          172.16.102.2    YES manual up               up

Serial0.103          172.16.101.9    YES manual up               up


Helena#sh ip int b

Interface            IP-Address      OK? Method Status           Protocol

Ethernet0            172.16.152.1    YES manual up               up

Serial0.101          172.16.102.3    YES manual up               up

Serial0.102          172.16.101.10   YES manual up               up
```

Output from `show frame-relay pvc` reveals that all of the PVCs between Bozeman, Livingston and Helena are also up.

```
Bozeman#sh frame-relay pvc


PVC Statistics for interface Serial0 (Frame Relay DTE)

DLCI = 102, DLCI USAGE = LOCAL, PVC STATUS = ACTIVE, INTERFACE = Serial0.101


   input pkts 156          output pkts 1          in bytes 19189

   out bytes 30            dropped pkts 0         in FECN pkts 0

   in BECN pkts 0          out FECN pkts 0        out BECN pkts 0

   in DE pkts 0            out DE pkts 0

   out bcast pkts 1         out bcast bytes 30

   pvc create time 00:39:02, last time pvc status changed 00:39:02
```

DLCI = 103, DLCI USAGE = LOCAL, PVC STATUS = ACTIVE, INTERFACE = Serial0.101

input pkts 461	output pkts 5	in bytes 52170
out bytes 150	dropped pkts 10	in FECN pkts 0
in BECN pkts 0	out FECN pkts 0	out BECN pkts 0
in DE pkts 0	out DE pkts 0	
out bcast pkts 5	out bcast bytes 150	

pvc create time 00:39:03, last time pvc status changed 00:17:33

Livingston#**show frame-relay pvc**

PVC Statistics for interface Serial0 (Frame Relay DTE)

DLCI = 201, DLCI USAGE = LOCAL, PVC STATUS = ACTIVE, INTERFACE = Serial0.101

input pkts 169	output pkts 573	in bytes 17260
out bytes 61830	dropped pkts 0	in FECN pkts 0
in BECN pkts 0	out FECN pkts 0	out BECN pkts 0
in DE pkts 0	out DE pkts 0	
out bcast pkts 573	out bcast bytes 61830	

pvc create time 01:36:25, last time pvc status changed 00:39:04

DLCI = 203, DLCI USAGE = LOCAL, PVC STATUS = ACTIVE, INTERFACE = Serial0.103

input pkts 1779	output pkts 830	in bytes 144517
out bytes 83521	dropped pkts 10	in FECN pkts 0
in BECN pkts 0	out FECN pkts 0	out BECN pkts 0
in DE pkts 0	out DE pkts 0	
out bcast pkts 712	out bcast bytes 73321	

pvc create time 01:36:25, last time pvc status changed 00:17:54

Helena#**show frame-relay pvc**
PVC Statistics for interface Serial0 (Frame Relay DTE)
DLCI = 301, DLCI USAGE = LOCAL, PVC STATUS = ACTIVE, INTERFACE = Serial0.101

```
input pkts 2          output pkts 119        in bytes 60

out bytes 12139       dropped pkts 1         in FECN pkts 0

in BECN pkts 0        out FECN pkts 0        out BECN pkts 0

in DE pkts 0          out DE pkts 0

out bcast pkts 119     out bcast bytes 12139

pvc create time 00:18:17, last time pvc status changed 00:18:06


DLCI = 302, DLCI USAGE = LOCAL, PVC STATUS = ACTIVE, INTERFACE = Serial0.102


input pkts 144        output pkts 141        in bytes 14835

out bytes 14299       dropped pkts 3         in FECN pkts 0

in BECN pkts 0        out FECN pkts 0        out BECN pkts 0

in DE pkts 0          out DE pkts 0

out bcast pkts 141     out bcast bytes 14299

pvc create time 00:18:17, last time pvc status changed 00:18:07
```

However, looking at the contents of the routing tables for all three routers reveals that there is a problem.

Bozeman router's table for OSPF configuration over Frame Relay using subinterfaces

```
Bozeman#sh ip route
Codes: C - connected,
Gateway of last resort is not set


     172.16.0.0/24 is subnetted, 2 subnets
C       172.16.150.0 is directly connected, Ethernet0
C       172.16.102.0 is directly connected, Serial0.101
```

Livingston router's table for OSPF configuration over Frame Relay using subinterfaces

```
Livingston#sh ip route
Codes: C - connected, S - static, I - IGRP, R - RIP, M - mobile, B - BGP
       D - EIGRP, EX - EIGRP external, O - OSPF,


Gateway of last resort is not set
```

```
    172.16.0.0/16 is variably subnetted, 4 subnets, 2 masks
O       172.16.152.0/24 [110/1572] via 172.16.101.10, 00:00:22, Serial0.103
C       172.16.151.0/24 is directly connected, Ethernet0
C       172.16.101.8/30 is directly connected, Serial0.103
C       172.16.102.0/24 is directly connected, Serial0.101
```

Helena router's table for OSPF configuration over Frame Relay using subinterfaces

```
Helena#show ip route
Codes: C - connected, S - static, I - IGRP, R - RIP, M - mobile, B - BGP
       D - EIGRP, EX - EIGRP external, O - OSPF,


Gateway of last resort is not set

    172.16.0.0/16 is variably subnetted, 4 subnets, 2 masks
C       172.16.152.0/24 is directly connected, Ethernet0
O       172.16.151.0/24 [110/1572] via 172.16.101.9, 00:00:42, Serial0.102
C       172.16.101.8/30 is directly connected, Serial0.102
C       172.16.102.0/24 is directly connected, Serial0.101
```

The routing tables for the preceding configurations reveal that the Bozeman router is only aware of the directly connected networks. The Livingston and Helena routers know about each other's Ethernet LANs (172.16.151.0 and 172.16.152.0), but neither one seems to know about the Bozeman router's Ethernet (172.16.150.0). The problem seems to lie with the Bozeman router.

What's different about the Bozeman router's configuration from those of the other two routers is that the Bozeman has defined its subinterface as a multipoint. Subinterfaces can be defined either as point-to-point or multipoint. From OSPF's point of view, a multipoint subinterface represents a different network type than a point-to-point subinterface. And network types must match between neighboring OSPF routers if they are to exchange routing updates, unlike protocols such as RIP and IGRP which don't have a concept of a network type. Several solutions to this problem scenario involving an OSPF network type mismatch are developed in the following section.

Network Type Mismatch

From OSPF's point of view, there are four types of networks that routers can be interfaced to:

- Non-broadcast
- Point-to-point
- Point-to-multipoint
- Broadcast

An OSPF router defaults to one of these four network types for every one of its interfaces. The default network type is a function of the router's physical interface and the Data Link Layer encapsulation. OSPF's behavior varies as a function of network type. Consequently, if two OSPF routers are going to exchange routing updates, it is vital that they are interfaced to the same network type. Conceptually, this is similar to the issue of encapsulation mismatches that was examined in Chapter 1. OSPF network type must match between neighboring routers, just like Data Link Layer encapsulation must match, if they expect to establish a FULL adjacency and exchange routing updates. The big difference between encapsulation mismatch and OSPF network type mismatch is that if there is an encapsulation mismatch, neighboring routers will not be able to exchange anything. When there is a mismatch in the OSPF network type, it's only the OSPF messages that are affected.

Cisco's IOS allows for the changing of the default OSPF network type, which comes in very handy. The four network types are examined next.

Non-broadcast Network Type

OSPF routers default to the non-broadcast network type when a router's physical interfaces (without being configured as subinterfaces) are connected to a WAN cloud. WAN clouds are used in reference to networking technologies such as Frame Relay, ATM, or X.25. These technologies rely on the use of virtual circuits for establishing connectivity between devices. In Frame Relay, Data Link Connection Identifiers, or DLCIs, identify virtual circuits. The non-broadcast network type is also the default when Frame Relay is configured using multipoint subinterfaces. However, when Frame Relay is configured using point-to-point subinterfaces, the default

OSPF network type is point-to-point. This is the key issue that's causing the problem in the scenario depicted in Figure 8.1.

Observe the partial output from the show ip ospf interface command displaying the information about the s0.101 subinterface on the Bozeman router.

```
Bozeman#sh ip ospf inter
Serial0.101 is up, line protocol is up
  Internet Address 172.16.102.1/24, Area 0.0.0.0
  Process ID 1, Router ID 172.16.150.1, Network Type NON_BROADCAST, Cost: 1562
  Transmit Delay is 1 sec, State DR, Priority 1
  Designated Router (ID) 172.16.150.1, Interface address 172.16.102.1
  No backup designated router on this network
  Timer intervals configured, Hello 30, Dead 120, Wait 120, Retransmit 5
    Hello due in 00:00:11
  Neighbor Count is 0, Adjacent neighbor count is 0
  Suppress hello for 0 neighbor(s)
```

Notice the Network Type showing up as NON_BROADCAST on Bozeman's s0.101. Now look at the output from the same commands for Livingston and Helena routers:

```
Livingston#sh ip ospf inter
Serial0.101 is up, line protocol is up
  Internet Address 172.16.102.2/24, Area 0.0.0.0
  Process ID 1, Router ID 172.16.151.1, Network Type POINT_TO_POINT, Cost: 1562
  Transmit Delay is 1 sec, State POINT_TO_POINT,
  Timer intervals configured, Hello 10, Dead 40, Wait 40, Retransmit 5
    Hello due in 00:00:09
  Neighbor Count is 0, Adjacent neighbor count is 0
  Suppress hello for 0 neighbor(s)
Serial0.103 is up, line protocol is up
  Internet Address 172.16.101.9/30, Area 0.0.0.0
  Process ID 1, Router ID 172.16.151.1, Network Type POINT_TO_POINT, Cost: 1562
  Transmit Delay is 1 sec, State POINT_TO_POINT,
  Timer intervals configured, Hello 10, Dead 40, Wait 40, Retransmit 5
    Hello due in 00:00:07
```

```
Neighbor Count is 1, Adjacent neighbor count is 1
  Adjacent with neighbor 172.16.152.1
Suppress hello for 0 neighbor(s)
Helena#sh ip ospf inter
Serial0.101 is up, line protocol is up
  Internet Address 172.16.102.3/24, Area 0.0.0.0
  Process ID 1, Router ID 172.16.152.1, Network Type POINT_TO_POINT, Cost: 1562
  Transmit Delay is 1 sec, State POINT_TO_POINT,
  Timer intervals configured, Hello 10, Dead 40, Wait 40, Retransmit 5
    Hello due in 00:00:09
  Neighbor Count is 0, Adjacent neighbor count is 0
  Suppress hello for 0 neighbor(s)
Serial0.102 is up, line protocol is up
  Internet Address 172.16.101.10/30, Area 0.0.0.0
  Process ID 1, Router ID 172.16.152.1, Network Type POINT_TO_POINT, Cost: 1562
  Transmit Delay is 1 sec, State POINT_TO_POINT,
  Timer intervals configured, Hello 10, Dead 40, Wait 40, Retransmit 5
    Hello due in 00:00:08
  Neighbor Count is 1, Adjacent neighbor count is 1
    Adjacent with neighbor 172.16.151.1
  Suppress hello for 0 neighbor(s)
```

The network type for all of the subinterfaces on Livingston and Helena routers is point-to-point.

What stands out from the preceding traces is that the Livingston and Helena routers are able to establish adjacency and exchange OSPF routing updates. Livingston has a neighbor on its subinterface s0.103, which has a PVC to Helena, and Helena has a neighbor on its subinterface s0.102, over which it has a PVC to Livingston. However, neither Livingston nor Helena are able to establish adjacency with the Bozeman router due to network type mismatch. Consequently, the Bozeman router will only be aware of the directly connected networks. Notice that the `Adjacent neighbor count` on the Bozeman router is 0, while it is 1 on the Helena and Livingston routers.

There are several ways in which the situation can be remedied. One is to configure the Bozeman router with two point-to-point subinterfaces instead of using a single multipoint subinterface. In this way, interfaces on all three routers connecting into the Frame Relay cloud will have the same network type, which is point-to-point.

Point-to-point Network Type

One characteristic of OSPF on point-to-point networks — whether physical point-to-point links or defined via point-to-point subinterfaces — is that it always establishes full adjacency without electing a Designated Router (DR) or a Backup Designated Router (BDR). DR/BDR is discussed further in the broadcast network type section. The catch here is that each point-to-point link consumes a separate subnet, which means that reconfiguration would have to take place on all three routers. Notice the changes to the configuration, the subsequent changes to the routing tables, and the display resulting from the `show ip ospf interface` command.

Reconfigured Bozeman router with point-to-point subinterfaces

```
!
hostname Bozeman
!
enable password cisco
!
interface Ethernet0
  ip address 172.16.150.1 255.255.255.0
!
interface Serial0
  no ip address
  encapsulation frame-relay
  no ip route-cache
  no ip mroute-cache
  frame-relay lmi-type cisco
!
interface Serial0.102 point-to-point
  description 64K link to Livingston
  ip address 172.16.101.1 255.255.255.252
  bandwidth 64
```

```
  frame-relay interface-dlci 102
!
interface Serial0.103 point-to-point
  description 64K link to Helena
  ip address 172.16.101.5 255.255.255.252
  bandwidth 64
  frame-relay interface-dlci 103
!
router ospf 1
  network 172.16.101.1 0.0.0.0 area 0.0.0.0
  network 172.16.101.5 0.0.0.0 area 0.0.0.0
  network 172.16.150.0 0.0.0.255 area 0.0.0.0
```

Reconfigured Livingston router following Bozeman's reconfiguration with point-to-point subinterfaces

```
!
hostname Livingston
!
enable password cisco
!
interface Ethernet0
  ip address 172.16.151.1 255.255.255.0
!
interface Serial0
  no ip address
  encapsulation frame-relay
  no ip mroute-cache
  no fair-queue
  frame-relay lmi-type cisco
!
interface Serial0.101 point-to-point
  description 64K frame link to Bozeman
  ip address 172.16.101.2 255.255.255.252   Note address change
  bandwidth 64
  frame-relay interface-dlci 201
```

```
!
interface Serial0.103 point-to-point

description 64k frame link to Helena

ip address 172.16.101.9 255.255.255.252

bandwidth 64

frame-relay interface-dlci 203
!
router ospf 1

network 172.16.101.2 0.0.0.0 area 0.0.0.0

network 172.16.101.9 0.0.0.0 area 0.0.0.0

network 172.16.151.0 0.0.0.255 area 0.0.0.0
!
```

Reconfigured Helena router following Bozeman's reconfiguration with point-to-point subinterfaces

```
!
hostname Helena
!
enable password cisco
!
ip subnet-zero
!
interface Ethernet0

ip address 172.16.152.1 255.255.255.0
!
interface Serial0

no ip address

encapsulation frame-relay

no ip mroute-cache

frame-relay lmi-type cisco
!
interface Serial0.101 point-to-point

description 64K frame link to Bozeman

ip address 172.16.101.6 255.255.255.252          Note address change

bandwidth 64
```

```
frame-relay interface-dlci 301
!
interface Serial0.102 point-to-point
 description 64K frame link to Livingston
 ip address 172.16.101.10 255.255.255.252
 bandwidth 64
 frame-relay interface-dlci 302
!
router ospf 1
 network 172.16.101.6 0.0.0.0 area 0.0.0.0
 network 172.16.101.10 0.0.0.0 area 0.0.0.0
 network 172.16.152.0 0.0.0.255 area 0.0.0.0
!
```

The routing table for Bozeman now looks a lot fuller. OSPF-derived routes for Ethernet networks attached to Livingston and Helena are now showing up in the Bozeman's routing table.

Bozeman's routing table following reconfiguration with point-to-point subinterfaces

```
Bozeman#sh ip route
Codes: C - connected, S - static, I - IGRP, R - RIP, M - mobile, B - BGP
       D - EIGRP, EX - EIGRP external, O - OSPF,

Gateway of last resort is not set

     172.16.0.0/16 is variably subnetted, 6 subnets, 2 masks
O        172.16.152.0/24 [110/1572] via 172.16.101.6, 00:04:01, Serial0.103
C        172.16.150.0/24 is directly connected, Ethernet0
O        172.16.151.0/24 [110/1572] via 172.16.101.2, 00:04:01, Serial0.102
O        172.16.101.8/30 [110/3124] via 172.16.101.2, 00:04:01, Serial0.102
                         [110/3124] via 172.16.101.6, 00:04:01, Serial0.103
C        172.16.101.0/30 is directly connected, Serial0.102
C        172.16.101.4/30 is directly connected, Serial0.103
```

The tables for the Livingston and Helena routers now show entries for the Ethernet attached to the Bozeman router (172.16.150.0/24).

Livingston's routing table following Bozeman's reconfiguration with point-to-point subinterfaces

```
Livingston#sh ip route
Codes: C - connected, S - static, I - IGRP, R - RIP, M - mobile, B - BGP
       D - EIGRP, EX - EIGRP external, O - OSPF,


Gateway of last resort is not set

     172.16.0.0/16 is variably subnetted, 6 subnets, 2 masks
O       172.16.152.0/24 [110/1572] via 172.16.101.10, 00:04:12, Serial0.103
O       172.16.150.0/24 [110/1572] via 172.16.101.1, 00:04:12, Serial0.101
C       172.16.151.0/24 is directly connected, Ethernet0
C       172.16.101.8/30 is directly connected, Serial0.103
C       172.16.101.0/30 is directly connected, Serial0.101
O       172.16.101.4/30 [110/3124] via 172.16.101.10, 00:04:12, Serial0.103
                        [110/3124] via 172.16.101.1, 00:04:12, Serial0.101
```

Helena's routing table following Bozeman's reconfiguration with point-to-point subinterfaces

```
Helena#sh ip route
Codes: C - connected, S - static, I - IGRP, R - RIP, M - mobile, B - BGP
       D - EIGRP, EX - EIGRP external, O - OSPF,


Gateway of last resort is not set

     172.16.0.0/16 is variably subnetted, 6 subnets, 2 masks
C       172.16.152.0/24 is directly connected, Ethernet0
O       172.16.150.0/24 [110/1572] via 172.16.101.5, 00:04:30, Serial0.101
O       172.16.151.0/24 [110/1572] via 172.16.101.9, 00:04:30, Serial0.102
C       172.16.101.8/30 is directly connected, Serial0.102
O       172.16.101.0/30 [110/3124] via 172.16.101.9, 00:04:30, Serial0.102
                        [110/3124] via 172.16.101.5, 00:04:30, Serial0.101
C       172.16.101.4/30 is directly connected, Serial0.101
```

Full connectivity has been re-established through the preceding recon-figuration. All of the routers show entries in their routing tables for all of the subnets in the internetwork. However, a note of caution about the re-configuration process may save you a few headaches.

Normally, a command that has been issued on a Cisco router can be negated by simply putting a no in front of it. If a subinterface s0.101 has been configured as a multipoint, it can be removed with a "no" statement as follows: no interface s0.101 multipoint. However, if you attempt to reconfigure the same subinterface number now as point-to-point, you will get an error message. What you should do is to save your configuration to NVRAM, reload the router, and then reconfigure your subinterface. The other option is to use a different subinterface number.

The following traces displaying OSPF on the routers' interfaces now in-dicate that the network type on each serial subinterface is point-to-point. All of the routers have an adjacent neighbor on each subinterface. Contrast this with the traces from the preceding section where the Bozeman router was configured with a multipoint subinterface.

```
Bozeman#sh ip ospf inter
Serial0.102 is up, line protocol is up
  Internet Address 172.16.101.1/30, Area 0.0.0.0
  Process ID 1, Router ID 172.16.150.1, Network Type POINT_TO_POINT, Cost: 1562
  Transmit Delay is 1 sec, State POINT_TO_POINT,
  Timer intervals configured, Hello 10, Dead 40, Wait 40, Retransmit 5
    Hello due in 00:00:08
  Neighbor Count is 1, Adjacent neighbor count is 1
    Adjacent with neighbor 172.16.151.1
  Suppress hello for 0 neighbor(s)
Serial0.103 is up, line protocol is up
  Internet Address 172.16.101.5/30, Area 0.0.0.0
  Process ID 1, Router ID 172.16.150.1, Network Type POINT_TO_POINT, Cost: 1562
  Transmit Delay is 1 sec, State POINT_TO_POINT,
  Timer intervals configured, Hello 10, Dead 40, Wait 40, Retransmit 5
    Hello due in 00:00:03
  Neighbor Count is 1, Adjacent neighbor count is 1
    Adjacent with neighbor 192.168.3.2
```

```
Suppress hello for 0 neighbor(s)


Livingston#sh ip ospf inter

Serial0.101 is up, line protocol is up

  Internet Address 172.16.101.2/30, Area 0.0.0.0

  Process ID 1, Router ID 172.16.151.1, Network Type POINT_TO_POINT, Cost: 1562

  Transmit Delay is 1 sec, State POINT_TO_POINT,

  Timer intervals configured, Hello 10, Dead 40, Wait 40, Retransmit 5

    Hello due in 00:00:08

  Neighbor Count is 1, Adjacent neighbor count is 1

    Adjacent with neighbor 172.16.150.1

  Suppress hello for 0 neighbor(s)

Serial0.103 is up, line protocol is up

  Internet Address 172.16.101.9/30, Area 0.0.0.0

  Process ID 1, Router ID 172.16.151.1, Network Type POINT_TO_POINT, Cost: 1562

  Transmit Delay is 1 sec, State POINT_TO_POINT,

  Timer intervals configured, Hello 10, Dead 40, Wait 40, Retransmit 5

    Hello due in 00:00:03

  Neighbor Count is 1, Adjacent neighbor count is 1

    Adjacent with neighbor 192.168.3.2

  Suppress hello for 0 neighbor(s)


Helena#sh ip ospf inter

Ethernet0 is up, line protocol is up

 Serial0.101 is up, line protocol is up

  Internet Address 172.16.101.6/30, Area 0.0.0.0

  Process ID 1, Router ID 192.168.3.2, Network Type POINT_TO_POINT, Cost: 1562

  Transmit Delay is 1 sec, State POINT_TO_POINT,

  Timer intervals configured, Hello 10, Dead 40, Wait 40, Retransmit 5

    Hello due in 00:00:06

  Neighbor Count is 1, Adjacent neighbor count is 1

    Adjacent with neighbor 172.16.150.1

  Suppress hello for 0 neighbor(s)

 Serial0.102 is up, line protocol is up

  Internet Address 172.16.101.10/30, Area 0.0.0.0
```

```
Process ID 1, Router ID 192.168.3.2, Network Type POINT_TO_POINT, Cost: 1562

Transmit Delay is 1 sec, State POINT_TO_POINT,

Timer intervals configured, Hello 10, Dead 40, Wait 40, Retransmit 5

    Hello due in 00:00:04

Neighbor Count is 1, Adjacent neighbor count is 1

    Adjacent with neighbor 172.16.151.1

Suppress hello for 0 neighbor(s)
```

Point-to-multipoint Network Type

The next OSPF network type that's considered here is point-to-multipoint. Interfaces configured for OSPF do not default to this network type; point-to-multipoint has to be configured explicitly on an interface via the configuration command `ip ospf network point-to-multipoint`.

Configuring OSPF as a point-to-multipoint network type enables the use of a single IP subnet for the entire WAN cloud, does not require a full PVC mesh, has a high degree of reliability, and at the same time is very easy to configure. The point-to-multipoint network type is typically configured on physical interfaces as opposed to subinterfaces. The implication here is that multiple DLCIs may be configured on a single physical interface. Configuring Frame Relay on a physical interface with multiple DLCIs and defining a point-to-multipoint OSPF network type works fine with OSPF. However, if multiple DLCIs are associated with a single physical interface and Frame Relay is used with distance vector protocols such as RIP or IGRP, you can run into a problem with split horizon. Split horizon is automatically disabled when Frame Relay encapsulation is used on a physical interface. This increases the probability of loops. If you enable split horizon, some networks may become unreachable.

The rule of thumb is that if you are running OSPF over Frame Relay as the only routing protocol, then point-to-multipoint is a viable option, given its advantages. If routing protocols other than OSPF are also used in your Frame Relay configuration, it's best to consider using point-to-point subinterfaces. With subinterfaces there is no need to use point-to-multipoint network type for OSPF if point-to-point subinterfaces are used. OSPF defaults to point-to-point network type for point-to-point subinterfaces. However, if only multipoint subinterfaces are used, OSPF will default to the non-broadcast network type. In this case, there is a choice.

Change the network type to point-to-multipoint or leave it as non-broadcast and start configuring neighbors, making sure that at least one router has PVCs to all other routers. Configuring neighbors with a non-broadcast OSPF network type is very labor intensive, and is certainly not the recommended choice for running OSPF over a WAN cloud.

A point-to-multipoint configuration example follows. Contrast this example with the subinterface point-to-point configuration in the preceding section. The point-to-multipoint configuration is a lot simpler. Interfaces serial0 on all three routers have an IP address assigned from the same subnet, and the OSPF point-to-multipoint network is specified on each interface. Inverse ARP, which is enabled on a Cisco router by default, provides the mapping between the DLCIs and the destination IP addresses. Unlike in the subinterface configuration example, DLCIs no longer have to be specified on each interface via the `frame-relay interface-dlci` *xxx* command, where *xxx* represents a DLCI number between 16 and 1022. The Frame Relay switch announces the DLCIs to the routers and they are mapped via Inverse ARP to the destination IP addresses. The net result is that the point-to-multipoint configuration is a lot simpler but the final outcome is the same as with the subinterface configuration in the preceding section. There is full reachability between all destinations.

Bozeman router configuration with point-to-multipoint OSPF network type

```
!
hostname Bozeman
!
enable password cisco
!
interface Ethernet0
 ip address 172.16.150.1 255.255.255.0
!
interface Serial0
 ip address 172.16.101.1 255.255.255.0
 encapsulation frame-relay
 ip ospf network point-to-multipoint
 frame-relay lmi-type cisco
!
router ospf 1
```

```
 network 172.16.101.1 0.0.0.0 area 0.0.0.0
 network 172.16.150.0 0.0.0.255 area 0.0.0.0
!
```

Livingston router configuration with point-to-multipoint OSPF network type

```
!
hostname Livingston
!
enable password cisco
!
interface Ethernet0
 ip address 172.16.151.1 255.255.255.0
!
interface Serial0
 ip address 172.16.101.2 255.255.255.0
 encapsulation frame-relay
 ip ospf network point-to-multipoint
 frame-relay lmi-type cisco
!
router ospf 1
 network 172.16.101.2 0.0.0.0 area 0.0.0.0
 network 172.16.151.0 0.0.0.255 area 0.0.0.0
!
```

Helena router configuration with point-to-multipoint OSPF network type

```
!
hostname Helena
!
enable password cisco
!
interface Ethernet0
 ip address 172.16.152.1 255.255.255.0
!
interface Serial0
```

```
ip address 172.16.101.3 255.255.255.0

encapsulation frame-relay

ip ospf network point-to-multipoint

frame-relay lmi-type cisco

!

router ospf 1

network 172.16.101.3 0.0.0.0 area 0.0.0.0

network 172.16.152.0 0.0.0.255 area 0.0.0.0
```

If the network type had not been specified on the serial0 interface of each router, OSPF would have defaulted to the non-broadcast type. Additional configuration of neighbors would have been required in order to make OSPF function. The show ip ospf interface s0 display on all three routers clearly reflects the point-to-multipoint network type and the fact that each router is fully adjacent with two neighbors.

```
Bozeman#sh ip ospf interface s0

Serial0 is up, line protocol is up

   Internet Address 172.16.101.1/24, Area 0.0.0.0

   Process ID 1, Router ID 172.16.150.1, Network Type POINT_TO_MULTIPOINT, Cost: 64

   Transmit Delay is 1 sec, State POINT_TO_MULTIPOINT,

   Timer intervals configured, Hello 30, Dead 120, Wait 120, Retransmit 5

     Hello due in 00:00:16

   Neighbor Count is 2, Adjacent neighbor count is 2

     Adjacent with neighbor 172.16.151.1

     Adjacent with neighbor 172.16.152.1

   Suppress hello for 0 neighbor(s)


Livingston#sh ip ospf interface s0

Serial0 is up, line protocol is up

   Internet Address 172.16.101.2/24, Area 0.0.0.0

   Process ID 1, Router ID 172.16.151.1, Network Type POINT_TO_MULTIPOINT, Cost: 64

   Transmit Delay is 1 sec, State POINT_TO_MULTIPOINT,

   Timer intervals configured, Hello 30, Dead 120, Wait 120, Retransmit 5

     Hello due in 00:00:20

   Neighbor Count is 2, Adjacent neighbor count is 2
```

```
Adjacent with neighbor 172.16.150.1

Adjacent with neighbor 172.16.152.1

Suppress hello for 0 neighbor(s)
```

```
Helena#sh ip ospf interface s0

Serial0 is up, line protocol is up

  Internet Address 172.16.101.3/24, Area 0.0.0.0

  Process ID 1, Router ID 172.16.152.1, Network Type POINT_TO_MULTIPOINT, Cost: 64

  Transmit Delay is 1 sec, State POINT_TO_MULTIPOINT,

  Timer intervals configured, Hello 30, Dead 120, Wait 120, Retransmit 5

    Hello due in 00:00:04

  Neighbor Count is 2, Adjacent neighbor count is 2

    Adjacent with neighbor 172.16.150.1

    Adjacent with neighbor 172.16.151.1

  Suppress hello for 0 neighbor(s)
```

Broadcast Network Type

Broadcast networks are LANs like Ethernet, Token Ring, or FDDI. When an OSPF router is interfaced to one of these networks, OSPF views it by default as a broadcast network type. When OSPF detects a broadcast network type, it also engages in a process of selecting a Designated Router (DR) and a Backup Designated Router (BDR) on that subnet. The idea behind a DR and a BDR is to reduce the amount of routing updates that are exchanged between routers attached to the same broadcast subnet. Broadcast subnets are considered to be transitive. This means that if router X can talk to router Y, and router Y can talk to router Z, then router X can talk to router Z. That's not the case with WAN clouds. X can have a PVC to Y and Y can have a PVC to Z, but there is no PVC from X to Z. Consequently, X cannot communicate directly with Z without going through Y.

Transitivity has its advantages. For example, a router only needs to transmit a single packet to reach all other routers on a broadcast subnet, whereas on a WAN cloud, the same packet has to be transmitted on every PVC. However, when it comes to exchanging routing updates between neighbors on a transitive network, transitivity can have disadvantages as well.

Consider the meaning of OSPF as a link-state protocol. A link is considered to be a router's interface to a network or, better yet, to a neighbor on that network. On a point-to-point physical subnet, a router is going to have a single neighbor. On a subnetwork, where a router is acting as a default gateway for hosts, it's not going to have any neighbors. However, on a transit broadcast subnet, it's going to have many neighbors. Having the potential for many neighbors on a broadcast subnet creates what's commonly referred to in more theoretical discussions of OSPF as the "n square" problem.

The "n square" stems from the fact that if there are "n" routers attached to a broadcast subnet, then each one of them would have a link to all of its neighbors, that is, each router would have (n-1) links just on that subnet. The formula for the total number of router connections on the broadcast network is n(n-1)/2. This is how the "n square" problem got its name Having a designated router on a broadcast subnet is intended to reduce the number of links, resulting in fewer routing update messages between neighboring routers.

The DR/BDR concept is an optimization technique. OSPF functions fine on point-to-point and point-to-multipoint networks without DR/BDR election, but on broadcast networks, DR/BDR election automatically takes place so that the DR and BDR will have FULL adjacency with all other routers on the broadcast subnet. But routers that are neither DR nor BDR (known as DROTHERs) will only have a 2-WAY relationship with one another. The 2-WAY relationship enables them to exchange Hello messages, but not link-state update messages which represent routing updates.

From a troubleshooting perspective, it's important to understand that if there are broadcast subnets in an OSPF internetwork, each one them should have a DR to function properly. A BDR is helpful in case of a DR failure. The DR synchronizes the link-state databases — from which routing tables are derived — with all of the other routers on a broadcast subnet. Without a DR on transit broadcast subnets, the neighboring routers will not have correct routing tables.

DR/BDR election takes place automatically on a broadcast subnet. It is influenced by the priority value, which is an interface parameter. The default OSPF priority is 1. The priority field, which is inside the OSPF Hello messages, can assume values from 0 to 255. The higher the priority, the more likely that a router will become a DR. A router with a 0 priority on an interface will never become a DR or BDR. The election of a DR is also influenced by the power-on order of routers on a broadcast subnet. Once a DR has been elected—the first router with non-zero priority that's powered up on a subnet—it will remain DR until its interface to that subnet has been shut down or priority value for that interface is changed to 0.

Consider the scenario depicted in Figure 8.2 where four routers have their Ethernet 0 interface attached to the same Ethernet subnet. Each router also has a serial link to other locations.

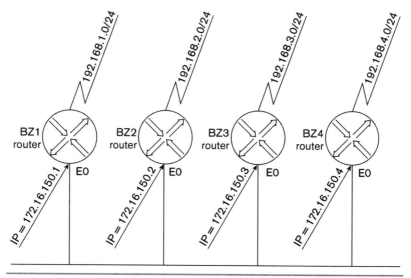

Figure 8.2 *OSPF on an Ethernet (broadcast) subnet with four routers attached*

Given this configuration, one of the routers should become a DR, another BDR, and the remaining two DROTHERs.

A `show ip ospf neighbor` command executed on the BZ4 router shows that BZ4 has three neighbors over its Ethernet 0 interface. One of the neighbors is DR, the other BDR, and the last one DROTHER. The relationship the BZ4 has on that subnet with the DROTHER (in the State column of the trace) is 2-WAY. This indicates that BZ4 is also a DROTHER on that subnet. A DR and BDR will always have a FULL adjacency with all other routers on a subnet.

```
BZ4#sh ip ospf neigh
```

Neighbor ID	Pri	State	Dead Time	Address	Interface
172.16.150.2	1	FULL/BDR	0:00:39	172.16.150.2	Ethernet0
172.16.150.1	1	FULL/DR	0:00:39	172.16.150.1	Ethernet0
172.16.150.3	1	2WAY/DROTHER	0:00:35	172.16.150.3	Ethernet0

Looking at the trace from `show ip ospf interface` e0 on router BZ4 reveals that it is interfaced to a broadcast network, it is a DROTHER, it has two adjacencies (with DR and BDR), and it has three neighbors (able to exchange Hello messages with DR, BDR, and DROTHER).

```
BZ4#sh ip ospf int e0
Ethernet0 is up, line protocol is up
  Internet Address 172.16.150.4 255.255.255.0, Area 0.0.0.0
  Process ID 1, Router ID 172.16.150.4, Network Type BROADCAST, Cost: 10
  Transmit Delay is 1 sec, State DROTHER, Priority 1
  Designated Router (ID) 172.16.150.1, Interface address 172.16.150.1
  Backup Designated router (ID) 172.16.150.2, Interface address 172.16.150.2
  Timer intervals configured, Hello 10, Dead 40, Wait 40, Retransmit 5
    Hello due in 0:00:01
  Neighbor Count is 3, Adjacent neighbor count is 2
    Adjacent with neighbor 172.16.150.2  (Backup Designated Router)
    Adjacent with neighbor 172.16.150.1  (Designated Router)
```

With regard to configuration, there is very little to misconfigure when configuring OSPF to run over a broadcast subnet, unless of course you are changing priorities. What can happen when changing priorities is discussed in the next section.

Zero Priority on All Routers on a Broadcast Subnet

There is a general misunderstanding about what happens to OSPF on a broadcast subnet when all routers interfaced to that subnet have the OSPF priority value set to a 0 for their interfaces to that subnet. The OSPF priority value for an interface is changed using the `ip ospf priority` *xx* command, where *xx* represents a value between 0 and 255. Consider what happens when the OSPF priority value is changed to 0 on the E0 interfaces on all routers in Figure 8.2.

The `show ip ospf neighbor` command executed on router BZ4 yields the following trace.

```
BZ4#sh ip ospf neigh


Neighbor ID    Pri   State          Dead Time   Address        Interface

172.16.150.2    0    2WAY/DROTHER   0:00:39     172.16.150.2   Ethernet0

172.16.150.1    0    2WAY/DROTHER   0:00:30     172.16.150.1   Ethernet0

172.16.150.3    0    2WAY/DROTHER   0:00:39     172.16.150.3   Ethernet0

BZ4#
```

There is no DR or BDR on this subnet. The 2-WAY relationship enables routers to exchange Hello messages but not routing updates. The implication is that this subnet is no longer a transit subnet. Router BZ1 (see Figure 8.2) will not be able to communicate to router BZ4 about the networks that it can reach via its serial interface, and vice versa. The same applies to all of the other routers. For example, BZ1 will not know about the serial networks 192.168.2.0, 192.168.3.0, or 192.168.4.0 connected to BZ2, BZ3, and BZ4, respectively.

Effectively, the transit subnet — now no longer a transit — has become a "firewall" of sorts between different portions of the OSPF internetwork interfaced to that subnet. This is usually not a desirable situation and is considered to be a misconfiguration. However, it may serve a useful purpose when portions of an internetwork need to be isolated from one another for other troubleshooting purposes. Note that this applies to OSPF only. Output from the command `sh ip ospf interface e0` confirms that BZ4 has neighbors but no adjacencies over which to exchange routing updates.

```
BZ4#sh ip ospf interface e0

Ethernet0 is up, line protocol is up

  Internet Address 172.16.150.4 255.255.255.0, Area 0.0.0.0

  Process ID 1, Router ID 172.16.150.4, Network Type BROADCAST, Cost: 10

  Transmit Delay is 1 sec, State DROTHER, Priority 0
```

```
No designated router on this network

No backup designated router on this network

Timer intervals configured, Hello 10, Dead 40, Wait 40, Retransmit 5

  Hello due in 0:00:05
```
Neighbor Count is 3, Adjacent neighbor count is 0
```
BZ4#
```

OSPF Configuration Models on Frame Relay WANs

The various ways of configuring OSPF on Frame Relay WANs were discussed in the context of OSPF network types. This section serves as a reinforcement and summary of the different techniques and potential pitfalls.

NBMA Model

Non-Broadcast Multi Access (NBMA) is used generically in reference to WAN clouds like Frame Relay or ATM. However, from OSPF's point of view, the NBMA model is used when OSPF considers the cloud either as a broadcast or non-broadcast network type. As discussed in the Network type mismatch section, OSPF defaults to certain network types for different interfaces and encapsulations, but it can also be "fooled" into thinking that what it would normally consider as a default is actually a different network type. This is done via the ip ospf network *network_type* command where *network_type* is broadcast, non-broadcast, point-to-point, or point-to-multipoint.

The characteristic of the NBMA model is that it requires a DR election. You've seen what happens without a DR on a broadcast subnet; only 2-WAY relationships are formed which do not allow for the exchange of routing updates. On a genuine broadcast subnet (shared media like Ethernet), the DR election can take place automatically. However, on a Frame Relay mesh presented to OSPF as a broadcast network, the DR election should take place automatically only when there is a full mesh.

Without a full mesh you have to disqualify routers that do not have PVCs to all other routers from becoming DR. This is done by setting their OSPF priority value to 0 on their interfaces into the cloud. With a partial mesh presented to OSPF as a broadcast network, a router that does not have a PVC to all other routers could become a DR if it was not disqualified from doing so by an administrator. What's emerging is that the NBMA model works best when the WAN cloud is fully meshed.

But even with a full mesh, the NBMA model is subject to strange failure modes. Consider a fully meshed WAN cloud between five routers with PVCs going from every router to every other router, as shown in Figure 8.3.

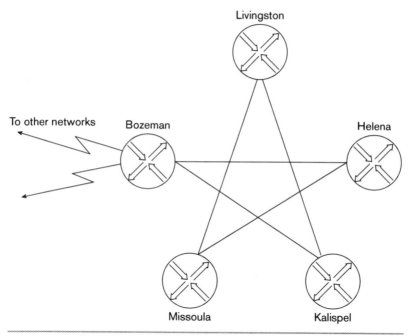

Figure 8.3 *OSPF over a fully meshed Frame Relay cloud*

Assume that the Bozeman router has become a DR. Assume also that there is no BDR—a conscious decision by the network administrator to conserve WAN bandwidth. Now, consider that the Missoula router loses its PVC to the Bozeman router. Even though Missoula has PVCs to all of the other routers, it will not be able to communicate any routing updates to them because all of the routing information about the networks that Missoula could reached was shared with all of the other routers via the DR. This is why configuring OSPF on a WAN cloud using the NBMA model is no longer popular. But it used to be the only way to configure OSPF on a WAN before there was IOS support for the point-to-multipoint model and subinterfaces.

Point-to-Multipoint Model

The strength of the point-to-multipoint model is that it functions well with partial meshes. This model has no DR/BDR election. With no DR issues to contend with, the failure of a PVC between Bozeman and Missoula has minimal impact on Missoula. Missoula can still share routing updates about the networks it can reach with all of the other routers to which it has PVCs. In a point-to-multipoint configuration, all neighboring routers automatically establish FULL adjacencies. The downside of the point-to-multipoint configuration is that there will be more traffic resulting from routing updates on the links.

But if bandwidth is not an issue and the resiliency of the WAN cloud is of primary concern, then the point-to-multipoint model should be your choice. Just like the NBMA model, the point-to-multipoint model also consumes only a single subnet. The point-to-multipoint network type must be configured explicitly. Watch out for network type mismatches because every interface into the cloud now requires that the point-to-multipoint network type be specified.

Subinterfaces Model

If you are running OSPF as the only routing protocol, then using subinterfaces does not offer any great advantage. If, however, OSPF is running side-by-side with a distance vector protocol, then using subinterfaces is the way to configure your WAN. Subinterfaces will split the cloud into point-to-point links. Each link will require a separate subnet. From OSPF's perspective, it's just like having a bunch of point-to-point physical links. The only difference is that subinterfaces are logical rather than physical interfaces.

OSPF views point-to-point subinterfaces as point-to-point network types. There is no DR/BDR election on point-to-point networks, and neighboring routers always form full adjacencies. The level of resiliency is comparable to the point-to-multipoint model, but there is more configuration and a router will consume more memory when it is configured with subinterfaces.

An additional benefit of using the subinterface model is that point-to-point subinterfaces will handle split horizon issues for distance vector protocols. With point-to-point subinterfaces, routing updates that arrive via one PVC and leave via another are still arriving and leaving via the same physical interface. However, from the perspective of a distance vector protocol, it looks like the updates are coming in via a different interface than they are leaving. Thus, split horizon is not violated and protocols such as IGRP or RIP can run side by side with OSPF.

Authentication Mismatch

OSPF supports three types of authentication:

- Null
- Simple
- MD5

OSPF authentication type is configured per area. All routers with interfaces belonging to a particular area must have the same type of authentication configured for that area. Routers with interfaces in multiple areas must have authentication configured for each area.

OSPF authentication is configured in two sections in the configuration file. Authentication type is configured in the OSPF process section. For routers belonging to multiple areas, that is, ABRs, multiple authentication type configuration statements are required. Passwords and MD5 keys are configured in the interface sections. There is usually one configuration statement per interface.

Correctly configured authentication between neighboring routers enables routers to discover each other and exchange routing updates. Authentication mismatches between neighbors prevent OSPF from operating properly.

Null Authentication

Null authentication means no authentication. This is the default authentication type with OSPF. No configuration is required either in the OSPF process section or in the interface sections.

Simple Authentication

Simple authentication relies on the use of clear text passwords. The key to the successful use of simple authentication is understanding that even though the authentication type must match per area, the passwords must match only between neighboring routers, that is, per subnet. Consequently, a router with three interfaces in the same area can have a different password configured on each interface. However, on each of the three subnets that this router is connected to, all of the neighboring routers must share the same password.

Consider a configuration as shown in Figure 8.4.

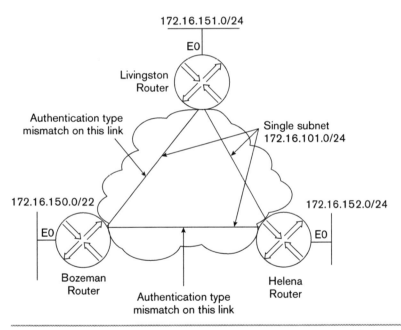

Figure 8-4 *Full Frame Relay mesh in NBMA mode with broadcast OSPF network type used for authentication mismatch analysis*

The configuration for the Bozeman, Livingston, and Helena routers follow. All routers initially implement Null authentication. There are no explicit authentication configuration statements. This is the base configuration that will be used to explore authentication mismatches using simple and MD5 authentication.

Bozeman router base configuration for analysis of authentication mismatches

```
hostname Bozeman
!
enable password cisco
!
interface Ethernet0
 ip address 172.16.150.1 255.255.255.0
!
interface Serial0
 ip address 172.16.101.1 255.255.255.0
 encapsulation frame-relay
 ip ospf network broadcast
 frame-relay lmi-type cisco
!
router ospf 1
 network 172.16.101.1 0.0.0.0 area 0.0.0.0
 network 172.16.150.0 0.0.0.255 area 0.0.0.0
```

Livingston router base configuration for analysis of authentication mismatches

```
hostname Livingston
!
enable password cisco
!
interface Ethernet0
 ip address 172.16.151.1 255.255.255.0
!
interface Serial0
 ip address 172.16.101.2 255.255.255.0
 encapsulation frame-relay
 ip ospf network broadcast
 frame-relay lmi-type cisco
```

```
!
router ospf 1
 network 172.16.101.2 0.0.0.0 area 0.0.0.0
 network 172.16.151.0 0.0.0.255 area 0.0.0.0
```

Helena router base configuration for analysis of authentication mismatches

```
hostname Helena
!
enable password cisco
!
interface Ethernet0
 ip address 172.16.152.1 255.255.255.0
!
interface Serial0
 ip address 172.16.101.3 255.255.255.0
 encapsulation frame-relay
 ip ospf network broadcast
 no ip mroute-cache
 frame-relay lmi-type cisco
!
router ospf 1
 network 172.16.101.3 0.0.0.0 area 0.0.0.0
 network 172.16.152.0 0.0.0.255 area 0.0.0.0
```

Since OSPF looks at the preceding configuration as a broadcast network, it will elect a DR and a BDR on the 172.16.101.0 subnet. A check for OSPF neighbors on each router reveals that each router has a full adjacency with the other two routers on the 172.16.101.0 subnet.

```
Bozeman#sh ip ospf neigh

Neighbor ID     Pri  State      Dead Time   Address       Interface
172.16.151.1     1   FULL/BDR   00:00:32    172.16.101.2   Serial0
172.16.152.1     1   FULL/DR    00:00:39    172.16.101.3   Serial0
```

```
Livingston#sh ip ospf neigh

Neighbor ID     Pri   State          Dead Time   Address        Interface

172.16.150.1     1    FULL/DROTHER   00:00:39    172.16.101.1   Serial0

172.16.152.1     1    FULL/DR        00:00:37    172.16.101.3   Serial0


Helena#sh ip ospf neigh

Neighbor ID     Pri   State          Dead Time   Address        Interface

172.16.150.1     1    FULL/DROTHER   00:00:34    172.16.101.1   Serial0

172.16.151.1     1    FULL/BDR       00:00:36    172.16.101.2   Serial0
```

An analysis of the preceding trace reveals that the Bozeman router has an ID of 172.16.150.1, the Livingston router has an ID of 172.16.151.1, and the Helena router, an ID of 172.16.152.1. The Bozeman router has a full adjacency with a DR and BDR. The conclusion is that the Bozeman router must be something other than DR or BDR, that is, DROTHER. In fact, the traces from Livingston and Helena reveal that each has a full adjacency with a DROTHER router, which matches the ID of the Bozeman router.

The routing tables for the preceding configurations reveal that there is a full reachability between all of the networks.

Bozeman's routing table from the base configuration for analysis of authentication mismatches

```
Bozeman#sh ip route

Codes: C - connected, S - static, I - IGRP, R - RIP, M - mobile, B - BGP

       D - EIGRP, EX - EIGRP external, O - OSPF,


Gateway of last resort is not set


      172.16.0.0/24 is subnetted, 4 subnets

O        172.16.152.0 [110/74] via 172.16.101.3, 00:11:44, Serial0

C        172.16.150.0 is directly connected, Ethernet0

O        172.16.151.0 [110/74] via 172.16.101.2, 00:11:44, Serial0

C        172.16.101.0 is directly connected, Serial0
```

Livingston's routing table from the base configuration for analysis of authentication mismatches

```
Livingston#sh ip route
Codes: C - connected, S - static, I - IGRP, R - RIP, M - mobile, B - BGP
       D - EIGRP, EX - EIGRP external, O - OSPF,


Gateway of last resort is not set


     172.16.0.0/24 is subnetted, 4 subnets
O       172.16.152.0 [110/74] via 172.16.101.3, 00:12:00, Serial0
O       172.16.150.0 [110/74] via 172.16.101.1, 00:12:00, Serial0
C       172.16.151.0 is directly connected, Ethernet0
C       172.16.101.0 is directly connected, Serial0
```

Helena's routing table from the base configuration for analysis of authentication mismatches

```
Helena#sh ip route
Codes: C - connected, S - static, I - IGRP, R - RIP, M - mobile, B - BGP
       D - EIGRP, EX - EIGRP external, O - OSPF,


Gateway of last resort is not set


     172.16.0.0/24 is subnetted, 4 subnets
C       172.16.152.0 is directly connected, Ethernet0
O       172.16.150.0 [110/74] via 172.16.101.1, 00:12:15, Serial0
O       172.16.151.0 [110/74] via 172.16.101.2, 00:12:15, Serial0
C       172.16.101.0 is directly connected, Serial0
```

Now comes the demonstration of the authentication mismatch problem. Notice the change to the Bozeman configuration and the effects of that change on the neighbor relationships or states, and the routing tables. The configuration for Livingston and Helena remains unchanged.

Reconfigured Bozeman router introducing authentication mismatch

```
hostname Bozeman
!
enable password cisco
!
interface Ethernet0
 ip address 172.16.150.1 255.255.255.0
!
interface Serial0
 ip address 172.16.101.1 255.255.255.0
 encapsulation frame-relay
 ip ospf authentication-key abc
 ip ospf network broadcast
 frame-relay lmi-type cisco
!
router ospf 1
 network 172.16.101.1 0.0.0.0 area 0.0.0.0
 network 172.16.150.0 0.0.0.255 area 0.0.0.0
 area 0.0.0.0 authentication
```

The effects of the preceding configuration change are devastating. Bozeman no longer has any relationships with any of its neighboring routers, and its routing table contains no OSPF entries at all.

```
Bozeman#sh ip ospf neigh
Bozeman#
```

Notice that nothing shows up here, no neighbor state between routers. This is in contrast to the previous example where the Bozeman router had no authentication configured and the state between the Bozeman router and the other two routers was FULL.

A check for OSPF neighbors on the Livingston and Helena routers shows a new state, INIT, between them and Bozeman.

```
Livingston#sh ip ospf neigh
```

Neighbor ID	Pri	State	Dead Time	Address	Interface
172.16.150.1	1	**INIT/DROTHER**	00:00:34	172.16.101.1	Serial0

```
172.16.152.1    1   FULL/DR       00:00:32   172.16.101.3   Serial0


Helena#sh ip ospf neigh


Neighbor ID    Pri  State         Dead Time  Address        Interface
172.16.150.1    1   INIT/DROTHER  00:00:37   172.16.101.1   Serial0
172.16.151.1    1   FULL/BDR      00:00:38   172.16.101.2   Serial0
Helena#
```

The INIT state between the Livingston and Helena routers and the Bozeman router is the result of authentication mismatch. The INIT state indicates lack of bi-directional communication between two routers, namely, the Hello packets are not being exchanged. If the Hello packets are not exchanged, there is no possibility for the routers to establish an adjacency (FULL state) which would enable them to exchange link-state updates. In the preceding configuration, the INIT state will not go away on the Livingston and Helena routers until either authentication is disabled on the Bozeman router, or authentication is configured on the Livingston and Helena routers.

A check of the routing tables on all three routers further confirms that there is a problem.

Bozeman's routing table following introduction of authentication mismatch

```
Bozeman#sh ip route
Codes: C - connected,


Gateway of last resort is not set


     172.16.0.0/24 is subnetted, 2 subnets
C       172.16.150.0 is directly connected, Ethernet0
C       172.16.101.0 is directly connected, Serial0
```

Livingston's routing table following introduction of authentication mismatch

```
Livingston#sh ip route
Codes: C - connected, S - static, I - IGRP, R - RIP, M - mobile, B - BGP
       D - EIGRP, EX - EIGRP external, O - OSPF,
```

```
Gateway of last resort is not set


    172.16.0.0/24 is subnetted, 3 subnets
O       172.16.152.0 [110/74] via 172.16.101.3, 00:06:22, Serial0
C       172.16.151.0 is directly connected, Ethernet0
C       172.16.101.0 is directly connected, Serial0
```

Helena's routing table following introduction of authentication mismatch

```
Helena#sh ip route

Codes: C - connected, S - static, I - IGRP, R - RIP, M - mobile, B - BGP
       D - EIGRP, EX - EIGRP external, O - OSPF,


Gateway of last resort is not set


    172.16.0.0/24 is subnetted, 3 subnets
C       172.16.152.0 is directly connected, Ethernet0
O       172.16.151.0 [110/74] via 172.16.101.2, 00:06:37, Serial0
C       172.16.101.0 is directly connected, Serial0
```

The Ethernet subnet, 172.16.150.0, attached to the Bozeman router is no longer visible to the Livingston and Helena routers. The Bozeman router does not see anything except the directly connected networks, as both of its neighbors have a different authentication type, namely, null authentication. The effects on the Bozeman router would have been the same if its neighbors (Livingston and Helena) were also configured with simple authentication but were using different passwords.

MD5 Authentication

The principles behind the simple authentication mismatch discussed in the preceding section apply to MD5 as well. MD5 is a stronger authentication method than the clear text password authentication. From a troubleshooting perspective, it's important to understand the additional keywords and syntax associated with configuring MD5 authentication. The syntax for configuring MD5 authentication for an area (area 0.0.0.0 in the example), which is done in the OSPF process section, is as follows:

```
area 0.0.0.0 authentication message-digest
```

The only difference here between the simple authentication configuration and MD5 authentication configuration is the message-digest keyword. This is another potential source of authentication mismatches. The MD5 configuration syntax per interface is

```
ip ospf message-digest-key keyid MD5 key
```

The *keyid* is a number between 1 and 255 and the *key* is an alphanumeric password up to 16 characters long. Just like in simple authentication, the keyid and the key must match between neighboring routers. However, MD5 authentication allows for the change of keys and keyids without disrupting routing update exchanges. This is in contrast to simple authentication, where you have up to the dead interval (see next section) to change a password on a neighboring router to the same password, otherwise adjacency between neighbors will fail.

With MD5, you can specify a new key and a keyid on an interface without displacing the old ones. A router with multiple MD5 authentication statements on an interface will send out more multiple OSPF messages authenticated with a different key/keyid combination. After you have changed all of the interfaces to the new key/keyid combination, the old ones can be removed.

Hello Interval Mismatch

The Hello interval represents the amount of time elapsed between two successive transmissions of Hello packets by an OSPF router. The Hello interval is coupled with the Dead interval, which is the amount of time that an OSPF router can tolerate not receiving Hello packets from its neighbor before declaring the neighbor as being down. By default, the Dead interval is four times the Hello interval. The Hello and Dead intervals vary as a function of OSPF network type. On broadcast and point-to-point networks, the value of the Hello interval is 10 seconds and the default value of the Dead interval is 4 times that, or 40 seconds. On non-broadcast and point-to-multipoint networks, the values of Hello and Dead intervals are 30 and 120 seconds, respectively.

The Hello and Dead intervals must match between neighboring routers for OSPF to function properly. As long as you follow the guidelines for avoiding mismatches in OSPF network types and you do not manually change the values of the Hello and Dead intervals, the chances of Hello and Dead interval mismatches between two neighboring routers are zero. Should you choose to manually adjust these two timers, be sure that you consider all of the neighbors.

The values of Hello and Dead intervals apply only to router interfaces; they are not global values. If you want to remove a router from participating in OSPF exchanges on a given interface, changing the Hello interval is probably the easiest way to do it. Such a router will lose adjacencies to its neighbors within the original Dead interval.

Summarization Pitfalls

One of the much-talked about features of OSPF is summarization. Correctly implemented summarization reduces the size of the link-state database, which in turn results in smaller routing tables. Summarization, however, only applies when an OSPF internetwork is broken into areas and the network addresses within each area are somewhat contiguous.

Summarization is implemented on Area Border Routers or ABRs, which connect one or more OSPF areas to the OSPF backbone area, 0.0.0.0. Typically, an ABR will summarize the networks within each area that it connects to the backbone. The ABR will then inject the summary records for these networks into the backbone area's link-state database. Summarization in the opposite direction is also possible. If there is a significant number of contiguous networks on the backbone, these networks can also be summarized by ABRs. When the backbone networks are summarized by ABRs, the summary records are injected into the respective areas.

A good visualization for an ABR implementing summarization is a router with two arrows; one arrow points toward the backbone and represents summarized non-backbone area networks being injected into the backbone's link-state database. The other arrow points away from the backbone into the non-backbone area, representing the backbone's networks being injected into the non-backbone's area link-state database. This summarization is represented visually in Figure 8.5.

Networks from area 0 are
injected into area 1

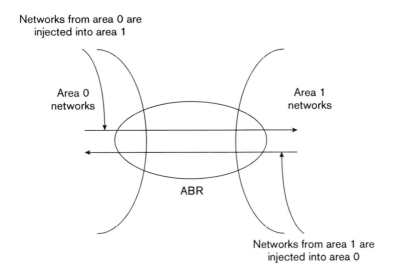

Figure 8.5 *Graphical representation of the OSPF summarization principle*

In Figure 8.5 the ABR injects summary records from the non-backbone area into the backbone (arrow pointing to the left) and vice versa (arrow pointing to the right).

There are two pitfalls to summarization:

- Summarizing non-existent networks
- Using incorrect summary masks

Summarizing Non-existent Networks

What makes summarization effective is a well-designed area-addressing scheme. Assume that there are eight different logical subnets in an area to be summarized. If these subnets are contiguous, summarization can be implemented with a single configuration statement, and the number of summary records in the backbone database coming from the area being summarized can be reduced from 8 to 1. If the subnets are not contiguous with network numbers being assigned to an area in a random fashion, implementing summarization may be completely useless.

Summarization is implemented via a configuration command:

```
area area_id range address mask
```

Where the *area_id* represents the area in which the networks are being summarized, *address* is the summary network representing all of the summarized individual networks, and the *mask*, when used in conjunction with the address, is used to identify which networks have been summarized. Consider the example shown in Figure 8.6.

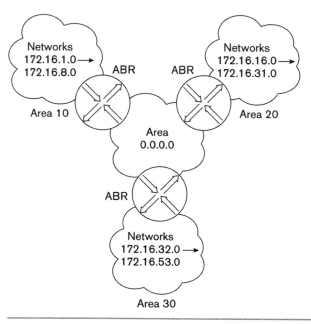

Figure 8.6 *Sample internetwork implementing summarization*

All three areas in Figure 8.6 use subnets derived from a private class B address, 172.16.0.0. This private address has been initially subnetted with a /24 mask creating 254 subnets excluding subnets that are all 0s and all 1s. These subnets range from 172.16.1.0 to 172.16.254.0. Subnets in the range from 172.16.1.0 to 172.16.8.0 have been assigned to area 10, subnets in the range from 172.16.16.0 to 172.16.31.0 have been assigned to area 20, and subnets in the range from 172.16.32.0 to 172.16.53.0 have been assigned to area 30. Since all of the subnets in each area are contiguous, this has the makings of a perfect scenario for implementing summarization. Let's review the process of arriving at the summary network and mask for each area.

When subnets need to be summarized, one of the easiest ways of finding the summarization network and mask is to find the same highest order bits between all of the networks being summarized. Convert the dotted decimal representation into binary, line up the binary values in a column, take a ruler, and slide it one bit at a time from left to right. Keep sliding the ruler as long as all of the bits in a column are the same. When at least one bit in column changes, then stop. The summary address in decimal is equivalent to the same high-order bits shared between all of the networks being summarized. The remaining bits are all set to 0s. The mask is set to all 1s wherever the high-order bits are the same and to 0 past the point where they begin to differ.

Consider the networks in area 10 of Figure 8.6. In the chart that follows, the dotted decimal values are converted into binary with four groups bit columns ranging from 7 to 0 corresponding to the 4 dotted decimals:

```
Bit          7 6 5 4 3 2 1 0   7 6 5 4 3 2 1 0   7 6 5 4 3 2 1 0   7 6 5 4 3 2 1 0

172.16.1.0=  1 0 1 0 1 1 0 0   0 0 0 1 0 0 0 0   0 0 0 0 0 0 0 1   0 0 0 0 0 0 0 0

172.16.2.0=  1 0 1 0 1 1 0 0   0 0 0 1 0 0 0 0   0 0 0 0 0 0 1 0   0 0 0 0 0 0 0 0

172.16.3.0=  1 0 1 0 1 1 0 0   0 0 0 1 0 0 0 0   0 0 0 0 0 0 1 1   0 0 0 0 0 0 0 0

172.16.4.0=  1 0 1 0 1 1 0 0   0 0 0 1 0 0 0 0   0 0 0 0 0 1 0 0   0 0 0 0 0 0 0 0

172.16.5.0=  1 0 1 0 1 1 0 0   0 0 0 1 0 0 0 0   0 0 0 0 0 1 0 1   0 0 0 0 0 0 0 0

172.16.6.0=  1 0 1 0 1 1 0 0   0 0 0 1 0 0 0 0   0 0 0 0 0 1 1 0   0 0 0 0 0 0 0 0

172.16.7.0=  1 0 1 0 1 1 0 0   0 0 0 1 0 0 0 0   0 0 0 0 0 1 1 1   0 0 0 0 0 0 0 0

172.16.8.0=  1 0 1 0 1 1 0 0   0 0 0 1 0 0 0 0   0 0 0 1 0 0 0 0   0 0 0 0 0 0 0 0

Address =    1 0 1 0 1 1 0 0   0 0 0 1 0 0 0 0   0 0 0 0 0 0 0 0   0 0 0 0 0 0 0 0

Mask =       1 1 1 1 1 1 1 1   1 1 1 1 1 1 1 1   1 1 1 1 0 0 0 0   0 0 0 0 0 0 0 0
```

In this example, the high-order bits stay the same until you get to column 4 in the third byte (third group of 7 to 0 bits). To arrive at the summary address value, retain the same high-order bits up to the column where they begin to differ, and then set all of the bits beginning with and to the right of that column to 0. The result is a summary address that you will substitute into the summarization configuration statement in place of the *address* variable. In the preceding example, the dotted decimal value of the summary address is 172.16.0.0.

Figuring out the summarization mask at this point is easy. Count the number of the same high-order bits. In the summary mask, the number of bits corresponding to the same high-order bits will be set to 1s, and the remaining bits will be set to 0s. The binary value of the mask is shown in the preceding example. In dotted decimal representation, the value of the mask is 255.255.240.0.

There is a potential problem lurking here, however. If you converted network numbers from 172.16.9.0 to 172.16.15.0 into binary and lined them in the preceding example, you would still end up with the same summarization address and mask. In effect, what has happened is that networks not assigned to area 10 have been summarized along with networks that are used in that area.

Assume now that the networks from 172.16.9.0 to 172.16.15.0 are assigned to a different area, either by mistake or out of necessity. If they are summarized, they will produce a summary record identical to that coming out of area 10. Then two identical summary records would be advertised onto the backbone by two different area border routers. Traffic destined for any subnets between 172.16.1.0 to 172.16.15.0 would follow the summary address that was advertised at the lowest cost. For example, traffic meant for subnet 172.16.10.0 could end up going to the ABR connecting area 10 to the backbone where 172.16.10.0 does not exist.

One way to avoid the problem in the example would be to summarize networks 172.16.1.0 though 172.16.7.0 with the address of 172.16.0.0 and the mask of 255.255.248.0, while leaving the subnet 172.16.8.0 unsummarized. Subnet 172.16.8.0 would then be advertised onto the backbone with its subnet mask of /24 or 255.255.255.0.

Contrast the summarization example from area 10 with a summarization of area 20. All of the subnets in area 20 neatly fit into a single summary address, which does not include any non-existent networks in that area. Using the same principle of finding the highest common order bits, the summary address for the range from 172.16.16.0 to 172.16.31.0 would be 172.16.16.0 with a mask of 255.255.240.0. No issue here at all with any non-existent networks in the range.

Summarization for area 30 is left for the reader as an exercise. The hint is that it's going to have problems similar to area 10. What can make the summarization for all of the areas even worse is the use of totally incorrect summarization masks.

Using Incorrect Summary Masks

Imagine that the summarization mask that was configured on all three ABRs in Figure 8.6 is 255.255.0.0. This means that all three ABRs would claim that they are summarizing all of the networks in the range from 172.16.1.0 to 172.16.254.0. Each one of them would be summarizing non-existent networks in its respective area, further increasing the chances of traffic not being delivered to the correct destination.

Making the summarization mask shorter than it's supposed to be means that non-existent networks will be summarized. If the summarization mask is made longer than it's supposed to be, the effects of summarization will be minimized, and fewer networks will be included in the summary record. This will make OSPF less efficient, but if you had to err on the mask, it's probably better to make it longer than shorter.

OSPF Metric on High-speed Interfaces

OSPF cost or metric is configured per router interface. When interfaces are assigned to the OSPF process, OSPF calculates a default cost of transmitting traffic via each interface. The default OSPF interface metric is defined as 100,000,000/bandwidth of an interface in bits/second. For 10Mbps Ethernet, the interface cost is 10, for a point-to-point T1 link, the cost is 64, and for a 64K link, the cost is 1,562. The total cost of reaching a destination — the metric of an OSPF route in a routing table — is the sum of the individual costs taken from the router's outbound interfaces along the path to the destination. The outbound interfaces are interfaces used by traffic to leave a router as opposed to the interfaces used to enter a router on the way to a destination. Consider a network as shown in Figure 8.7.

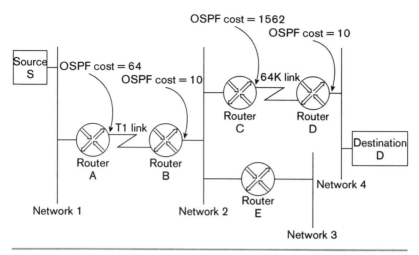

Figure 8.7 *OSPF network for cost calculation example*

In the internetwork represented in Figure 8.7, the cost of transmitting from source station S on network N1 to a destination station D on network N4 is the sum of the individual costs associated with outbound interfaces along the way from S to D. Numerically, the cost is derived by adding 64 (leaving router A) + 10 (leaving router B) +1,562 (leaving router C) + 10 (leaving router D). The return total cost would be the same, derived from 1,562 (leaving router D), +10 (leaving router C) + 64 (leaving router B) + 10 (leaving router A).

What network administrators need to be mindful of regarding cost in OSPF networks is that on interfaces where the transmission speed is greater than 100Mbps, the cost is going to remain at 1. The 100Mbps transmission pipe may seem like a big pipe, but with ATM backbones operating at gigabit speeds, 100Mbps seems insignificant. If you implement OSPF in environments where transmission speeds exceed 100Mbps, it's advisable to scale the OSPF metric throughout the internetwork by some multiplication factor. For example, if you scale the OSPF metric by a 100, then traditional Ethernet metric becomes1000 (10x100), Fast Ethernet becomes 100 (1x100), and gigabit Ethernet would correspondingly be 10. This would allow for the growth and introduction of even faster technologies into an OSPF internetwork.

The process of scaling a metric as described previously is by no means trivial and requires considerable amount of administration. It means the `ip ospf cost` command would have to be executed on every interface assigned to the OSPF process, which can be prone to errors. For example, a very low metric indicating a desirable path from OSPF's point of view could be accidentally assigned to a low speed interface. The effect could be congestion on a low speed link, while a higher speed link is underutilized.

Unlike IGRP and EIGRP, OSPF does not have the capability to facilitate unequal-cost load sharing. OSPF will place routes of equal cost to same destination into the routing table facilitating equal-cost load sharing, but if there are multiple paths to the same destination but of varying costs, only the lowest cost path will be used. The others will not be used and will only act as backups.

OSPF Link State Database

The OSPF link-state database can be displayed via the `show ip ospf database` command. The link-state database is a collection of link-state records from which routing tables are derived. Link-state databases are the same per OSPF area. Link-state databases can be displayed in a summary format or in a detail format. If you choose to look at the details of different types of records in the database you must enter the `show ip ospf database` command followed by keywords corresponding to the different types of records that can be found in the link-state database. Troubleshooting OSPF by looking at the link-state database requires a clear understanding of which routers create what records, and what the contents of different records represent.

Troubleshooting OSPF by looking at the link-state database can be tricky, but here are some hints:

- Link-state databases must be the same per area.
- Area border routers will have a link-state database for each area.

Every router creates a router link-state record, which describes the status of its interfaces (links). Router link-state records contain multiple links. You should expect as many router link-state records in the database as there are routers in an OSPF area, and as many links in a router link-state record as there are interfaces on a router. The exception is that two links are used to describe a serial interface. A simple internetwork consisting of two routers via a point-to-point serial link and each having a single Ethernet interface ought to result in a link-state database consisting of two router link-state records, with each record having three links in it.

Designated routers create network link-state records. You ought to expect as many network link-state records in the database as there are transit networks in an internetwork. Note that if a router is connected to a subnetwork (there are no other routers connected to that network), it will be elected as DR on that subnetwork but it will not create a network link-state record.

Only ABRs create summary and summary-ASB records. If you only have a single OSPF area, you will not have any ABRs and consequently no summary or summary-ASB records. Summary records can be numerous in the link-state database if OSPF internetwork is broken into multiple areas and summarization has not been implemented. The trick here is that summary records will exist in a multi-area OSPF internetwork with or without summarization. They will be more numerous without summarization. Summary-ASB records will exist only if there is an Autonomous System Border Router connecting the OSPF internetwork to another routing domain or the Internet.

Autonomous System Border Routers (ASBRs) create external records. These records are present only when an OSPF internetwork is interfaced to other routing domains. OSPF areas can be configured to restrict the importation of external records, which could end up being most numerous in the database.

Chapter Summary

OSPF is a hierarchical, highly scalable link-state routing protocol. When OSPF internetwork is broken into multiple areas, the backbone area 0.0.0.0 must be configured for routing updates to be exchanged between all of the areas. OSPF network type, area ID, Hello and Dead intervals, and authentication must match between neighboring routers. OSPF authentication type is configured per area in the OSPF process section. Passwords and MD5 keys have to match between neighbors and are configured in the interface sections. The `show ip ospf` command that can be executed by itself or with optional keywords (neighbor, interface, database) is an excellent IOS-based tool for troubleshooting OSPF problems.

Chapter 9

Troubleshooting RIP

Routing Information Protocol (RIP) is a very simple routing protocol when compared to EIGRP, OSPF, or even IGRP. RIP version 1 is one of the oldest routing protocols that's still commonly deployed and supported in the TCP/IP internetworking arena. It's a distance vector protocol with all of the limitations and workarounds associated with the distance-vector routing algorithm. The limitations of RIP include its slow convergence and propensity toward routing loops. The workarounds addressing RIP's limitations are split horizon (simple or with poison reverse), hold down, and triggered updates.

It might seem that after troubleshooting EIGRP, IGRP and OSPF, troubleshooting RIP would be easy. But as a classful protocol, RIP can be troublesome if you are not aware of its peculiarities. RIP updates do not carry subnet masks, which implies automatic summarization on major network boundaries and lack of support for Variable Length Subnet Masks (VLSM). Automatic summarization on major network boundaries, in turn, leads to reachability problems when subnets of a major network are separated by another major network.

Accidental application of variable length subnetting in a RIP internetwork will not totally disable RIP operation, but it will make certain destinations unreachable in the same way as demonstrated with IGRP.

Refer to Chapter 7 for the discussion of automatic summarization and variable length subnetting in the context of troubleshooting IGRP. RIP and IGRP are both classful protocols with lack of support for VLSM.

The misconfiguration problems in RIP networks discussed in this chapter are concerned with the assignment of networks to the RIP routing process and the effects of mismatches in subnets and masks between RIP neighbors.

Missing Network Statements

Network administrators must assign the networks, which are going to be advertised by RIP, to the RIP routing process. These are usually the networks to which a router is directly connected. The procedure for assigning networks to the routing process in RIP is the same as in IGRP or EIGRP. A major network number follows the `network` statement.

If you are running RIP within a single subnetted major network, there is going to be only one network statement to put in. If you don't assign at least one network to RIP, the RIP process will not even be activated. This behavior is no different than in IGRP or EIGRP. The activation of the RIP process is the simplest of all of the routing protocols discussed thus far. From the global configuration mode, execute the command `router rip`. Remember, it does have to be followed with at least one network statement for the RIP process to become active.

When a router is attached to multiple major networks, a separate network statement is required for each network. If a network statement is missing for one of the networks to which the router is attached, it means that network may become unreachable from other routers.

Consider the internetwork depicted in Figure 9.1.

Given the addressing scheme in the scenario depicted in Figure 9.1, each router must have a network statement for each major network that it's connected to. In the case of Boston, that's four network statements, in the case of Atlanta, it's three, and in the case of Chicago, it's two.

If you are going to run RIP, the address assignment and interface configurations as shown in Figure 9.1 are ideal. All physical subnets have their own major network assigned to them. Major networks are not subnetted, avoiding reachability problems when separated by another major network. Cisco default HDLC encapsulation is used on point-to-point serial links avoiding problems with split horizon, which tend to crop up in NBMA environments. The only requirement to ensure the proper functioning of this internetwork is that all the networks be properly assigned to the RIP process.

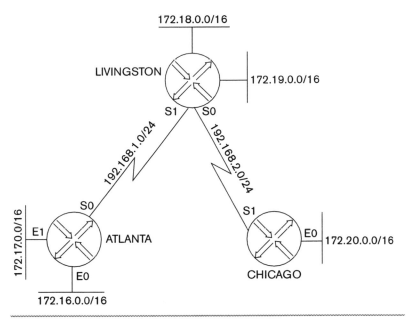

Figure 9.1 *RIP internetwork with multiple major networks*

The initial router configurations and the routing tables that follow reflect a properly functioning RIP internetwork. These correct initial configurations will be used as a baseline to identify problems with missing network statements and misconfigured subnets and masks.

Atlanta router correct initial RIP configuration

```
!
hostname Atlanta
!
enable password cisco
!
interface Ethernet0
 ip address 172.16.0.1 255.255.0.0
 no shut
!
interface Ethernet1
 ip address 172.17.0.1 255.255.0.0
```

```
 no shut
!
interface Serial0
 ip address 192.168.1.1 255.255.255.0
 no shut
!
interface Serial1
 shut
!
router rip
 network 172.16.0.0
 network 172.17.0.0
 network 192.168.1.0
```

Boston router correct initial RIP configuration

```
!
hostname Boston
!
enable password cisco
!
interface Ethernet0
 ip address 172.18.0.1 255.255.0.0
 no shut
!
interface Ethernet1
 ip address 172.19.0.1 255.255.0.0
 no shut
!
interface Serial0
 ip address 192.168.2.1 255.255.255.0
 no shut
!
interface Serial1
 ip address 192.168.1.2 255.255.255.0
```

```
clockrate 64000

no shut

!

router rip

network 172.18.0.0

network 172.19.0.0

network 192.168.1.0

network 192.168.2.0
```

Chicago router correct initial RIP configuration

```
hostname Chicago

!

enable password cisco

!

interface Ethernet0

 ip address 172.20.0.1 255.255.0.0

 no shut

!

interface Serial0

 no ip address

 shut

!

interface Serial1

 ip address 192.168.2.2 255.255.255.0

 clockrate 64000

 no shut

!

router rip

 network 172.20.0.0

 network 192.168.2.0
```

The routing tables that follow result from the preceding RIP configurations. Every destination in the internetwork in Figure 9.1 is reachable from every router. The RIP-derived routes are boldfaced.

Atlanta router's table for the initial RIP configuration

```
Atlanta#sh ip route
Codes: C - connected, S - static, I - IGRP, R - RIP,


Gateway of last resort is not set


C    172.17.0.0/16 is directly connected, Ethernet1
C    172.16.0.0/16 is directly connected, Ethernet0
R    172.19.0.0/16 [120/1] via 192.168.1.2, 00:00:11, Serial0
R    172.18.0.0/16 [120/1] via 192.168.1.2, 00:00:11, Serial0
R    172.20.0.0/16 [120/2] via 192.168.1.2, 00:00:11, Serial0
C    192.168.1.0/24 is directly connected, Serial0
R    192.168.2.0/24 [120/1] via 192.168.1.2, 00:00:11, Serial0
```

Boston router's table for the initial RIP configuration

```
Boston#sh ip route
Codes: C - connected, S - static, I - IGRP, R - RIP,


Gateway of last resort is not set


R    172.17.0.0/16 [120/1] via 192.168.1.1, 00:00:05, Serial1
R    172.16.0.0/16 [120/1] via 192.168.1.1, 00:00:05, Serial1
C    172.19.0.0/16 is directly connected, Ethernet1
C    172.18.0.0/16 is directly connected, Ethernet0
R    172.20.0.0/16 [120/1] via 192.168.2.2, 00:00:26, Serial0
C    192.168.1.0/24 is directly connected, Serial1
C    192.168.2.0/24 is directly connected, Serial0
```

Chicago router's table for the initial RIP configuration

```
Chicago#sh ip route
Codes: C - connected, S - static, I - IGRP, R - RIP,


Gateway of last resort is not set
```

```
R    172.17.0.0/16 [120/2] via 192.168.2.1, 00:00:23, Serial1

R    172.16.0.0/16 [120/2] via 192.168.2.1, 00:00:23, Serial1

R    172.19.0.0/16 [120/1] via 192.168.2.1, 00:00:23, Serial1

R    172.18.0.0/16 [120/1] via 192.168.2.1, 00:00:23, Serial1

C    172.20.0.0/16 is directly connected, Ethernet0

R    192.168.1.0/24 [120/1] via 192.168.2.1, 00:00:23, Serial1

C    192.168.2.0/24 is directly connected, Serial1
```

Now, observe what happens when two network statements are removed from the Boston router's initial configuration. The network statements that are removed are for Boston's serial links to Atlanta and Chicago. Configurations for the Atlanta and Chicago routers remain unchanged.

Boston router with two missing network statements from the initial configuration

```
hostname Boston
!
enable password cisco
!
interface Ethernet0
 ip address 172.18.0.1 255.255.0.0
 no shut
!
interface Ethernet1
 ip address 172.19.0.1 255.255.0.0
 no shut
!
interface Serial0
 ip address 192.168.2.1 255.255.255.0
 no shut
!
interface Serial1
 ip address 192.168.1.2 255.255.255.0
 clockrate 64000
 no shut
!
```

```
router rip
  network 192.168.1.0
  network 192.168.2.0
```

The missing network statements on the Boston router have a dramatic impact on the reachability throughout the internetwork in Figure 9.1. Note the changes in the routing tables on all three routers.

Atlanta router's table following removal of two network statements on the Boston router

```
Atlanta#sh ip route
Codes: C - connected, S - static, I - IGRP, R - RIP


Gateway of last resort is not set


C    172.17.0.0/16 is directly connected, Ethernet1
C    172.16.0.0/16 is directly connected, Ethernet0
C    192.168.1.0/24 is directly connected, Serial0
```

Boston router's table following removal of two network statements on the Boston router

```
Boston#sh ip route
Codes: C - connected, S - static, I - IGRP, R - RIP,


Gateway of last resort is not set


C    172.19.0.0/16 is directly connected, Ethernet1
C    172.18.0.0/16 is directly connected, Ethernet0
C    192.168.1.0/24 is directly connected, Serial1
C    192.168.2.0/24 is directly connected, Serial0
```

Chicago router's table following removal of two network statements on the Boston router

```
Chicago#sh ip route
Codes: C - connected, S - static, I - IGRP, R - RIP,
```

```
Gateway of last resort is not set
```

```
C    172.20.0.0/16 is directly connected, Ethernet0
C    192.168.2.0/24 is directly connected, Serial1
```

The only entries that now show up in the routing tables on all three routers are for the directly connected networks. And yet, there has been no change to the Atlanta or Chicago configurations, and only two out of the four network statements have been removed on the Boston router. But the removal of those two statements disabled RIP from running on the two serial links between Boston–Atlanta and Boston–Chicago. For the purposes of routing, RIP was effectively disabled throughout the entire internetwork in Figure 9.1.

What's demonstrated in the preceding example is not so much how a network administrator could deliberately cause problems by making changes to a correctly functioning configuration, but rather what can happen when the network statements that were removed never made it into the configuration in the first place.

Missing network statements should not be difficult to troubleshoot. Look at the following debug trace for RIP on the Boston router. The boldfaced messages in the trace clearly point you in the direction of the problem. The Boston router is ignoring updates from its serial neighbors (Atlanta and Chicago) because RIP is not enabled on the links to those neighbors. Also, notice in the debug trace that even though RIP advertises updates over its Ethernet interfaces, it does not advertise anything over its serial interfaces.

Debug trace on Boston following removal of two network statements

```
Boston#debug ip rip
RIP protocol debugging is on
Boston#
01:01:01: RIP: sending v1 update to 255.255.255.255 via Ethernet0 (172.18.0.1)
01:01:02:     network 172.19.0.0, metric 1
01:01:02: RIP: sending v1 update to 255.255.255.255 via Ethernet1 (172.19.0.1)
01:01:02:     network 172.18.0.0, metric 1
01:01:05: RIP: ignored v1 packet from 192.168.1.1 (not enabled on Serial1)
01:01:24: RIP: ignored v1 packet from 192.168.2.2 (not enabled on Serial0)
01:01:30: RIP: sending v1 update to 255.255.255.255 via Ethernet0 (172.18.0.1)
```

```
01:01:30:      network 172.19.0.0, metric 1
Boston#undebug all
All possible debugging has been turned off
```

Several conclusions can be drawn about the missing network statements in RIP. First, selectively absent network statements in RIP configurations can produce the appearance that RIP is not running at all in an internetwork. For example, when the Boston router ignored routing updates received over its serial links, and at the same time did not advertise its own networks over the same links, every router in the internetwork in Figure 9.1 knew only about its directly connected networks. From the routing point of view, all of the RIP traffic generated in that misconfigured internetwork served no purpose.

Second, using the `debug ip rip` command can be very useful in troubleshooting RIP problems. Given the misconfiguration with the missing network statements on the Boston router, debugging RIP on the Atlanta and Chicago routers would reveal that they are both advertising their routes correctly on every interface, but are not receiving any routing updates from their Boston neighbor. And when a router is not receiving any RIP updates, it's a given that it's not going to know about any networks via RIP. In OSPF, you could check for the presence of fully adjacent neighbors to determine if an OSPF router is receiving routing updates. But since RIP does not acquire neighbors, you have to know from whom a RIP router expects to receive updates and over which interfaces it is supposed to be advertising its own networks. Then it's a matter of verifying that updates are being received and sent out correctly.

Subnet Mask Mismatches

Subnet mask mismatches are not unique to RIP; they are a problem in any TCP/IP configuration. What makes subnet mask mismatches interesting is that their impact on the operation of routing protocols varies from one protocol to another. Given the large number of potential misconfigurations that can occur in the routing protocols discussed thus far, subnet mask mismatches are best covered in the context of a simple protocol like RIP.

The initial configurations for the internetwork in Figure 9.1 are correct. Subnet mask mismatches will be gradually introduced into the internetwork. At first, subnet masks will be changed on the serial links on the

Boston router. The Boston router initial configuration for s0 and s1 is as follows:

Boston router correct initial configuration for serial links

```
interface Serial0
 ip address 192.168.2.1 255.255.255.0
!
interface Serial1
 ip address 192.168.1.2 255.255.255.0
 clockrate 64000
```

Observe what happens, however, when an attempt is made to reconfigure the serial interfaces on the Boston router with subnet masks other than the default Class C mask.

```
Boston#conf t
Boston(config)#inter s0
Boston(config-if)#ip address 192.168.2.1 255.255.255.240
Bad mask /28 for address 192.168.2.1
Boston(config-if)#
Boston(config-if)#inter s1
Boston(config-if)#ip address 192.168.1.2 255.255.255.252
Bad mask /30 for address 192.168.1.2
Boston(config-if)#
```

A message about a bad mask is returned. At first, you might think that the message has something to do with the fact that you are changing the subnet mask to begin with, but it actually has to do with the fact that the IP addresses assigned to s0 and s1, when used in conjunction with the new masks (/28 and /30), come out of subnets 0 on both 192.168.2.0 and 192.168.1.0. IP address 192.168.2.1 is the first valid host address on subnet 0 or 192.168.1.0/28 when a /28 mask is applied to 192.168.1.0. Other subnets resulting from the application of /28 mask to 192.168.1.0 are 192.168.1.16/28, 192.168.1.32/28, and so on. If a host address from one of the subnets other than subnet 0 were assigned to s0, the "Bad mask" message would not be returned.

For s1, the host address of 192.168.1.2 with a /30 mask becomes the second valid host on 192.168.1.0/30 or subnet 0. The other valid subnets resulting from applying /30 mask to 192.168.1.0 are 192.168.1.4/30, 192.168.1.8/30, 192.168.1.12/30, and so on. Again, if a host from one of the other subnets other than subnet 0 were assigned to s1, the "Bad mask" message would not appear.

In order for the attempted subnet mask changes to work, a global command ip subnet-zero has to be executed first. Observe that the statements assigning IP addresses to interfaces are now successful.

```
Boston#conf t
Boston(config)#ip subnet-zero
Boston(config)#inter s0
Boston(config-if)#ip address 192.168.2.1 255.255.255.240
Boston(config-if)#inter s1
Boston(config-if)#ip address 192.168.1.2 255.255.255.252
Boston(config-if)#
```

No "Bad mask" error messages are returned when addresses from subnet 0 are assigned to the serial interfaces following the execution of the ip subnet-zero command. The configuration for the Boston router now appears as follows. The configurations of Atlanta and Chicago remain unchanged from the initial correct configurations.

Boston router reconfigured with new subnet masks

```
!
hostname Boston
!
enable password cisco
!
ip subnet-zero
!
interface Ethernet0
 ip address 172.18.0.1 255.255.0.0
!
interface Ethernet1
 ip address 172.19.0.1 255.255.0.0
```

```
!
interface Serial0
 ip address 192.168.2.1 255.255.255.240
!
interface Serial1
 ip address 192.168.1.2 255.255.255.252
 clockrate 64000
!
router rip
 network 172.18.0.0
 network 172.19.0.0
 network 192.168.1.0
 network 192.168.2.0
```

The serial link between Atlanta and Boston is now configured with 192.168.1.1/24 on the Atlanta side and 192.168.1.2/28 on the Boston side. The serial link between Boston and Chicago is now configured with 192.168.2.1/30 on the Boston side and 192.168.2.2/24 on the Chicago side. The results of these mismatches in the subnet mask are not what you might expect.

These particular mismatches in the mask have no impact on the routing tables and the operations of RIP on all three routers. This lack of impact has to do with the fact that even though the masks differ between neighboring routers, the addresses are still derived from the same subnet, subnet 0, in all cases. Think about it — RIP is a classful protocol. It has no idea what mask is configured on a neighboring router. If a router receives an update from a neighbor, it will apply its own mask to determine whether or not the neighbor is on the same subnet. As long as a RIP router thinks that the neighbor is on the same subnet, it will accept an update from that neighbor.

From an administrator's point of view, there is a big difference between subnet 0 with a /30, /28, or /24 mask. But from the point of view of RIP, subnet 0 is the same regardless of the length of the mask. It has to do with the number of valid host addresses that can be derived from each subnet. As long as IP addresses between neighboring routers are derived from the same subnet, the length of the mask does not matter.

Consider another example where host addresses between RIP neighbors are derived from the same (this time non-zero) subnets of varying sizes. If IP addresses between serial neighbors in the scenario in Figure 9.1

are 192.168.1.17/240 and 192.168.1.21/248, this kind of a mask mismatch is not going to have an impact on routing. 192.168.1.17 is a valid IP address on subnet 192.168.1.16 with a /28 mask. 192.168.1.21 is a valid IP address on subnet 192.168.1.16, but this time with a /29 mask. So as long as the subnets are the same, there is no problem, and everything still works fine. What it means is that there will be times when you will get lucky with subnet mask mismatches. But don't count on being lucky all the time.

The following configurations show the lucky subnet mask mismatch for non-zero subnets. The corresponding routing tables that follow reflect full reachability throughout the internetwork.

Atlanta router configuration with mismatched masks but matching subnets

```
hostname Atlanta
!
enable password cisco
!
interface Ethernet0
 ip address 172.16.0.1 255.255.0.0
!
interface Ethernet1
 ip address 172.17.0.1 255.255.0.0
!
interface Serial0
 ip address 192.168.1.17 255.255.255.240
!
interface Serial1
 no ip address
!
router rip
 network 172.16.0.0
 network 172.17.0.0
 network 192.168.1.0
```

Boston router configuration with mismatched masks but matching subnets

```
hostname Boston
!
enable password cisco
!
 interface Ethernet0
 ip address 172.18.0.1 255.255.0.0
!
interface Ethernet1
 ip address 172.19.0.1 255.255.0.0
!
interface Serial0
 ip address 192.168.2.33 255.255.255.224
!
interface Serial1
 ip address 192.168.1.21 255.255.255.248
 clockrate 64000
!
router rip
 network 172.18.0.0
 network 172.19.0.0
 network 192.168.1.0
 network 192.168.2.0
```

Chicago router configuration with mismatched masks but matching subnets

```
hostname Chicago
!
enable password cisco
!
interface Ethernet0
 ip address 172.20.0.1 255.255.0.0
!
interface Serial0
 no ip address
```

```
!
interface Serial1
  ip address 192.168.2.38 255.255.255.240
  clockrate 64000
!
router rip
  network 172.20.0.0
  network 192.168.2.0
```

Atlanta's routing table for configuration with mismatched masks but matching subnets

```
Atlanta#sh ip route
Codes: C - connected, S - static, I - IGRP, R - RIP,


Gateway of last resort is not set


C    172.17.0.0/16 is directly connected, Ethernet1
C    172.16.0.0/16 is directly connected, Ethernet0
R    172.19.0.0/16 [120/1] via 192.168.1.21, 00:00:19, Serial0
R    172.18.0.0/16 [120/1] via 192.168.1.21, 00:00:19, Serial0
R    172.20.0.0/16 [120/2] via 192.168.1.21, 00:00:19, Serial0
     192.168.1.0/28 is subnetted, 1 subnets
C       192.168.1.16 is directly connected, Serial0
R    192.168.2.0/24 [120/1] via 192.168.1.21, 00:00:19, Serial0
```

Boston's routing table for configuration with mismatched masks but matching subnets

```
Boston#sh ip route
Codes: C - connected, S - static, I - IGRP, R - RIP,


Gateway of last resort is not set


R    172.17.0.0/16 [120/1] via 192.168.1.17, 00:00:02, Serial1
R    172.16.0.0/16 [120/1] via 192.168.1.17, 00:00:03, Serial1
```

```
C    172.19.0.0/16 is directly connected, Ethernet1

C    172.18.0.0/16 is directly connected, Ethernet0

R    172.20.0.0/16 [120/1] via 192.168.2.38, 00:00:19, Serial0

     192.168.1.0/29 is subnetted, 1 subnets

C        192.168.1.16 is directly connected, Serial1

     192.168.2.0/27 is subnetted, 1 subnets

C        192.168.2.32 is directly connected, Serial0
```

Chicago's routing table for configuration with mismatched masks but matching subnets

```
Chicago#sh ip route

Codes: C - connected, S - static, I - IGRP, R - RIP,


Gateway of last resort is not set


R    172.17.0.0/16 [120/2] via 192.168.2.33, 00:00:22, Serial1

R    172.16.0.0/16 [120/2] via 192.168.2.33, 00:00:22, Serial1

R    172.19.0.0/16 [120/1] via 192.168.2.33, 00:00:22, Serial1

R    172.18.0.0/16 [120/1] via 192.168.2.33, 00:00:23, Serial1

C    172.20.0.0/16 is directly connected, Ethernet0

R    192.168.1.0/24 [120/1] via 192.168.2.33, 00:00:23, Serial1

     192.168.2.0/28 is subnetted, 1 subnets

C        192.168.2.32 is directly connected, Serial1
```

Note that in the preceding configurations, the Atlanta router is a serial neighbor with the Boston router over its serial0 interface. Boston is a neighbor with Atlanta over its serial1 interface. The routing tables show that the directly connected networks on Atlanta's serial0 and Boston's serial1 are the same, 192.168.1.16. So even though the masks vary, RIP is still functioning. If you want to convince yourself that subnet mask mismatches don't work all the time (they usually don't work), take a look at the following configurations and routing tables.

Changing the mask on the Boston's serial1 mask from /29 to /30 will change the subnet for 192.168.1.21 from 192.168.1.16/28 to 192.168.1.20/30. Changing the mask on Chicago's serial1 from /28 to /30 will change the subnet for 192.168.2.38 from 192.168.2.32/28 to 192.168.2.36/30. With mismatched subnets between neighbors, the results in the internetwork are drastically different. In fact the results are strange.

Atlanta router configuration with mismatched masks and subnets

```
hostname Atlanta
!
enable password cisco
!
ip subnet-zero
!
interface Ethernet0
 ip address 172.16.0.1 255.255.0.0
!
interface Ethernet1
 ip address 172.17.0.1 255.255.0.0
!
interface Serial0
 ip address 192.168.1.17 255.255.255.240
!
interface Serial1
 no ip address
!
router rip
 network 172.16.0.0
 network 172.17.0.0
 network 192.168.1.0
```

Boston router configuration with mismatched masks and subnets

```
hostname Boston
!
enable password cisco
!
ip subnet-zero
!
```

```
interface Ethernet0
 ip address 172.18.0.1 255.255.0.0
!
interface Ethernet1
 ip address 172.19.0.1 255.255.0.0
!
interface Serial0
 ip address 192.168.2.33 255.255.255.224
!
interface Serial1
 ip address 192.168.1.21 255.255.255.252
 clockrate 64000
!
router rip
 network 172.18.0.0
 network 172.19.0.0
 network 192.168.1.0
 network 192.168.2.0
```

Chicago router configuration with mismatched masks and subnets

```
hostname Chicago
!
enable password cisco
!
ip subnet-zero
!
interface Ethernet0
 ip address 172.20.0.1 255.255.0.0
!
interface Serial0
 no ip address
!
interface Serial1
 ip address 192.168.2.38 255.255.255.252
```

```
clockrate 64000
!
router rip
  network 172.20.0.0
  network 192.168.2.0
```

Atlanta's routing table for configuration with mismatched masks and subnets

```
Atlanta#sh ip route
Codes: C - connected, S - static, I - IGRP, R - RIP,

Gateway of last resort is not set

C    172.17.0.0/16 is directly connected, Ethernet1
C    172.16.0.0/16 is directly connected, Ethernet0
R    172.19.0.0/16 [120/1] via 192.168.1.21, 00:00:03, Serial0
R    172.18.0.0/16 [120/1] via 192.168.1.21, 00:00:03, Serial0
R    172.20.0.0/16 [120/2] via 192.168.1.21, 00:00:03, Serial0
     192.168.1.0/28 is subnetted, 1 subnets
C       192.168.1.16 is directly connected, Serial0
R    192.168.2.0/24 [120/1] via 192.168.1.21, 00:00:04, Serial0
```

Boston's routing table for configuration with mismatched masks and subnets

```
Boston#sh ip route
Codes: C - connected, S - static, I - IGRP, R - RIP,

Gateway of last resort is not set

C    172.19.0.0/16 is directly connected, Ethernet1
C    172.18.0.0/16 is directly connected, Ethernet0
R    172.20.0.0/16 [120/1] via 192.168.2.38, 00:00:17, Serial0
     192.168.1.0/30 is subnetted, 1 subnets
C       192.168.1.20 is directly connected, Serial1
```

```
     192.168.2.0/27 is subnetted, 1 subnets
C       192.168.2.32 is directly connected, Serial0
```

Chicago's routing table for configuration with mismatched masks and subnets

```
Chicago#sh ip route
Codes: C - connected, S - static, I - IGRP, R - RIP,


Gateway of last resort is not set


C    172.20.0.0/16 is directly connected, Ethernet0
     192.168.2.0/30 is subnetted, 1 subnets
C       192.168.2.36 is directly connected, Serial1
```

The only way to make sense out of the preceding tables, is to look at debug traces of RIP.

Rip debug trace on Boston for mismatched masks and subnets configuration

```
Boston#debug ip rip
RIP protocol debugging is on
Boston#
04:53:03: RIP: received v1 update from 192.168.2.38 on Serial0
04:53:03:      172.20.0.0 in 1 hops
04:53:10: RIP: ignored v1 update from bad source 192.168.1.17 on Serial1
04:53:27: RIP: sending v1 update to 255.255.255.255 via Ethernet0 (172.18.0.1)
04:53:27:      network 172.19.0.0, metric 1
04:53:27:      network 172.20.0.0, metric 2
04:53:27:      network 192.168.1.0, metric 1
04:53:27:      network 192.168.2.0, metric 1
04:53:27: RIP: sending v1 update to 255.255.255.255 via Ethernet1 (172.19.0.1)
04:53:27:      network 172.18.0.0, metric 1
04:53:27:      network 172.20.0.0, metric 2
04:53:28:      network 192.168.1.0, metric 1
04:53:28:      network 192.168.2.0, metric 1
```

```
04:53:28: RIP: sending v1 update to 255.255.255.255 via Serial0 (192.168.2.33)

04:53:28:      network 172.19.0.0, metric 1

04:53:28:      network 172.18.0.0, metric 1

04:53:28:      network 192.168.1.0, metric 1

04:53:28: RIP: sending v1 update to 255.255.255.255 via Serial1 (192.168.1.21)

04:53:28:      network 172.19.0.0, metric 1

04:53:28:      network 172.18.0.0, metric 1

04:53:28:      network 172.20.0.0, metric 2

04:53:28:      network 192.168.2.0, metric 1

04:53:32: RIP: received v1 update from 192.168.2.38 on Serial0

04:53:32:      172.20.0.0 in 1 hops

04:53:39: RIP: ignored v1 update from bad source 192.168.1.17 on Serial1
```

Rip debug trace on Chicago for mismatched masks and subnets configuration

```
Chicago#debug ip rip

RIP protocol debugging is on

Chicago#

06:05:45: RIP: ignored v1 update from bad source 192.168.2.33 on Serial1

06:05:46: RIP: sending v1 update to 255.255.255.255 via Ethernet0 (172.20.0.1)

06:05:46:      network 192.168.2.0, metric 1

06:05:46: RIP: sending v1 update to 255.255.255.255 via Serial1 (192.168.2.38)

06:05:46:      network 172.20.0.0, metric 1

06:06:14: RIP: ignored v1 update from bad source 192.168.2.33 on Serial1

06:06:14: RIP: sending v1 update to 255.255.255.255 via Ethernet0 (172.20.0.1)

06:06:14:      network 192.168.2.0, metric 1

06:06:14: RIP: sending v1 update to 255.255.255.255 via Serial1 (192.168.2.38)

06:06:14:      network 172.20.0.0, metric 1

06:06:41: RIP: ignored v1 update from bad source 192.168.2.33 on Serial1

06:06:42: RIP: sending v1 update to 255.255.255.255 via Ethernet0 (172.20.0.1)

06:06:42:      network 192.168.2.0, metric 1

06:06:42: RIP: sending v1 update to 255.255.255.255 via Serial1 (192.168.2.38)

06:06:42:      network 172.20.0.0, metric 1

06:07:08: RIP: sending v1 update to 255.255.255.255 via Ethernet0 (172.20.0.1)

06:07:08:      network 192.168.2.0, metric 1
```

```
06:07:08: RIP: sending v1 update to 255.255.255.255 via Serial1 (192.168.2.38)
06:07:08:     network 172.20.0.0, metric 1
06:07:10: RIP: ignored v1 update from bad source 192.168.2.33 on Serial1
```

Rip debug trace on Atlanta for mismatched masks and subnets configuration

```
Atlanta#debug ip rip
RIP protocol debugging is on
Atlanta#
04:37:36: RIP: received v1 update from 192.168.1.21 on Serial0
04:37:36:     172.18.0.0 in 1 hops
04:37:36:     172.20.0.0 in 2 hops
04:37:36:     192.168.2.0 in 1 hops
04:37:59: RIP: sending v1 update to 255.255.255.255 via Ethernet0 (172.16.0.1)
04:37:59:     network 172.17.0.0, metric 1
04:37:59:     network 172.18.0.0, metric 2
04:37:59:     network 172.20.0.0, metric 3
04:38:00:     network 192.168.1.0, metric 1
04:38:00:     network 192.168.2.0, metric 2
04:38:00: RIP: sending v1 update to 255.255.255.255 via Ethernet1 (172.17.0.1)
04:38:00:     network 172.16.0.0, metric 1
04:38:00:     network 172.18.0.0, metric 2
04:38:00:     network 172.20.0.0, metric 3
04:38:00:     network 192.168.1.0, metric 1
04:38:00:     network 192.168.2.0, metric 2
04:38:00: RIP: sending v1 update to 255.255.255.255 via Serial0 (192.168.1.17)
04:38:00:     network 172.17.0.0, metric 1
04:38:00:     network 172.16.0.0, metric 1
04:38:03: RIP: received v1 update from 192.168.1.21 on Serial0
04:38:03:     172.18.0.0 in 1 hops
04:38:03:     172.20.0.0 in 2 hops
04:38:03:     192.168.2.0 in 1 hops
Atlanta#undebug all
All possible debugging has been turned off
```

What the debug traces reveal is that Boston is accepting an update from Chicago (see Boston debug trace), but Chicago is ignoring an update from Boston (see Chicago debug trace). The serial link between Boston and Chicago is 192.168.2.33/27 on the Boston side and 192.168.2.38/30 on the Chicago side. From Boston's point of view (according to its /27 mask), both IP addresses 192.168.2.33 and 192.168.2.38 are on the same subnet, 192.168.2.32/27. However, from Chicago's point of view, the two IP addresses are on different subnets. When Chicago applies its mask of /30 to an update coming from Boston's 192.168.2.33, it recognizes that the update is coming from a router that's not on the same subnet and it ignores the update. Consequently, Chicago does not have any RIP-derived entries.

Atlanta is accepting an update from Boston (see the Atlanta debug trace), but Boston is ignoring the update from Atlanta (see Boston debug trace). The serial link between Atlanta and Boston is 192.168.1.17/28 on the Atlanta side and 192.168.1.21/30 on the Boston side. It's a similar situation as on the Boston-Chicago link. From the point of view of Atlanta (according to its /28 mask), the addresses 192.168.1.17 and 192.168.1.21 are on the subnet, 192.168.1.16/28. From the point of view of Boston (according to its /30 mask), its address of 192.168.1.21 is on subnet 192.168.1.20/30 but Atlanta's IP address of 192.168.1.17 is on subnet 192.168.1.16/30. The net result is that Boston will not accept an update from Atlanta.

The oddest thing about this sequence of events is that Boston will accept an update from Chicago and pass it on to Atlanta, which will end up with a RIP-derived entry for Chicago's Ethernet in its routing table. However, pings from Atlanta to hosts on Chicago's Ethernet (172.20.0.0) will fail. That's because Chicago does not have any RIP-derived routes because it is not accepting anything from Boston. When the ping packet arrives on Chicago's Ethernet, it will have no way of returning since Chicago knows only about its directly connected networks.

The bottom line of mismatched masks and subnets is that if you want to avoid spending a lot of time troubleshooting really strange problems, then ensure that subnets and masks match between neighboring routers. The most difficult thing about mismatched subnets and masks is that the results are not always the same or predictable.

RIP, Split Horizon, and NBMA

One way to think about split horizon is as an IOS feature that's associated with router interfaces. By default, split horizon is enabled on most interfaces configured with IP. One instance where split horizon is disabled is when Frame Relay encapsulation is used on a physical serial interface. To check if split horizon is enabled or disabled, execute the `show ip interface` command.

Split horizon is intended to speed up convergence and minimize the potential for routing loops in internetworks deploying distance vector protocols like RIP. The issue of split horizon was first addressed in Chapter 7 in the context of troubleshooting IGRP. Split horizon applies to RIP in the same way as it applies to IGRP. You are encouraged to review the Chapter 7 section "Split Horizon Issue in IGRP on a Frame Relay WAN," substituting RIP whenever you see IGRP.

Split horizon is a mixed bag. You should consider whether you are better off with or without split horizon. On LANs and dedicated leased lines, having split horizon enabled is advantageous; it prevents routing loops between neighboring routers and reduces the size of routing updates. But in NBMA environments — when multiple Data Link Layer VCs are configured on a single physical serial interface or a multipoint subinterface — enabled split horizon will cause some networks to become invisible.

Frame Relay clouds are generically referred to as NBMA networks. When routers in a Frame Relay cloud are configured with a single PVC per interface (whether a physical or a point-to-point subinterface), split horizon works to your advantage. However, split horizon works to your disadvantage when there are multiple PVCs configured on a single interface. In those instances, it may be better to disable split horizon.

What you need to keep in mind regarding split horizon is that it only works to improve stability in unstable networks where links between routers tend to fail. In stable networks, the key advantage of split horizon is that it reduces the size of routing updates. You will have to decide whether to choose between the ability to reach all destinations or have a more stable network in those rare instances where split horizon becomes a problem in NBMA environments using distance vector protocols.

Chapter Summary

Remember to tell RIP about networks that it will route for via the `network` command. Avoid subnet mask mismatches at all costs. Use point-to-point subinterfaces in NBMA clouds to avoid split horizon problems. In larger internetworks, use a more sophisticated protocol like OSPF or EIGRP rather than RIP.

Chapter 10

Troubleshooting BGP

The routing protocols discussed thus far (IGRP, EIGRP, OSPF, and RIP) are referred to as Interior Gateway Protocols or IGPs. They vary in scalability and operational characteristics, but they share a common purpose: they operate within (interior to) routing domains. A routing domain may consist of a few or a few hundred routers. It may be a corporate network, a university network, a regional ISP's network, or a major Internet backbone. Multiple IGPs may operate within a routing domain performing route redistribution. Occasionally, an IGP like OSPF may be used to interconnect several routing domains deploying another IGP like IGRP or RIP. These situations arise during migrations from one IGP to another. However, it's not the primary purpose of any one IGP to interconnect a large number of routing domains that are deploying other IGPs. Also, IGPs were not designed to support a large number of routes.

Another type of routing protocol is needed to carry the tens of thousands of routes that result from interconnecting all of the routing domains comprising today's Internet. The protocols that have been designed specifically to route between multiple routing domains capable of carrying large numbers of routes are generically referred to as Exterior Gateway Protocols or EGPs. BGP version 4 is the most popular member of the EGP family in use on today's Internet. The Internet routing domains interconnected via BGP are known as autonomous systems (AS) and the process of interconnecting autonomous systems via BGP is known as peering.

BGP Autonomous Systems

The concept of a BGP autonomous system or AS is quite different from the autonomous systems used in IGRP and EIGRP. The BGP autonomous systems are the building blocks of the global Internet. They represent collections of routers and networks with routing policies that are driven by economic, political, and security considerations.

Not every routing domain — whether it's part of the Internet or not — is automatically a BGP autonomous system. A BGP autonomous system entails BGP being configured on one or more routers within a routing domain. The activation of the BGP process on a router requires the use of an autonomous system number (ASN). This means that network administrators must know their ASN at the time of BGP configuration. The ASN that's used to activate the BGP process identifies the AS in which a router resides.

ASNs must be registered and unique throughout the global Internet, just like IP addresses. In certain configurations, though, the use of private (non-registered) ASNs is allowed. Conceptually, this is similar to the use of private (non-registered) IP addresses on internal networks, which are then connected to the Internet via a proxy. Valid ASNs range from 1 to 65,535.

Routing between Autonomous Systems

Routing within a domain via an IGP is often referred to as destination-based routing. It's based on the principle of finding the shortest path between a source and a destination. The shortest path implies the lowest IGP metric. As seen in previous chapters, the IGP metric is a function of network bandwidth (OSPF), number of hops (RIP), or a combination of bandwidth and delay (IGRP/EIGRP). When an IGP router is aware that multiple paths exist to reach a destination, choosing the best route is simple — the route with the lowest metric is best.

Routing between the BGP autonomous systems is no longer a matter of finding the shortest path between a source and a destination based on the IGP criteria. When a BGP router has multiple paths available to reach a destination, the selection of a best BGP route becomes complex. The selection process involves the examination and comparison of up to a dozen parameters. Some of these parameters are used to configure AS routing policies, which have a significant impact on the traffic flow between autonomous systems.

An example of an AS routing policy may be the denial of entry to traffic originating within a certain autonomous system. Or, the policy may influence which way traffic enters and leaves an autonomous system if there are multiple ingress/egress points. Another policy example might be to ensure that traffic entering an autonomous system is not allowed to pass through it. The opposite of not allowing any traffic to pass through an AS is a policy to allow all traffic to pass through. AS policies are implemented through BGP configuration. IOS tools like route maps and access control lists are applied to BGP update messages to implement policy-based routing between autonomous systems.

Impact of the BGP Update Message Structure on Routing

The routing update messages exchanged between BGP-speaking routers have a structure that facilitates routing policy implementations. A component of the BGP update message is the destination network, which in BGP jargon is referred to as Network Layer Reachability Information (NLRI). This is nothing more than one or more (aggregate) Internet destination represented in a prefix/length notation. The BGP attributes occupy the remainder of the update message and, in effect, "describe" how the destination or NLRI is to be reached.

One of the BGP attributes is the AS_path attribute, which represents the collection or a list of all of the autonomous system numbers through which a BGP update has traversed. An AS_path can be used to filter traffic that originated in or has passed through certain autonomous systems. Traffic filtering means denial of entry to traffic. Also, the length of the AS_path (the number of AS numbers in the list) influences BGP route selection process; the longer the path, the less preferable the route.

Two BGP attributes known as local preference and multi-exit discriminator (MED) can be configured to influence which way traffic will come into and leave an AS if there are multiple entry and exit points. Seven BGP attributes have been defined in RFC 1771, including the three mentioned here. Additionally, router vendors have created proprietary attributes that are not part of the formal BGP specification.

What makes BGP powerful and flexible is that the BGP routing update message can carry varying numbers of attributes, some of the attribute fields can have a variable length, and all of the attributes can assume a wide range of values. Think now about the numerous ways in which a destination can be described through the use of BGP attributes. And each way that a destination is described represents an implementation of a routing policy.

When you consider the BGP message structure and couple it with how many individual destinations and autonomous systems there are in the global Internet, the possibilities of routing policies seem endless. However, from a broad perspective, all of those policies can ultimately be reduced to a simple principle. Traffic is either permitted or denied entry into an AS and can be influenced which way it enters and leaves an AS. Still, there is significant potential for misconfigurations in implementing this relatively simple principle.

When reading about BGP, think Internet. The Internet represents many things to many people, but in the context of this discussion, the best way to view the Internet is as a collection of interconnected autonomous systems with the BGP protocol operating between them. In contrast, the IGRP/EIGRP autonomous systems are internal to the BGP autonomous systems.

Potential BGP misconfigurations are discussed next. They include misconfiguration of neighbors, improper aggregation, routing policy misconfigurations, creation of routing loops, and more.

Misconfigured IP Addresses of Neighbors

The BGP routing process is activated on a Cisco router via a global configuration command: `router bgp` *as_number,* where the *as_number* is the number of the autonomous system to which a router belongs. The next step in BGP configuration is to define neighbor(s) with which the router will exchange BGP updates. The concept of defining neighbors in BGP is in stark contrast to the IGPs discussed so far. For example, OSPF and EIGRP discover their neighbors dynamically. In rare instances on a non-broadcast network type, OSPF can be configured with neighbors, but that's the least-recommended approach to OSPF configuration. The option of defining neighbors in EIGRP does not exist.

RIP and IGRP don't care about neighbors. They broadcast their updates on all active interfaces, whether a neighbor is there to hear them or not. RIP can be configured with neighbors, but again, that's only an option to reduce the level of broadcast traffic. With a manual definition of neighbors there is always a greater potential for misconfigurations. In BGP, neighbor configuration is not an option, it's a must. And in the initial stages of BGP configuration, configuring neighbors can be a source of errors.

The configuration command for defining neighbors is executed in the BGP process section. The syntax is `neighbor ip_address remote-as as_number`, where the *ip_address* is the neighbor's IP address and the *as_number* is the ASN assigned to the AS in which the neighbor resides.

Given that neighbors must be configured manually and that neighboring routers will often reside in different autonomous systems, it follows that BGP configurations require cooperation between network administrators managing the different ASs. It is useless to configure a BGP router with neighbors if the neighbors have not been configured with BGP or have not defined the original router as their neighbor.

Consider an internetwork as shown in Figure 10.1.

In the scenario in Figure 10.1, customer X in AS 90 has links to providers A and B. X's routing policy is driven by the nature of its business. X is operating an online store with tens of thousands of clients visiting its site daily, and must provide its clients with reliable access to its network. Consequently, X has decided to be multihomed, which means that X is using more than one provider to offer its clients access to its network. In fact, there are multiple levels of multihoming going on in the scenario in Figure 10.1. First, X is multihomed to provider B. There are two ways of reaching X via B. Second, X is multihomed between A and B, which means that X can be reached through both providers. With several levels of multihoming, X is improving its chances that in the event of failures, access to its site can be maintained.

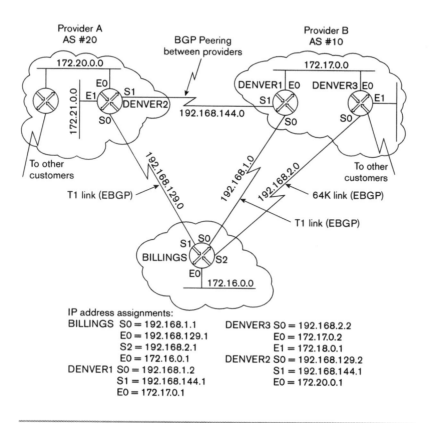

Figure 10.1 *A sample BGP internetwork*

The providers A and B depicted in Figure 10.1 are transit providers. They have dozens of customers like X and they operate Internet backbones spanning the globe. Figure 10.1 represents a small slice of their overall network structure. The providers' routing policy is simple: Pass traffic through. They make their living by allowing their customers' traffic to travel over their backbones. Major transit providers like A and B can also have smaller regional ISPs as their customers. In turn, the regional ISPs can provide Internet access to clients of customers like X. The bottom line for the transit providers is that the more traffic that passes over their backbones, the more likely they are to stay in business.

Following are the initial configuration files for routers Billings, Denver1, Denver2, and Denver3 in Figure 10.1 before BGP has been activated or neighbors defined. These partial configurations show the IP address assignments and the IGP routing processes. Customer X is running IGRP internally. Providers A and B are running OSPF on their internal networks. However, A and B are not exchanging routing updates via OSPF and X is not sharing updates about its network with either A or B. Initially there is total isolation between all three parties involved. Each provider and customer X know only about their internal networks.

Billings initial configuration before BGP activation (Customer X)

```
hostname billings
!
interface Ethernet0
 ip address 172.16.0.1 255.255.0.0
 no shut
!
interface Serial0
 description T1 link to Denver1 (Provider B)
 ip address 192.168.1.1 255.255.255.0
 clockrate 2000000
 no shut
!
interface Serial1
 description T1 link to Denver2 (Provider A)
 ip address 192.168.129.1 255.255.255.0
 clockrate 2000000
 no shut
!
interface Serial2
 description 64K link (backup) to Denver3 (Provider B)
 ip address 192.168.2.1 255.255.255.0
 clockrate 64000
 no shut
!
router igrp 99
 network 172.6.0.0
!
```

Denver1 initial configuration before BGP activation (Provider B)

```
hostname Denver1
!
enable password cisco
!
ip subnet-zero
!
interface Ethernet0
 ip address 172.17.0.1 255.255.0.0
 no shut
!
interface Serial0
 description T1 link to Billings (Customer X)
 ip address 192.168.1.2 255.255.255.0
 no shut
!
interface Serial1
 description T1 link to Denver2 (Provider A)
 ip address 192.168.144.1 255.255.255.0
 clockrate 2000000
 no shut
!
router ospf 10
 network 172.17.0.0 0.0.255.255 area 0.0.0.0
!
```

Denver3 initial configuration before BGP activation (Provider B)

```
hostname Denver3
!
enable password cisco
!
interface Ethernet0
 ip address 172.17.0.2 255.255.0.0
 no shut
```

```
!

interface Ethernet1

 ip address 172.18.0.1 255.255.0.0

 no shut

!

interface Serial0

 description 64K link to Billings (Customer X)

 ip address 192.168.2.2 255.255.255.0

 no shut

!

interface Serial1

 shut

!

router ospf 10

 network 172.17.0.0 0.0.255.255 area 0.0.0.0

 network 172.18.0.0 0.0.255.255 area 0.0.0.0

!
```

Denver2 initial configuration before BGP activation (Provider A)

```
hostname Denver2

!

enable password cisco

!

interface Ethernet0

 ip address 172.20.0.1 255.255.0.0

 no shut

!

interface Ethernet1

 ip address 172.21.0.1 255.255.0.0

 no shut

!

interface Serial0

 description T1 link to Billings (Customer X)

 ip address 192.168.129.2 255.255.255.0
```

```
 no shut
 !
 interface Serial1
   description T1 link to Denver1 (Provider B)
   ip address 192.168.144.2 255.255.255.0
   no shut
 !
 router ospf 20
   network 172.20.0.0 0.0.255.255 area 0.0.0.0
   network 172.21.0.0 0.0.255.255 area 0.0.0.0
 !
```

The routing tables for the preceding initial configuration confirm the isolation between the three autonomous systems.

Billings routing table for the initial configuration before activation of BGP

```
billings#sh ip route
Codes: C - connected, S - static, I - IGRP, R - RIP, M - mobile, B - BGP
       D - EIGRP, EX - EIGRP external, O - OSPF,


Gateway of last resort is not set


C    192.168.1.0 is directly connected, Serial0
C    192.168.2.0 is directly connected, Serial2
C    172.16.0.0 is directly connected, Ethernet0
C    192.168.129.0 is directly connected, Serial1
billings#
```

Denver1 routing table for the initial configuration before activation of BGP

```
Denver1#sh ip route
Codes: C - connected, S - static, I - IGRP, R - RIP, M - mobile, B - BGP
       D - EIGRP, EX - EIGRP external, O - OSPF,


Gateway of last resort is not set
```

```
C    192.168.144.0/24 is directly connected, Serial1

C    172.17.0.0/16 is directly connected, Ethernet0

O    172.18.0.0/16 [110/20] via 172.17.0.2, 02:51:57, Ethernet0

C    192.168.1.0/24 is directly connected, Serial0
```

Denver3 routing table for the initial configuration before activation of BGP

```
Denver3#sh ip route

Codes: C - connected, S - static, I - IGRP, R - RIP, M - mobile, B - BGP

       D - EIGRP, EX - EIGRP external, O - OSPF,


Gateway of last resort is not set


C    172.17.0.0/16 is directly connected, Ethernet0

C    172.18.0.0/16 is directly connected, Ethernet1

C    192.168.2.0/24 is directly connected, Serial0

Denver3#
```

Denver2 routing table for the initial configuration before activation of BGP

```
Denver2#sh ip route

Codes: C - connected, S - static, I - IGRP, R - RIP, M - mobile, B - BGP

       D - EIGRP, EX - EIGRP external, O - OSPF,


Gateway of last resort is not set


C    192.168.144.0/24 is directly connected, Serial1

C    192.168.129.0/24 is directly connected, Serial0

C    172.21.0.0/16 is directly connected, Ethernet1

C    172.20.0.0/16 is directly connected, Ethernet0
```

Given the preceding initial configurations, a minimum of three steps must now be taken to make BGP functional in the internetwork in Figure 10.1. The BGP process must be activated, neighbors defined, and networks that BGP will route for injected into BGP. Each one of these three steps has its own potential for errors, but neighbor definition is probably the most error-prone. That's because there are two flavors of BGP, External BGP (EBGP) and Internal BGP (IBGP). EBGP operates between neighbors in different ASs, whereas IBGP neighbors operate within the same AS. Depending on where a BGP neighbor resides — same or different AS — the rules for choosing the neighbor's IP address vary.

The fundamental rule that applies to defining BGP neighbors is that there must be IP connectivity between the networks from which the neighbor addresses are derived before the `neighbor` command will have any effect. When BGP is activated and neighbors are correctly defined via the `neighbor` command, a TCP session is established between the neighboring routers using a TCP port 179. BGP uses the connection-oriented reliable transport protocol, TCP, to exchange updates between neighbors. This is again in contrast to all of the IGPs, which deploy connectionless IP or UDP as their transport mechanism. If a TCP session must be established before any updates can be exchanged between BGP neighbors, it implies that IP connectivity must already exist between them. IP connectivity between BGP neighbors can be provided via an IGP, static routes, or sharing the same physical subnets.

External BGP Neighbors

Typically, the IP address that's used with the `neighbor` command to define external BGP sessions is the neighbor's interface IP address on the subnet that's shared between them. External BGP has a rule that requires neighbors to share the same physical subnet. Otherwise, BGP updates received from an external neighbor that's not physically connected to the same subnet are dropped. Of course, every rule is confirmed by an exception, and this rule is no different. A BGP `ebgp-multihop` command allows for configuration of external neighbors that are not physically connected. Under the typical circumstances for external BGP neighbors, IP connectivity is there because neighbors are sharing the same subnet. In the case of `ebgp-multihop` configuration, IP connectivity has to be provided via an IGP or static routes.

In the scenario in Figure 10.1, the Billings router is going to have external BGP sessions with Denver1, Denver 2, and Denver3.

Observe what happens when BGP is activated and external neighbors are defined on all four routers. The configuration files showing the correct definitions follow.

Billings configuration following BGP activation and definition of external neighbors

```
hostname billings
!
interface Ethernet0
 ip address 172.16.0.1 255.255.0.0
 no shut
!
interface Serial0
 description T1 link to Denver1 (Provider B)
 ip address 192.168.1.1 255.255.255.0
 clockrate 2000000
 no shut
!
interface Serial1
 description T1 link to Denver2 (Provider A)
 ip address 192.168.129.1 255.255.255.0
 clockrate 2000000
 no shut
!
interface Serial2
 description 64K link to Denver3 (Provider B)
 ip address 192.168.2.1 255.255.255.0
 clockrate 64000
 no shut
!
router igrp 99
 network 172.16.0.0
!
router bgp 90
 neighbor 192.168.1.2 remote-as 10    Note: EBGP session Denver1
```

```
neighbor 192.168.2.2 remote-as 10     Note: EBGP session to Denver3
neighbor 192.168.129.2 remote-as 20   Note: EBGP session to Denver2
!
```

Denver1 configuration following BGP activation and definition of external neighbors

```
hostname Denver1
!
enable password cisco
!
ip subnet-zero
!
interface Ethernet0
 ip address 172.17.0.1 255.255.0.0
 no shut
!
interface Serial0
 description T1 link to Billings (Customer X)
 ip address 192.168.1.2 255.255.255.0
 no shut
!
interface Serial1
 description T1 link to Denver2 (Provider A)
 ip address 192.168.144.1 255.255.255.0
 clockrate 2000000
 no shut
!
router ospf 10
 network 172.17.0.0 0.0.255.255 area 0.0.0.0
!
router bgp 10
 neighbor 192.168.1.1 remote-as 90     Note: EBGP session to Billings
 neighbor 192.168.144.2 remote-as 20   Note: EBGP session to Denver2
!
```

Denver3 configuration following BGP activation and definition of external neighbors

```
hostname Denver3
!
enable password cisco
!
interface Ethernet0
 ip address 172.17.0.2 255.255.0.0
 no shut
!
interface Ethernet1
 ip address 172.18.0.1 255.255.0.0
 no shut
!
interface Serial0
 description 64K link to Billings (Customer X)
 ip address 192.168.2.2 255.255.255.0
 no shut
!
interface Serial1
 shut
!
router ospf 10
 network 172.17.0.0 0.0.255.255 area 0.0.0.0
 network 172.18.0.0 0.0.255.255 area 0.0.0.0
!
router bgp 10
 neighbor 192.168.2.1 remote-as 90        Note: EBGP session to Billings
!
```

Denver2 configuration following BGP activation and definition of external neighbors

```
hostname Denver2
!
```

```
enable password cisco
!
interface Ethernet0
 ip address 172.20.0.1 255.255.0.0
 no shut
!
interface Ethernet1
 ip address 172.21.0.1 255.255.0.0
 no shut
!
interface Serial0
 description T1 link to Billings (Customer X)
 ip address 192.168.129.2 255.255.255.0
 no shut
!
interface Serial1
 description T1 link to Denver1 (Provider A)
 ip address 192.168.144.2 255.255.255.0
 no shut
!
router ospf 20
 network 172.20.0.0 0.0.255.255 area 0.0.0.0
!
router bgp 20
 neighbor 192.168.129.1 remote-as 90  Note: EBGP session to Billings
 neighbor 192.168.144.1 remote-as 10  Note: EBGP session to Denver1
!
```

To verify that BGP sessions have been correctly established between neighbors, you should use the command show ip bgp neighbors, which will result in the display of a considerable amount of information. The output from the show ip bgp neighbors command executed on the Billings router follows. Key information related to correct configuration of neighbors is boldfaced.

```
billings#sh ip bgp neighbors
                                Note: Info about link to Denver1
```

BGP neighbor is 192.168.1.2,   remote AS 10, external link

 BGP version 4, **remote router ID 192.168.144.1**

 BGP state = Established, table version = 1, up for 0:22:26

 Last read 0:00:26, hold time is 180, keepalive interval is 60 seconds

 Minimum time between advertisement runs is 30 seconds

 Received 25 messages, 0 notifications, 0 in queue

 Sent 25 messages, 0 notifications, 0 in queue

 Connections established 1; dropped 0

Connection state is ESTAB, I/O status: 1, unread input bytes: 0

Local host: 192.168.1.1, Local port: 179

Foreign host: 192.168.1.2, Foreign port: 11007

Enqueued packets for retransmit: 0, input: 0, saved: 0

Event Timers (current time is 7343540):

Timer:	Retrans	TimeWait	AckHold	SendWnd	KeepAlive
Starts:	26	0	25	0	0
Wakeups:	0	0	0	0	0
Next:	0	0	0	0	0

iss: 149263248 snduna: 149263734 sndnxt: 149263734   sndwnd: 15899
irs: 179746550 rcvnxt: 179747036 rcvwnd: 15899 delrcvwnd: 485

SRTT: 324 ms, RTTO: 989 ms, RTV: 170 ms, KRTT: 0 ms

minRTT: 8 ms, maxRTT: 304 ms, ACK hold: 300 ms

Flags: passive open, nagle, gen tcbs

Datagrams (max data segment is 1460 bytes):

Rcvd: 50 (out of order: 0), with data: 25, total data bytes: 485

Sent: 26 (retransmit: 0), with data: 25, total data bytes: 485

                    Note: Info about link to Denver3

BGP neighbor is 192.168.2.2,   remote AS 10, external link

 BGP version 4, **remote router ID 192.168.2.2**

 BGP state = Established, table version = 1, up for 0:22:57

Last read 0:00:57, hold time is 180, keepalive interval is 60 seconds

Minimum time between advertisement runs is 30 seconds

Received 25 messages, 0 notifications, 0 in queue

Sent 25 messages, 0 notifications, 0 in queue

Connections established 1; dropped 0

Connection state is ESTAB, I/O status: 1, unread input bytes: 0

Local host: 192.168.2.1, Local port: 179

Foreign host: 192.168.2.2, Foreign port: 11001

Enqueued packets for retransmit: 0, input: 0, saved: 0

Event Timers (current time is 7359432):

Timer:	Retrans	TimeWait	AckHold	SendWnd	KeepAlive
Starts:	27	0	26	0	0
Wakeups:	0	0	0	0	0
Next:	0	0	0	0	0

iss: 150941742 snduna: 150942247 sndnxt: 150942247   sndwnd: 15880

irs: 2654198023 rcvnxt: 2654198528 rcvwnd: 15880 delrcvwnd: 504

SRTT: 319 ms, RTTO: 941 ms, RTV: 151 ms, KRTT: 0 ms

minRTT: 16 ms, maxRTT: 300 ms, ACK hold: 300 ms

Flags: passive open, nagle, gen tcbs

Datagrams (max data segment is 1460 bytes):

Rcvd: 52 (out of order: 0), with data: 26, total data bytes: 504

Sent: 27 (retransmit: 0), with data: 26, total data bytes: 504

                              Note: Info about link to Denver2

BGP neighbor is 192.168.129.2, remote AS 20, external link

  BGP version 4, **remote router ID 192.168.144.2**

  BGP state = Established, table version = 1, up for 0:23:01

  Last read 0:00:01, hold time is 180, keepalive interval is 60 seconds

  Minimum time between advertisement runs is 30 seconds

  Received 26 messages, 0 notifications, 0 in queue

```
Sent 26 messages, 0 notifications, 0 in queue

Connections established 1; dropped 0

Connection state is ESTAB, I/O status: 1, unread input bytes: 0

Local host: 192.168.129.1, Local port: 179

Foreign host: 192.168.129.2, Foreign port: 11002


Enqueued packets for retransmit: 0, input: 0, saved: 0


Event Timers (current time is 7364292):

Timer:        Retrans   TimeWait    AckHold   SendWnd  KeepAlive

Starts:          27         0          26         0         0

Wakeups:          0         0           7         0         0

Next:             0         0           0         0         0


iss:  152314902  snduna:  152315407  sndnxt:  152315407     sndwnd:  15880

irs:  187017839  rcvnxt:  187018344  rcvwnd:     15880  delrcvwnd:    504


SRTT: 319 ms, RTTO: 941 ms, RTV: 151 ms, KRTT: 0 ms

minRTT: 8 ms, maxRTT: 300 ms, ACK hold: 300 ms

Flags: passive open, nagle, gen tcbs


Datagrams (max data segment is 1460 bytes):

Rcvd: 52 (out of order: 0), with data: 26, total data bytes: 504

Sent: 34 (retransmit: 0), with data: 26, total data bytes: 504

billings#
```

Note that the preceding trace displays information about three neighbors. The IP addresses of the three neighbors correspond to the IP addresses used with the `neighbor` command in the BGP section of the Billings router. What you are looking for from a troubleshooting perspective is `BGP state = Established`. When you see an established BGP state after configuring neighbors, you are in good shape. If you don't, it's time to verify that you are following the rules for neighbor configuration.

Observe what happens on the Billings router when the rule for defining external neighbors is violated. Rather than using the IP addresses from the serial subnets which are shared between Billings and all of the providers' routers, the neighbor IP addresses are derived from the Ethernet subnets on the providers' routers.

The configuration steps and the corresponding display resulting from `show ip bgp neighbors` follow:

```
billings#conf t
Enter configuration commands, one per line.  End with CNTL/Z.
billings(config)#router bgp 90
billings(config-router)#no neighbor 192.168.1.2 remote-as 10
billings(config-router)#no neighbor 192.168.2.2 remote-as 10
billings(config-router)#no neighbor 192.168.129.2 remote-as 20
billings(config-router)#neighbor 172.17.0.1 remote-as 10
billings(config-router)#neighbor 172.18.0.1 remote-as 10
billings(config-router)#neighbor 172.20.0.1 remote-as 20
billings(config-router)#^Z
billings#
%SYS-5-CONFIG_I: Configured from console by console
billings#
```

Notice that IOS offers no warnings or error messages when an IP address is used in the `neighbor` configuration command that will not allow an external BGP session to be established. The IP addresses 172.17.0.1, 172.18.0.1, and 172.20.0.1 are valid IP addresses on routers Denver1, Denver 3, and Denver2, respectively. However, their use in the `neighbor` command on Billings violates the rule that for external neighbors, IP addresses must be derived from subnets shared by the neighbors.

The telltale signs of problems are clearly visible in the `show ip bgp neighbor` display.

```
billings#sh ip bgp neighbors

                            Note: External link to Denver1
BGP neighbor is 172.17.0.1,  remote AS 10, external link
  BGP version 4, remote router ID 0.0.0.0
  BGP state = Idle, table version = 0

  Last read 0:00:10, hold time is 180, keepalive interval is 60 seconds
```

Minimum time between advertisement runs is 30 seconds

Received 0 messages, 0 notifications, 0 in queue

Sent 0 messages, 0 notifications, 0 in queue

Connections established 0; dropped 0

External BGP neighbor not directly connected.

No active TCP connection

                                Note: External link to Denver3

BGP neighbor is 172.18.0.1, remote AS 10, external link

  BGP version 4, **remote router ID 0.0.0.0**

  BGP state = Idle, table version = 0

  Last read 0:00:11, hold time is 180, keepalive interval is 60 seconds

  Minimum time between advertisement runs is 30 seconds

  Received 0 messages, 0 notifications, 0 in queue

  Sent 0 messages, 0 notifications, 0 in queue

  Connections established 0; dropped 0

  External BGP neighbor not directly connected.

  No active TCP connection

                                Note: External link to Denver2

  BGP neighbor is 172.20.0.1, remote AS 20, external link

  BGP version 4, **remote router ID 0.0.0.0**

  BGP state = Idle, table version = 0

  Last read 0:00:01, hold time is 180, keepalive interval is 60 seconds

  Minimum time between advertisement runs is 30 seconds

  Received 0 messages, 0 notifications, 0 in queue

  Sent 0 messages, 0 notifications, 0 in queue

  Connections established 0; dropped 0

  External BGP neighbor not directly connected.

  No active TCP connection

billings#

The newly configured IP addresses of neighbors (172.17.0.1, 172.18.0.1, and 172.20.0.1) still show up in the display as the neighbors' addresses. The autonomous system numbers and the link type (external) are still displayed the same way as for the correct configuration. What's

different is that the router ID is all zeros, the BGP state = Idle, and at
the bottom of the display for each neighbor there is a clear statement about
no active TCP connection and the fact that the external neighbor is not
directly connected. This is in contrast to the correct configuration where
the IP addresses and the ports and the local and foreign hosts (the neighboring routers) are displayed. When the BGP state is idle and there is no
TCP connection between neighbors, no BGP updates will be exchanged
between them, that is, no BGP routing will take place.

Assume at this point that the neighbor IP addresses on the Billings
router have been changed back to the correct addresses used in the initial
neighbor configuration. What periodically throws off even those who
have worked with BGP for a while is the fact that after BGP has been
activated and neighbors correctly defined, there is still no impact on the
routing tables on any of the routers. Take a look at the routing tables for
all four routers following the activation of BGP and the correct configuration of external neighbors. They are identical to the routing tables
before any BGP configuration took place. The three autonomous systems
are still isolated from one another.

Billings routing table following BGP activation and definition of external neighbors

```
billings#sh ip route
Codes: C - connected, S - static, I - IGRP, R - RIP, M - mobile, B - BGP
       D - EIGRP, EX - EIGRP external, O - OSPF,


Gateway of last resort is not set


C    192.168.1.0 is directly connected, Serial0
C    192.168.2.0 is directly connected, Serial2
C    172.16.0.0 is directly connected, Ethernet0
C    192.168.129.0 is directly connected, Serial1
billings#
```

Denver1 routing table following BGP activation and definition of external neighbors

```
Denver1#sh ip route
Codes: C - connected, S - static, I - IGRP, R - RIP, M - mobile, B - BGP
       D - EIGRP, EX - EIGRP external, O - OSPF,


Gateway of last resort is not set


C    192.168.144.0/24 is directly connected, Serial1
C    172.17.0.0/16 is directly connected, Ethernet0
O    172.18.0.0/16 [110/20] via 172.17.0.2, 02:51:57, Ethernet0

C    192.168.1.0/24 is directly connected, Serial0
```

Denver3 routing table following BGP activation and definition of external neighbors

```
Denver3#sh ip route
Codes: C - connected, S - static, I - IGRP, R - RIP, M - mobile, B - BGP
       D - EIGRP, EX - EIGRP external, O - OSPF,


Gateway of last resort is not set


C    172.17.0.0/16 is directly connected, Ethernet0
C    172.18.0.0/16 is directly connected, Ethernet1
C    192.168.2.0/24 is directly connected, Serial0
Denver3#
```

Denver2 routing table following BGP activation and definition of external neighbors

```
Denver2#sh ip route
Codes: C - connected, S - static, I - IGRP, R - RIP, M - mobile, B - BGP
       D - EIGRP, EX - EIGRP external, O - OSPF,


Gateway of last resort is not set
```

```
C    192.168.144.0/24 is directly connected, Serial1
C    192.168.129.0/24 is directly connected, Serial0
C    172.21.0.0/16 is directly connected, Ethernet1
C    172.20.0.0/16 is directly connected, Ethernet0
```

The only routing table entries present are for the directly connected networks and a single OSPF-derived route on Denver1. What's missing from the current BGP configurations are statements telling BGP what networks to route for. BGP can be told about networks to route for either statically or dynamically. Static injection of networks into BGP is accomplished via the `network` command and is referred to as advertising. Dynamic injection of networks into the BGP process is accomplished via the `redistribute` command and is referred to as redistribution. Examples of advertising and redistribution follow later on in this chapter. Chapter 11 is dedicated in its entirety to problems relating to redistribution.

Internal BGP Neighbors

For internal BGP sessions (BGP neighbors within the same autonomous system), there is no longer the requirement for physical connectivity between neighbors. However, there still has to be IP connectivity between the internal BGP neighbors either via an IGP or static routes if they are not directly connected.

The purpose of having internal BGP sessions is to be able to preserve BGP route characteristics in transit autonomous systems. In Figure 10.1, both providers A and B operate transit autonomous systems.

Observe the IBGP configuration between Denver1 and Denver3. Each router will add one neighbor statement to its existing BGP configuration. Given that OSPF is running inside of AS 10, resulting in full IP connectivity inside the AS, it might seem hard to make a mistake. But the serial networks in use by Denver1 and Denver3 are not advertised into OSPF. If the neighbor addresses for Denver1 and Denver3 are mistakenly derived from their serial subnets, there is going to be a problem.

Following are the configurations for Denver1 and Denver3 with the addition of neighbor statements for IBGP with IP addresses of neighbors derived from their serial subnets.

Denver1 misconfiguration of internal neighbor

```
hostname Denver1
!
enable password cisco
!
ip subnet-zero
!
interface Ethernet0
 ip address 172.17.0.1 255.255.0.0
 no shut
!
interface Serial0
 description T1 link to Billings (Customer X)
 ip address 192.168.1.2 255.255.255.0
 no shut
!
interface Serial1
 description T1 link to Denver2 (Provider A)
 ip address 192.168.144.1 255.255.255.0
 clockrate 2000000
 no shut
!
router ospf 10
 network 172.17.0.0 0.0.255.255 area 0.0.0.0
!
router bgp 10
 neighbor 192.168.1.1 remote-as 90      Note: EBGP session to Billings
 neighbor 192.168.2.2 remote-as 10      Note: IBGP session to Denver3?
 neighbor 192.168.144.2 remote-as 20    Note: EBGP session to Denver2
!
```

Denver3 misconfiguration of internal neighbor

```
hostname Denver3
!
```

```
enable password cisco
!
interface Ethernet0
 ip address 172.17.0.2 255.255.0.0
 no shut
!
interface Ethernet1
 ip address 172.18.0.1 255.255.0.0
 no shut
!
interface Serial0
 description 64K link to Billings (Customer X)
 ip address 192.168.2.2 255.255.255.0
 no shut
!
interface Serial1
 shut
!
router ospf 10
 network 172.17.0.0 0.0.255.255 area 0.0.0.0
 network 172.18.0.0 0.0.255.255 area 0.0.0.0
!
router bgp 10
 neighbor 192.168.1.2 remote-as 10    Note: IBGP session to Denver1?
 neighbor 192.168.2.1 remote-as 90    Note: EBGP session to Billings
!
```

The results are disappointing, but in line with expectations. Show ip
bgp neighbors on both Denver1 and Denver3 clearly indicates lack of
TCP connection between the two routers. Due to space considerations, a
portion of the trace is displayed describing only the links to the internal
neighbors. Links to external neighbors from Denver1 and Denver3 are
configured correctly and are not displayed here.

```
Denver1#sh ip bgp neighbors
.
```

.

.

```
BGP neighbor is 192.168.2.2, remote AS 10, internal link
 Index 3, Offset 0, Mask 0x8
  BGP version 4, remote router ID 0.0.0.0
  BGP state = Active, table version = 0
  Last read 00:17:33, hold time is 180, keepalive interval is 60 seconds
  Minimum time between advertisement runs is 5 seconds
  Received 0 messages, 0 notifications, 0 in queue
  Sent 0 messages, 0 notifications, 0 in queue
  Connections established 0; dropped 0
  Last reset never
  No. of prefix received 0
  No active TCP connection
```

.

.

.

```
Denver3#sh ip bgp neighbors
BGP neighbor is 192.168.1.2, remote AS 10, internal link
 Index 2, Offset 0, Mask 0x4
  BGP version 4, remote router ID 0.0.0.0
  BGP state = Active, table version = 0
  Last read 00:17:17, hold time is 180, keepalive interval is 60 seconds
  Minimum time between advertisement runs is 5 seconds
  Received 0 messages, 0 notifications, 0 in queue
  Sent 0 messages, 0 notifications, 0 in queue
  Connections established 0; dropped 0
  Last reset never
  No. of prefix received 0
  No active TCP connection
```

.

.

One way to verify that your IBGP neighbor configurations are going to work is to ping the IP address of the neighbor. If the ping fails, investigate what the problem is with IP connectivity. If the ping works, you are closer to success but not necessarily there yet. What you really have to do is to use an extended ping and specify the target address and the source address. The target address should be the neighbor IP address configured on your router. The source address should be the address on your router that is configured as the neighbor address on your neighbor's router. If the extended ping works, then you are in good shape.

When the IP address of the neighbor on Denver1 is changed from 192.168.2.2 to 172.18.0.1, the normal ping from Denver1 to 172.18.0.1 works fine. However, the extended ping specifying the source address as 192.168.1.2 and the target address of 172.18.0.1 fails as shown in the trace that follows:

```
Normal ping from Denver1

Denver1#ping 172.18.0.1

Type escape sequence to abort.

Sending 5, 100-byte ICMP Echos to 172.18.0.1, timeout is 2 seconds:

!!!!!

Success rate is 100 percent (5/5), round-trip min/avg/max = 4/4/4 ms
```

Extended ping from Denver1

```
Denver1#ping

Protocol [ip]:

Target IP address: 172.18.0.1

Repeat count [5]:

Datagram size [100]:

Timeout in seconds [2]:

Extended commands [n]: y

Source address or interface: 192.168.1.2

Type of service [0]:

Set DF bit in IP header? [no]:

Validate reply data? [no]:

Data pattern [0xABCD]:

Loose, Strict, Record, Timestamp, Verbose[none]:

Sweep range of sizes [n]:

Type escape sequence to abort.
```

```
Sending 5, 100-byte ICMP Echos to 172.18.0.1, timeout is 2 seconds:
.....
Success rate is 0 percent (0/5)
```

If the neighbor IP address on Denver1 is changed from 192.168.2.2 to 172.18.0.1, but no change takes place on Denver3, the result will still be a non-existent IBGP session between them due to lack of IP connectivity as confirmed by the preceding extended ping. Only when the change on Denver1 is coupled with the change on Denver3 will the internal BGP session work fine. Observe what happens when the `neighbor` commands with incorrect addresses are removed and replaced with correct ones.

```
Denver1#conf t
Enter configuration commands, one per line.  End with CNTL/Z.
Denver1(config)#router bgp 10
Denver1(config-router)#no neighbor 192.168.2.2 remote-as 10
Denver1(config-router)#neighbor 172.18.0.1 remote-as 10
Denver1(config-router)#^Z
Denver1#


Denver3#conf t
Enter configuration commands, one per line.  End with CNTL/Z.
Denver3(config)#router bgp 10
Denver3(config-router)#no neighbor 192.168.1.2 remote-as 10
Denver3(config-router)#neighbor 172.17.0.1 remote-as 10
Denver3(config-router)#^Z
Denver3#


Denver1#sh ip bgp neighbors
BGP neighbor is 172.18.0.1, remote AS 10, internal link
  Index 1, Offset 0, Mask 0x2
    BGP version 4, remote router ID 192.168.2.2
    BGP state = Established, table version = 8, up for 00:14:16
    Last read 00:00:16, hold time is 180, keepalive interval is 60 seconds
    Minimum time between advertisement runs is 5 seconds
    Received 20 messages, 0 notifications, 0 in queue
```

```
Sent 21 messages, 0 notifications, 0 in queue

Connections established 1; dropped 0

Last reset never

No. of prefix received 0

Connection state is ESTAB, I/O status: 1, unread input bytes: 0
```
Local host: 172.17.0.1, Local port: 11001

Foreign host: 172.18.0.1, Foreign port: 179
```
Denver1#
```

```
Denver3#sh ip bgp neighbors
```
BGP neighbor is 172.17.0.1, remote AS 10, internal link
```
  Index 3, Offset 0, Mask 0x8

  BGP version 4, remote router ID 192.168.144.1

  BGP state = Established, table version = 2, up for 00:00:11

  Last read 00:00:11, hold time is 180, keepalive interval is 60 seconds

  Minimum time between advertisement runs is 5 seconds

  Received 3 messages, 0 notifications, 0 in queue

  Sent 3 messages, 0 notifications, 0 in queue

  Connections established 1; dropped 0

  Last reset never

  No. of prefix received 0

  Connection state is ESTAB, I/O status: 1, unread input bytes: 0
```
Local host: 172.18.0.1, Local port: 179

Foreign host: 172.17.0.1, Foreign port: 11042

All of the signs of a properly established internal BGP session between Denver1 and Denver3 are now present. Each router correctly identifies the valid router ID of the neighbor, the BGP state = Established and the IP addresses (used in the neighbor configuration) along with the TCP port numbers on both routers are identified.

What's tricky about IBGP neighbor configuration is that no error messages are generated when a wrong IP address is used in the neighbor command. Consequently, if the BGP neighbor configuration guidelines are not followed, BGP sessions will not be established and BGP will not work.

The IBGP neighbor configuration guidelines can be summarized as follows. First, the neighbor's IP address must be reachable via IP. Use ping and extended ping to verify this. Second, the IP addresses used should be of the most stable interfaces on the neighboring routers. Loopback addresses can be used for internal neighbors as long as they are reachable via IP. An additional command, `neighbor` *ip_address* `update-source` *interface* (where interface represents the loopback interface), may be required when only loopbacks are used. Third, in the case of external BGP neighbors, neighbor IP addresses need to be derived from the shared subnet over which BGP updates will be exchanged. In certain situations, loopback addresses can also be used for external neighbors, typically in combination with the `ebgp-multihop` command.

Aggregating Someone Else's Routes

The discussion about aggregation of someone else's routes assumes first and foremost that BGP is being told about networks that it's going to route. Secondly, the BGP process is being told about so many networks that an administrator decides to implement aggregation to reduce the number of routes that a BGP router will advertise to its neighbors. The concept of BGP aggregation is similar to OSPF summarization: A single route is used to represent multiple networks. OSPF summarization pitfalls have already been discussed in Chapter 8. Problems with BGP aggregation are not much different.

Assume a backbone/customer configuration as shown in Figure 10.2. A global Internet provider is operating a global backbone which has peering sessions with other global backbones and several regional backbones operated by regional ISPs.

Customers C1 through C6 have peering sessions with the regional providers ISP1 and ISP2. Customers C1 through C3 are multihomed to both regional providers. The global ISP has assigned ranges of network addresses to the regional ISPs, who in turn assign them to their customers. For the purpose of this example, private addresses are used.

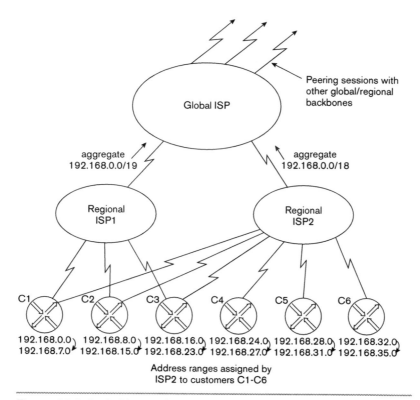

Figure 10.2 *Logical layout of a typical global/regional backbone configuration operated by major ISPs*

The address ranges assigned to the customers by each provider are shown in Figure 10.2. The problem in this configuration occurs when regional ISP1 decides to aggregate addresses that have been assigned to customers C1, C2, and C3 by regional ISP2.

Take a look at the arithmetic. Addresses 192.168.0.0 through 192.168.63.0 belong to regional ISP2, who in turn assigned them to its customers as shown in Figure 10.2. Addresses 192.168.64.0 through 192.168.127.0 belong to regional ISP1 who also assigned some of them to its customers. ISP2 has more customers than ISP1, and some of ISP2's customers (C4, C5, and C6) are not peering with ISP1.

When ISP2 performs aggregation on the addresses that have been assigned to its customers, the aggregate address is 192.168.0.0/18, which encompasses all addresses in the range from 192.168.0.0 to 192.168.63.0 that are owned by ISP2. Now, when ISP1 decides to aggregate ISP2's addresses that are advertised to it by customers C1, C2, and C3, ISP1 comes up with an aggregate of 192.168.0.0/19. This aggregate encompasses addresses in the range from 192.168.0.0 to 192.168.31.0. This would not be a problem if ISP1 had a peering session with all customers using the addresses from the range 192.168.0.0 to 192.168.31.0. However, customers C4 and C5 have networks in the range 192.168.0.0/19, but they are not peering with ISP1.

It still might not seem like there is a problem here because, after all, ISP2 is advertising an aggregate toward the global backbone that encompasses the networks that are assigned to C4 and C5. The problem is that ISP1's aggregate is more specific (it has a longer mask) than ISP2's aggregate: ISP1's aggregate is 192.168.0.0/19 whereas ISP2's aggregate is 192.168.0.0/18. BGP favors the route with a longer or more specific prefix, consequently, the traffic from the global backbone destined for networks of C4 and C5 will be directed to regional ISP1. Since ISP1 has no connectivity to C4 or C5, except though the global backbone, that traffic destined for C4 and C5 will never reach them. In BGP jargon, a "black hole" has been created.

The problem resulting from the aggregation of someone else's routes is easily avoidable. First and foremost, ISP1 does not have to aggregate ISP2's networks. Second, if ISP1 insists on aggregating networks assigned to its customers by ISP2, ISP1 ought to recognize that there are networks included in the aggregate that it does not know about. Instead of issuing a single aggregate toward the global backbone, ISP1 could issue two aggregates that would cover only the networks that it knows about. The two aggregates would be 192.168.0.0/20 encompassing 192.168.0.0 through 192.168.15.0 (C1 and C2's networks) and 192.168.16.0/21 encompassing 192.168.16.0 through 192.168.23.0 (C3's networks).

Third, ISP2 can advertise toward the global backbone an aggregate of its networks along with all of the individual networks that it owns. That way, the routers on the global backbone will have an aggregate to pass on to other global peering partners, but they will also have the individual networks from ISP2. Having the individual entries for all of ISP2's networks would ensure that even with ISP1's improper aggregation, the traffic destined for C4 and

C5 would still reach them. The networks in C4 and C5 would simply be visible in the routers on the global backbone with a /24 mask, which is longer than the /19 mask coming from ISP1.

The command for implementing aggregation is `aggregate-address` *address mask* [options]. The *address* represents the aggregated prefix and the *mask* the length of the prefix. One of the options is *summary-only*. When summary-only is used, only the aggregate itself will be advertised. Without the summary-only, the aggregate along with the individual routes composing the aggregate will be advertised. Advertising the aggregate along with the individual networks composing the aggregate is recommended in the preceding paragraph as a way to avoid the consequences of improper aggregation by other providers.

Improper Use of Route Maps

Route maps are generic IOS tools that are well suited to implementing BGP routing policies. The purpose of a route map is to identify a condition that's used in defining a routing policy and then to take action on that condition. An example of a condition may be the presence of a certain autonomous system number inside the AS_path attribute. The identification of the condition is done via a *match* keyword. One example of an action that's taken on that condition may be the setting a value for the local_preference attribute. Route map actions are implemented via the use of a *set* keyword.

Take a look at the configuration depicted in Figure 10.3.

The configuration files for all routers in Figure 10.3 are shown next. The BGP portion of the configuration includes the activation of the BGP process, definition of neighbors, and redistribution of routes from the IGPs into BGP. The routing tables on all routers now show BGP routes. Compare the routing tables resulting from this configuration with those from the configuration in the "Misconfigured IP Addresses of Neighbors" section, Figure 10.1. Whereas before there was total isolation between the autonomous systems because the BGP processes were not told about which networks to route, now there is full reachability between all three autonomous systems.

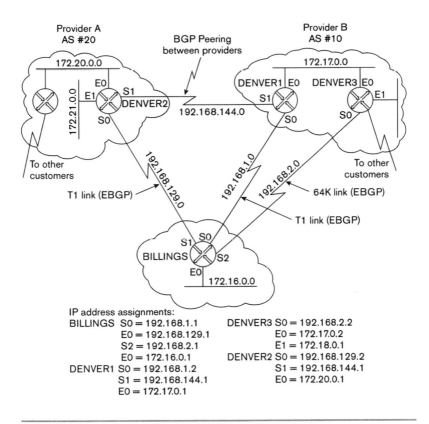

Figure 10.3 *BGP configuration for use with route map examples*

Billings router configuration following IGP redistribution into BGP

```
hostname billings
!
interface Ethernet0
 ip address 172.16.0.1 255.255.0.0
 no shut
!
interface Serial0
 description T1 link to Denver1 (Provider B)
 ip address 192.168.1.1 255.255.255.0
 clockrate 2000000
```

```
 no shut
!
interface Serial1
 description T1 link to Denver2 (Provider A)
 ip address 192.168.129.1 255.255.255.0
 clockrate 2000000
 no shut
!
interface Serial2
 description 64K link to Denver3 (Provider B)
 ip address 192.168.2.1 255.255.255.0
 clockrate 64000
 no shut
!
router igrp 99
 network 172.16.0.0
!
router bgp 90
 redistribute igrp 99          Note: redistribution of IGRP into BGP
 neighbor 192.168.1.2 remote-as 10
 neighbor 192.168.2.2 remote-as 10
 neighbor 192.168.129.2 remote-as 20
!
```

Denver1 router configuration following IGP redistribution into BGP

```
hostname Denver1
!
ip subnet-zero
!
interface Ethernet0
 ip address 172.17.0.1 255.255.0.0
 no shut
!
interface Serial0
```

```
 description T1 link to Billings (Customer X)
 ip address 192.168.1.2 255.255.255.0
 no shut
!
interface Serial1
 description T1 link to Denver2 (Provider A)
 ip address 192.168.144.1 255.255.255.0
 clockrate 2000000
 no shut
!
router ospf 10
 network 172.17.0.0 0.0.255.255 area 0.0.0.0
!
router bgp 10
 redistribute ospf 10              Note: redistribution of OSPF into BGP
 neighbor 192.168.1.1 remote-as 90
 neighbor 192.168.144.2 remote-as 20
 neighbor 172.18.0.1 remote-as 10
!
```

Denver3 router configuration following IGP redistribution into BGP

```
hostname Denver3
!
enable password cisco
!
interface Ethernet0
 ip address 172.17.0.2 255.255.0.0
 no shut
!
interface Ethernet1
 ip address 172.18.0.1 255.255.0.0
 no shut
!
interface Serial0
```

```
 description 64K link to Billings (Customer X)
 ip address 192.168.2.2 255.255.255.0
 no shut
!
interface Serial1
 shut
!
router ospf 10
 network 172.17.0.0 0.0.255.255 area 0.0.0.0
 network 172.18.0.0 0.0.255.255 area 0.0.0.0
!
router bgp 10
 redistribute ospf 10            Note: redistribution of OSPF into BGP
 neighbor 192.168.2.1 remote-as 90
 neighbor 172.17.0.1 remote-as 10
!
```

Denver2 router configuration following IGP redistribution into BGP

```
hostname Denver2
!
enable password cisco
!
interface Ethernet0
 ip address 172.20.0.1 255.255.0.0
 no shut
!
interface Ethernet1
 ip address 172.21.0.1 255.255.0.0
 no shut
!
interface Serial0
 description T1 link to Billings (Customer X)
 ip address 192.168.129.2 255.255.255.0
 no shut
!
```

```
interface Serial1

 description T1 link to Denver1 (Provider B)

 ip address 192.168.144.2 255.255.255.0

 no shut

!

router ospf 20

 network 172.20.0.0 0.0.255.255 area 0.0.0.0

 network 172.21.0.0 0.0.255.255 area 0.0.0.0

!

router bgp 20

 redistribute ospf 20            Note: redistribution of OSPF into BGP

 neighbor 192.168.129.1 remote-as 90

 neighbor 192.168.144.1 remote-as 10

!
```

Billings routing table showing BGP routes

```
billings#sh ip route

Codes: C - connected, S - static, I - IGRP, R - RIP, M - mobile, B - BGP

       D - EIGRP, EX - EIGRP external, O - OSPF,


Gateway of last resort is not set


C    192.168.1.0 is directly connected, Serial0

C    192.168.2.0 is directly connected, Serial2

B    172.20.0.0 [20/0] via 192.168.129.2, 01:45:12

B    172.21.0.0 [20/0] via 192.168.129.2, 01:38:08

C    172.16.0.0 is directly connected, Ethernet0

B    172.17.0.0 [20/0] via 192.168.2.2, 01:44:07

B    172.18.0.0 [20/0] via 192.168.2.2, 01:42:25

C    192.168.129.0 is directly connected, Serial1
```

Denver1 routing tables showing BGP routes

```
Denver1#sh ip route

Codes: C - connected, S - static, I - IGRP, R - RIP, M - mobile, B - BGP
```

```
         D - EIGRP, EX - EIGRP external, O - OSPF,


Gateway of last resort is not set


C    192.168.144.0/24 is directly connected, Serial1
C    172.17.0.0/16 is directly connected, Ethernet0
B    172.16.0.0/16 [20/0] via 192.168.1.1, 01:42:07
O    172.18.0.0/16 [110/20] via 172.17.0.2, 01:45:58, Ethernet0
B    172.21.0.0/16 [20/0] via 192.168.144.2, 01:38:32
B    172.20.0.0/16 [20/0] via 192.168.144.2, 01:45:36
C    192.168.1.0/24 is directly connected, Serial0
Denver1#
```

Denver3 routing tables showing BGP routes

```
Denver3#sh ip route
Codes: C - connected, S - static, I - IGRP, R - RIP, M - mobile, B - BGP
         D - EIGRP, EX - EIGRP external, O - OSPF,


Gateway of last resort is not set


C    172.17.0.0/16 is directly connected, Ethernet0
B    172.16.0.0/16 [20/0] via 192.168.2.1, 01:42:26
C    172.18.0.0/16 is directly connected, Ethernet1
B    172.21.0.0/16 [20/0] via 192.168.2.1, 01:38:50
B    172.20.0.0/16 [20/0] via 192.168.2.1, 01:45:54
C    192.168.2.0/24 is directly connected, Serial0
Denver3#
```

Denver2 routing tables showing BGP routes

```
Denver2#sh ip route
Codes: C - connected, S - static, I - IGRP, R - RIP, M - mobile, B - BGP
         D - EIGRP, EX - EIGRP external, O - OSPF,


Gateway of last resort is not set
```

```
C    192.168.144.0/24 is directly connected, Serial1

C    192.168.129.0/24 is directly connected, Serial0

B    172.17.0.0/16 [20/0] via 192.168.144.1, 01:45:05

B    172.16.0.0/16 [20/0] via 192.168.129.1, 01:42:42

B    172.18.0.0/16 [20/20] via 192.168.144.1, 01:45:06

C    172.21.0.0/16 is directly connected, Ethernet1

C    172.20.0.0/16 is directly connected, Ethernet0

Denver2#
```

What's interesting to note in the routing table on the Billings router is that the networks residing in AS 10 are reachable via the slower 64K backup link. The next hop for 172.17.0.0 and 172.18.0.0 is 192.168.2.2. That's the serial0 interface on Denver3. The link between Billings and Denver3 is a 64K link, whereas the link between Billings and Denver1 is configured as a T1 link. To detemine why this is happening, it is necessary to look at the BGP table on the Billings router.

Once BGP has been activated and BGP updates are exchanged between routers, BGP creates its own table for all of the reachable destinations. The entries in the BGP table become subject to a rather complex route selection process. The best entry for each destination makes it into the IP routing table. As mentioned earlier in this chapter, the BGP route selection process does not take into account parameters like bandwidth of the links.

Billings BGP table

```
billings#sh ip bgp

BGP table version is 9, local router ID is 192.168.129.1

Status codes: s suppressed, d damped, h history, * valid, > best, i - internal

Origin codes: i - IGP, e - EGP, ? - incomplete
```

	Network	Next Hop	Metric	LocPrf	Weight	Path
*>	172.16.0.0	0.0.0.0	0		32768	?
*	172.17.0.0	192.168.1.2	0		0	10 ?
*>		192.168.2.2	0		0	10 ?
*		192.168.129.2			0	20 10 ?
*	172.18.0.0	192.168.1.2	20		0	10 ?

```
*                    192.168.129.2                    0 20 10 ?
*>                   192.168.2.2         0            0 10 ?
*> 172.20.0.0        192.168.129.2       0            0 20 ?
*                    192.168.1.2                      0 10 20 ?
*> 172.21.0.0        192.168.129.2       0            0 20 ?
*                    192.168.1.2                      0 10 20 ?
billings#
```

The BGP table has more information in it than the IP routing or forwarding table. Before the Network column, which identifies the destinations, there is a column with status codes, which are explained in the table legend. The two status codes that appear in the Billings table are "*" and ">", which represent valid and best routes, respectively. The interpretation of the Billings table is that all of the routes present in the table are valid, but only one out of the valid routes for each destination is best. When the Billings BGP table is compared to the Billings routing table, it's clear that the best routes from the BGP table appear in the routing table.

The BGP attributes, which are carried inside the BGP update messages, are used to determine which BGP routes are best. Some of those attributes include the local preference, the AS_path, the multi-exit discriminator (MED), and the origin code. All of these attributes appear in the BGP table. Local preference appears in the LocPrf column, the AS_path in the Path column, the MED in the Metric column, and the origin codes follow the path values. There is no column heading in the table for the origin codes.

The detailed review of the complete BGP route selection process is outside the scope of this book. Refer to other reference material listed in Appendix A. However, for the purpose of the discussion on route maps, it's important to know that out of the attributes referenced thus far, local preference takes precedence. The higher the local preference, the better the route.

After local preference comes the AS_path. If two routes exist to the same destination with the same local preference, the route with the shorter path (fewer ASNs in the list) will be preferable. If the two preceding conditions are the same, the route with a lower origin code is more desirable. Two common origin codes are IGP represented by "I" and incomplete represented by "?". The IGP or "I" code is the result of a network advertised into BGP via a network command. The incomplete code (?) results from redistribution implemented via a `redistribute` command. In the case of the Billings router, all entries in the BGP table are a result of redistribution as reflected in the configuration files for the scenario in Figure 10.3 and the "?" origin code in the Billings BGP table.

The MED value is the tiebreaker if the values of all of the preceding attributes are the same. Administrators can set the MED values or they can be carried into BGP from redistribution. The lower the MED value, the more preferable the route. And finally if the local preference, the AS_path, the origin, and the MED values are the same, the tiebreaker becomes the router ID. If two routers are advertising routes to the same destination with all of the preceding conditions being equal, the path that leads through the router with a lower router ID will be chosen.

The routes in the Billing routing table resulting from the default configuration in the scenario in Figure 10.3 are clearly not desirable. From the Billings router, the administrator wants to ensure that networks 172.17.0.0 and 172.18.0.0 are reachable via the faster T1 link. Let's concentrate on reaching 172.17.0.0 via the T1 link to Denver1.

The BGP table for the Billings router shows that there are actually three ways of reaching 172.17.0.0. Since the local preference is not set for any of the three routes, the next attribute that takes precedence is the AS_path. The route with the longest AS_path going through AS 20 can be eliminated. The remaining two routes have the same length AS_path, the same origin code, and the same MED. This means that the router with a lower ID will be chosen. A display of BGP neighbors on the Billings router confirms that the neighbor with the next hop of 192.168.2.2 has a lower router ID than the neighbor with the next hop of 192.168.1.2.

Partial display of BGP neighbors on the Billings router to verify router IDs

```
billings#sh ip bgp neighbor
BGP neighbor is 192.168.1.2,   remote AS 10, external link
  BGP version 4, remote router ID 192.168.144.1
  BGP state = Established, table version = 10, up for 2:19:10
  .
  .
  .
BGP neighbor is 192.168.2.2,   remote AS 10, external link
  BGP version 4, remote router ID 192.168.2.2
```

```
BGP state = Established, table version = 10, up for 2:17:33
.

.

.

billings#
```

At this point, the administrator has a choice as to how to influence the traffic from Billings destined for 172.17.0.0. In fact, there are so many choices that the process becomes more error-prone. Given the precedence of the attributes in the BGP route selection process, it seems natural that changing the local preference should be the number one choice. The configuration process on the Billings router to accomplish the change of local preference is as follows.

```
billings#conf t
Enter configuration commands, one per line.  End with CNTL/Z.
billings(config)#router bgp 90
billings(config-router)#neighbor 192.168.1.2 route-map set_lp in
billings(config-router)#exit
billings(config)#route-map set_lp permit 1
billings(config-route-map)#set local-preference 300
billings(config-route-map)#^Z
billings#
```

The preceding reconfiguration effectively told Billing's neighbor (Denver1) that Billings is going to apply a routing policy to all of the updates received from it. The policy is identified via a route map named *set_lp*. The action that *set_lp* takes is to flag all of the updates received from Denver1 with the local preference value of 300. The default local preference value is 100. And here is where the pitfalls begin.

First, the resulting BGP table and IP routing table do not show anything different after this reconfiguration. This is illustrated in the traces that follow.

Billings BGP table following the application of a route map

```
billings#sh ip bgp
BGP table version is 9, local router ID is 192.168.129.1
Status codes: s suppressed, d damped, h history, * valid, > best, i - internal
```

```
Origin codes: i - IGP, e - EGP, ? - incomplete
```

Network	Next Hop	Metric	LocPrf	Weight	Path
*> 172.16.0.0	0.0.0.0	0		32768	?
*> **172.17.0.0**	**192.168.2.2**	**0**		**0**	**10 ?**
*	192.168.1.2	0		0	10 ?
*	192.168.129.2			0	20 10 ?
*> **172.18.0.0**	**192.168.2.2**	**0**		**0**	**10 ?**
*	192.168.1.2	20		0	10 ?
*	192.168.129.2			0	20 10 ?
*> 172.20.0.0	192.168.129.2	0		0	20 ?
*	192.168.1.2			0	10 20 ?
*> 172.21.0.0	192.168.129.2	0		0	20 ?
*	192.168.1.2			0	10 20 ?

```
billings#
```

The best BGP routes to 172.17.0.0 and 172.18.0.0 are still via
192.168.2.2, which is the slow 64K serial link between Billings and
Denver3. The Billings IP routing table confirms that traffic from Billings to
all networks in autonomous system 10 will continue to go via the slow link.

Billings routing table following the application of a route map

```
billings#sh ip route
Codes: C - connected, S - static, I - IGRP, R - RIP, M - mobile, B - BGP
       D - EIGRP, EX - EIGRP external, O - OSPF,


Gateway of last resort is not set


C    192.168.1.0 is directly connected, Serial0

C    192.168.2.0 is directly connected, Serial2

B    172.20.0.0 [20/0] via 192.168.129.2, 01:45:12

B    172.21.0.0 [20/0] via 192.168.129.2, 01:38:08

C    172.16.0.0 is directly connected, Ethernet0

B    172.17.0.0 [20/0] via 192.168.2.2, 01:44:07

B    172.18.0.0 [20/0] via 192.168.2.2, 01:42:25

C    192.168.129.0 is directly connected, Serial1
```

Naturally, there is a problem here. The BGP connection between Billings and Denver3 needs to be cleared before the route map is going to have any effect. Clearing of the connection is shown next.

```
billings#clear ip bgp *
billings#
```

Clearing the BGP connection as shown accomplishes the purpose of allowing the *set_lp* route map to take effect, but it is quite dangerous. This is the second potential pitfall to watch out for in the course of applying route maps in a live production environment. All of the BGP sessions between Billings and all of its neighbors—not just the connection between Billings and Denver—have been cleared.

In live production environments, the execution of `clear ip bgp *` will cause a serious disruption in routing as all of the BGP routes are removed from the IP routing table upon its execution. The correct way to clear the connection between Billings and Denver1 would be to specify the neighbor IP address of Denver1 as opposed to a "*". Assume for a moment that a correct clearing of the connection between Billings and Denver1 took place via `clear ip bgp 192.168.1.2`.

Now observe the BGP and IP routing tables on Billings.

Billings BGP table following the clearing of BGP connection between Billings and Denver1

```
billings#sh ip bgp
BGP table version is 8, local router ID is 192.168.129.1
Status codes: s suppressed, d damped, h history, * valid, > best, i - internal
Origin codes: i - IGP, e - EGP, ? - incomplete
```

Network	Next Hop	Metric	LocPrf	Weight	Path
*> 172.16.0.0	0.0.0.0	0		32768	?
* 172.17.0.0	192.168.2.2	0		0	10 ?
*>	192.168.1.2	0	300	0	10 ?
*	192.168.129.2			0	20 10 ?
* 172.18.0.0	192.168.2.2	0		0	10 ?
*>	192.168.1.2	20	300	0	10 ?
*	192.168.129.2			0	20 10 ?

```
*> 172.20.0.0      192.168.1.2                    300      0 10 20 ?
*                  192.168.129.2          0                0 20 ?
*> 172.21.0.0      192.168.1.2                    300      0 10 20 ?
*                  192.168.129.2          0                0 20 ?
billings#
```

The best BGP routes for destinations in AS 10 are boldfaced in the table. The local preference setting took effect and the networks 172.17.0.0 and 172.18.0.0 in AS 10 are now reachable from Billings via the desired faster link. The Billings IP routing table reflects this condition.

Billings routing table after the clearing of BGP connection between Billings and Denver1

```
billings#sh ip route
Codes: C - connected, S - static, I - IGRP, R - RIP, M - mobile, B - BGP
       D - EIGRP, EX - EIGRP external, O - OSPF,


Gateway of last resort is not set

C    192.168.1.0 is directly connected, Serial0
C    192.168.2.0 is directly connected, Serial2
B    172.20.0.0 [20/0] via 192.168.1.2, 00:01:31
B    172.21.0.0 [20/0] via 192.168.1.2, 00:01:31
C    172.16.0.0 is directly connected, Ethernet0
B    172.17.0.0 [20/0] via 192.168.1.2, 00:01:31
B    172.18.0.0 [20/20] via 192.168.1.2, 00:01:31
C    192.168.129.0 is directly connected, Serial1
billings#
```

There is, however, an undesirable side effect to this reconfiguration. Notice that networks in AS 20, 172.20.0.0, and 172.21.0.0 are now also reachable via Denver1. One problem has been fixed, another introduced. It's clear that there are pitfalls associated with the use of route maps.

The undesirable side effect can be remedied by setting the local preference on the Billings router for updates received from Denver2 to be 300 as well. This way, both high-speed links from Billings to Denver1 and Denver2 will have the same local preference of 300. The same higher local preference

on both high-speed links will make them equally preferable over the slow
backup link from Billings to Denver3. The next BGP attribute, which is the
AS_path, will then kick in to break the ties for reaching destinations in AS
10 and AS 20.

With the same local preference for routes advertised via the Billings T1
links, the routes with fewer ASNs in the AS_path attribute will be more
desirable. This means that routes in AS 10 will be reachable via Billings'
T1 link to AS 10. The routes in AS 20 will be reachable via Billings' T1
link to AS 20.

Observe what happens after Billings is again reconfigured (with setting the local preference for routes received from Denver2 to 300) and a
connection between Billings and Denver2 has been cleared following the
reconfiguration.

```
billings#conf t
Enter configuration commands, one per line.  End with CNTL/Z.
billings(config)#router bgp 90
billings(config-router)#neighbor 192.168.129.2 route-map set_lp_again in
billings(config-router)#exit
billings(config)#route-map set_lp_again permit 1
billings(config-route-map)#set local-preference 300
billings(config-route-map)#^Z
billings#


billings#clear ip bgp 192.168.129.2


billings#sh ip BGP
BGP table version is 18, local router ID is 192.168.129.1
Status codes: s suppressed, d damped, h history, * valid, > best, i - internal
Origin codes: i - IGP, e - EGP, ? - incomplete


   Network          Next Hop          Metric LocPrf Weight Path
*> 172.16.0.0       0.0.0.0                0         32768 ?
*  172.17.0.0       192.168.2.2            0             0 10 ?
```

```
*>                  192.168.1.2         0    300    0 10 ?

*                   192.168.129.2            300    0 20 10 ?

*   172.18.0.0      192.168.2.2         0           0 10 ?

*>                  192.168.1.2        20    300    0 10 ?

*                   192.168.129.2            300    0 20 10 ?

*   172.20.0.0      192.168.1.2              300    0 10 20 ?

*>                  192.168.129.2       0    300    0 20 ?

*   172.21.0.0      192.168.1.2              300    0 10 20 ?

*>                  192.168.129.2       0    300    0 20 ?

billings#
```

```
billings#sh ip route
Codes: C - connected, S - static, I - IGRP, R - RIP, M - mobile, B - BGP
       D - EIGRP, EX - EIGRP external, O - OSPF,

Gateway of last resort is not set

C    192.168.1.0 is directly connected, Serial0
C    192.168.2.0 is directly connected, Serial2
B    172.20.0.0 [20/0] via 192.168.129.2, 00:01:01
B    172.21.0.0 [20/0] via 192.168.129.2, 00:01:01
C    172.16.0.0 is directly connected, Ethernet0
B    172.17.0.0 [20/0] via 192.168.1.2, 00:19:02
B    172.18.0.0 [20/20] via 192.168.1.2, 00:19:02
C    192.168.129.0 is directly connected, Serial1
billings#
```

Notice that the Billings routing table now reflects the desired results. Traffic for networks in AS 20 is going through the desired high-speed link, connecting Billings with AS 20. Traffic for networks in AS 10 will flow through the high-speed link, linking Billings with AS 10. The slow backup link between Billings and AS 10 will be used only in the event that both high-speed links go down.

The final Billings configuration is shown below.

Final Billings BGP configuration with route maps

```
hostname billings
!
interface Ethernet0
 ip address 172.16.0.1 255.255.0.0
 no shut
!
interface Serial0
 ip address 192.168.1.1 255.255.255.0
 clockrate 2000000
 no shut
!
interface Serial1
 ip address 192.168.129.1 255.255.255.0
 clockrate 2000000
 no shut
!
interface Serial2
 ip address 192.168.2.1 255.255.255.0
 clockrate 64000
 no shut
!
router igrp 99
 network 172.16.0.0
!
router bgp 90
 redistribute igrp 99
 neighbor 192.168.1.2 remote-as 10
 neighbor 192.168.1.2 route-map set_lp in
 neighbor 192.168.2.2 remote-as 10
 neighbor 192.168.129.2 remote-as 20
```

```
neighbor 192.168.129.2 route-map set_lp_again in

!

route-map set_lp_again permit 1

 set local-preference 300

!

route-map set_lp permit 1

 set local-preference 300
```

The concept of route maps is simple: Identify a condition and then act upon it. The possibilities for the use of route maps are almost limitless — but so is the potential for errors. The preceding example of setting a local preference was very simple, and yet if implemented improperly, it could either have had no impact at all or have serious routing disruptions.

Partial IBGP Mesh inside a Transit Autonomous System

Transit autonomous systems are operated by major ISPs. These providers are also referred to as tier 1 ISPs. Companies like MCI/Worldcom, Concert, BBN Planet, Level 3 Communications, or PSInet fall into the category of tier-1 transit providers. A transit provider operating a global backbone will have multiple POPs that are linked together via high-speed connections. POPs include routers that connect to other POP routers, as well as routers that are used for customer access to the backbone.

The key to the successful implementation of a transit autonomous system is to understand the rules that govern the operation of routing protocols used inside of it. A transit AS will typically run an IGP and IBGP. The IGP offers connectivity between networks internal to the AS. IBGP ensures that the BGP attributes in updates received from external neighbors are preserved. Without IBGP, redistribution of external BGP routes would be required into IGP, and then back into BGP. Clearly, a double redistribution is a very undesirable proposition, as will be discussed in the next chapter.

Consider a logical representation of a backbone as shown in Figure 10.4.

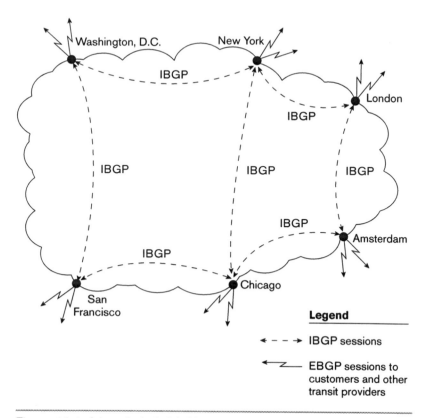

Figure 10.4 *A hypothetical global backbone with IBGP sessions*

All of the routers shown in Figure 10.4 belong to the same autonomous system 100. Each location is a major POP aggregating feeds from customers, peering with regional backbones and other global providers. The dotted lines shown in Figure 10.4 represent internal BGP sessions between routers at each location. For example, the Chicago router has IBGP sessions with San Francisco, New York, and Amsterdam. The London router peers with New York and Amsterdam. At first it might seem like everything is in order in the transit AS 100. There is a major problem here, however.

The IBGP is used for the purpose of preserving the BGP attributes associated with routes learned from customers and other providers. As discussed in the previous section, BGP attributes are used in determining the path that traffic coming from other autonomous systems will take.

IBGP has a rule that if a route is learned from an IBGP peer, it cannot be passed to another IBGP peer. Here's the practical implication of this rule. Chicago learns its customers' and other providers' routes and shares them with San Francisco, New York, and Amsterdam. Chicago does not have a peering session with London or Washington, DC. Amsterdam cannot pass the updates received from Chicago to London or it would be violating the IBGP rule. Consequently, if London has not learned about Chicago's customers' through other means — from another provider — traffic destined from London's customers to Chicago's customers will not be able to reach them.

The solution to this problem is straightforward. Each BGP router inside a transit AS must peer with every other BGP router inside the AS. With six routers forming the AS in Figure 10.4, it means that every router would have five neighbors. The total number of IBGP sessions would be 15. The formula for determining the number of IBGP sessions inside a transit AS is $n(n-1)/2$, where n is the number of BGP routers inside the AS. When the number of routers inside the AS is relatively small, the number of IBGP sessions is tolerable. However, when the number of routers is 50, 60, or even 100, the number of IBGP sessions begins to skyrocket. For 50 routers, the number of IBGP sessions would be 1225, for 60 routers, 1770, and for 100 routers, 4950. Also, imagine the reconfiguration headaches involved with adding a new POP to the backbone.

A large number of IBGP sessions could pose a serious performance problem and reconfiguration headaches. At least two solutions have been proposed to deal with a large number of IBGP sessions inside a transit AS: confederations and route reflectors. The proposed specifications for confederations and route reflectors are described in RFCs 1965 and 1966, respectively.

The concept of route reflectors is that routers inside an AS are divided into groups or clusters. One router in each cluster is configured as a "reflector," others are configured as clients of the reflector. The reflector can "break" the IBGP rule and re-advertise or reflect the routes that it has learned from its other peers. For example, assume that a transit AS with 50 routers is broken into five clusters of ten routers each.

Within each cluster, there are going to be nine IBGP sessions. One router in each cluster is configured as a reflector, all others as clients. The reflector peers with all clients but the clients do not peer with each other. There still has to be a full mesh between the clusters. The total number of

IBGP sessions inside that AS would be 60 (5×9=45 from the 5 clusters of 10 routers + 15 sessions between the 5 clusters). That's a big reduction from the 1225 that would be required to implement a full IBGP mesh between 50 routers.

The concept of confederations involves the break up of an autonomous system into smaller, mini-ASs. This breakup, however, is only internal. From the outside, the transit AS still appears as a single AS. Private AS numbers can be used to identify the mini-ASs. Each mini-AS would still have to have a full IBGP mesh inside of it.

The key point of this discussion is that when you are operating a transit AS, you have three choices: a full IBGP mesh, use of route reflectors, or confederations. For smaller number of routers, a full IBGP mesh seems simplest. For backbones with a larger number of routers, use of route reflectors seems to be the trend.

Default Routes Resulting in Routing Loops

Going around in circles is not a very appealing thought, except perhaps in an amusement park. But that's exactly what can happen to Internet traffic when routers are misconfigured. Preventing routing loops is an issue that must always be foremost in every network administrator's mind.

BGP has a very simple loop prevention mechanism. The AS_path variable accumulates the numbers of all ASs through which a BGP update has traversed. Take a look at Figure 10.5.

Billings will advertise 172.16.0.0 to Denver2. When Denver2 receives it, the AS_path variable will include ASN 90. Denver 2 will advertise 172.16.0.0 to Denver1. When the update about 172.16.0.0 reaches Denver1 from Denver2, the AS_path variable will include 90 and 20. Denver1 will attempt to advertise 172.16.0.0 back to Billings. When Billings receives the update about 172.16.0.0, it recognizes that ASN 90 is already in the AS_path variable and rejects the update.

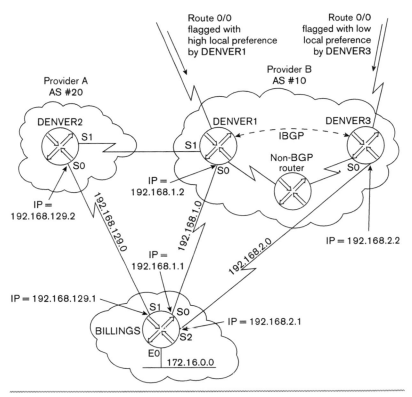

Figure 10.5 *BGP configuration for routing loop analysis*

Observe a portion of debug trace resulting from debug ip bgp updates. After the debug command has been executed, all BGP connections on Billings were cleared via the clear ip bgp * command. The purpose of clearing the BGP connections was to allow for the full exchange of BGP routing updates. Once BGP creates its table, only incremental updates are exchanged. In a steady state environment when no changes that impact routing are taking place, the results of debug ip bgp updates yield nothing.

BGP updates exchange demonstrating loop prevention

```
billings#debug ip bgp updates
BGP updates debugging is on
billings#
```

```
billings#clear ip bgp *
.
.
.
BGP: 192.168.1.2 rcv UPDATE about 172.20.0.0 255.255.0.0, next hop 192.168.1.2,
path 10 20 metric 0
BGP: 192.168.1.2 rcv UPDATE about 172.21.0.0 255.255.0.0, next hop 192.168.1.2,
path 10 20 metric 0
BGP: 192.168.1.2 rcv UPDATE about 172.18.0.0 255.255.0.0, next hop 192.168.1.2,
path 10 metric 20
BGP: 192.168.1.2 rcv UPDATE about 172.17.0.0 255.255.0.0, next hop 192.168.1.2,
path 10 metric 0
BGP: nettable_walker 172.17.0.0/255.255.0.0 calling revise_route
BGP: revise route installing 172.17.0.0/255.255.0.0 -> 192.168.1.2
BGP: nettable_walker 172.18.0.0/255.255.0.0 calling revise_route
BGP: revise route installing 172.18.0.0/255.255.0.0 -> 192.168.1.2
```
BGP: nettable_walker 172.16.0.0/255.255.0.0 route sourced locally
```
BGP: 192.168.129.2 computing updates, neighbor version 1, table version 8,
starting at 0.0.0.0
```
BGP: 192.168.129.2 send UPDATE 172.16.0.0 255.255.0.0, next 192.168.129.1,
metric 0, path 90
```
BGP: 192.168.129.2 send UPDATE 172.17.0.0 255.255.0.0, next 192.168.129.1,
metric 0, path 90 10
BGP: 192.168.129.2 send UPDATE 172.18.0.0 255.255.0.0, next 192.168.129.1,
metric 0, path 90 10
.
.
.
```
BGP: 192.168.1.2 rcv UPDATE about 172.16.0.0 255.255.0.0 -- denied
```
BGP: 192.168.2.2 computing updates, neighbor version 5, table version 8,
starting at 0.0.0.0
```
BGP: 192.168.2.2 send UPDATE 172.16.0.0 255.255.0.0, next 192.168.2.1, metric 0,
path 90
```
BGP: 192.168.2.2 send UPDATE 172.17.0.0 255.255.0.0, next 192.168.2.1, metric 0,
path 90 10
```

```
BGP: 192.168.2.2 send UPDATE 172.18.0.0 255.255.0.0, next 192.168.2.1, metric 0,

path 90 10

.

.

.

billings#undebug all

All possible debugging has been turned off

billings#
```

Due to a large volume of information resulting from the debug ip
bgp updates command, only a portion of the trace is displayed. The
lines relating to the 172.16.0.0 update are boldfaced. First, the BGP process on the Billings router recognizes that 172.16.0.0 is local (attached) to
Billings (*route sourced locally* in the trace). Next, Billings advertises
172.16.0.0 to Denver2 (to 192.168.129.2 neighbor) with a next-hop of
192.168.129.1 (Billings' serial1 interface) with a metric of 0 and AS_path
variable of 90. The next boldfaced line shows that Denver1 is attempting
to pass the update about 172.16.0.0 to Billings — after receiving it from
Denver2 — but Billings rejects the update (*denied* in the trace). BGP loop
prevention is simple and effective.

Routing loops become a problem when BGP has to interact with
IGPs, static, or default routes. Indiscriminate implementation of default
routes will definitely cause problems. Consider, for example, what would
happen if the Billings router was advertising a default route to Denver1,
and Denver1 was advertising a default route to Billings. Traffic for destinations not in Billings' routing table would be forwarded to Denver1. If
Denver1 did not have entries in its routing table for those destinations, it
would forward the traffic back to Billings.

The classic routing loop occurs when there is a mix of BGP and IGP
routers along with the use of default routes. AS 10 in Figure 10.5 affords
just such a combination. Denver1 and Denver3 are BGP border routers
peering with larger providers. Both Denver1 and Denver3 receive defaults
from their providers. It is the policy of AS 10, however, that all default traffic leaves through Denver1. Consequently, the default router received by
Denver1 from its provider is tagged with a higher local preference through
the use of a route map. Denver1 and Denver3 will exchange IBGP updates
about their defaults and agree that traffic for destinations not present in

their tables should leave via Denver1. This means that any traffic that Denver3 receives from its customers that is meant for destinations not present in its routing table will be forwarded to Denver1.

This is the crux of the problem. Denver1 and Denver3 have an IBGP session, but no direct physical connection. Traffic between them must flow through the non-BGP router. The non-BGP router has a default route that's accidentally pointing toward Denver3, and a loop occurs between the non-BGP router and Denver3. There could be several reasons why the non-BGP router has a default route pointing toward Denver3; anything from plain oversight if it's a static default to the IGP metric for the link between the non-BGP router and Denver3 being lower than its link to Denver1 if it's an IGP default.

The issue that network administrators must be aware of in such situations is that routing policies between BGP and IGPs must be consistent inside an autonomous system. It's best to avoid having non-BGP routers between BGP border routers, but if that's not possible, then the next best thing is to be informed about how the routing protocols operate.

Chapter Summary

Default BGP configuration is relatively simple. The BGP process must be activated, neighbors defined, and routes injected into BGP. IP connectivity must exist between BGP neighbors before a BGP session can be established. External BGP neighbors typically share a physical subnet. Implementing BGP policies is complex. Route maps and access control lists are commonly used to implement BGP routing policies. Improper route aggregation can result in undeliverable traffic. A full IBGP mesh is required inside a transit AS. The alternative is to use route reflectors or confederations. Autonomous systems that rely on the use of default routes in combination with BGP and non-BGP routers are prone to routing loops.

Chapter 11

Route Redistribution Pitfalls

Different routing protocols do not talk to one another unless forced to do so by network administrators through configuration. The communication process between routing protocols is referred to as redistribution. Redistribution can occur between any two protocols. Troubleshooting techniques for five routing protocols (IGRP, EIGRP, OSPF, RIP, and BGP) were discussed in previous chapters. This chapter focuses on troubleshooting interactions between some of these protocols.

Why Redistribution?

Primary reasons for redistribution are protocol migrations, network merges, and interactions between IGPs and EGPs. Rapid growth and expansion at installations deploying an older protocol like RIP often forces a migration to a more scalable protocol like EIGRP or OSPF. If the conversion from one routing protocol to another cannot be accomplished all at once, a period of coexistence is required during which both protocols are operational. And when multiple routing protocols are present in an internetwork, it's a given that some routers will perform redistribution in order to maintain reachability to all destinations.

When companies using different routing protocols merge their networks, a period of coexistence between the protocols is again required. It's possible that a task of converting the merged network to a single protocol is simply too resource-intensive. In that case, redistribution is there to stay.

The other major reason for redistribution is the interaction between IGPs and EGPs. IGPs like RIP, OSPF, or IGRP were not designed to operate between autonomous systems or carry a large number of routes; those functions are reserved for EGPs. BGP version 4 is the premier EGP for maintaining reachability between Internet locations. But BGP has to be told about the networks inside an autonomous system, which is typically accomplished via redistribution of IGP routes into BGP.

Theoretically, any routing protocol can be redistributed into any other routing protocol. In practice, some redistributions make more sense than others. It's generally accepted that a redistribution of IGPs into BGP is a must. But going the other way around is often not necessary, and if you decide to redistribute BGP into an IGP, it's recommended that you exercise caution.

Due to the large numbers of BGP routes that exist in the core Internet routers (at the major Internet exchanges), redistribution of all BGP routes into an IGP protocol like RIP, IGRP, or OSPF could easily crash the routers running these protocols. Limited BGP redistribution that's implemented via route maps and access control lists may be an option. A general guideline regarding redistribution of BGP into an IGP is to avoid it if you can and perform it with care if you must.

Different Routing Metrics

You will recall from previous chapters that different routing protocols calculate the cost of reaching a destination in different ways. In a sense, comparing the routing costs derived via one routing protocol to that of another is like comparing apples and oranges. However, if you have to perform redistributions, you will be forced to develop some sort of a relationship between the apples and oranges.

IGP Routing Costs

RIP's routing metric is by far the simplest. It's the hop count representing the number of routers that a packet has to cross to reach a destination. Destinations with a hop count of 16 are considered to be unreachable.

In OSPF, each router interface has a cost associated with it. The cost is a function of interface speed and ranges from 1 to 65,635. The default

OSPF interface cost is equal to 100,000,000 divided by the speed of the interface in bits/second. But network administrators have the option of setting the OSPF cost manually or manipulating it through the use of the `bandwidth` command. The total OSPF metric is derived from adding the costs of all of the outbound interfaces on routers that a packet must cross to reach its destination. There is no theoretical limit on the number of routers in an OSPF network, so the total OSPF metric can be very large. Compare this to the RIP hop count with a maximum of 16.

Assume, for example, that in a hypothetical internetwork the OSPF cost of reaching a destination is 70,000. When OSPF is deactivated and RIP is turned on in the same internetwork, the RIP cost of reaching the same destination is 5. It's tempting to divide 70,000 by 5 to come up with a ratio between OSPF and RIP costs for that internetwork. But that would be meaningless considering how the costs are derived.

It's also possible that traffic patterns within an internetwork will change when a conversion takes place from one routing protocol to another. From OSPF's point of view, it's cheaper to go through five T1 links than through a single 56K link. But from RIP's point of view, going through a single 56K link (one hop) is less expensive than going through five T1 links (five hops). If both paths were available, each protocol operating within that internetwork would use a different path. This is another example of the difficulty in relating routing metrics between routing protocols.

In IGRP and EIGRP, the metrics are more complex than in RIP or OSPF. The default cost of reaching a destination is a function of bandwidth and delay. Optionally it can be made to be a function of the network load and reliability. Trying to compare these costs to the equivalent RIP or OSPF costs is very difficult and not necessarily practical.

BGP Routing Cost

The routing cost in BGP is more involved than in any of the IGPs. With the IGPs, the cost of reaching a destination is ultimately reduced to a single number. That number may be a function of several variables depending on the routing protocol, but it's still a single number. In BGP, destination reachability is described by attributes. Attributes like the AS_path, local preference, origin, weight, or community, simply do not have an equivalent in IGPs.

One of the BGP attributes is the multi-exit discriminator (MED). If there are multiple paths leading into an autonomous system (AS), MED can influence which way the traffic will enter the AS. MED comes the closest to being the equivalent of the IGP metric. When an IGP like OSPF is redistributed into BGP, the OSPF metric becomes the MED value. But when you think about redistributing BGP into an IGP, there is simply no vehicle inside of an IGP to preserve all of the attributes associated with a route. That's one of the reasons for configuring IBGP inside of transit autonomous systems, as discussed in Chapter 10.

Given the complexity of translating the metrics between different routing protocols, a metric translation mechanism that's transcendentally simple is required to make redistribution work at all.

Reconciling Routing Costs between Protocols

When redistribution takes place between two IGPs, it's common to consider each IGP cloud as having a basic unit cost associated with it. For RIP, the basic unit cost of crossing another IGP's cloud may be considered as 1, or the equivalent of crossing a single router. For OSPF, the cost of crossing a RIP cloud could be considered the equivalent of passing through an Ethernet subnet, which would represent a cost of 10.

Consider a generic redistribution scenario as shown in Figure 11.1.

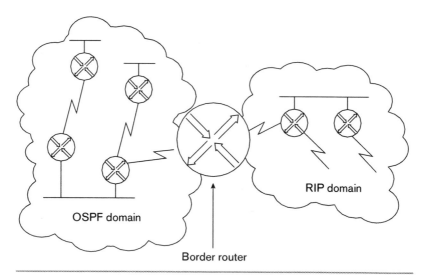

RIP domain

OSPF domain

Border router

Figure 11.1 *Generic redistribution scenario between IGPs*

Applying the principle of each IGP routing domain having a basic unit cost, the border router in Figure 11.1 can redistribute RIP routes into the OSPF domain with a cost of 10, and the OSPF routes into the RIP domain with a cost of 1. The RIP cost of 1 represents one hop and the OSPF cost of 10 represents the cost of crossing an Ethernet subnet. From the point of view of each IGP, all of the networks in the other IGP domains are either an extra hop or an extra subnet away from what it costs to get to the border router.

If you think about it, this technique could be used to stretch out a RIP network that's grappling with the maximum 16-hop count limit. You could break the RIP internetwork into two parts and insert a mini-OSPF domain between them. There would be two border routers performing redistribution between three domains, as shown in Figure 11.2.

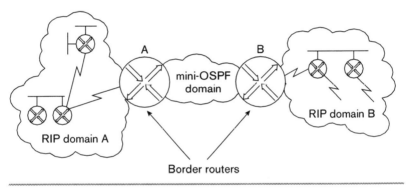

Figure 11.2 *Extending a RIP internetwork via redistribution*

From the point of view of RIP routers inside the A domain, all networks to the right of the border router A are an extra hop away. From the point of view of RIP routers in the B domain, all networks to the left of the border router B are also an extra hop away.

If you assume, for example, that each RIP domain has a diameter of 10 (maximum of 10 hops between any two networks within the domain), then combining the two RIP domains into a single domain could exceed the maximum 16-hop count limit. Whereas with another small IGP domain between two smaller RIP domains, the internetwork can still function via redistribution without an immediate need to migrate to another IGP.

Redistribution between IGPs

Redistribution between IGPs is typically the result of protocol migration or network merges. Whatever the business reasons, the technical implementation is the same. When performing redistribution between IGPs you must know the nature of each IGP. Specifically, you need to consider whether an IGP supports fixed-length or variable-length subnetting.

Another issue to consider is that redistribution is a two-way street. When two protocols are involved, it's not enough to redistribute just one into the other. That does not ensure full reachability throughout the internetwork; mutual redistribution or use of defaults is required.

Problems in mutual redistribution occur when one protocol carries a disproportionately larger number of routes than the other. When redistribution occurs between IGPs, this is not normally the case. But when redistribution occurs between an IGP and an EGP like BGP, then the danger of mutual redistribution is very real. This is explored in a later section in this chapter.

Redistribution between RIP and OSPF

When performing redistribution between RIP and OSPF, you must remember to specify a metric for the OSPF routes being redistributed into RIP. In the event that RIP routes are subnetted, you have to use the *subnets* keyword when redistributing them into OSPF. If you forget about the metric for routes being redistributed into RIP or the subnets for routes redistributed into OSPF, the IOS will accept your configuration statements but redistribution will not work. Consider an internetwork as shown in Figure 11.3, where the administrator initially forgets about those two important points.

The border router (BR) in Figure 11.3 will perform redistribution. The networks in the RIP domain are subnetted. The initial configurations for all routers in Figure 11.3 are shown next.

BR router initial configuration for RIP/OSPF redistribution analysis

```
!
hostname BR
!
```

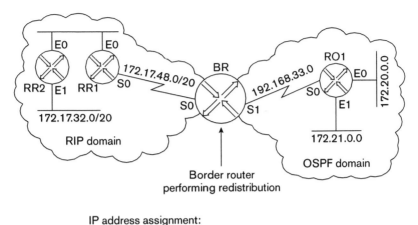

Figure 11.3 *Internetwork for RIP/OSPF redistribution analysis*

```
interface Ethernet0

 no ip address

 shutdown

!

interface Serial0

 ip address 172.17.48.1 255.255.240.0

 no fair-queue

 clockrate 2000000

!

interface Serial1

 ip address 192.168.33.1 255.255.255.0

 clockrate 2000000

!

router ospf 33

 network 192.168.33.0 0.0.0.255 area 0.0.0.0

!

router rip

 network 172.17.0.0

!
```

RR1 router initial configuration for RIP/OSPF redistribution analysis

```
!
hostname RR1
!
enable password cisco
!
ip subnet-zero
!
interface Ethernet0
 ip address 172.17.16.1 255.255.240.0
!
interface Serial0
 ip address 172.17.48.2 255.255.240.0
!
router rip
 network 172.17.0.0
!
ip classless
!
```

RR2 router initial configuration for RIP/OSPF redistribution analysis

```
!
hostname RR2
!
enable password cisco
!
interface Ethernet0
 ip address 172.17.16.2 255.255.240.0
!
interface Ethernet1
 ip address 172.17.32.1 255.255.240.0
!
router rip
 network 172.17.0.0
```

```
!
ip classless
!
```

RO1 router initial configuration for RIP/OSPF redistribution analysis

```
!
hostname RO1
!
enable password cisco
!
interface Ethernet0
 ip address 172.20.0.1 255.255.0.0
!
interface Ethernet1

 ip address 172.21.0.1 255.255.0.0
!
interface Serial0
 ip address 192.168.33.2 255.255.255.0
!
router ospf 33
 network 172.20.0.0 0.0.255.255 area 0.0.0.0
 network 172.21.0.0 0.0.255.255 area 0.0.0.0
 network 192.168.33.0 0.0.0.255 area 0.0.0.0
!
ip classless
!
```

The routing tables on the BR router have entries to all networks throughout the internetwork in Figure 11.3, but the remaining routers know only about networks in their own domain. The BR router shows both RIP and OSPF entries.

```
BR#sh ip route
Codes: C - connected, S - static, I - IGRP, R - RIP, M - mobile, B - BGP
       D - EIGRP, EX - EIGRP external, O - OSPF,
```

```
Gateway of last resort is not set


C    192.168.33.0 is directly connected, Serial1
O    172.20.0.0 [110/74] via 192.168.33.2, 00:32:21, Serial1
O    172.21.0.0 [110/74] via 192.168.33.2, 00:32:21, Serial1
     172.17.0.0 255.255.240.0 is subnetted, 3 subnets
C       172.17.48.0 is directly connected, Serial0
R       172.17.32.0 [120/2] via 172.17.48.2, 00:00:06, Serial0
R       172.17.16.0 [120/1] via 172.17.48.2, 00:00:06, Serial0
BR#




RR1#sh ip route
Codes: C - connected, S - static, I - IGRP, R - RIP, M - mobile, B - BGP
       D - EIGRP, EX - EIGRP external, O - OSPF,


Gateway of last resort is not set


     172.17.0.0/20 is subnetted, 3 subnets
C       172.17.48.0 is directly connected, Serial0
R       172.17.32.0 [120/1] via 172.17.16.2, 00:00:23, Ethernet0
C       172.17.16.0 is directly connected, Ethernet0
RR1#




RR2#sh ip route
Codes: C - connected, S - static, I - IGRP, R - RIP, M - mobile, B - BGP
       D - EIGRP, EX - EIGRP external, O - OSPF,


Gateway of last resort is not set


     172.17.0.0/20 is subnetted, 3 subnets
R       172.17.48.0 [120/1] via 172.17.16.1, 00:00:13, Ethernet0
C       172.17.32.0 is directly connected, Ethernet1
C       172.17.16.0 is directly connected, Ethernet0
```

```
RR2#
```

```
RO1#sh ip route
Codes: C - connected, S - static, I - IGRP, R - RIP, M - mobile, B - BGP
       D - EIGRP, EX - EIGRP external, O - OSPF,

Gateway of last resort is not set

C    172.21.0.0/16 is directly connected, Ethernet1
C    172.20.0.0/16 is directly connected, Ethernet0
C    192.168.33.0/24 is directly connected, Serial0
RO1#
```

The idea behind redistribution is to turn the RIP routes on BR into OSPF routes on routers in the OSPF domain and the OSPF routes on BR into RIP routes on routers in the RIP domain. The administrator performed the initial redistribution and since there are no errors from the IOS, the administrator considers his job done.

```
BR#conf t
Enter configuration commands, one per line.  End with CNTL/Z.
BR(config)#router rip
BR(config-router)#redistribute ospf 33
BR(config-router)#
BR(config-router)#router ospf 33
BR(config-router)#redistribute rip
BR(config-router)#^Z
BR#
```

But when the routing tables are checked, none of the OSPF routes present on BR are showing up on routers in the RIP domain, and no RIP routes from BR show up in the OSPF domain. The one exception is the network 192.168.33.0 over which OSPF is active and which is also directly connected to the border router. This network is redistributed into RIP, but it's not the main focus of this discussion. Needless to say, something was missed in the preceding configuration.

```
RR1#sh ip route
Codes: C - connected, S - static, I - IGRP, R - RIP, M - mobile, B - BGP
       D - EIGRP, EX - EIGRP external, O - OSPF,


Gateway of last resort is not set


     172.17.0.0/20 is subnetted, 3 subnets


C      172.17.48.0 is directly connected, Serial0
R      172.17.32.0 [120/1] via 172.17.16.2, 00:00:10, Ethernet0
C      172.17.16.0 is directly connected, Ethernet0
R    192.168.33.0/24 [120/1] via 172.17.48.1, 00:00:21, Serial0
RR1#


RR2#sh ip route
Codes: C - connected, S - static, I - IGRP, R - RIP, M - mobile, B - BGP
       D - EIGRP, EX - EIGRP external, O - OSPF,


Gateway of last resort is not set


     172.17.0.0/20 is subnetted, 3 subnets
R      172.17.48.0 [120/1] via 172.17.16.1, 00:00:22, Ethernet0
C      172.17.32.0 is directly connected, Ethernet1
C      172.17.16.0 is directly connected, Ethernet0
R    192.168.33.0/24 [120/2] via 172.17.16.1, 00:00:22, Ethernet0
RR2#


RO1#sh ip route
Codes: C - connected, S - static, I - IGRP, R - RIP, M - mobile, B - BGP
       D - EIGRP, EX - EIGRP external, O - OSPF,


Gateway of last resort is not set


C    172.21.0.0/16 is directly connected, Ethernet1
C    172.20.0.0/16 is directly connected, Ethernet0
```

```
C    192.168.33.0/24 is directly connected, Serial0
RO1#
```

When redistribution takes place into RIP you must specify the metric. When subnetted routes are being redistributed into OSPF you must use the *subnets* keyword. The following trace shows the removal of the incorrect statements and the correct configuration of redistribution between RIP and OSPF.

```
BR#conf t
Enter configuration commands, one per line.  End with CNTL/Z.
BR(config)#router rip
BR(config-router)#no red ospf 33
BR(config-router)#redistribute ospf 33 metric 1
BR(config-router)#
BR(config-router)#router ospf 33
BR(config-router)#no red rip
BR(config-router)#redistribute rip subnets
BR(config-router)#^Z
BR#
```

Notice the change in the routing tables. The RIP routers now show routing table entries for all networks present in the OSPF domain. Before the metric was configured, only the network over which OSPF was active and which was directly connected to the border router was present. On the OSPF side, all of the RIP subnets are now showing up as OSPF External Type 2 routes (E2).

```
RR2#sh ip route
Codes: C - connected, S - static, I - IGRP, R - RIP, M - mobile, B - BGP
       D - EIGRP, EX - EIGRP external, O - OSPF,

Gateway of last resort is not set

     172.17.0.0/20 is subnetted, 3 subnets
R       172.17.48.0 [120/1] via 172.17.16.1, 00:00:07, Ethernet0
C       172.17.32.0 is directly connected, Ethernet1
C       172.17.16.0 is directly connected, Ethernet0
```

```
R    172.21.0.0/16 [120/2] via 172.17.16.1, 00:00:07, Ethernet0

R    172.20.0.0/16 [120/2] via 172.17.16.1, 00:00:07, Ethernet0

R    192.168.33.0/24 [120/2] via 172.17.16.1, 00:00:07, Ethernet0

RR2#


RO1#sh ip route

Codes: C - connected, S - static, I - IGRP, R - RIP, M - mobile, B - BGP
       D - EIGRP, EX - EIGRP external, O - OSPF,


Gateway of last resort is not set


     172.17.0.0/20 is subnetted, 3 subnets
O E2    172.17.48.0 [110/20] via 192.168.33.1, 00:03:14, Serial0

O E2    172.17.32.0 [110/20] via 192.168.33.1, 00:03:14, Serial0

O E2    172.17.16.0 [110/20] via 192.168.33.1, 00:03:14, Serial0

C    172.21.0.0/16 is directly connected, Ethernet1

C    172.20.0.0/16 is directly connected, Ethernet0

C    192.168.33.0/24 is directly connected, Serial0

RO1#
```

Redistribution between OSPF and EIGRP

In the previous section, you learned that the one pitfall of redistribution into OSPF is forgetting about the *subnets* keyword. When redistributing into EIGRP, you must remember about the metric, just as with RIP. Redistribution between OSPF and EIGRP is no different than that between OSPF and RIP, except for the structure of the EIGRP metric. The EIGRP metric is more complex than that of RIP.

Take a look again at Figure 11.3 and substitute EIGRP AS #44 for the RIP domain. All addressing stays the same. The configuration on the border router BR will appear as follows:

```
BR#conf t
Enter configuration commands, one per line.  End with CNTL/Z.
BR(config)#router eigrp 44
BR(config-router)#redistribute ospf 33 metric 10000 100 255 1 1500
BR(config-router)#
BR(config-router)#router ospf 33
BR(config-router)#redistribute eigrp 44 subnets
BR(config-router)#^Z
BR#
```

The EIGRP metric definition requires the use of five parameters: band-width in Kbps, delay in 10 microsecond units, percent reliability (255 = max, 1=min), percent load (1=min, 255=max), and MTU in octets (bytes). The numbers 10000, 100, 255, 1, 1500 used with the *metric* keyword in the preceding configuration are the representative values for a reliable, mini-mally loaded Ethernet network.

As a result of this configuration, the OSPF routes will appear in the EIGRP domain as external EIGRP routes. Routing tables with external EIGRP routes are shown in the next section. The EIGRP routes will ap-pear in the OSPF domain as E2 OSPF routes, just like in the RIP/OSPF redistribution in the preceding section.

Redistribution between IGRP and EIGRP

Redistribution between IGRP and EIGRP is the easiest to configure of all the redistributions between routing protocols. It's almost automatic. No need to be concerned about metric or subnets. Consider the internetwork in Figure 11.4. The layout and the IP address assignments are the same as in Figure 11.3. The change is that the RIP domain is replaced with IGRP AS 33 and the OSPF domain is replaced with EIGRP AS 44.

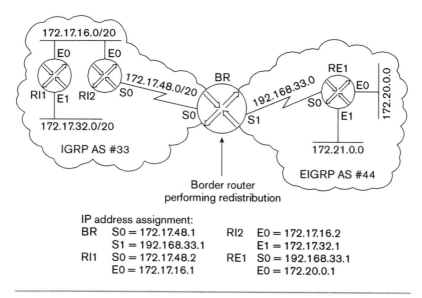

Figure 11.4 *Internetwork for IGRP/EIGRP redistribution analysis*

The redistribution configuration on the border router (BR) is as follows:

```
BR#conf t
Enter configuration commands, one per line.  End with CNTL/Z.
BR(config)#router igrp 33
BR(config-router)#redistribute eigrp 44
BR(config-router)#
BR(config-router)#router eigrp 44
BR(config-router)#redistribute igrp 33
BR(config-router)#^Z
BR#
```

The final configuration for BR and the routing tables for RI2 and RE1 are shown next.

BR configuration following redistribution between IGRP and EIGRP

```
!
hostname BR
!
```

```
interface Ethernet0

 ip address 172.16.0.1 255.255.0.0

 shutdown

!

interface Serial0

 ip address 172.17.48.1 255.255.240.0

 no fair-queue

 clockrate 2000000

!

interface Serial1

 ip address 192.168.33.1 255.255.255.0

 clockrate 2000000

!

router eigrp 44

 redistribute igrp 33

 network 192.168.33.0

!

router igrp 33

 redistribute eigrp 44

 network 172.17.0.0

!


RR2#sh ip route

Codes: C - connected, S - static, I - IGRP, R - RIP, M - mobile, B - BGP
       D - EIGRP, EX - EIGRP external, O - OSPF,


Gateway of last resort is not set


     172.17.0.0/20 is subnetted, 3 subnets
I       172.17.48.0 [100/8576] via 172.17.16.1, 00:00:25, Ethernet0
C       172.17.32.0 is directly connected, Ethernet1
C       172.17.16.0 is directly connected, Ethernet0
I    172.21.0.0/16 [100/10676] via 172.17.16.1, 00:00:25, Ethernet0
I    172.20.0.0/16 [100/10676] via 172.17.16.1, 00:00:25, Ethernet0
I    192.168.33.0/24 [100/10576] via 172.17.16.1, 00:00:25, Ethernet0
```

```
RR2#


RO1#sh ip route
Codes: C - connected, S - static, I - IGRP, R - RIP, M - mobile, B - BGP
       D - EIGRP, EX - EIGRP external, O - OSPF,


Gateway of last resort is not set


     172.17.0.0/20 is subnetted, 3 subnets
D EX    172.17.48.0 [170/2169856] via 192.168.33.1, 00:22:07, Serial0
D EX    172.17.32.0 [170/2733056] via 192.168.33.1, 00:22:07, Serial0
D EX    172.17.16.0 [170/2707456] via 192.168.33.1, 00:22:07, Serial0
C    172.21.0.0/16 is directly connected, Ethernet1
C    172.20.0.0/16 is directly connected, Ethernet0
C    192.168.33.0/24 is directly connected, Serial0
RO1#
```

It's hard to do something wrong when performing IGRP/EIGRP re-distribution. The clue that redistribution is even taking place is that the routes that are redistributed from IGRP into EIGRP show up as External EIGRP routes in the EIGRP domain.

Redistribution of IGPs into BGP

The redistribution of IGPs into BGP is a necessity. The BGP process must be told about the networks to route for, which can be accomplished either via redistribution or advertising. The process of advertising networks into BGP is discussed in the context of mask misconfigurations in Chapter 6. In this section, the focus is on redistribution.

The IGP numeric routing metric is very simple when compared to the BGP route description via the BGP attributes. The simplicity of IGP's metric makes the configuration of IGP redistribution into BGP relatively straightforward, more so than redistribution between IGPs. But as you will see throughout this section, there are pitfalls to watch out for any time that redistribution takes place into BGP.

The One-Way Redistribution Pitfall

Consider the internetwork shown in Figure 11.5.

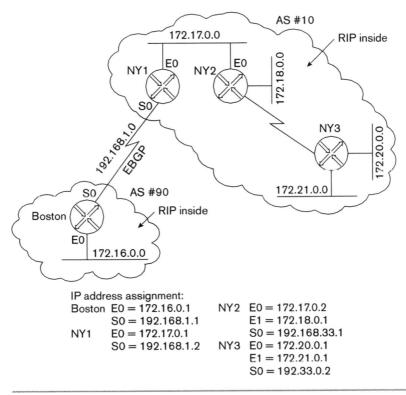

IP address assignment:
Boston E0 = 172.16.0.1   NY2 E0 = 172.17.0.2
           S0 = 192.168.1.1   E1 = 172.18.0.1
NY1 E0 = 172.17.0.1   S0 = 192.168.33.1
     S0 = 192.168.1.2   NY3 E0 = 172.20.0.1
                        E1 = 172.21.0.1
                        S0 = 192.33.0.2

Figure 11.5 *Internetwork for analysis of IGP redistribution into BGP*

The internetwork in Figure 11.5 consists of two BGP autonomous systems, AS 10 and AS 90. An external BGP session is established between the Boston and NY1 routers. An IGP (RIP) is activated on every router in each AS. All networks internal to each AS are correctly assigned to the RIP processes. The BGP border routers (Boston and NY1) perform redistribution of RIP into BGP.

Additionally, the border routers are advertising the network between them into BGP via the `network` command. The network administrator is acutely aware that the IP address in the Next_hop attribute in a BGP update message is derived from that network. This network is referred to as the Demilitarized Zone (DMZ). The first step in the BGP route selection process is that the Next_hop of an update received from a neighbor must be reachable via IP. The administrator wants to make sure that no BGP updates are dropped.

The goal behind the redistribution in the internetwork in Figure 11.5 is to have full reachability between the two ASs. Any subnet should be reachable from any other subnet. The configurations for all routers in Figure 11.5 are shown next. Upon their examination and review of the Boston routing table, it seems like everything is in order.

Boston router initial configuration for RIP into BGP redistribution

```
hostname Boston
!
interface Ethernet0
 ip address 172.16.0.1 255.255.0.0
!
interface Serial0
 ip address 192.168.1.1 255.255.255.0
 no fair-queue
 clockrate 2000000
!
router rip
 network 172.16.0.0
!
router bgp 90
 network 192.168.1.0
 redistribute rip
 neighbor 192.168.1.2 remote-as 10
!
```

NY1 router initial configuration for RIP into BGP redistribution

```
hostname NY1
!
enable password cisco
!
```

```
ip subnet-zero
!
interface Ethernet0
 ip address 172.17.0.1 255.255.0.0
!
interface Serial0
 ip address 192.168.1.2 255.255.255.0
!
interface Serial1
 no ip address
 shutdown
!
router rip
 network 172.17.0.0
!
router bgp 10
 network 192.168.1.0
 redistribute rip
 neighbor 192.168.1.1 remote-as 90
!
```

NY2 router initial configuration for RIP into BGP redistribution

```
hostname NY2
!
enable password cisco
!
interface Ethernet0
 ip address 172.17.0.2 255.255.0.0
!
interface Ethernet1
 ip address 172.18.0.1 255.255.0.0
!
interface Serial0
 ip address 192.168.33.1 255.255.255.0
```

```
!
interface Serial1
 no ip address
 shutdown
!
router rip
 network 172.17.0.0
 network 172.18.0.0
 network 192.168.33.0
!
```

NY3 router initial configuration for RIP into BGP redistribution

```
hostname NY3
!
enable password cisco
!
interface Ethernet0
 ip address 172.20.0.1 255.255.0.0
!
interface Ethernet1
 ip address 172.21.0.1 255.255.0.0
!
interface Serial0
 ip address 192.168.33.2 255.255.255.0
 clockrate 2000000
!
interface Serial1
 no ip address
 shutdown
!
router rip
 network 172.20.0.0
 network 172.21.0.0
 network 192.168.33.0
```

Boston's routing table resulting from initial RIP into BGP redistribution

```
Boston#

Boston#sh ip route

Codes: C - connected, S - static, I - IGRP, R - RIP, M - mobile, B - BGP



Gateway of last resort is not set

B    192.168.33.0 [20/1] via 192.168.1.2, 00:30:54

C    192.168.1.0 is directly connected, Serial0

B    172.20.0.0 [20/2] via 192.168.1.2, 00:30:53

B    172.21.0.0 [20/2] via 192.168.1.2, 00:30:53

C    172.16.0.0 is directly connected, Ethernet0

B    172.17.0.0 [20/0] via 192.168.1.2, 00:30:53

B    172.18.0.0 [20/1] via 192.168.1.2, 00:30:53

Boston#
```

Boston's routing table has entries for all of the networks in AS 10. But look what happens when an attempt is made to ping some router interfaces on those networks.

```
Boston#ping 172.18.0.1

Type escape sequence to abort.

Sending 5, 100-byte ICMP Echos to 172.18.0.1, timeout is 2 seconds:

.....

Success rate is 0 percent (0/5)



Boston#ping 172.21.0.1

Type escape sequence to abort.

Sending 5, 100-byte ICMP Echos to 172.21.0.1, timeout is 2 seconds:

.....

Success rate is 0 percent (0/5)
```

The pings fail. The reasons for the failure are the common redistribution pitfalls. BGP is operating correctly between the ASs. RIP is working correctly within each AS. RIP is being correctly redistributed into BGP. But there are two elements of the redistribution configuration that have either been misconfigured or not yet configured. They relate to the DMZ and the redistribution of BGP into an IGP.

The DMZ Pitfall

Think for a moment why the pings from Boston to any subnet in AS 10 fail. After all, every subnet from AS 10 shows up in Boston's routing table. To come up with the solution to this problem, you may find it helpful to examine the routing table for NY3. NY3 is directly attached to subnet 172.21.0.0 to which the ping from Boston fails.

```
NY3#sh ip route

Codes: C - connected, S - static, I - IGRP, R - RIP, M - mobile, B - BGP


Gateway of last resort is not set


R     172.17.0.0/16 [120/1] via 192.168.33.1, 00:00:25, Serial0

R     172.18.0.0/16 [120/1] via 192.168.33.1, 00:00:26, Serial0

C     172.21.0.0/16 is directly connected, Ethernet1

C     172.20.0.0/16 is directly connected, Ethernet0

C     192.168.33.0/24 is directly connected, Serial0

NY3#
```

Notice the absence here of the DMZ, 192.168.1.0, in NY3's routing table. This may seem perplexing. After all, you made sure that the DMZ is advertised into BGP on both border routers. And redistribution between RIP and BGP is also occurring on both border routers. The redistribution, however, is only from RIP to BGP. The border routers are not redistributing BGP into RIP.

Consider again the ping traffic originating from Boston that's meant for a host on network 172.21.0.0. It is actually possible for the echo request component of the ping to reach subnet 172.21.0.0, but it's not possible for the echo reply to return back to Boston.

Router NY3 is only a RIP router. It knows only about the RIP networks inside the AS 10. Boston knows that to get to 172.21.0.0 it must go to

NY1. And NY1 has a RIP route to 172.21.0.0. Consequently, the echo request component of ping reaches 172.21.0.1.

But when the echo reply component of the ping tries to find a path back to a subnet from which the ping originated, it can't find that subnet in NY3's table. If you are pinging 172.21.0.1 from the Boston router, the ping's source IP address is derived either from the DMZ (192.168.1.0) or a subnet within AS 90 (172.16.0.0). Neither of those networks is present in NY3's table. NY3 has no way of replying back and the ping fails.

It seems that the obvious solution is to redistribute BGP routes into RIP. There is some validity to this, and the next section will cover this topic. But redistribution of BGP into RIP will not do anything for the DMZ. The DMZ is directly connected to the border routers and it shows up as such in their routing tables. For the RIP routers throughout each AS to know about the DMZ, they must be told about it via a `redistribute connected` command.

Observe the configuration of the `redistribute connected` command. Then look again at NY3's routing table after the `redistribute connected` has been added to the RIP section of NY1.

```
NY1# conf t
Enter configuration commands, one per line.  End with CNTL/Z.
NY1(config)#router rip
NY1(config-router)#redistribute connected
NY1(config-router)#^Z
NY1#
```

NY3 routing table following configuration of redistribute connected on NY1

```
NY3#sh ip route
Codes: C - connected, S - static, I - IGRP, R - RIP, M - mobile, B - BGP


Gateway of last resort is not set


R     172.17.0.0/16 [120/1] via 192.168.33.1, 00:00:05, Serial0

R     172.18.0.0/16 [120/1] via 192.168.33.1, 00:00:05, Serial0

C     172.21.0.0/16 is directly connected, Ethernet1

C     172.20.0.0/16 is directly connected, Ethernet0
```

```
R    192.168.1.0/24 [120/2] via 192.168.33.1, 00:00:05, Serial0
C    192.168.33.0/24 is directly connected, Serial0
NY3#
```

The DMZ network 192.168.1.0 now appears in NY3's routing table.
This means that if a ping from Boston originates with an IP address derived from the DMZ, the ping should work. Two pings to different subnets
are executed from Boston to confirm this.

```
Boston#
Boston#ping 172.18.0.1
Type escape sequence to abort.
Sending 5, 100-byte ICMP Echos to 172.18.0.1, timeout is 2 seconds:
!!!!!
Success rate is 100 percent (5/5), round-trip min/avg/max = 4/5/8 ms

Boston#ping 172.21.0.1
Type escape sequence to abort.
Sending 5, 100-byte ICMP Echos to 172.21.0.1, timeout is 2 seconds:
!!!!!
Success rate is 100 percent (5/5), round-trip min/avg/max = 4/7/12 ms
Boston#
```

But what happens if an extended ping is used from Boston, forcing the
source IP address of the ping to be derived from a subnet with the AS 90?
Take the Boston router's e0 interface, 172.16.0.1 for example.

```
Boston#ping
Protocol [ip]:
Target IP address: 172.21.0.1
Repeat count [5]:
Datagram size [100]:
Timeout in seconds [2]:
Extended commands [n]: y
Source address: 172.16.0.1
Type of service [0]:
Set DF bit in IP header? [no]:
```

```
Validate reply data? [no]:

Data pattern [0xABCD]:

Loose, Strict, Record, Timestamp, Verbose[none]:

Sweep range of sizes [n]:

Type escape sequence to abort.

Sending 5, 100-byte ICMP Echos to 172.21.0.1, timeout is 2 seconds:

.....
```

Success rate is 0 percent (0/5)

```
Boston#
```

The extended ping fails. This means that any other subnets within AS
90 will not be able to reach subnets within AS 10 unless the situation is
remedied via further redistribution or the use of default routes. RIP-only
routers in AS 10 still do not know about the networks in AS 90 and vice
versa. Only the BGP border routers (running RIP and BGP) know about
all the networks, and that's not enough to ensure full reachability between
all of the subnets through that internetwork.

The Mutual Redistribution Remedy

Further redistribution means mutual redistribution. RIP is redistributed
into BGP and BGP into RIP. But this kind of indiscriminate mutual redistribution can lead to routing loops. Policies have to be implemented to
prevent looping; the policies that you want to implement on each border
router should prevent the RIP routes that are redistributed into BGP from
being redistributed back from BGP into RIP.

Observe the configuration of a redistribution policy on the NY1 router.
It's implemented via a route map and access control list.

```
NY1#conf t

Enter configuration commands, one per line.  End with CNTL/Z.

NY1(config)#router rip

NY1(config-router)#redistribute bgp 10 route-map block_internal metric 1

NY1(config-router)#

NY1(config-router)#route-map block_internal permit 1

NY1(config-route-map)#match ip address 88

NY1(config-route-map)#access-list 88 deny 172.18.0.0 0.0.255.255
```

```
NY1(config)#access-list 88 deny 172.20.0.0 0.0.255.255

NY1(config)#access-list 88 deny 172.21.0.0 0.0.255.255

NY1(config)#access-list 88 permit any

NY1(config)#^Z

NY1#
```

The preceding configuration tells the RIP process to accept all BGP routes except the ones that have been injected into BGP from RIP in the first place.

The result of this configuration is shown next in the configuration file on NY1.

```
NY1#show run
Building configuration...


Current configuration:
!
version 11.3
service timestamps debug uptime
service timestamps log uptime
no service password-encryption
!
hostname NY1
!
enable password cisco
!
ip subnet-zero
!
interface Ethernet0
 ip address 172.17.0.1 255.255.0.0
!
interface Serial0
 ip address 192.168.1.2 255.255.255.0
!
interface Serial1
 no ip address
```

```
  shutdown
 !
 router rip
  redistribute connected
  redistribute bgp 10 metric 1 route-map block_internal
  network 172.17.0.0
 !
 router bgp 10
  redistribute rip
  neighbor 192.168.1.1 remote-as 90
 !
 no ip classless
 !
 access-list 88 deny    172.18.0.0 0.0.255.255
 access-list 88 deny    172.20.0.0 0.0.255.255
 access-list 88 deny    172.21.0.0 0.0.255.255
 access-list 88 permit any
 route-map block_internal permit 1
  match ip address 88
 !
```

Route map *block_internal* is invoked from the `redistribute` command. Within a route map, a match condition is identified for access control list 88. Access control list 88 denies all of the networks that are internal to AS 10 and permits all others. The net result is that the subnets advertised from Boston to NY1 via BGP are now visible in NY2 and NY3. A look at the NY3 routing table confirms that 172.16.0.0 is present there.

```
NY3#sh ip route
Codes: C - connected, S - static, I - IGRP, R - RIP, M - mobile, B - BGP


Gateway of last resort is not set


R    172.17.0.0/16 [120/1] via 192.168.33.1, 00:00:07, Serial0
R    172.16.0.0/16 [120/2] via 192.168.33.1, 00:00:08, Serial0
R    172.18.0.0/16 [120/1] via 192.168.33.1, 00:00:08, Serial0
```

```
C    172.21.0.0/16 is directly connected, Ethernet1
C    172.20.0.0/16 is directly connected, Ethernet0
R    192.168.1.0/24 [120/2] via 192.168.33.1, 00:00:08, Serial0
C    192.168.33.0/24 is directly connected, Serial0
NY3#
```

The final confirmation that everything in the internetwork is now working correctly comes from the extended ping that failed before. The extended ping is executed from the Boston router using its interface to the 172.16.0.0 subnet as the source address.

```
Boston#ping
Protocol [ip]:
Target IP address: 172.21.0.1
Repeat count [5]:
Datagram size [100]:
Timeout in seconds [2]:
Extended commands [n]: y
Source address: 172.16.0.1
Type of service [0]:
Set DF bit in IP header? [no]:
Validate reply data? [no]:
Data pattern [0xABCD]:
Loose, Strict, Record, Timestamp, Verbose[none]:
Sweep range of sizes [n]:
Type escape sequence to abort.
Sending 5, 100-byte ICMP Echos to 172.21.0.1, timeout is 2 seconds:
!!!!!
Success rate is 100 percent (5/5), round-trip min/avg/max = 4/5/8 ms
Boston#
```

The ping works, confirming that redistribution in Figure 11.5 has been configured correctly and there is now full reachability throughout the internetwork. However, if you think about the preceding configuration of redistributing BGP routes into RIP, it can prove to be quite dangerous.

The Mutual Redistribution Danger

The danger of mutual redistribution lies in redistributing all BGP routes into an IGP such as RIP. In the scenario in Figure 11.5, mutual redistribution is a workable solution because there are not many routes in either AS. But assume for a moment that each AS in Figure 11.5 had several hundred RIP routes. RIP routes from each AS would then be translated into BGP routes (for transit between the ASs) and then redistributed back into RIP in the other AS. That would double the number of RIP routes in each AS. That's quite unnecessary.

Consider another possibility where the border routers Boston and NY1 had links to other ASs and were receiving thousands of BGP routes from them. All of those routes would be redistributed into RIP and very likely cause the RIP routers in each AS to choke. Of course, additional policies via the use of route maps and access control lists could be applied to minimize the number of routes redistributed from BGP into RIP. You can see where all this is leading: a large number of routes in an IGP, or an intensive configuration to screen them all out.

The guideline regarding mutual redistribution between BGP and IGPs is that it's workable in an environment where the border routers do not carry a large number of BGP routes. When the number of BGP routes starts getting into the thousands, mutual IGP/BGP redistribution is no longer a viable solution. Another alternative is needed.

The Static Defaults Remedy

The alternative to mutual IGP/BGP redistribution is the use of default routes inside an AS. There is already full reachability between subnets inside each AS via IGP. Additionally, each border router carries full routes for both ASs resulting from IGP redistribution into BGP. Since the border routers represent entry and exit points into and out of each AS, a default route can be defined on each of them (Boston and NY1 in Figure 11.5) and redistributed into RIP.

The default routes will allow full reachability between AS 10 and AS 90 in Figure 11.5 without the redistribution of BGP into RIP. A note of caution about the default routes is in order. In the case of RIP, a default route is automatically redistributed into RIP, but that's not the case with all IGPs. Assume the initial configuration for the internetwork in Figure 11.5

as shown at the beginning of this section. The redistribution of BGP into RIP has not taken place yet. The default route configuration on the Boston and NY1 routers is as follows:

```
Boston#conf t
Enter configuration commands, one per line.  End with CNTL/Z.
Boston(config)#ip route 0.0.0.0 0.0.0.0 s0
Boston(config)#^Z
Boston#


NY1#conf t
Enter configuration commands, one per line.  End with CNTL/Z.
NY1(config)#ip route 0.0.0.0 0.0.0.0 s0
NY1(config)#^Z
NY1#
```

That's the extent of the additional configuration that's required for full reachability between the ASs in Figure 11.5. It's a lot easier than redistribution of BGP into RIP, which required implementation of policies to prevent loops and control the number of BGP routes being redistributed into RIP. The routing tables on Boston and NY1 show the default route as a static route.

```
Boston#sh ip route
Codes: C - connected, S - static, I - IGRP, R - RIP, M - mobile, B - BGP
       D - EIGRP, EX - EIGRP external, O - OSPF, IA - OSPF inter area
       E1 - OSPF external type 1, E2 - OSPF external type 2, E - EGP
       i - IS-IS, L1 - IS-IS level-1, L2 - IS-IS level-2, * - candidate default


Gateway of last resort is 0.0.0.0 to network 0.0.0.0


B    192.168.33.0 [20/1] via 192.168.1.2, 02:06:32
C    192.168.1.0 is directly connected, Serial0
B    172.20.0.0 [20/2] via 192.168.1.2, 02:06:32
B    172.21.0.0 [20/2] via 192.168.1.2, 02:06:32
C    172.16.0.0 is directly connected, Ethernet0
B    172.17.0.0 [20/0] via 192.168.1.2, 02:07:24
B    172.18.0.0 [20/1] via 192.168.1.2, 01:19:01
```

```
S*   0.0.0.0 0.0.0.0 is directly connected, Serial0
Boston#
```

```
NY1#sh ip route
Codes: C - connected, S - static, I - IGRP, R - RIP, M - mobile, B - BGP
       D - EIGRP, EX - EIGRP external, O - OSPF, IA - OSPF inter area
       N1 - OSPF NSSA external type 1, N2 - OSPF NSSA external type 2
       E1 - OSPF external type 1, E2 - OSPF external type 2, E - EGP
       i - IS-IS, L1 - IS-IS level-1, L2 - IS-IS level-2, * - candidate default
       U - per-user static route, o - ODR


Gateway of last resort is 0.0.0.0 to network 0.0.0.0


C    172.17.0.0/16 is directly connected, Ethernet0
B    172.16.0.0/16 [20/0] via 192.168.1.1, 02:07:27
R    172.18.0.0/16 [120/1] via 172.17.0.2, 00:00:00, Ethernet0
R    172.21.0.0/16 [120/2] via 172.17.0.2, 00:00:00, Ethernet0
R    172.20.0.0/16 [120/2] via 172.17.0.2, 00:00:00, Ethernet0
C    192.168.1.0/24 is directly connected, Serial0
R    192.168.33.0/24 [120/1] via 172.17.0.2, 00:00:00, Ethernet0
S*   0.0.0.0/0 is directly connected, Serial0
NY1#
```

If you look at the routing table on a RIP-only router like NY3, the static default route from NY1 was translated into RIP default. When a static default was defined on NY1, it was automatically redistributed into RIP without any additional configuration.

```
NY3#sh ip route
Codes: C - connected, S - static, I - IGRP, R - RIP, M - mobile, B - BGP
       D - EIGRP, EX - EIGRP external, O - OSPF, IA - OSPF inter area
       N1 - OSPF NSSA external type 1, N2 - OSPF NSSA external type 2
       E1 - OSPF external type 1, E2 - OSPF external type 2, E - EGP
       i - IS-IS, L1 - IS-IS level-1, L2 - IS-IS level-2, * - candidate default
       U - per-user static route, o - ODR
```

```
Gateway of last resort is 192.168.33.1 to network 0.0.0.0


R    172.17.0.0/16 [120/1] via 192.168.33.1, 00:00:09, Serial0

R    172.18.0.0/16 [120/1] via 192.168.33.1, 00:00:09, Serial0

C    172.21.0.0/16 is directly connected, Ethernet1

C    172.20.0.0/16 is directly connected, Ethernet0

C    192.168.33.0/24 is directly connected, Serial0

R*   0.0.0.0/0 [120/2] via 192.168.33.1, 00:00:09, Serial0

NY3#
```

To confirm full reachability between the ASs, a ping is executed from NY3 to a subnet in AS 10. The ping is successful.

```
NY3#ping 172.16.0.1

Type escape sequence to abort.

Sending 5, 100-byte ICMP Echos to 172.16.0.1, timeout is 2 seconds:

!!!!!

Success rate is 100 percent (5/5), round-trip min/avg/max = 4/8/16 ms

NY3#
```

Traceroute from NY3 to Boston's interface to the subnet 172.16.0.0 in AS 10 verifies that the traffic path goes through the networks in AS 10 and the DMZ: the s0 interface on NY2 (192.168.33.1), the e0 interface on NY1 (172.17.0.1), and the s0 interface on Boston (192.168.1.1). The only way this can happen is if both NY3 and NY2 have defaults pointing them in the direction of NY1.

```
NY3#traceroute 172.16.0.1

Type escape sequence to abort.

Tracing the route to 172.16.0.1


  1 192.168.33.1 0 msec 0 msec 4 msec

  2 172.17.0.1 4 msec 4 msec 4 msec

  3 192.168.1.1 8 msec 8 msec *

NY3#
```

The final test that the default route configuration did its job is the extended ping from Boston to NY3's interface to subnet 172.21.0.0. You will recall from previous sections that this ping was failing before the mutual redistribution was configured.

```
Boston#ping

Protocol [ip]:

Target IP address: 172.21.0.1

Repeat count [5]:

Datagram size [100]:

Timeout in seconds [2]:

Extended commands [n]: y

Source address: 172.16.0.1

Type of service [0]:

Set DF bit in IP header? [no]:

Validate reply data? [no]:

Data pattern [0xABCD]:

Loose, Strict, Record, Timestamp, Verbose[none]:

Sweep range of sizes [n]:

Type escape sequence to abort.

Sending 5, 100-byte ICMP Echos to 172.21.0.1, timeout is 2 seconds:

!!!!!

Success rate is 100 percent (5/5), round-trip min/avg/max = 4/7/12 ms

Boston#
```

The use of static defaults inside ASs to direct traffic to border routers is a preferable technique when large numbers of BGP routes are involved. It has to be understood that no one technique is foolproof or can be applied in every situation. The indiscriminate use of defaults can lead to routing loops as well, as discussed in Chapter 10.

Redistribution of OSPF into BGP

Conceptually, the redistribution of OSPF into BGP is similar to the redistribution of RIP into BGP. There are some differences, however, that make configuration of mutual redistribution easier, but the configuration of default routes more tricky.

Consider the internetwork as shown in Figure 11.6. The difference between this internetwork and the internetwork in Figure 11.5 is that OSPF is running as the IGP inside the ASs instead of RIP.

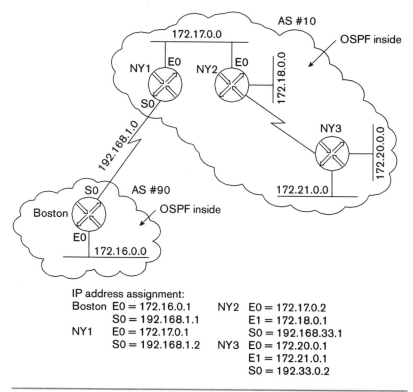

IP address assignment:
Boston E0 = 172.16.0.1   NY2 E0 = 172.17.0.2
          S0 = 192.168.1.1   E1 = 172.18.0.1
NY1   E0 = 172.17.0.1   S0 = 192.168.33.1
          S0 = 192.168.1.2   NY3 E0 = 172.20.0.1
                                     E1 = 172.21.0.1
                                     S0 = 192.33.0.2

Figure 11.6 *Internetwork for analysis of OSPF/BGP redistributions*

The initial configuration files for all routers highlighting the OSPF configuration and the redistribution into BGP are shown next.

Boston router initial configuration for OSPF into BGP redistribution

```
!
hostname Boston
!
interface Ethernet0
 ip address 172.16.0.1 255.255.0.0
!
interface Serial0
 ip address 192.168.1.1 255.255.255.0
 no fair-queue
```

```
 clockrate 2000000
!
router ospf 90
 network 172.16.0.0 0.0.255.255 area 0.0.0.0
!
router bgp 90
 redistribute ospf 90 match internal
 neighbor 192.168.1.2 remote-as 10
!
```

NY1 router initial configuration for OSPF into BGP redistribution

```
!
hostname NY1
!
enable password cisco
!
ip subnet-zero
!
interface Ethernet0
 ip address 172.17.0.1 255.255.0.0
!
interface Serial0
 ip address 192.168.1.2 255.255.255.0
!
interface Serial1
 no ip address
 shutdown
!
router ospf 10
 network 172.17.0.0 0.0.255.255 area 0.0.0.0
!
router bgp 10
 redistribute ospf 10 match internal
 neighbor 192.168.1.1 remote-as 90
!
```

NY2 router initial configuration for OSPF into BGP redistribution

```
!
hostname NY2
!
enable password cisco
!
interface Ethernet0
 ip address 172.17.0.2 255.255.0.0
!
interface Ethernet1
 ip address 172.18.0.1 255.255.0.0
!
interface Serial0
 ip address 192.168.33.1 255.255.255.0
!
interface Serial1
 no ip address
 shutdown
!
router ospf 10
 network 172.17.0.0 0.0.255.255 area 0.0.0.0
 network 172.18.0.0 0.0.255.255 area 0.0.0.0
 network 192.168.33.0 0.0.0.255 area 0.0.0.0
!
```

NY3 router initial configuration for OSPF into BGP redistribution

```
!
hostname NY3
!
enable password cisco
!
interface Ethernet0
 ip address 172.20.0.1 255.255.0.0
!
```

```
interface Ethernet1

 ip address 172.21.0.1 255.255.0.0

 !

interface Serial0

 ip address 192.168.33.2 255.255.255.0

 clockrate 2000000

 !

interface Serial1

 no ip address

 shutdown

 !

router ospf 10

 network 172.20.0.0 0.0.255.255 area 0.0.0.0

 network 172.21.0.0 0.0.255.255 area 0.0.0.0

 network 192.0.0.0 0.255.255.255 area 0.0.0.0

 !
```

Notice the difference between the `redistribute` command used with RIP and the `redistribute` command used with OSPF. The *match internal* keywords in OSPF specify that only routes that are internal OSPF to the AS will be redistributed into BGP. In the event that BGP was redistributed back into OSPF, it would not be necessary to set up policies with route maps and access control lists.

BGP routes redistributed into OSPF appear as OSPF external routes, type 2 or E2. The *match internal* keywords are effectively a loop prevention mechanism. Those keywords are optional because OSPF redistributes only internal routes by default. But it doesn't hurt you to include them in the configuration as a reminder that that is indeed what's happening.

The redistribution by default of only the internal OSPF routes is the first major difference between RIP and OSPF when it comes to redistribution into BGP. Observe now the Boston and NY1 routing tables following the initial configurations for OSPF into BGP redistribution.

Boston's routing table resulting from initial OSPF into BGP redistribution

```
Boston#sh ip route

Codes: C - connected, S - static, I - IGRP, R - RIP, M - mobile, B - BGP

       D - EIGRP, EX - EIGRP external, O - OSPF, IA - OSPF inter area
```

```
E1 - OSPF external type 1, E2 - OSPF external type 2, E - EGP
i - IS-IS, L1 - IS-IS level-1, L2 - IS-IS level-2, * - candidate default

Gateway of last resort is not set

B    192.168.33.0 [20/74] via 192.168.1.2, 00:16:24
C    192.168.1.0 is directly connected, Serial0
B    172.20.0.0 [20/84] via 192.168.1.2, 00:14:46
B    172.21.0.0 [20/84] via 192.168.1.2, 00:14:46
C    172.16.0.0 is directly connected, Ethernet0
B    172.17.0.0 [20/0] via 192.168.1.2, 00:18:11
B    172.18.0.0 [20/20] via 192.168.1.2, 00:16:51
Boston#
```

NY1's routing table resulting from initial OSPF into BGP redistribution

```
NY1#sh ip route
Codes: C - connected, S - static, I - IGRP, R - RIP, M - mobile, B - BGP
       D - EIGRP, EX - EIGRP external, O - OSPF,

Gateway of last resort is not set

C    172.17.0.0/16 is directly connected, Ethernet0
B    172.16.0.0/16 [20/0] via 192.168.1.1, 00:20:49
O    172.18.0.0/16 [110/20] via 172.17.0.2, 00:15:18, Ethernet0
O    172.21.0.0/16 [110/84] via 172.17.0.2, 00:15:18, Ethernet0
O    172.20.0.0/16 [110/84] via 172.17.0.2, 00:15:18, Ethernet0
C    192.168.1.0/24 is directly connected, Serial0
O    192.168.33.0/24 [110/74] via 172.17.0.2, 00:15:18, Ethernet0
NY1#
```

It should not surprise you that the routing tables show entries for all routes throughout the internetwork in Figure 11.6. It should also not surprise you that the NY3 routing table does not have any entries for networks in AS 90 and it does not have a default route.

NY3's routing table resulting from initial OSPF into BGP redistribution

```
NY3#sh ip route
Codes: C - connected, S - static, I - IGRP, R - RIP, M - mobile, B - BGP
       D - EIGRP, EX - EIGRP external, O - OSPF,


Gateway of last resort is not set


O    172.17.0.0/16 [110/74] via 192.168.33.1, 00:16:09, Serial0

O    172.18.0.0/16 [110/74] via 192.168.33.1, 00:16:10, Serial0

C    172.21.0.0/16 is directly connected, Ethernet1

C    172.20.0.0/16 is directly connected, Ethernet0

C    192.168.33.0/24 is directly connected, Serial0

NY3#
```

Mutual redistribution or default routes have not been configured yet. Needless to say, pings from NY3 to 172.16.0.0 will fail. The OSPF/BGP redistribution configuration needs to be finished. The choice at this point is between redistribution of the DMZ network and of BGP routes into OSPF versus the use of default routes. The configuration of the first choice is shown next on the NY1 router.

```
NY1#
NY1#conf t
Enter configuration commands, one per line.  End with CNTL/Z.
NY1(config)#router ospf 10
NY1(config-router)#redistribute connected
NY1(config-router)#redistribute bgp 10
NY1(config-router)#^Z
NY1#
The NY3 table now shows entries for networks in AS 90 and the DMZ. Similar
configuration on the Boston router would ensure full reachability throughout the
internetwork in Figure 11.6.


NY3#sh ip route
Codes: C - connected, S - static, I - IGRP, R - RIP, M - mobile, B - BGP
       D - EIGRP, EX - EIGRP external, O - OSPF, IA - OSPF inter area
```

```
N1 - OSPF NSSA external type 1, N2 - OSPF NSSA external type 2

E1 - OSPF external type 1, E2 - OSPF external type 2, E - EGP

i - IS-IS, L1 - IS-IS level-1, L2 - IS-IS level-2, * - candidate default

U - per-user static route, o - ODR


Gateway of last resort is not set


O    172.17.0.0/16 [110/74] via 192.168.33.1, 00:02:59, Serial0

O E2 172.16.0.0/16 [110/1] via 192.168.33.1, 00:01:49, Serial0

O    172.18.0.0/16 [110/74] via 192.168.33.1, 00:03:00, Serial0

C    172.21.0.0/16 is directly connected, Ethernet1

C    172.20.0.0/16 is directly connected, Ethernet0

O E2 192.168.1.0/24 [110/20] via 192.168.33.1, 00:03:00, Serial0

C    192.168.33.0/24 is directly connected, Serial0

NY3#
```

The danger of mutual redistribution was discussed in a previous section. To recap, as the number of BGP routes increases on the border routers, they will be redistributed into the IGP-only routers, eventually causing performance problems. The second choice to reach full connectivity here is to use defaults. But OSPF differs in the way it handles defaults.

Assume at this point that the preceding commands performing redistribution of the DMZ and BGP into OSPF have been removed on the NY1 and Boston routers. The configurations on all of the routers are those as shown at the beginning of this section (the initial OSPF into BGP redistribution).

The next step is to define the default routes. But if you define default routes on Boston and NY1 and think that that's all you have to do, you will be disappointed. Observe the configuration of a default route on NY1 and the resulting routing table on NY1 and NY3.

```
NY1#conf t

Enter configuration commands, one per line.  End with CNTL/Z.

NY1(config)#ip route 0.0.0.0 0.0.0.0 s0

NY1(config)#^Z

NY1#
```

NY1's routing table following default route configuration

```
NY1#sh ip route
Codes: C - connected, S - static, I - IGRP, R - RIP, M - mobile, B - BGP
       D - EIGRP, EX - EIGRP external, O - OSPF, IA - OSPF inter area
       N1 - OSPF NSSA external type 1, N2 - OSPF NSSA external type 2
       E1 - OSPF external type 1, E2 - OSPF external type 2, E - EGP
       i - IS-IS, L1 - IS-IS level-1, L2 - IS-IS level-2, * - candidate default
       U - per-user static route, o - ODR


Gateway of last resort is 0.0.0.0 to network 0.0.0.0


C    172.17.0.0/16 is directly connected, Ethernet0
B    172.16.0.0/16 [20/0] via 192.168.1.1, 00:20:49
O    172.18.0.0/16 [110/20] via 172.17.0.2, 00:15:18, Ethernet0
O    172.21.0.0/16 [110/84] via 172.17.0.2, 00:15:18, Ethernet0
O    172.20.0.0/16 [110/84] via 172.17.0.2, 00:15:18, Ethernet0
C    192.168.1.0/24 is directly connected, Serial0
O    192.168.33.0/24 [110/74] via 172.17.0.2, 00:15:18, Ethernet0
S*   0.0.0.0/0 is directly connected, Serial0
NY1#
```

NY3's routing table following default route configuration on NY1

```
NY3#sh ip route
Codes: C - connected, S - static, I - IGRP, R - RIP, M - mobile, B - BGP
       D - EIGRP, EX - EIGRP external, O - OSPF,


Gateway of last resort is not set


O    172.17.0.0/16 [110/74] via 192.168.33.1, 00:02:59, Serial0
O    172.18.0.0/16 [110/74] via 192.168.33.1, 00:03:00, Serial0
C    172.21.0.0/16 is directly connected, Ethernet1
C    172.20.0.0/16 is directly connected, Ethernet0
C    192.168.33.0/24 is directly connected, Serial0
NY3#
```

The definition of a default route on NY1 has no impact on NY3. That's the big difference between OSPF and RIP handling defaults. When RIP finds a default route in the routing tables it automatically redistributes it into itself and communicates it to other RIP routers in the internetwork. OSPF does nothing when it finds a default route in the routing table. Perhaps you are thinking of the default route that you just configured as a static route. But if you are also thinking that *redistribute static* in the OSPF section might do the trick, you are in for another disappointment.

What you have to do here is use the `default-information origi-nate` command in the OSPF section of the Boston and NY1 routers. That command has an *always* keyword as an option. The action without the *always* keyword is to redistribute a default route into OSPF when a default route already exists in the routing table. When the *always* keyword is used, a default route will always be redistributed into OSPF regardless of whether there is already one in the routing table.

The subtlety here is that if you use `default-information origi-nate always`, the router that's performing the redistribution itself will not have a default. In this case, the Boston and NY1 routers would end up not having a default route. To duplicate the reachability achieved with RIP, you have to define the static defaults on Boston and NY1 and then use the `default-information originate` without the *always* keyword.

Observe the completion of this configuration on the Boston and NY1 routers. Then look at the resulting routing table on the NY3 router.

```
Boston#conf t
Enter configuration commands, one per line.  End with CNTL/Z.
Boston(config)#ip route 0.0.0.0 0.0.0.0 s0
Boston(config)#router ospf 90
Boston(config-router)#default-information originate
Boston(config-router)#^Z
Boston#


NY1#conf t
Enter configuration commands, one per line.  End with CNTL/Z.
NY1(config)#router ospf 10
NY1(config-router)#default-information originate
NY1(config-router)#^Z
```

```
NY1#


NY3#sh ip route

Codes: C - connected, S - static, I - IGRP, R - RIP, M - mobile, B - BGP

       D - EIGRP, EX - EIGRP external, O - OSPF, IA - OSPF inter area

       N1 - OSPF NSSA external type 1, N2 - OSPF NSSA external type 2

       E1 - OSPF external type 1, E2 - OSPF external type 2, E - EGP

       i - IS-IS, L1 - IS-IS level-1, L2 - IS-IS level-2, * - candidate default

       U - per-user static route, o - ODR


Gateway of last resort is 192.168.33.1 to network 0.0.0.0


O    172.17.0.0/16 [110/74] via 192.168.33.1, 00:00:25, Serial0

O    172.18.0.0/16 [110/74] via 192.168.33.1, 00:00:26, Serial0

C    172.21.0.0/16 is directly connected, Ethernet1

C    172.20.0.0/16 is directly connected, Ethernet0

C    192.168.33.0/24 is directly connected, Serial0

O*E2 0.0.0.0/0 [110/1] via 192.168.33.1, 00:00:26, Serial0

NY3#
```

The default route now shows up as an OSPF Type 2 External route in the NY3 routing table. Remember that with the redistribution of BGP into OSPF, NY3's routing table had the entry for the DMZ and for all of the networks internal to AS 90. If the number of networks in AS 90 continued to grow, so would the routing tables in the neighboring AS 10. With the use of the default route, the growth of AS 90 has no impact on AS 10. All networks in AS 90 can still be reached from AS 10, but the routing tables on the AS 10 OSPF-only routers remain small.

To verify that the default configuration worked, a normal ping is executed from NY3 to an interface on subnet 172.16.0.0. An extended ping is executed from Boston to 172.21.0.1.

```
NY3#ping 172.16.0.1


Type escape sequence to abort.

Sending 5, 100-byte ICMP Echos to 172.16.0.1, timeout is 2 seconds:

!!!!!
```

```
Success rate is 100 percent (5/5), round-trip min/avg/max = 4/7/12 ms
NY3#
```

```
Boston#ping
Protocol [ip]:
Target IP address: 172.21.0.1
Repeat count [5]:
Datagram size [100]:
Timeout in seconds [2]:
Extended commands [n]: y
Source address: 172.16.0.1
Type of service [0]:
Set DF bit in IP header? [no]:
Validate reply data? [no]:
Data pattern [0xABCD]:
Loose, Strict, Record, Timestamp, Verbose[none]:
Sweep range of sizes [n]:
Type escape sequence to abort.
Sending 5, 100-byte ICMP Echos to 172.21.0.1, timeout is 2 seconds:
!!!!!
Success rate is 100 percent (5/5), round-trip min/avg/max = 4/11/32 ms
Boston#
```

Both pings are successful. Redistribution between OSPF and BGP has been configured correctly. OSPF is redistributed into BGP on the border routers and OSPF-only routers rely on the use of default routes.

Redistribution of IGRP into BGP

When redistributing IGRP into BGP — with the intent of ensuring full reachability throughout the BGP autonomous systems — you face the same choices as you do with RIP or OSPF: mutual redistribution or use of defaults. Either way, the configuration of IGRP/BGP interactions is the same in principal, each with its own peculiarities.

Consider the internetwork as shown in Figure 11.7. The layout of this internetwork is similar to that in Figures 11.5 and 11.6, but IGRP is running inside the BGP autonomous systems instead of RIP or OSPF.

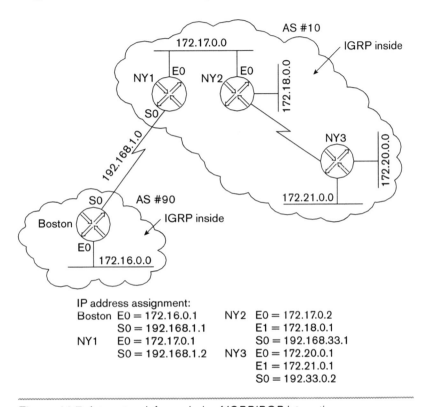

IP address assignment:

Boston	E0 = 172.16.0.1	NY2	E0 = 172.17.0.2
	S0 = 192.168.1.1		E1 = 172.18.0.1
NY1	E0 = 172.17.0.1		S0 = 192.168.33.1
	S0 = 192.168.1.2	NY3	E0 = 172.20.0.1
			E1 = 172.21.0.1
			S0 = 192.33.0.2

Figure 11.7 *Internetwork for analysis of IGRP/BGP interactions*

The initial configuration files for all routers in the internetwork in Figure 11.7 are shown next.

NY3 router initial configuration for IGRP into BGP redistribution

```
!
hostname Boston
!
interface Ethernet0
 ip address 172.16.0.1 255.255.0.0
```

```
!
interface Serial0
 ip address 192.168.1.1 255.255.255.0
 no fair-queue
 clockrate 2000000
!
router igrp 66
 network 172.16.0.0
!
router bgp 90
 network 192.168.1.0
 redistribute igrp 66
 neighbor 192.168.1.2 remote-as 10
!
```

NY1 router initial configuration for IGRP into BGP redistribution

```
!
hostname NY1
!
enable password cisco
!
ip subnet-zero
!
interface Ethernet0
 ip address 172.17.0.1 255.255.0.0
!
interface Serial0
 ip address 192.168.1.2 255.255.255.0
!
interface Serial1
 no ip address
 shutdown
!
router igrp 55
```

```
 network 172.17.0.0
!
router bgp 10
 redistribute igrp 55
 neighbor 192.168.1.1 remote-as 90
!
ip classless
!
```

NY2 router initial configuration for IGRP into BGP redistribution

```
!
hostname NY2
!
enable password cisco
!
interface Ethernet0
 ip address 172.17.0.2 255.255.0.0
!
interface Ethernet1
 ip address 172.18.0.1 255.255.0.0
!
interface Serial0
 ip address 192.168.33.1 255.255.255.0
!
interface Serial1
 no ip address
 shutdown
!
router igrp 55
 network 172.17.0.0
 network 172.18.0.0
 network 192.168.33.0
!
ip classless
!
```

NY3 router initial configuration for IGRP into BGP redistribution

```
hostname NY3
!
enable password cisco
!
interface Ethernet0
 ip address 172.20.0.1 255.255.0.0
!
interface Ethernet1
 ip address 172.21.0.1 255.255.0.0
!
interface Serial0
 ip address 192.168.33.2 255.255.255.0
 clockrate 2000000
!
interface Serial1
 no ip address
 shutdown
!
router igrp 55
 network 172.20.0.0
 network 172.21.0.0
 network 192.168.33.0
!
ip classless
!
```

If you have gone through the previous sections describing BGP/RIP and BGP/OSPF interactions, the results of the initial configuration from the preceding traces should no longer surprise you. The border routers (Boston and NY1) know about all of the routes in the internetwork. The IGRP-only routers have no idea how to reach destinations in other ASs.

The routing table on NY3 confirms that it only knows about its directly connected networks and networks within the IGRP AS 55 or BGP AS 10.

```
NY3#show ip route
Codes: C - connected, S - static, I - IGRP, R - RIP, M - mobile, B - BGP

       D - EIGRP, EX - EIGRP external, O - OSPF,


Gateway of last resort is not set


I    172.17.0.0/16 [100/8576] via 192.168.33.1, 00:00:33, Serial0

I    172.18.0.0/16 [100/8576] via 192.168.33.1, 00:00:33, Serial0

C    172.21.0.0/16 is directly connected, Ethernet1

C    172.20.0.0/16 is directly connected, Ethernet0

C    192.168.33.0/24 is directly connected, Serial0

NY3#
```

If you decide to go the mutual redistribution route, you must be aware
that when redistributing BGP into IGRP, you must specify the IGRP
metric. IOS does not force you to do so, but if you don't do it, your configuration will not work. The BGP routes redistributed into IGRP are per-
ceived by IGRP as system routes. The three IGRP route types are interior,
system, and exterior. Observe the configuration of BGP redistribution into
IGRP with and without the metric. The use of debug is required to see exactly what's happening.

First, take a look at NY1's routing table. There is only one BGP route.
Normally, there would be thousands, but they are not shown here due to
space considerations.

```
NY1#sh ip route
Codes: C - connected, S - static, I - IGRP, R - RIP, M - mobile, B - BGP

       D - EIGRP, EX - EIGRP external, O - OSPF,


Gateway of last resort is not set


C    172.17.0.0/16 is directly connected, Ethernet0

B    172.16.0.0/16 [20/0] via 192.168.1.1, 01:33:54

I    172.18.0.0/16 [100/1200] via 172.17.0.2, 00:01:00, Ethernet0

I    172.21.0.0/16 [100/8676] via 172.17.0.2, 00:01:00, Ethernet0

I    172.20.0.0/16 [100/8676] via 172.17.0.2, 00:01:00, Ethernet0
```

```
C    192.168.1.0/24 is directly connected, Serial0
I    192.168.33.0/24 [100/8576] via 172.17.0.2, 00:01:00, Ethernet0
NY1#
```

Next, redistribution of BGP into IGRP is configured on the NY1 router with the idea of having the redistributed BGP routes propagated to the IGRP-only routers inside AS 10.

```
NY1#conf t
Enter configuration commands, one per line.  End with CNTL/Z.
NY1(config)#router igrp 55
NY1(config-router)#redistribute bgp 10
NY1(config-router)#^Z
NY1#
```

The problem with this configuration is that when the administrator checks the routing table on NY3, it's the same as it was before the redistribution of BGP into IGRP took place on NY1 router. the network 172.16.0.0 that the administrator expected to see in the NY3's table is not there. The administrator decides that it's time to use debug (see Chapter 3 for more details on debug).

```
NY1#debug ip igrp transactions
IGRP protocol debugging is on
NY1#
01:39:12: IGRP: sending update to 255.255.255.255 via Ethernet0 (172.17.0.1)
01:39:13:       network 172.16.0.0, metric=4294967295
01:39:34: IGRP: received update from 172.17.0.2 on Ethernet0
01:39:34:       network 172.18.0.0, metric 1200 (neighbor 1100)
01:39:34:       network 172.21.0.0, metric 8676 (neighbor 8576)
01:39:34:       network 172.20.0.0, metric 8676 (neighbor 8576)
01:39:34:       network 192.168.33.0, metric 8576 (neighbor 8476)
NY1#undebug all
All possible debugging has been turned off
NY1#
```

The debug trace reveals that NY1 advertises 172.16.0.0 with a metric of 4294967295. That's a very high number (2 raised to the power of 32 less 1). An IGRP route advertised with that metric is considered unreachable.

The simple rule about redistributing BGP into IGRP is that you must define a metric for the redistribution to work. In the trace that follows, the incorrect configuration is removed and replaced with the correct one.

```
NY1#conf t

Enter configuration commands, one per line.  End with CNTL/Z.

NY1(config)#

NY1(config)#router igrp 55

NY1(config-router)#no redistribute bgp 10

NY1(config-router)#redistribute bgp 10 metric 10000 100 255 1 1500

NY1(config-router)#^Z
```

The IGRP/EIGRP metric is derived from several variables. The components of the metric include bandwidth, delay, reliability, load, and MTU. When you look at the output from debug again, you can see that route 172.16.0.0 is now advertised with a metric that's understandable to other IGRP routers. The metric is 1100 instead of 4294967295.

```
NY1#debug ip igrp trans

IGRP protocol debugging is on

NY1#

01:45:34: IGRP: sending update to 255.255.255.255 via Ethernet0 (172.17.0.1)

01:45:34:       network 172.16.0.0, metric=1100

01:45:34: IGRP: received update from 172.17.0.2 on Ethernet0

01:45:34:       network 172.18.0.0, metric 1200 (neighbor 1100)

01:45:34:       network 172.21.0.0, metric 8676 (neighbor 8576)

01:45:34:       network 172.20.0.0, metric 8676 (neighbor 8576)

01:45:34:       network 192.168.33.0, metric 8576 (neighbor 8476)
```

Debugging of IGRP events reveals that the redistributed route is treated as a system route.

```
NY1#debug ip igrp events

IGRP event debugging is on

NY1#

01:46:46: IGRP: sending update to 255.255.255.255 via Ethernet0 (172.17.0.1)

01:46:47: IGRP: Update contains 0 interior, 1 system, and 0 exterior routes.

01:46:47: IGRP: Total routes in update: 1

NY1#undebug all
```

The routing table on NY3 now shows an entry for 172.16.0.0. Had there been more BGP routes on NY1 rather than 172.16.0.0 only, they would all be showing up in the NY3 routing table as IGRP routes at this point.

```
NY3#sh ip route

Codes: C - connected, S - static, I - IGRP, R - RIP, M - mobile, B - BGP

       D - EIGRP, EX - EIGRP external, O - OSPF,


Gateway of last resort is not set


I    172.17.0.0/16 [100/8576] via 192.168.33.1, 00:00:29, Serial0

I    172.16.0.0/16 [100/8676] via 192.168.33.1, 00:00:29, Serial0

I    172.18.0.0/16 [100/8576] via 192.168.33.1, 00:00:29, Serial0

C    172.21.0.0/16 is directly connected, Ethernet1

C    172.20.0.0/16 is directly connected, Ethernet0

C    192.168.33.0/24 is directly connected, Serial0

NY3#
```

You can leave the configuration as is and face the danger of a large number of BGP routes, or you can decide to rely on defaults as with RIP and OSPF. The configuration of defaults is, again, quite different from that of RIP or OSPF. Assume that the entire configuration related to BGP redistribution into IGRP has been removed. There are several ways to handle the configuration of defaults in IGRP.

You'll recall that IGRP defines three types of routes. Interior routes are for subnets of a major network advertised to a neighbor sharing a subnet of the same network. System routes are for major networks from within the same IGRP AS that are not shared with neighbors, and exterior routes are for networks outside the IGRP AS.

The default route has to be an exterior route and unlike RIP or OSPF, in IGRP it's not 0.0.0.0. In the internetwork in Figure 11.7, the default IGRP route has to be a network that's either connected to the border router, or entirely outside the AS. This network also has to be defined via the `default-network` command before IGRP will recognize it as a candidate default.

If a `redistribute connected` command is executed on the NY1 router, the DMZ network 192.168.1.0 will be redistributed into IGRP as a system route. This means that all of the routers in AS 10 would know how to get to the DMZ but would still not be able to get to networks in AS 90.

If, on the other hand, `redistribute connected` is used in conjunction the `with ip default-network` command, then the route to the DMZ will be viewed as an exterior route — and a candidate default — and all traffic to AS 90 will follow the path to the NY1 border router. When the NY1 router is reached, it knows about all destinations in AS 90.

To ensure full reachability between both ASs, the configuration of a candidate default must take place on both the Boston and NY1 routers in Figure 11.7.

Observe the configuration of a candidate default on the Boston and NY1 routers.

```
Boston#conf t
Enter configuration commands, one per line.  End with CNTL/Z.
Boston(config)#ip default-network 192.168.1.0
Boston(config)#router igrp 66
Boston(config-router)#redistribute connected
Boston(config-router)#^Z
Boston#


NY1#conf t
Enter configuration commands, one per line.  End with CNTL/Z.
NY1(config)#ip default-network 192.168.1.0
NY1(config)#router igrp 55
NY1(config-router)#redistribute connected
NY1(config-router)#^Z
NY1#
```

A look at the NY1 routing table following the preceding configuration shows that 192.168.1.0 is now considered a candidate default.

```
NY1#sh ip route
Codes: C - connected, S - static, I - IGRP, R - RIP, M - mobile, B - BGP
       D - EIGRP, EX - EIGRP external, O - OSPF, IA - OSPF inter area
```

```
N1 - OSPF NSSA external type 1, N2 - OSPF NSSA external type 2
E1 - OSPF external type 1, E2 - OSPF external type 2, E - EGP
i - IS-IS, L1 - IS-IS level-1, L2 - IS-IS level-2, * - candidate default
U - per-user static route, o - ODR


Gateway of last resort is not set


C    172.17.0.0/16 is directly connected, Ethernet0
B    172.16.0.0/16 [20/0] via 192.168.1.1, 02:55:05
I    172.18.0.0/16 [100/1200] via 172.17.0.2, 00:01:03, Ethernet0
I    172.21.0.0/16 [100/8676] via 172.17.0.2, 00:01:03, Ethernet0
I    172.20.0.0/16 [100/8676] via 172.17.0.2, 00:01:03, Ethernet0
C*   192.168.1.0/24 is directly connected, Serial0
I    192.168.33.0/24 [100/8576] via 172.17.0.2, 00:01:03, Ethernet0
NY1#
```

Debugging IGRP events reveals that NY1 is now advertising an exterior route.

```
NY1#debug ip igrp events
IGRP event debugging is on
NY1#
02:58:39: IGRP: sending update to 255.255.255.255 via Ethernet0 (172.17.0.1)
02:58:40: IGRP: Update contains 0 interior, 0 system, and 1 exterior routes.
02:58:40: IGRP: Total routes in update: 1
NY1#undebug all
```

And a look at the NY3 routing table shows that it also has a default route. Note that the gateway of last resort is defined as the address of the last router to advertise the default network to NY3.

```
NY3#sh ip route
Codes: C - connected, S - static, I - IGRP, R - RIP, M - mobile, B - BGP
       D - EIGRP, EX - EIGRP external, O - OSPF, IA - OSPF inter area
       N1 - OSPF NSSA external type 1, N2 - OSPF NSSA external type 2
       E1 - OSPF external type 1, E2 - OSPF external type 2, E - EGP
       i - IS-IS, L1 - IS-IS level-1, L2 - IS-IS level-2, * - candidate default
```

```
     U - per-user static route, o - ODR

Gateway of last resort is 192.168.33.1 to network 192.168.1.0

I    172.17.0.0/16 [100/8576] via 192.168.33.1, 00:00:09, Serial0

I    172.18.0.0/16 [100/8576] via 192.168.33.1, 00:00:09, Serial0

C    172.21.0.0/16 is directly connected, Ethernet1

C    172.20.0.0/16 is directly connected, Ethernet0

I*   192.168.1.0/24 [100/10576] via 192.168.33.1, 00:00:09, Serial0

C    192.168.33.0/24 is directly connected, Serial0

NY3#
```

The preceding steps involving the use of the ip default-network and the redistribute connected commands offered one way to configure defaults inside of an IGRP AS. In the internetwork in Figure 11.7, the IGRP ASs coincide with the BGP ASs.

Another approach to defaults in IGRP/BGP interactions is to use one of the BGP routes on NY1 as a default route and propagate it to all routers in AS 10. This approach involves redistributing BGP into IGRP with a route map, along with defining one BGP route with the ip default-network command.

The final results of this approach are identical to what you have seen with the use of the DMZ as a default route. The route map that's used with the BGP redistribution into IGRP permits only one route to be redistributed, the route that's used with the ip default-network command. Observe this configuration on the NY1 router, and the corresponding routing tables on the NY1, NY2, and NY3 routers.

```
NY1#conf t

Enter configuration commands, one per line.  End with CNTL/Z.

NY1(config)#ip default-network 172.16.0.0

NY1(config)#router igrp 55

NY1(config-router)#redistribute bgp 10 route-map one_only

NY1(config-router)#exit

NY1(config)#route-map one_only permit 1

NY1(config-route-map)#match ip address 33

NY1(config-route-map)#exit
```

```
NY1(config)#access-list 33 permit 172.16.0.0 0.0.255.255
NY1(config)#^Z
NY1#
```

To make the results more interesting, an extra BGP route, 172.33.0.0, has been introduced into the NY1's table. Consider this route as representing thousands of routes that will be screened out by the route map.

```
NY1#sh ip route
Codes: C - connected, S - static, I - IGRP, R - RIP, M - mobile, B - BGP
       D - EIGRP, EX - EIGRP external, O - OSPF, IA - OSPF inter area
       N1 - OSPF NSSA external type 1, N2 - OSPF NSSA external type 2
       E1 - OSPF external type 1, E2 - OSPF external type 2, E - EGP
       i - IS-IS, L1 - IS-IS level-1, L2 - IS-IS level-2, * - candidate default
       U - per-user static route, o - ODR

Gateway of last resort is 192.168.1.1 to network 172.16.0.0

C     172.17.0.0/16 is directly connected, Ethernet0
B*    172.16.0.0/16 [20/0] via 192.168.1.1, 05:05:43
I     172.18.0.0/16 [100/1200] via 172.17.0.2, 00:00:13, Ethernet0
I     172.21.0.0/16 [100/8676] via 172.17.0.2, 00:00:13, Ethernet0
I     172.20.0.0/16 [100/8676] via 172.17.0.2, 00:00:13, Ethernet0
B     172.33.0.0/16 [20/0] via 192.168.1.1, 01:32:30
C     192.168.1.0/24 is directly connected, Serial0
I     192.168.33.0/24 [100/8576] via 172.17.0.2, 00:00:13, Ethernet0
NY1#
```

NY1's table now has all of the BGP routes with 172.16.0.0 flagged as candidate default. This is correct because NY1 is a border router. But on the IGRP-only routers, NY2 and NY3, you would expect the route map to screen out all routes except 172.16.0.0.

```
NY2#sh ip route
Codes: C - connected, S - static, I - IGRP, R - RIP, M - mobile, B - BGP
       D - EIGRP, EX - EIGRP external, O - OSPF, IA - OSPF inter area
       N1 - OSPF NSSA external type 1, N2 - OSPF NSSA external type 2
```

```
        E1 - OSPF external type 1, E2 - OSPF external type 2, E - EGP

        i - IS-IS, L1 - IS-IS level-1, L2 - IS-IS level-2, * - candidate default

        U - per-user static route, o - ODR


Gateway of last resort is 172.17.0.1 to network 172.16.0.0


C     172.17.0.0/16 is directly connected, Ethernet0

I*    172.16.0.0/16 [100/1200] via 172.17.0.1, 00:00:37, Ethernet0

C     172.18.0.0/16 is directly connected, Ethernet1

I     172.21.0.0/16 [100/8576] via 192.168.33.2, 00:00:29, Serial0

I     172.20.0.0/16 [100/8576] via 192.168.33.2, 00:00:29, Serial0

C     192.168.33.0/24 is directly connected, Serial0

NY2#

NY2#



NY3#sh ip route

Codes: C - connected, S - static, I - IGRP, R - RIP, M - mobile, B - BGP

        D - EIGRP, EX - EIGRP external, O - OSPF, IA - OSPF inter area

        N1 - OSPF NSSA external type 1, N2 - OSPF NSSA external type 2

        E1 - OSPF external type 1, E2 - OSPF external type 2, E - EGP

        i - IS-IS, L1 - IS-IS level-1, L2 - IS-IS level-2, * - candidate default

        U - per-user static route, o - ODR


Gateway of last resort is 192.168.33.1 to network 172.16.0.0


I     172.17.0.0/16 [100/8576] via 192.168.33.1, 00:00:38, Serial0

I*    172.16.0.0/16 [100/8676] via 192.168.33.1, 00:00:38, Serial0

I     172.18.0.0/16 [100/8576] via 192.168.33.1, 00:00:38, Serial0

C     172.21.0.0/16 is directly connected, Ethernet1

C     172.20.0.0/16 is directly connected, Ethernet0

C     192.168.33.0/24 is directly connected, Serial0

NY3#
```

Route 172.16.0.0 has been redistributed from BGP into IGRP. In the IGRP-only routers it appears as a candidate default route. This approach of redistributing BGP routes into IGRP—with a route map screening out all routes except the one that's used as default—is another way of implementing BGP/IGRP redistribution.

Chapter Summary

Interaction between routing protocols is implemented via redistribution. the most common reasons for redistribution are protocol migration, network merges, and IGP/EGP interactions. Redistribution can be one-way or two-way. Two-way redistribution is referred to as mutual redistribution. Mutual redistribution is dangerous when it occurs between an IGP and an EGP (like BGP). The number of BGP routes in the Internet is over 69,000 and is growing. A large number of BGP routes redistributed into an IGP can cause the IGP to crash.

Mutual redistribution can be controlled via route maps. Under some circumstances, the use of default routes is an alternative to mutual or one-way redistribution. Redistribution into OSPF requires the use of the *subnets* keyword for its subnetted routes to be redistributed from another protocol. Protocols like RIP, IGRP, and EIGRP require the use of the *metric* keyword with the appropriate parameters when accepting routes from other protocols. Configuration of redistribution is easiest between IGRP and EIGRP.

Appendix A

Bibliography

Recommended Reading

The following titles are arranged by topic.

Cabling

Vacca, John. *The Cabling Handbook*. Prentice Hall Inc., 1999.

BGP

Halabi, Bassam. *Internet Routing Architectures*. New Riders Publishing, 1997.

IGRP/EIGRP/RIP

Doyle, Jeff. *Routing TCP/IP*. Vol. 1. Macmillan Technical Publishing, 1998.

NetWare

Siyan, Karanjit S. *Novell Intranetware Professional Reference*. New Riders Publishing, 1997.

OSPF

Moy, John. *OSPF Anatomy of an Internet Routing Protocol*. Addison Wesley Longman Inc., 1998.

RFCs

1771, "A Border Gateway Protocol 4 (BGP-4)", Y. Rekher and T. Li, March 1995.

1965, "Autonomous System Confederations for BGP", P. Traina, June 1996.

1966, "BGP Route Reflection: An Alternative to Full Mesh IBGP", T. Bates, R. Chandrasekeran, June 1996.

Routers

Rybaczyk, Peter. *Novell's Internet Plumbing Handbook*. Novell Press and IDG Books Worldwide, 1998.

Appendix B

Acronym and Abbreviation Guide

Acronym/Abbreviation	Meaning
ABR	Area Border Router
AC	Alternating Current
ACL	Access Control List
AMI	Alternate Mark Inversion
ARP	Address Resolution Protocol
ARPA	Advanced Research Projects Agency
AS	Autonomous System
ASBR	Autonomous System Border Router
ASN	Autonomous System Number
ATM	Asynchronous Transfer Mode
B8ZS	Bipolar, with 8 Zero Substitution
BDR	Backup Designated Router
BGP	Border Gateway Protocol
BRI	Basic Rate Interface
CDP	Cisco Discovery Protocol
CPE	Customer Premises Equipment
CPU	Central Processing Unit

Continued

Appendix B *Continued*

Acronym/Abbreviation	Meaning
CSC	Clock and Scheduler Card
CSMA/CD	Carrier Sense Multiple Access/Collision Detection
CSU/DSU	Channel Service Unit/Data Service Unit
CTS	Clear To Send
DC	Direct Current
DCD	Data Carrier Detect
DCE	Data Circuit-Terminating Equipment
DHCP	Dynamic Host Configuration Protocol
DDP	Datagram Delivery Protocol
DEC	Digital Equipment Corporation
DLCI	Data Link Connection Identifier
DMZ	Demilitarized Zone
DR	Designated Router
DSAP	Destination Service Access Point
DSR	Data Set Ready
DTE	Data Terminal Equipment
DTR	Data Terminal Ready
EBGP	External BGP
ED	Early Deployment
EGP	Exterior Gateway Protocol
EIA/TIA	Electronics Industry Association/Telecommunications Industry Association
EIGRP	Enhanced Interior Gateway Routing Protocol
ESF	Extended Super Frame
FCS	First Commercial Shipment, First Customer Shipment
FDDI	Fiber Distributed Data Interface
GD	General Deployment
GRP	Gigabit Route Processor
GSR	Gigabit Switch Router
HDLC	High-Level Data Link Control
IEEE	Institute of Electrical and Electronics Engineers
IBGP	Internal BGP
ICMP	Internet Control Message Protocol

Acronym/Abbreviation	Meaning
IGP	Interior Gateway Protocol
IGRP	Interior Gateway Routing Protocol
IOS	Internetwork Operating System
IP	Internet Protocol
IPX	Internet Packet Exchange
IPX/SPX	Internet Packet Exchange/Sequenced Packet Exchange
ISDN	Integrated Services Digital Network
ISP	Internet Service Provider
LAN	Local Area Network
LANCE	LAN Controller Ethernet
LAT	Local Area Transport
LC	Line Card
LED	Light Emitting Diode
LLC	Logical Link Control
LMI	Local Management Interface
MD5	Message Digest 5
MED	Multi-Exit Discriminator
MTU	Maximum Transmission Unit
NBMA	Non-Broadcast Multi Access
NETBEUI	NETBIOS Extended User Interface
NETBIOS	Network Basic Input Output Service
NEXT	Near-End Cross Talk
NIC	Network Interface Card
NLRI	Network Layer Reachability Information
NVRAM	Non-Volatile Random Access Memory
OC	Optical Carrier
OSI	Open-Systems Interconnection
OSPF	Open Shortest Path First
POP	Point of Presence
POS	Packet-Over-SONET
POST	Power-On-Self-Test
PVC	Permanent Virtual Circuit

Continued

Appendix B *Continued*

Acronym/Abbreviation	Meaning
PPP	Point-to-Point Protocol
RIP	Routing Information Protocol
RTS	Request to Send
ROM	Read Only Memory
RSP	Route Switch Processor
RTO	Retransmission Timeout
SAP	Service Access Point
SFC	Switch Fabric Card
SNAP	Subnetwork Access Protocol
SNMP	Simple Network Management Protocol
SONET	Synchronous Optical Network
SSAP	Source Service Access Point
STM	Synchronous Transfer Mode
STM-N	Synchronous Transmission Module level N
TCP	Transmission Control Protocol
TCP/IP	Transmission Control Protocol/Internet Protocol
TIA	Telecommunications Industry Association
TTL	Time To Live
UDP	User Datagram Protocol
UPS	Uninterruptible Power Supply
UTP	Unshielded Twisted Pair
VC	Virtual Circuit
VLSM	Variable-Length Subnet Mask
XNS	Xerox Network Service

Appendix C

Summary of Troubleshooting Tips and Issues

ACL Configuration Tips

- The order of statements in an access control list is important.
- There is an implicit *Deny all* statement at the end of a list.
- An ACL including only *deny* statements will deny everything.
- An ACL with a *Deny all* at the beginning of the list will deny everything regardless of what follows.
- Wild card mask in an ACL is an inverted mask where zero bits compare.
- ACLs are applied to interfaces, not entire routers.
- Keywords *in* and *out* are used with the `ip access-group` command to implement inbound and outbound ACL filters on interfaces.

BGP

- Default BGP configuration is simple: Activate the BGP process, define neighbors, and inject routes into BGP.
- Route maps and ACLs are used to implement BGP routing policies, which tend to be complex.

- Misconfigured IP addresses of neighbors are a common problem in BGP configurations.
- IP connectivity must exist between BGP neighbors before a BGP session can be established.
- EBGP operates between ASs, IBGP within an AS.
- External BGP neighbors typically share a physical subnet.
- Transit AS needs to be configured with a full IBGP mesh, route reflectors, or confederations.
- Routing loops can readily occur in ASs that rely on the use of defaults and deploy a combination of BGP/non-BGP routers.
- Improper route aggregation can result in undeliverable traffic.

Classful Routing Protocols

- IGRP and RIP are classful routing protocols.
- Classful routing protocols do not support VLSM.
- Separation of major network subnets with another major network leads to problems with classful routing protocols.

Data Link Layer Problems (and Remedies)

- Encapsulation mismatches (reconfigure correctly).
- Excessive link utilization (increase link's capacity).
- Interface controller failure (replace).
- An LMI type mismatch between a router and a Frame Relay switch will disable Frame Relay links.
- Non-routable protocols can be bridged.
- Excessive fragmentation resulting from drastically mismatched MTUs impacts router's performance.

Duplicate IP Addresses

- Address duplication can occur within a subnet or between subnets.

- Routing protocols like OSPF and BGP fail to operate between neighbors with duplicate addresses.
- Duplicate addresses within a subnet can result in lost connections and "hangs" for the user of a network.
- Duplicate subnets within a larger internetwork can result in misdelivered traffic.
- Review of ARP tables and output from CDP helps with location of duplicate addresses within a subnet.
- Avoid address duplication at all costs.

EIGRP

- EIGRP routers will not become neighbors if there is an authentication or an ASN mismatch between them.
- A mismatch in EIGRP timers causes sporadic appearance and disappearance of neighbors resulting in frequent route re-computations and network instability.
- Improperly configured bandwidth parameter on EIGRP serial links may lead to underutilization on some links and congestion on others.
- Auto summarization in EIGRP can lead to the same problems as the deployment of classful protocols.

Encapsulation Mismatches

- Encapsulation must match between neighboring routers.
- An encapsulation mismatch will disable a WAN link.
- An encapsulation mismatch will disable communication between a router and a LAN device but not across the entire LAN.
- Keywords like *ARPA, SAP, SNAP* or *NOVELL-ETHER* are used to indicate encapsulation type, which corresponds to LAN frame types.
- Encapsulation on a router's LAN interfaces should match the frame types configured on other LAN devices.

IGRP/EIGRP ASN Mismatch

- The ASNs in IGRP/EIGRP must match between neighboring routers for routing updates to be exchanged.
- Mismatch in the ASN can be accidental or purposeful.
- Purposeful use of different ASNs combined with redistribution allows for breakup of large IGRP/EIGRP internetworks into smaller domains.
- Accidental mismatch in ASN causes reachability problems.

IOS Tips

- Be mindful of the feature set supported by your IOS.
- Over 60 image files are available in the IOS Release 12.0 for a wide range of Cisco product lines.
- IOS is a complex operating system that is going to have some bugs in it.
- When you bump into a strange problem and you've made sure that your configuration is correct, it's possible that you are discovering an IOS bug.

IOS troubleshooting tools

- IOS-supported troubleshooting tools include *ping, telnet, show,* and *debug.*
- Show and debug commands can be used to troubleshoot the Physical, Data Link, and Network Layers.
- Show and debug commands are available with hundreds of keywords.
- Review Cisco documentation available on the Web and on the Cisco Documentation CD for a complete listing of all available troubleshooting commands.

Masks

- Masks can be normal or inverted.
- Common uses of normal masks are with assignment of addresses to interfaces, aggregation and summarization.
- Normal masks are ultimately reflected in routing tables, defining the length of routing prefixes.
- Inverted masks are used as wild cards.
- Inverted masks are used with ACLs and when assigning interfaces to areas in OSPF.
- The use of less specific inverted masks can reduce the number of configuration statements in ACLs.
- IOS issues some warnings about bad masks, but misconfigurations involving masks are common.

OSPF

- Router interfaces are assigned to areas using inverted masks.
- Routing updates between areas are exchanged through the backbone area in a multi-area internetwork.
- The backbone area, 0.0.0.0, must be configured in a multi-area internetwork if routing updates are to be exchanged between areas.
- Area 0.0.0.0 does not have to be configured in a single area OSPF network, however, it is recommended that area 0.0.0.0 be always configured to avoid future problems.
- A mismatch in OSPF area ID, network type, authentication, or Hello/Dead intervals will prevent routers from becoming neighbors.
- On NBMA WANs, OSPF can be configured using the NBMA, point-to-multipoint, or subinterface models.
- Transit broadcast subnets must have a DR which implies that at least one router must have a non-zero priority on the subnet.

Physical Layer Problems and Issues

- Physical Layer problems can be related to power, router hardware components, cabling, and misconfiguration.

- Troubleshooting the Physical Layer is accomplished via a combination of visual inspections, review of console messages, and the use of IOS commands.

- Several pinouts are in use for RJ-45 connectorized cables.

- Good RJ-45 connectorized cables can be used in wrong places if cables are not clearly labeled.

- CSU/DSU can be built into a router or it can be an external device.

- Encoding, framing, and clocking are Physical Layer configuration parameters that are configured on a CSU/DSU.

Redistribution

- Interaction between routing protocols is implemented via redistribution.

- Common reasons for redistribution are protocol migration, network merges, and IGP/EGP interactions.

- Redistribution can be one-way or two-way.

- Two-way redistribution is referred to as mutual redistribution.

- Mutual redistribution between an IGP and an EGP (like BGP) can be dangerous because a large number of BGP routes redistributed into an IGP can cause it to crash.

- Mutual redistribution can be controlled via route maps.

- Use of default routes is an alternative to mutual or one-way redistribution.

- Be mindful of the differences in metrics when performing redistribution between routing protocols.

- Redistribution into OSPF requires the use of the *subnet* keyword for subnetted routes to be redistributed from another protocol.

- RIP, IGRP, and EIGRP require the use of the *metric* keyword with the appropriate parameters when accepting routes from other protocols.

RIP

- Missing *network* statements are a common problem in RIP configurations.

- RIP will work with mismatched subnet masks as long as neighboring routers perceive each other as belonging to the same subnet.

- Mismatched subnet masks between RIP neighbors are not recommended and should be avoided.

- Mismatched subnets in RIP result in routing tables that are difficult to understand.

- Debugging RIP helps with troubleshooting RIP problems.

- Use point-to-point subinterfaces in NBMA clouds running RIP to avoid problems with split horizon.

Split Horizon on WANs

- Split horizon is enabled by default on point-to-point and multipoint subinterfaces using Frame Relay encapsulation.

- Classful protocols like RIP or IGRP when deployed in Frame Relay networks with multipoint subinterfaces will result in partial reachability due to split horizon.

Troubleshooting Philosophy

- The four broad categories of problems with routers and internetworks are hardware, buggy IOS, misconfigurations, and interactions with other routers.

- Sectional and layered approaches can be used when troubleshooting misconfigurations.

- In the layered approach, check for problems beginning with the Physical Layer and using the OSI model as a reference.

- In the sectional approach, check each configuration section.

- "Let's fix it" holds the key to successful troubleshooting. The "Let's" stands for Locate, Eliminate, Test, and Support. Locate the problem, eliminate it, test your work, and support your installation in a pro-active way.

- Reasonable documentation and system baseline are a great aid in troubleshooting.

Index

Symbols and Numbers

?

    incomplete code, 388-389

    question mark, 79

2-WAY relationships, routers, 298

802.2 frame, 5

    DSAP (Destination SAP), 6

    SAPs (Service Access Points), 6

802.3 "Raw" frame, 7

2500 series non-modular routers

    interfaces, 110-111

    power problems, 104-105

12000 series modular routers

    interfaces, 107-110

    power problems, 105-106

<-4294967295> keyword, 94

A

A.B.C.D. keyword, 94

ABRs (Area Border Routers), 312-313

AC outlets, 104-105

access control list masks, 189192

Access Control Lists. *See* ACLs

access-expression keyword, 79

access-lists keyword, 79, 93

accounting keyword, 93

ACLs (Access Control Lists)

    Deny all statement, 21, 22

    improper use of, 18-25

    permit/deny statements, 22

    traces, router licensed for Enterprise edition of IOS, 18-19

    types of, 18-19

ACLs (Access Control Lists) IP (Internet Protocol), 20

    configuration format, 19

    configuration verification, 24-25

    inbound versus outbound filtering, 24

    incorrect list order, 21-22

    wild card mask improper application, 23-24

addresses, IP (Internet Protocol)

    CDP (Cisco Discovery Protocol), 159

    duplication, 157-160

addresses, networks, listing, 67

adjacencies, FULL, 271

Advanced Research Projects Agency (ARPA), 9

advertising of networks into BGP, 181-188

aggregate-address address masks [options] command, 176, 380

aggregation masks, BGP, 176-181

aggregations, routes, 377-380

alarm cards, 109

aliases keyword, 79, 93

alps keyword, 79

Alternate Mark Inversion (AMI), 124

always keyword, 448

AMI (Alternate Mark Inversion), 124

analyses

    BGP internetwork for mask aggregation, 177

    EIGRP internetwork for missing neighbors, 229

    IGRP internetwork for metric analysis, 255

    IGRP/BGP interactions, 451

    internetwork of IOS (Internetworking Operating System) troubleshooting tools, 70

    internetwork of OSPF/BGP redistributions, 440

    mask usage, BGP network command, 182, 185

Continued

Continued

Continued

Continued

Continued

Printed in the United States
79920LV00002B/49